Lecture Notes of the Institute for Computer Sciences, Social Informatics and Telecommunications Engineering 671

The LNICST series publishes ICST's conferences, symposia and workshops.

LNICST reports state-of-the-art results in areas related to the scope of the Institute.

The type of material published includes

- Proceedings (published in time for the respective event)
- Other edited monographs (such as project reports or invited volumes)

LNICST topics span the following areas:

- General Computer Science
- E-Economy
- E-Medicine
- Knowledge Management
- Multimedia
- Operations, Management and Policy
- Social Informatics
- Systems

Didier Bassole · Assane Gueye ·
Tiguiane Yélémou · Dame Diongue
Editors

Innovations and Interdisciplinary Solutions for Underserved Areas

8th International Conference, InterSol 2025
Ouagadougou, Burkina Faso, July 3–4, 2025
Proceedings

Editors
Didier Bassole
Université Joseph KI-ZERBO
Ouagadougou, Burkina Faso

Assane Gueye
Carnegie Mellon University Africa
Kigali, Rwanda

Tiguiane Yélémou
Université Nazi BONI
Bobo-Dioulasso, Burkina Faso

Dame Diongue
Université Gaston Berger de Saint Louis
Saint-Louis, Senegal

ISSN 1867-8211 ISSN 1867-822X (electronic)
Lecture Notes of the Institute for Computer Sciences, Social Informatics and Telecommunications Engineering
ISBN 978-3-032-15153-7 ISBN 978-3-032-15154-4 (eBook)
https://doi.org/10.1007/978-3-032-15154-4

This Springer imprint is published by the registered company Springer Nature Switzerland AG
The registered company address is: Gewerbestrasse 11, 6330 Cham, Switzerland

Preface

We are delighted to introduce the proceedings of the eighth edition of the European Alliance for Innovation (EAI) International Conference on Innovations and Interdisciplinary Solutions for Underserved Areas (InterSol 2025). Hosted by Joseph Ki-Zerbo University of Ouagadougou, Burkina Faso, the conference was held from July 3–4, 2025. This conference brought together researchers, developers, and practitioners around the world who are leveraging and developing innovative interdisciplinary solutions to address critical challenges in underserved areas. InterSol provided a platform to collaborate, innovate, and inspire meaningful change in underserved communities. This year's conference focused on the intersection of ICT, IoT, Energy, Environment, and Agriculture, with the goal of driving impactful, sustainable progress.

The technical program of InterSol 2025 consisted of 11 full papers and 3 short papers selected for publication and oral presentation sessions at the main conference tracks. These papers were selected from 56 submissions. Each submission was reviewed following a double-blind process with a minimum of 3 reviews per paper. This volume also includes 8 CNRIA workshop papers selected from 54 workshop track submissions. Aside from the high-quality technical paper presentations, the technical program of InterSol 2025 also featured two keynote speakers. The two keynote speakers were Robert Laurini from INSA Lyon, University of Lyon, France and Franklin Tchakounte, from the University of Ngaoundere in Cameroon.

Coordination with the General Chair, Oumarou Sié, and General Co-chair, Alain Mille, was essential for the success of the conference. We sincerely appreciate their constant support and guidance. It was also a great pleasure to work with such an excellent organizing committee team for their hard work in organizing and supporting the conference. In particular, the Program Chair, Tiguiane Yelemou, and the Technical Program Committee, led by our TPC Co-Chairs, Assane Gueye and Cheikh Mouhamed Fadel Kebe, have completed the peer-review process of technical papers and made a high-quality technical program. We are also grateful to Conference Manager, Katarína Antalová for her support and to all the authors who submitted their papers to the InterSol 2025 conference and CNRIA workshop.

We strongly believe that EAI InterSol provides a good forum for all researchers, developers, and practitioners to discuss all science and technology aspects that are relevant to ICT, IoT, Energy, Environment, and Agriculture. This volume will enable the scientific work presented at InterSol 2025 and CNRIA workshop to be widely disseminated, including the solutions proposed by the scientists who took part in this scientific event dedicated primarily to the problems of underserved areas. We also expect that the future EAI InterSol conferences will be as successful and stimulating, as indicated by the contributions presented in this volume.

Didier Bassole
Assane Gueye
Tiguiane Yélémou
Dame Diongue

Organization

Steering Committee

Didier Bassole	Université Joseph Ki-Zerbo, Burkina Faso
Assane Gueye	Carnegie Mellon University Africa, Rwanda
Tiguiane Yelemou	Université Nazi Boni, Burkina Faso
Cheikh Mouhamed Fadel Kebe	École Supérieure Polytechnique de Dakar, Senegal
Alain Mille	Université Lyon 1, France

Organizing Committee

General Chair

Oumarou Sie	Université Aube Nouvelle, Burkina Faso

General Co-chair

Alain Mille	Université Lyon 1, France

Program Chairs

Didier Bassole	Université Joseph Ki-Zerbo, Burkina Faso
Assane Gueye	Carnegie Mellon University Africa, Rwanda
Tiguiane Yelemou	Université Nazi Boni, Burkina Faso
Dame Diongue	Université Gaston Berger de Saint Louis, Senegal

TPC Chair and Co-chair

Assane Gueye	Carnegie Mellon University Africa, Rwanda
Cheikh Mouhamed Fadel Kebe	École Supérieure Polytechnique de Dakar, Senegal

Sponsorship and Exhibit Chair

Yaya Traore	Université Joseph Ki-Zerbo, Burkina Faso

Local Chair

Didier Bassole | Université Joseph Ki-Zerbo, Burkina Faso

Workshops Chairs

Boureima Zerbo | Université Thomas Sankara, Burkina Faso
Dame Diongue | Université Gaston Berger de Saint Louis, Senegal

Publicity and Social Media Chair

Ousmane Seidou | University of Ottawa, Canada

Publications Chair

Tiguiane Yelemou | Université Nazi Boni, Burkina Faso

Web Chair

Abdoulaye Sere | Université Nazi Boni, Burkina Faso

Posters and PhD Track Chair

Gervais Mendy | École Supérieure Polytechnique de Dakar, Senegal

Panels Chair

Gaoussou Camara | Université Alioune Diop, Senegal

Demos Chair

Narcisse Talla | University of Dschang, Cameroon

Tutorials Chair

Ghada Basioni | Ain Shams University, Egypt

Technical Program Committee

Kodjo Agbossuo	Université du Québec à Trois-Rivières, Canada
Abdelaziz Bacaoui	University Cadi Ayyad of Marrakech, Morocco
Ghada Basioni	Ain Shams University, Egypt
Didier Bassole	Université Joseph Ki-Zerbo, Burkina Faso
Gaoussou Camara	Université Alioune Diop, Senegal
Mesmin T. Dandjinou	Université Nazi Boni, Burkina Faso
Melissa R. Densmore	University of Cape Town, South Africa
Dame Diongue	Université Gaston Berger de Saint Louis, Senegal
Rodney Genga	Witts University, South Africa
Bi Tra Goore	Institut National Polytechnique Félix Houphouët-Boigny, Côte d'Ivoire
Assane Gueye	Carnegie Mellon University Africa, Rwanda
Cheikh Ahamadou B. Gueye	Université Cheikh Anta Diop de Dakar, Senegal
Cheikh Mouhamed Fadel Kebe	École Supérieure Polytechnique de Dakar, Sénégal
Amadou Seidou Maiga	Université Gaston Berger de Saint Louis, Senegal
Hicham Mastouri	University Mohammed VI Polytechnic, Morocco
Gervais Mendy	École Supérieure Polytechnique de Dakar, Sénégal
Alain Mille	Université Lyon 1, France
Amresh Phokeer	Internet Society, Mauritius
Jessica C. Rivas	WindAid Institute, Peru
Vincent Sambou	Université Cheikh Anta Diop of Dakar, Senegal
Ousmane Seidou	University of Ottawa, Canada
Abdoulaye Sere	Université Nazi Boni, Burkina Faso
Narcisse Talla	University of Dschang, Cameroon
Hamidou Tembine	University of New York, USA
Jessica Thorn	University of St. Andrews, UK
Yaya Traore	Université Joseph Ki-Zerbo, Burkina Faso
Tiguiane Yelemou	Université Nazi Boni, Burkina Faso
Boureima Zerbo	Université Thomas Sankara, Burkina Faso

Contents

Short Papers

Artificial Intelligence and Applications

Emergency Severity Index Protocol with Machine Learning

Manegaouindé Roland Tougma[1(✉)], Boureima Zerbo[2], Désiré Guel[1], Salah Idriss Seif Traore[3], and Salifou Napon[3]

[1] Université Joseph Ki Zerbo, Ouagadougou, Burkina Faso
{roland.tougma,desire.guel}@ujkz.bf
[2] Université Thomas SANKARA, Ouagadougou, Burkina Faso
boureima.zerbo@uts.bf
[3] Centre Hospitalier Universitaire de Bogodogo, Ouagadougou, Burkina Faso
seif_tis@yahoo.fr, salifou.napon@gmail.com

Abstract. Effective triage in emergency departments is vital for optimizing patient outcomes and resource use, especially in resource-limited contexts like Burkina Faso. This study presents an automated triage system using machine learning (ML) to predict patient priority levels and appropriate medical services based on the Emergency Severity Index (ESI) protocol. We analyzed electronic hospital records from 23,695 patients across three major Burkina Faso health centers collected from 2021 to 2024. Data, including physiological measures (e.g., blood pressure, temperature, SpO2, pulse) and patient complaints, were preprocessed using TF-IDF vectorization. The supervised ML algorithms XGBoost, LightGBM, RandomForest, Logistic Regression, and SVM were developed and tested in a loop to select the best performing model after each training session. Our results highlighted the potential of ML to streamline emergency triage in Burkina Faso (85% accuracy (precision) for priority class (1 to 5) and 74% accuracy (precision) for services class). Particularly for improving the detection of critical cases through further data integration and model refinement.

Keywords: ESIv4 · Machine Learning · Priority Prediction · Service Prediction · Electronic Health Records (EHR) · Physiological Data

1 Introduction

Emergency departments (EDs) worldwide face significant challenges in promptly assessing and prioritizing patients, especially in resource-limited environments [11]. In Burkina Faso, where medical infrastructure is scarce and acute health needs are high [13], efficient triage is critical to improving outcomes and managing limited resources. The Emergency Severity Index (ESI) [6], a five-level triage system, offers a structured approach to classify patients by urgency and resource requirements. Yet, manual ESI application can be error-prone and inefficient under stress. Advances in machine learning (ML) present an opportunity to

D. Bassole et al. (Eds.): InterSol 2025, LNICST 671, pp. 3–17, 2026.
https://doi.org/10.1007/978-3-032-15154-4_1

automate triage using electronic health records (EHRs) [14], potentially improving decision-making and patient flow. Although ML has shown success in predicting chronic disease onset and COVID-19 outcomes [1], its application to ED triage in low-resource settings remains underexplored. This study addresses that gap by developing an ML-based triage system tailored to Burkina Faso's context. Based on EHR data from 23,695 patients (20212024) across three hospitals, supervised ML algorithms were used to predict ESI levels and required services. By integrating physiological indicators and patient complaints, this work aims to improve triage precision, reduce delays, and support equitable care delivery in developing countries.

2 Literature Review

The integration of Machine Learning (ML) and Deep Learning (DL) into Electronic Health Records (EHR) analysis has significantly advanced health risk prediction. In France, Nevoret et al. [12] predicted asthma exacerbations using SNDS and CONSTANCES data, testing several algorithms. SVM achieved the highest sensitivity (0.82), while RF yielded the highest specificity (0.86). However, overall accuracy remained moderate (65%, 75%), and generalizability was not assessed. Mavrogiorgou et al. [10] reviewed supervised ML methods (e.g., Naïve Bayes, KNN, RF) across multiple diseases. Although some models reached 100% accuracy, concerns were raised about inconsistent data quality and evaluation standards. Grout et al. [7] applied a bidirectional GRU model with Word2Vec to 50 million U.S. EHRs to predict major diagnoses, achieving a mean ROC AUC of 0.920. Despite high performance, model explainability and long-term reliability remained challenging. A follow-up study confirmed benefits over a 3-year horizon but stressed the importance of interpretable outputs. For hypertension prediction, Datta et al. [5] used LSTM on longitudinal data from 233,000+ patients. It outperformed XGBoost and logistic regression (AUROC: 0.94 vs. 0.87 and 0.78), but performance dropped slightly over two years (0.90), indicating temporal drift. In oncology, Si et al. [17] developed a CNN-based method using PPD tensor overlays for predicting CLL treatment initiation. Though innovative, its dependency on tensor construction limits broader applicability. Wynants et al. [9] reviewed 66 COVID-19 prediction models, noting strong diagnostic potential but widespread methodological flaws. Despite strong results, recurring limitations persist—namely data quality, reproducibility, and clinical validation. Finally, Wynants et al. [9] reviewed 66 COVID-19 ML models, highlighting both promising diagnostics and widespread methodological limitations.

3 Theoretical Framework

This study is grounded in a hybrid framework combining clinical reasoning with machine learning (ML) for automating triage based on the Emergency Severity

Index (ESI). Traditional reasoning in emergency settings involves hypothetico-deductive logic [18], yet time pressure and resource constraints, such as in Burkina Faso, demand efficient, data-driven decision-making. ML aligns with automated decision theories emphasizing accuracy and replicability [19]. We adopt a supervised learning strategy [20] using five classification models: *RandomForest*, *XGBoost*, *LightGBM*, *Logistic Regression*, and *SVM*. Ensemble methods like *XGBoost* and *LightGBM* are chosen for handling missing values and non-linearities; *RandomForest* is robust and interpretable. Simpler models like *Logistic Regression* and *SVM* provide essential clinical transparency. Table 1 summarizes each algorithm's suitability. **Input features** include age, sex, HR, RR, SpO_2, BP, ECG, weight, and height—key indicators of acuity per guidelines like FRENCH [21]. Textual complaints were numerically encoded using TF-IDF [15]. Data were cleaned, normalized, and enriched (e.g., SpO_2/temperature ratio) to optimize predictions.

Table 1. Comparative Overview of Selected ML Algorithms for ESI-based Triage

Algorithm	Strengths	Limitations	ESI Relevance
XGBoost [9]	Flexible with non-linear data; handles missing values well; high predictive performance	Complex hyperparameter tuning; less interpretable	Best suited for learning complex distinctions across all ESI levels
LightGBM [9]	Fast and memory-efficient; effective for imbalanced classes (ESI 45)	Can overfit without conservative tuning (e.g., max_depth)	Efficient for detecting rare triage cases and scalable prediction
Random Forest [8]	Robust, easy to implement; stable baseline for multiclass tasks	Slower inference; less fine-grained control than boosting methods	Reliable benchmark across ESI 15 with interpretability
SVM [4]	Handles non-linear class boundaries; good in high-dimensional space	Scaling issues with large datasets; harder to interpret	Useful for modeling subtle boundaries between ESI levels
Logistic Regression	Simple, fast, interpretable; applicable to multiclass classification [24]	Assumes linearity; limited in complex feature spaces	Provides baseline for transparent triage predictions

4 Research Methodology

4.1 Research Design

This study uses a retrospective approach, analyzing historical electronic health records to train machine learning models for Emergency Severity Index (ESI)-based triage. By identifying patterns in past clinical data, it supports accurate prediction of patient priority and care needs, reflecting real-world emergency department practices and enhancing model relevance and reliability.

4.2 Participants and Data

This study draws on electronic medical records collected between 2021 and 2024 from three major hospitals in Burkina Faso: Tengandogo [2], Bogodogo [3], and Schiphra [16]. The dataset includes 23,695 patients from all 45 provinces, with 90% originating from Kadiogo-Ouagadougou (Fig. 1). Patients were 60% male and 40% female. Inclusion required complete physiological data; incomplete records were excluded regardless of weather or seasonal factors.

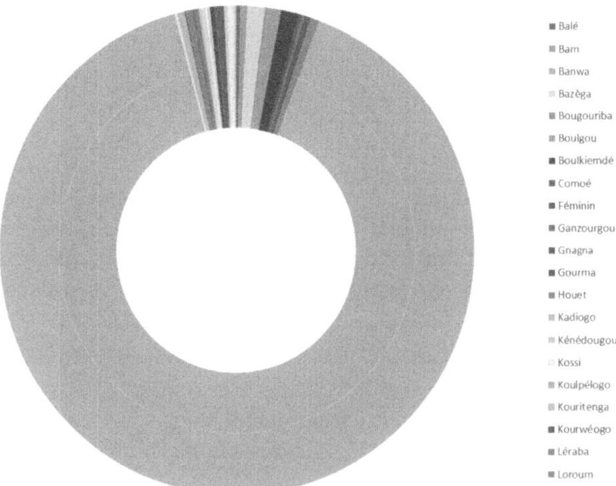

Fig. 1. 90% of come from Kadiogo.

4.3 Choice of Algorithms

The selection of the five supervised learning algorithms—*XGBoost*, *LightGBM*, *RandomForest*, *Logistic Regression*, and *SVM*, is guided by their suitability for predicting the five ESI priority levels (1 to 5) and corresponding medical services. *XGBoost* was selected for its strong performance in modeling complex, non-linear patterns across all ESI levels [9]. *LightGBM*, with its high efficiency on heterogeneous and imbalanced data, is particularly well-suited for detecting underrepresented classes such as ESI 4 and 5. *RandomForest* serves as a robust, interpretable baseline for multiclass classification in EHR settings [8]. *Logistic Regression* provides a transparent and fast linear benchmark, useful for clinical validation. *SVM* is capable of learning non-linear decision boundaries, complementing the ensemble methods in cases with more complex class separations [4]. To prevent overfitting, conservative hyperparameter settings—such as limiting tree depth—were applied across models. A detailed comparison of each algorithm's strengths, weaknesses, and ESI relevance is presented in Table 1.

4.4 Selected of Performance Metrics

To assess the five algorithms for triage prediction, we utilized Accuracy, F1-Score, Recall, ROC, Learning Curve, and Confusion Matrix, where TP (True Positives) is the number of correctly predicted positive cases, TN (True Negatives) is the number of correctly predicted negative cases, FP (False Positives) is the number of incorrectly predicted positive cases, and FN (False Negatives) is the number of incorrectly predicted negative cases. The following metrics ensure a robust evaluation:

- **Accuracy**: $\frac{TP+TN}{TP+TN+FP+FN}$ provides an overall performance snapshot across all classes.
- **F1-Score**: $2 \cdot \frac{\text{Precision}\cdot\text{Recall}}{\text{Precision}+\text{Recall}}$, where Precision $= \frac{TP}{TP+FP}$ and Recall $= \frac{TP}{TP+FN}$, balances precision and recall for rare classes like Priority 1.
- **Recall**: $\frac{TP}{TP+FN}$ prioritizes critical case detection by minimizing false negatives.
- **ROC (Receiver Operating Characteristic)**: Plots the True Positive Rate (TPR, $\frac{TP}{TP+FN}$) against the False Positive Rate (FPR, $\frac{FP}{FP+TN}$) across thresholds, with the Area Under the Curve (AUC) summarizing discriminative power; a high AUC (e.g., near 1) indicates strong separation of critical from non-critical cases.
- **Learning Curve**: Training score ($\text{Score}_{\text{train}} = \frac{\text{Correct Predictions}_{\text{train}}}{\text{Total Samples}_{\text{train}}}$) versus cross-validation score ($\text{Score}_{\text{CV}} = \frac{\text{Correct Predictions}_{\text{CV}}}{\text{Total Samples}_{\text{CV}}}$) assesses generalization, showing initial overfitting that improves with data.
- **Confusion Matrix**: A $k \times k$ matrix, where C_{ij} is the number of samples with true label i predicted as j, details class-specific predictions and correlations, guiding feature engineering.

4.5 Instruments and Analysis Tools

Data Preprocessing. Text preprocessing transforms patients' complaints into machine-readable input using vectorization techniques from `scikit-learn`. For instance, a 31-year-old woman admitted on 25 June 2024 with symptoms like cramps, paresthesia, chest pain, and vomiting, along with vital signs (BP 161/85, pulse 107, temperature 37.5°C), illustrates this process. Key clinical terms are extracted and irrelevant words removed. The text is segmented into symptom and vital sign categories, then vectorized using TF-IDF [15]. This assigns weights to terms based on importance e.g., "vomiting" scores higher than frequent, less meaningful words. The result is a structured numerical matrix, where each row encodes a patient's profile, enabling pattern recognition by machine learning models.

Verification of the Integrity and Consistency of Vectorized Data. To validate the vectorized dataset from patient complaints, 20% of the data (23,695 records) was compared with 4,739 raw records from Schiphra Protestant Hospital. The age distribution (Fig. 2), a key clinical variable, was analyzed using histograms, showing strong alignment between vectorized (red) and raw (gray) data. This confirms the vectorization process's robustness in preserving data characteristics. The validated dataset is reliable for downstream applications and suitable for model training, ensuring high-quality, representative data for subsequent analyses.

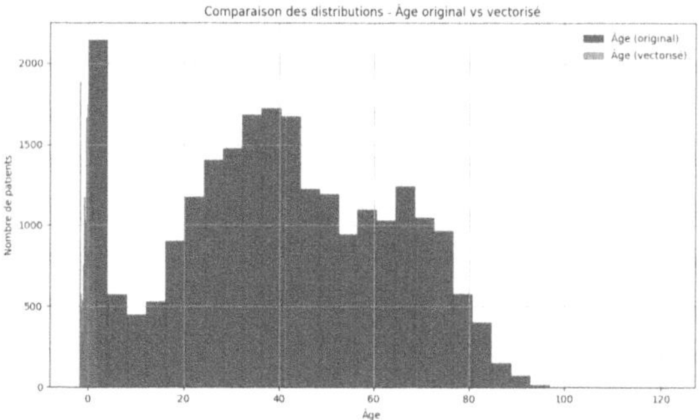

Fig. 2. Verification of the integrity and consistency of vectorized data.

Data Processing. A supervised learning approach was adopted to predict both triage levels and required medical services of ESI [6]. Five algorithms were iteratively trained and evaluated; the best-performing model was retained during each execution. The implementation used Python with libraries such as TensorFlow and Pandas for training, Scikit-learn for modeling, and Matplotlib for visualization. All source code was developed in Google Colab. To address missing triage levels, emergency physicians at Bogodogo Hospital contributed expert annotations. Clinical features such as age, gender, and critical conditions (e.g., coma, severe trauma, imminent delivery) triggered automatic classification as ESI level 1.

5 Results and Interpretations

In this section, we present the performance of our model according to the metrics defined in Sect. 4.4.

5.1 Accuracy

This section reports two key outcomes. A first model predicts patient priority using the ESI protocol (levels 1 to 5) with 82.3% accuracy [6], while a second model estimates the most appropriate post-triage department with 74% accuracy. Both models rely on a loop selecting the best algorithm at each run. Performance varies by model, but *XGBoost* and *LightGBM* consistently deliver the highest accuracies (Figs. 3, 8, 9, 12 and Table 2).

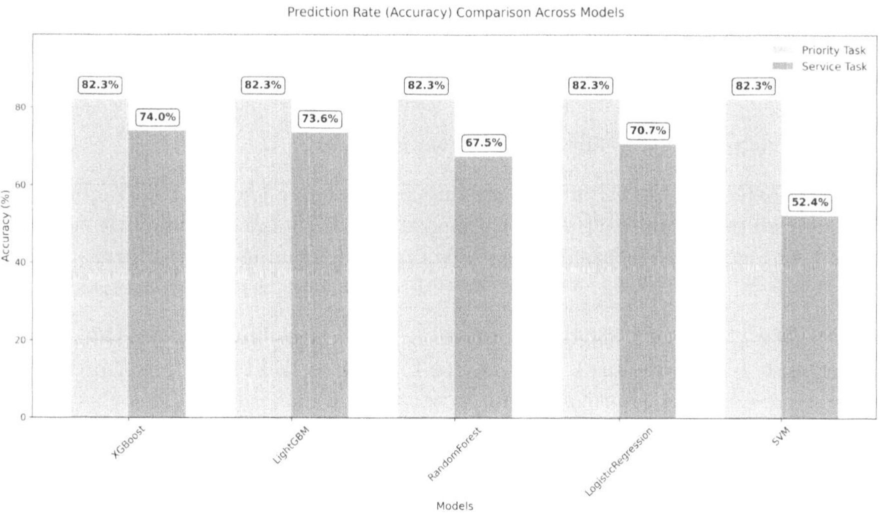

Fig. 3. Both models accuracy.

Interpretation: *XGBoost* and *LightGBM* outperform other models due to their robustness and adaptability. While patient priority prediction nears practical use, service allocation requires refinement. Iterative learning and enriched data—e.g., lab results and imaging—are expected to enhance performance and improve the system's predictive accuracy in future developments.

5.2 F1-Score

After training, the data according to the F1 score illustrate the behavior of the priority model based on the F1 score and recall (Fig. 4) and the graph (Fig. 5) compares the average macro F1 scores of different models for predicting the next service (`Service_Suivant`) :

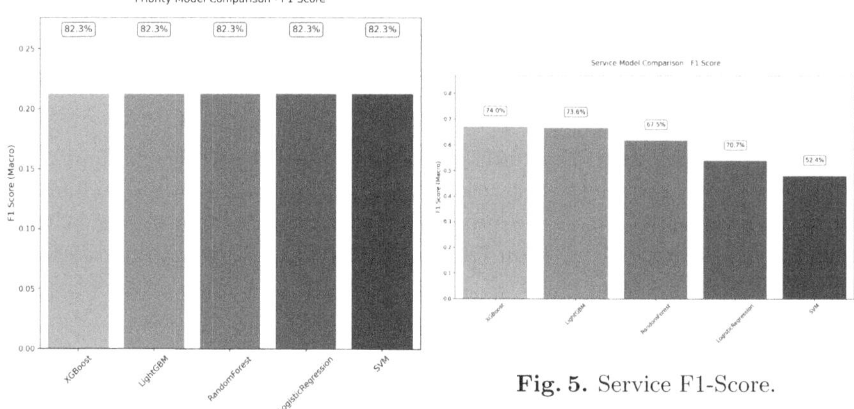

Fig. 4. Priority F1-Score.

Fig. 5. Service F1-Score.

Interpretation. Test results suggest two insights.

Priority Model (Fig. 4): All five algorithms reached an F1 score of 82.3%, indicating balanced performance. However, integrating additional clinical data—such as patient and caregiver complaints, lab results, and imaging—could further refine predictions [6].

Service Model (Fig. 5): Medical variables show non-linear interactions (e.g., SpO_2, pulse, blood pressure), making tree-based models like *XGBoost* and *LightGBM* more effective. However, some hyperparameters (e.g., `max_depth`=2) may limit learning. *Logistic Regression* and *SVM* lacked optimization. Finally, macro F1 scoring penalizes poorly predicted rare classes, such as radiotherapy.

5.3 Recall Performance for Priority and Service Prediction Models

Given the strong performance of XGBoost and LightGBM among the five algorithms, we selected LightGBM to illustrate the recall metric's behavior, specifically through precision-recall curves, for both the Priority Prediction Model (ESI levels 1 to 5) in Fig. 6 and the Service Prediction Model (medical service assignments) in Fig. 7 below.

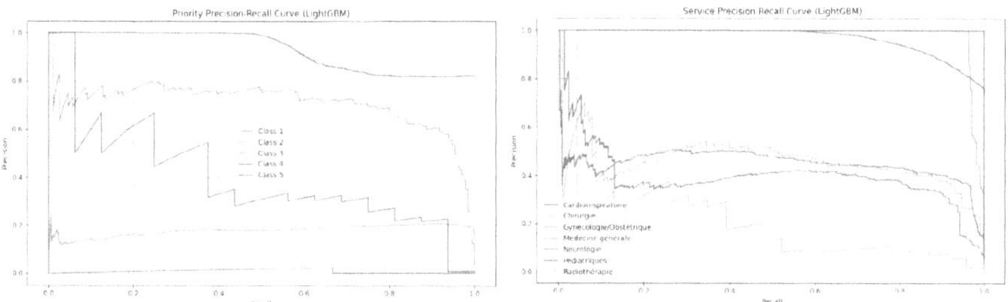

Fig. 6. Priority Recall. **Fig. 7.** Service Recall.

Interpretations: *LightGBM* demonstrated consistent strengths and limitations across both models. For priority prediction, recall improved for critical cases (e.g., Priority 1 at 28%) but at the cost of precision, while rare classes (Priorities 4 and 5) suffered from instability due to data scarcity. In service prediction, Pediatrics and Gynecology/Obstetrics achieved high precision and recall (up to 100%), unlike Cardiorespiratory and Neurology, which showed misclassifications due to overlapping features (Section ??). Surgery and Radiotherapy performed poorly for similar reasons. Learning curves revealed early overfitting (95% training, 75% validation), reduced as sample size increased, highlighting the benefit of richer data and improved feature engineering.

5.4 ROC Curve for both Models

The ROC curve of the Priority Prediction Model (LightGBM, one-vs-rest) reveals moderate AUC scores for Priority 13 (69%, 65%, 65%), and excellent values for rarer classes: Priority 4 (99%) and Priority 5 (93%). In the Service Prediction Model, AUCs were highest for Gynecology/Obstetrics and Pediatrics (100%), followed by Surgery (99%), Radiotherapy (97%), and General Medicine (96%). Cardiorespiratory (91%) and Neurology (92%) showed good, though slightly less precise, separation due to overlapping clinical profiles [6].

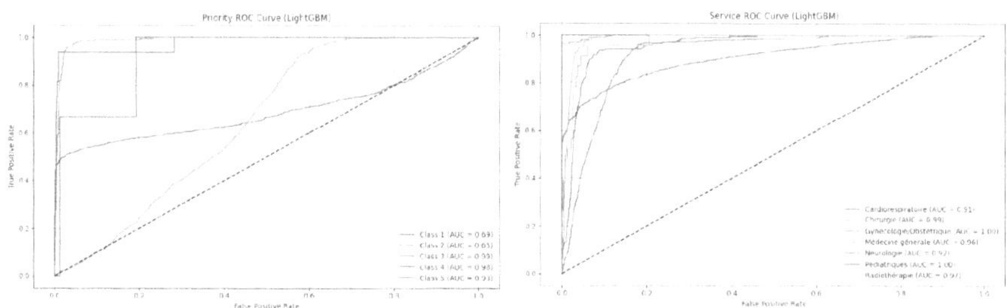

Fig. 8. Priority ROC curve. **Fig. 9.** Service ROC curve.

Interpretation

5.5 Learning Curve for both Models

The learning curve for both the Priority Prediction Model (Fig. 10) and the Service Prediction Model (Fig. 11) tracks the evolution of performance as training data increases. For the Priority Prediction Model, the prediction curve is at 100% (blue curve), and the training score starts at $\sim$ 72% and continuously rises to $\sim$ 85% (dark green color). On the other hand, the Service Prediction Model also has a prediction curve at 100% (blue curve) and a training score that starts at around 72% and continuously increases to $\sim$ 86% (dark green color). This demonstrates that the model is still learning and improving as we conduct training and reinforce the data.

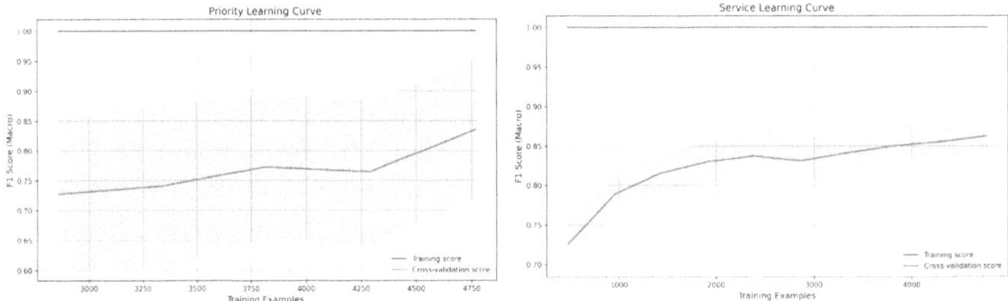

Fig. 10. Priority Learning curve.

Fig. 11. Service Learning curve.

5.6 Confusion Matrix

The Emergency Severity Index model assigns priorities from 1 (highest) to 5 (lowest). For priority 1, 1,542 cases were accurately predicted, but 3,257 were mistaken for priority 2, 71 for priority 3, 28 for priority 4, and 10 for priority 5. Priority 2 had 818 correct predictions, with minor confusions across priorities 3 to 5. Priority 3 saw 160 correct predictions, with some misclassifications as priorities 2 and 4. Priority 4 and 5 had 15 and 2 correct predictions, respectively, with minimal errors. For the Next_Service model, Cardiorespiratory had 2,791 correct predictions but was confused with Surgery (187 cases), General Medicine (299), Neurology (1,025), and Radiotherapy (107). Surgery had 106 correct predictions, Gynecology/Obstetrics 315, General Medicine 168, and Neurology 566, each with minor confusions. Pediatrics achieved perfect prediction (293 cases). Radiotherapy had 14 correct predictions, with 9 mistaken for Surgery.

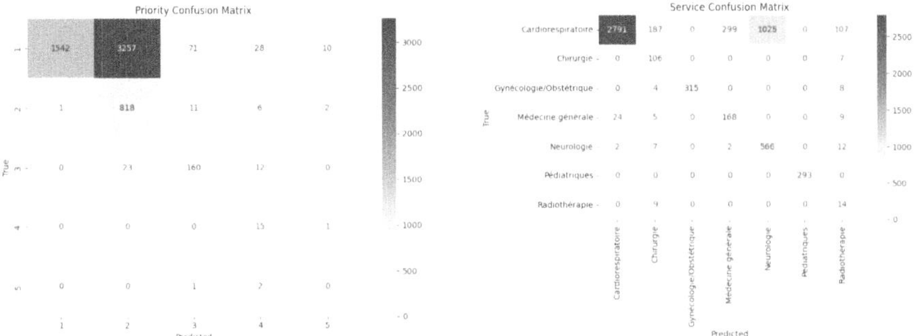

Fig. 12. Priority Confusion Matrix.

Fig. 13. Service Confusion Matrix.

Interpretation. The confusion matrix for the priority model shows strong Level 1 predictions (1,542 correct, 3,257 misclassified as Level 1) in Burkina Faso's tertiary hospitals (CHU-T, Bogodogo, SCHIPHRA), which focus on severe emergencies. Misclassifications between Levels 1 and 2 (3,257 and 818 cases) highlight challenges in distinguishing high-risk patients using only physiological data. Integrating clinical assessments and imaging could improve accuracy. Lower-priority levels (4 and 5) are underrepresented, with only 15 and 2 correct predictions, as non-urgent cases are filtered at primary/secondary levels.

Forservice Model (Fig. 13): Services like cardiology, neurology, and general medicine rely on variables (SpO2, pulse, blood pressure) with often similar ranges. For example, SpO2 < 92 suggests a cardiorespiratory condition, but a pulse $< 110 >$ may indicate a neurological issue. Data from CHU Tengandogo (20212014) show surgery (113 samples) and radiotherapy (23 samples) are underrepresented, limiting model learning.

6 Tests and Validation

For testing and validation, we relied on the French Emergency Nurses Classification in-Hospital, which defines the critical patient data that allows us to determine a patient's priority level. The Table 2 below presents the first three (3) levels (1, 2, 3) of the ESI protocol, with the two (2) others defined in agreement with emergency physicians from the Bogodogo University Hospital Center in Burkina Faso. Based on this, our web application, which we developed, integrates the best performance of the five algorithms developed in the loop, as described in the supervised model outlined in Sect. 3.2.2. Our model accurately detects the priority level and the subsequent services to direct the patient to for appropriate care.

Priority 1 and 2 Detected. After entering the values for a patient named OUEDRAOGO Boureima (borrowed name), whose oxygen saturation (SpO2) is 80%, his case is very critical, so the model classifies him as a Priority 1 patient

Table 2. Priority Classification for Adults

Adults	Priority 1	Priority 2	Priority 3
PAS (mmHg)	< 70	70–90 or 90–100 + FC > 100	< 90
FC/mn	> 180 or < 40	130–180	> 130
SpO_2(%)		86–90	< 90
FR/mn	< 86	30–40	
Blood glucose	> 40	≤ 20 and ketosis > 2 mmol/l	> 20 mmol/l & ketosis or nul
Glasgow	≤ 8	9–13	14

who should be directed to a cardiovascular service (Fig. 14). In the Fig. 15 shows a pregnant woman named DAO Aichata (still a borrowed name), who is pregnant and has normal physiological data except for her heart rate (pulse) which is equal to 151 bpm. She is classified as Priority 2, as shown in Table 6 and should be directed to the gynecology-obstetrics services.

Fig. 14. Priority 1 detected. **Fig. 15.** Priority 2 detected.

Priority 3 and 4/5 Detected. Here, SANOU Issouf, who has a blood pressure of 89 mmHg, is classified as Priority 3 and should be directed to cardiorespiratory services (Fig. 16. In the same time, the 12-year-old boy, SANOU Elvis, whose data is almost normal but who is suffering from pain, is classified as Priority 4 and should be directed to the pediatric services (Fig. 17)

Fig. 16. Priority 3 detected. **Fig. 17.** Priority 4 and 5 detected.

Patient Dashboard. A dashboard (Fig. 18: Patient's statuses and priority) is displayed on a giant screen for the emergency department staff to visualize the patients' statuses and their priority levels in real time. The data is dynamic (indicating whether the patient's condition is improving or deteriorating).

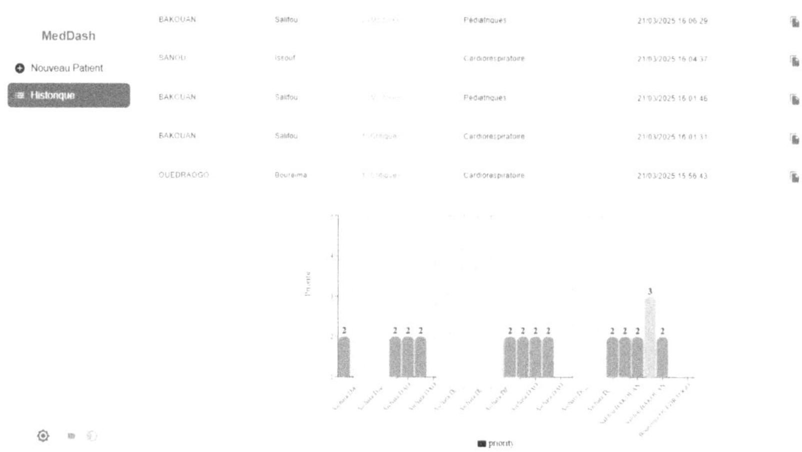

Fig. 18. Patient dashboard.

7 Conclusion and Future Works

The results confirm the feasibility of automating triage in Burkina Faso's emergency departments using ML models based on the ESI protocol. From 23,695 records (2021 – 2024), two models were developed for predicting ESI levels and appropriate services. *XGBoost* and *LightGBM* achieved promising results, notably a 40% F1-score for Priority 1 and ≈ 65% for service assignment. Despite data limitations and class imbalance, the models show potential for scalable deployment, especially with enriched datasets including imaging and laboratory results.

7.1 Future Works

To enhance the utility and robustness of the automated triage system, we propose in our future work:

- **Add data**: Integrate imaging (e.g., X-rays) and laboratory results (e.g., blood glucose) to better detect critical cases (Priority 1).
- **Expand data**: Increase the sample size and geographic diversity by including lower-level centers (Levels 2 and 3) and better (4 and 5) represent rare classes, beyond University Hospital Centers.

Data Availability Statement. The data that support the findings of this study are openly available online at https://bit.ly/medecal_data.

Ethical Statement. All ethical standards were respected throughout this study. Authorization for data collection and clinical testing was granted by the Health Research Ethics Committee of Burkina Faso (Deliberation No. 2024-03-76). Additional approvals were obtained from CHU-T (Receipt No. 2024_093/MSHP/SG/CHU-T/DG) and SCHIPHRA Hospital (Ref/DG/DAM 150724). All patient data were anonymized to preserve confidentiality and protect personal health information, in compliance with applicable ethical and legal regulations.

Conflicts of Interest. Manegaouindé Roland TOUGMA, Boureima ZERBO, Désiré GUEL, Salah Idriss Seif TRAORE, and Salifou NAPON declare that the research was conducted in the absence of any commercial or financial relationships that could be construed as a potential conflict of interest.

References

1. Chen, R., et al.: Prediction of prognosis in COVID-19 patients using machine learning: a systematic review and meta-analysis. Int. J. Med. Inf. **177**, 105151 September (2023). ISSN 13865056. https://doi.org/10.1016/j.ijmedinf.2023.105151. https://linkinghub.elsevier.com/retrieve/pii/S1386505623001697
2. Tengandogo CHU. Centre Hospitalier Universitaire Tengandogo (2025). https://hnbc-bf.org
3. CHU-B. Centre Hospitalier Universiataire de Bogodogo (2025). https://chubogodogo.gov.bf/index.php/fr/
4. Cortes, C., Vapnik, V.: Support-vector networks. Mach. Learn. **20**(3), 273–297 (1995). ISSN 0885-6125, 1573-0565. https://doi.org/10.1007/BF00994018. http://link.springer.com/10.1007/BF00994018
5. Datta, S.,et al.: Predicting hypertension onset from longitudinal electronic health records with deep learning. JAMIA Open **5**(4), ooac097 (2022.) ISSN 2574-2531. https://doi.org/10.1093/jamiaopen/ooac097. https://academic.oup.com/jamiaopen/article/doi/10.1093/jamiaopen/ooac097/6847194
6. ESI. Emergency Severity Index Version 4, ImplementationHandbook. https://www.sgnor.ch/fileadmin/user_upload/Dokumente/Downloads/Esi_Handbook.pdf
7. Grout, R., et al.: Predicting disease onset from electronic health records for population health management: a scalable and explainable Deep Learning approach. Front. Artif. Intell. **6**, 1287541 (2024). ISSN 2624-8212. https://doi.org/10.3389/frai.2023.1287541. https://www.frontiersin.org/articles/10.3389/frai.2023.1287541/full
8. Hosmer, D.W., Lemeshow, S.: Applied Logistic Regression. Wiley, 1st edn (2000). ISBN 978-0-471-35632-5 978-0-471-72214-4. https://doi.org/10.1002/0471722146. https://onlinelibrary.wiley.com/doi/book/10.1002/0471722146
9. Ke, G., et al.: Advances in Neural Information Processing Systems. (2017). https://urlr.me/dpbTGE
10. Mavrogiorgou, A., et al.: A catalogue of machine learning algorithms for healthcare risk predictions. Sensors **22**(22), 8615 (2022). ISSN 1424-8220. https://doi.org/10.3390/s22228615, https://www.mdpi.com/1424-8220/22/22/8615

11. Mostafa, R., El-Atawi, K.: Strategies to measure and improve emergency department performance: a review. Cureus (2024). ISSN 2168-8184. https://doi.org/10.7759/cureus.52879, https://www.cureus.com/articles/215396-strategies-to-measure-and-improve-emergency-department-performance-a-review
12. Nevoret, C., et al.: Apports et limites du machine learning dans la prédiction du changement de stade dans l'asthme en France: une analyse du Système national des données de santé (SNDS). Revue d'Épidémiologie et de Santé Publique, 70: S292–S293 (2022). ISSN 03987620. https://doi.org/10.1016/j.respe.2022.09.031, https://linkinghub.elsevier.com/retrieve/pii/S039876202200788X
13. Geneva based NGO. Urgence sanitaire au Burkina Faso. https://www.impact-initiatives.org/stories/urgence-sanitaire-au-burkina-faso/
14. Ramakrishnaiah, Y., Macesic, N., Webb, G.I., Peleg, A.Y., Tyagi, S.: EHR-ML: a data-driven framework for designing machine learning applications with electronic health records. Int. J. Med. Inf. **196**, 105816 (2025). ISSN 13865056. https://doi.org/10.1016/j.ijmedinf.2025.105816, https://linkinghub.elsevier.com/retrieve/pii/S1386505625000334
15. TF–IDF. In: Sammut, C., Webb, G.I. (eds) Encyclopedia of Machine Learning, pp. 986–987. Springer US, Boston, MA, 2011. ISBN 978-0-387-30768-8 978-0-387-30164-8. https://doi.org/10.1007/978-0-387-30164-8_832, https://link.springer.com/10.1007/978-0-387-30164-8_832
16. Schiphra. Hopital Protestant SCHIPHRA (2025). https://schiphra.org/
17. Si, Y., et al.: Deep representation learning of patient data from Electronic Health Records (EHR): a systematic review. J. Biomed. Inf. **115**, 103671 (2021). ISSN 15320464. https://doi.org/10.1016/j.jbi.2020.103671, https://linkinghub.elsevier.com/retrieve/pii/S1532046420302999
18. Siponen, M., Klaavunlemi, T.: Why is the hypothetico-deductive (H-D) method in information systems not an H-D method? Inf. Organ. **30**(1), 100287 (2020). ISSN 14717727. https://doi.org/10.1016/j.infoandorg.2020.100287, https://linkinghub.elsevier.com/retrieve/pii/S1471772720300117
19. Soori, M., Jough, F.K.G., Dastres, R., Arezoo, B.: AI-Based decision support systems in industry 4.0, a review. J. Econ. Technol. S2949948824000374 (2024). ISSN 29499488. https://doi.org/10.1016/j.ject.2024.08.005, https://linkinghub.elsevier.com/retrieve/pii/S2949948824000374
20. Southwest Jiaotong University, China, Iqbal Muhammad, Zhu Yan, and Southwest Jiaotong University, China. SUPERVISED MACHINE LEARNING APPROACHES: A SURVEY. IJSC, 05(03): 946–952, April 2015. ISSN 09766561, 22296956. https://doi.org/10.21917/ijsc.2015.0133. URL http://ictactjournals.in/ArticleDetails.aspx?id=1785
21. Taboulet, P., et al.: Triage des patients à l'accueil d'une structure d'urgences. Présentation de l'échelle de tri élaborée par la Société française de médecine d'urgence : la FRench Emergency Nurses Classification in Hospital (FRENCH). Ann. Fr. Med. Urgence **9**(1), 51–59 (2019). ISSN 2108-6524, 2108-6591. https://doi.org/10.3166/afmu-2018-0101, https://afmu.revuesonline.com/10.3166/afmu-2018-0101

Multi-label Classification of Plant Diseases Using the Binary Relevance Approach: An Application for Tomato

Hamandé Koursangama[1], Zakaria Cheick Oumar Keita[2(✉)], and Yaya Traore[1]

[1] Joseph KI-ZERBO University, Ouagadougou, Burkina Faso
[2] Nazi Boni University, Bobo-Dioulasso, Burkina Faso
zakariacheickoumarkeita@gmail.com

Abstract. Burkinabe agriculture is a fundamental pillar of the national economy. It plays a crucial role in the economic, social, and food security sectors, contributing to the stability and development of the country. However, this sector faces several challenges, particularly plant diseases, which lead to yield losses, inflated production costs, and food insecurity. As part of the agropastoral offensive aimed at improving agricultural production to achieve food self-sufficiency, combating these plant diseases is of paramount importance. Today, artificial intelligence (AI) offers significant advancements in the fight against these agricultural problems. In this article, we propose an approach using machine learning, focusing on multi-label classification for the simultaneous detection of multiple diseases on a plant. We used the EfficientNetB3 [1] neural network as a feature extractor for plant images and applied a technique based on the Binary Relevance approach with different base algorithms including Multi-Layer Perceptron (MLP), Support Vector Machine (SVM) Random Forest, Perceptron and Decision Tree. Our experiments showed that the MLP algorithm provided satisfactory performance, with an F1-Score of 86.06%, a Hamming Loss of 5.34%, and an accuracy of 80.02%. This approach represents an important step towards the rapid and accurate diagnosis of plant diseases in Burkina Faso.

Keywords: Plant diseases · Machine learning · Multi-label classification · Binary relevance

1 Introduction

Burkina Faso, like many other countries in West Africa, is highly dependent on agriculture for its economy and the survival of its population. The agricultural sector plays a vital role in Burkina Faso, serving as a source of income and livelihood for a large portion of the population. More than 80% of the country's population is employed in agriculture, which contributes almost 40% to the gross domestic product [2]. Despite this strong dependence on agriculture, the country

D. Bassole et al. (Eds.): InterSol 2025, LNICST 671, pp. 18–31, 2026.
https://doi.org/10.1007/978-3-032-15154-4_2

has not yet achieved food self-sufficiency. Despite efforts through various policies and strategies aimed at improving agricultural production, yields remain below the population's food needs. This situation can be explained by several interconnected factors [3]. First, unfavorable climatic conditions, marked by recurrent droughts and irregular rainfall, significantly affect agricultural production. Then, the gradual degradation of soils due to erosion, land depletion, and inappropriate farming practices reduces soil fertility and limits yields. In addition, the lack of access to modern agricultural inputs such as improved seeds, fertilizers, and pesticides hampers the optimization of production.

However, one of the main challenges remains the prevalence of crop diseases, which severely compromise harvests and exacerbate food insecurity. Plant diseases are complex and cover a wide range of pathologies that affect various species. These diseases can be fungal, bacterial, viral, or even related to physiological disorders, representing a major challenge for plants worldwide [4,5]. Diseases such as tomato blight, maize fusarium wilt, peanut rust, drying, bacterial wilt, and mango anthracnose cause significant yield losses, threatening the livelihoods of farmers. Currently, disease detection in Burkina Faso relies on manual methods, often lengthy and tedious, carried out by farmers, agronomists, or phytopathologists. However, this approach [6] is often late, costly, and can lack precision. It is also important to note that some areas are no longer accessible to agricultural experts due to the security situation in Burkina Faso. The lack of effective early detection strategies and integrated disease management exacerbates the situation, calling for innovative solutions, including the use of new technologies like artificial intelligence for faster and more accurate diagnostics. Advances in AI, particularly in Machine Learning (ML) and Deep Learning (DL), offer new opportunities to automate the detection of plant disease from images [7,8].

2 Problem Statement

In the field of plant disease detection, a major challenge lies in the fact that a single leaf can be affected by multiple diseases simultaneously. This issue cannot be effectively addressed using traditional multi-class classification, which assigns only one label per image. Therefore, we define our problem as a multi-label classification task, allowing multiple labels to be assigned to a single observation.

Advances in machine learning have sparked growing interest in multi-label classification (MLC), leading to the development of several approaches. These methods are generally categorized into three main groups [9,10]:

- Problem transformation methods, which convert multi-label classification into single-label classification (binary or multi-class). Among them are Binary Relevance (BR), Classifier Chains (CC), and Label Powerset (LP).
- Ensemble learning approaches, which combine multiple models from the first category, such as Random k-label sets (RAkEL), Ensemble of Binary Relevance (EBR), Ensemble of Classifier Chains (ECC), and Hierarchy Of Multilabel classifiERs (HOMER).

- Algorithm adaptation methods, which modify existing algorithms to suit multi-label classification, including decision trees, multi-label k-NN, multi-label SVMs, and neural networks.

In this study, we chose to explore the Binary Relevance (BR) approach, which transforms the problem into multiple independent binary classification sub-problems. This choice is motivated by the ease of implementation of BR [11] and its compatibility with various base classifiers, which provide a flexible and efficient solution for the detection of plant disease.

3 Related Works

The automatic identification of plant diseases has attracted significant attention in the scientific literature, with approaches based on deep learning, hybrid methods, and multi-label classification. Several studies have used classical or modified CNN architectures for disease detection. For example, Priyanka Kulkarni et al. [12] proposed a model based on Convolutional Neural Networks (CNN) to detect rice diseases such as blast and blight, achieving an accuracy of 95%. Similarly, Hafedh Mahmoud et al. [13] experimented with the YoloV8 model to identify tomato diseases, obtaining an overall accuracy of 66.67%. In a different approach, Hepzibah Elizabeth D. et al. [14] combined a CNN with a recurrent neural network (RNN) to improve the detection of tomato diseases, achieving an accuracy of 81.75%. Hande Yuksel Bayram et al. [15] tested six CNN architectures (AlexNet, GoogLeNet, ShuffleNet, EfficientNetB0, ResNet50, InceptionV3), and achieved the best results by combining AlexNet and GoogLeNet into a hybrid model, which reached an impressive accuracy of 99.50%. S. Poornima et al. [16] proposed an innovative hybrid model combining Region-based Convolutional Neural Network (RCNN) and the Region-based Fully Convolutional Network (RFCN) architectures for the detection of plant leaf diseases. By identifying regions of interest through selective search and extracting features using a CNN, their model achieved a remarkable accuracy of 98.88% in crops such as tomatoes, potatoes, and bell peppers.

Other studies have attempted to combine CNNs with traditional machine learning algorithms. Rashmi Ashtagi et al. [4] introduced two hybrid models: CNN+RF and CNN+SVM. The features extracted by CNN were optimized using a particle swarm optimization algorithm, then classified by Random Forest or SVM. The CNN+RF model outperformed CNN+SVM, achieving an accuracy of 95%, a recall of 93%, an F1-score of 96%, and a precision of 94%. A similar approach was undertaken by Obed Appiah et al. [6] in Burkina Faso. They used EfficientNetB3 for feature extraction and an artificial neural network (ANN) to classify diseases that affect maize, onion, and tomato crops. The results showed accuracy rates exceeding 96% in all crops studied.

Most previous approaches rely on single-label classification, which does not account for the possibility that a plant may be affected by multiple diseases simultaneously. A notable exception is the study by Kavitha Natarajan et al. [17], who implemented a multi-label classification combining an enhanced CNN with the Bat Algorithm optimization. Their model was able to handle the co-occurrence of diseases on the same leaf, achieving an accuracy of 96%, outperforming classical methods such as SVM and standard CNNs. Similarly, Abou Sanou et al. [18] developed a computer vision-based diagnostic system, using DenseNet and EfficientNetB7 to process leaves that potentially present multiple diseases. DenseNet achieved 97% accuracy during training and 93% during testing, while EfficientNetB7 obtained 91% and 70% respectively. Miaomiao Ji et al. [19] proposed a series of networks called BR-CNN, combining the Binary Relevance (BR) method with CNN, to simultaneously recognize crop species, classify leaf diseases, and estimate their severity from images. The BR-CNN based on ResNet50 achieved a test accuracy of 86.70%, while BR-CNN based on lightweight NasNet reached 85.28%.

Although the results obtained are promising, most studies do not take into account real-world field conditions or the need to handle multiple diseases simultaneously (multi-label). In addition, few studies address the challenges of applicability in African contexts, particularly Burkina Faso, where issues such as limited connectivity and restricted access to computational resources present significant obstacles. The objective of this research is therefore to propose an approach based on multi-label classification using the Binary Relevance method to simultaneously detect multiple plant diseases in Burkina Faso. This solution aims to improve agricultural productivity in the country's regions by allowing early and accurate disease identification.

4 Methods

Our architecture (Fig. 1) is divided into three main stages: data collection and processing, followed by model construction, where we train a multi-label classification algorithm based on the Binary Relevance approach, and finally, the development of the mobile application integrating our solution.

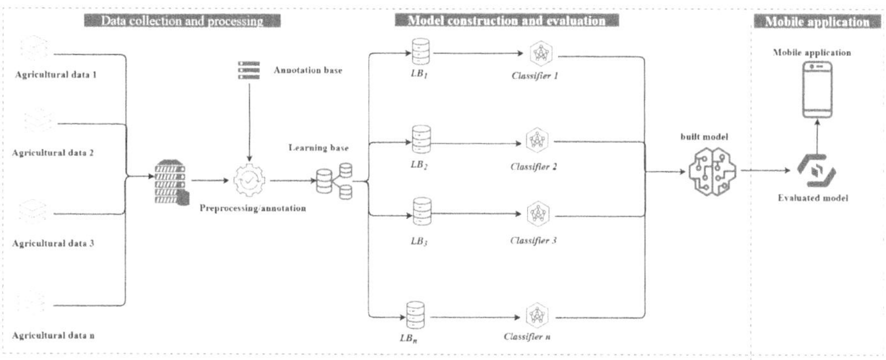

Fig. 1. Method architecture.

4.1 Data Collection and Processing

We used a dataset available on Kaggle [20], consisting of 5,653 images of tomato leaves designed for multi-label classification. The dataset includes eight classes representing different health conditions of tomato leaves (Fig. 2, 3, 4, 5, 6 and 7). Two fungal diseases, initially separated as early blight and late blight, were merged into a single class called blight, due to their visual similarity and common pathological origin. The remaining classes include leaf miner, which refers to insect damage forming visible tunnels on the leaves; magnesium deficiency, characterized by interveinal chlorosis; spotted wilt virus, a viral infection causing ring-shaped spots; nitrogen deficiency and potassium deficiency, which respectively manifest as generalized yellowing and browning of leaf edges; and finally, the healthy class, which includes leaves showing no visible symptoms of disease or deficiency.

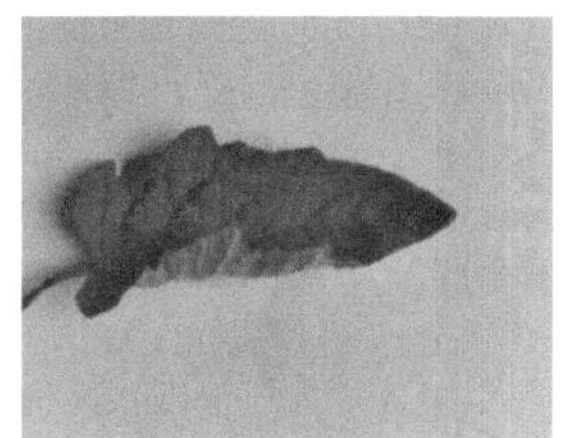

Fig. 2. Healthy.

Fig. 3. Late blight.

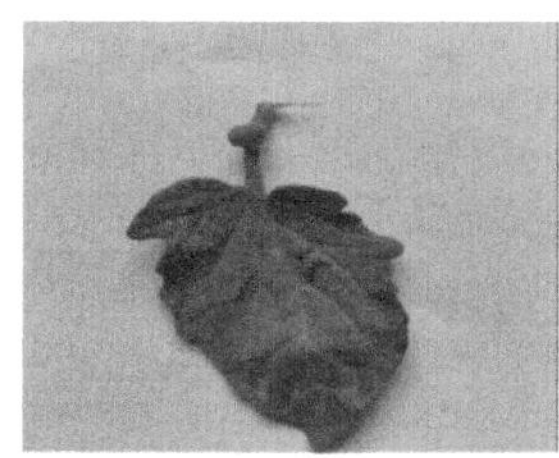

Fig. 4. Leaf miner.

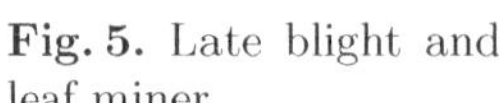

Fig. 5. Late blight and leaf miner.

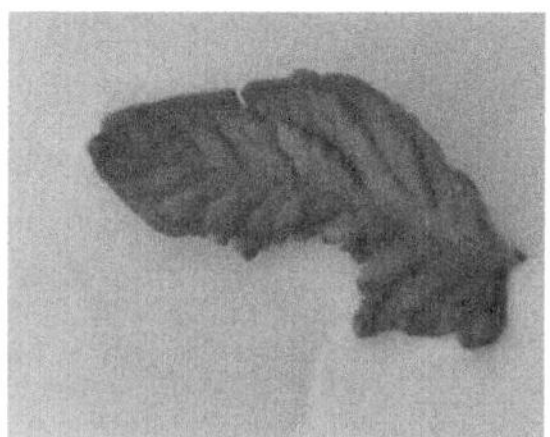

Fig. 6. Nitrogen deficiency.

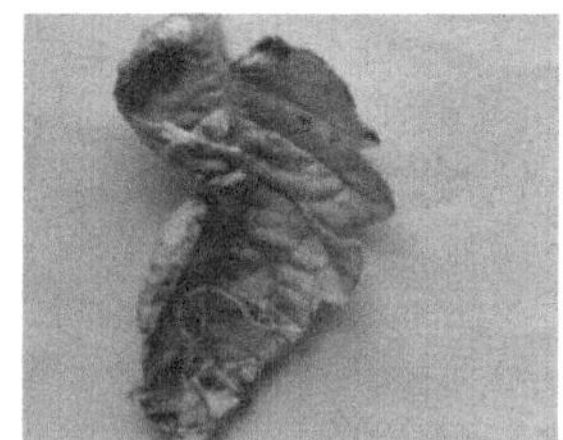

Fig. 7. Magnesium deficiency.

The data underwent a rigorous preprocessing pipeline prior to model training. The initial dataset exhibited significant class imbalance, with certain diseases being heavily underrepresented. To address this issue, data augmentation techniques were employed, including geometric transformations (rotation, horizontal flipping, zooming) and photometric adjustments (brightness modification, filter application). The images were then resized to a uniform dimension of 224×224 pixels. A Gaussian filter (5×5 kernel, standard deviation 0) was applied to reduce noise and eliminate irrelevant visual information. Pixel values were normalized between 0 and 1 to ensure numerical stability during training. For segmentation purposes, the RGB images were converted to the HSV (Hue, Saturation, Value) color space. Thresholds of [10, 30, 30] to [100, 255, 255] were set to identify pixels belonging to the region of interest. A binary mask was then generated and applied to the original image to isolate only the relevant areas. Each image in the dataset was then annotated with one or more visible diseases, and the labels were encoded in a one-hot format to enable direct use in our multi-label classification architecture. Visual features were extracted using the Efficient-NetB3 [1] network pre-trained on ImageNet, with only the convolutional layers retained. The resulting 3D outputs were flattened into 1D feature vectors to be used by traditional classifiers such as MLP, SVM, and Random Forests. Finally, the dataset was split in a stratified way into three subsets: 80% for training, 10% for validation, and 10% for testing.

4.2 Model Construction

The construction of our model is based on the BR approach, which transforms a multi-label classification problem into a set of independent binary classification tasks. In this context, where an image may be associated with several diseases simultaneously, the BR approach (Fig. 8) trains a separate binary classifier for each pathology.Thus, each base algorithm classifier is specialized in detecting a specific disease. The independent outputs of these classifiers are then combined to form a final binary vector (e.g. [1, 0, 1, 0, 0, 1, 0]), indicating the presence or absence of each disease in the image. For this implementation, we explored several base algorithms, including MLP, SVM, Random Forests, Perceptron, and Decision Trees. Therefore, each of these base algorithms was used to train a binary classifier for each disease.

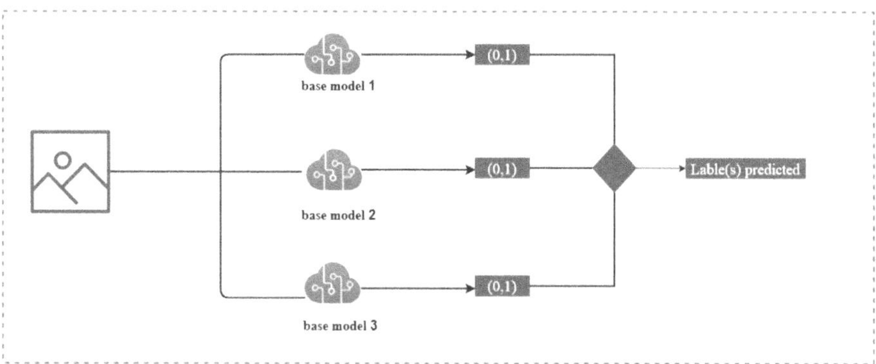

Fig. 8. Binary relevance functioning.

4.3 Usage of Our Solution

To make our solution accessible and easy to use for farmers, we provide a mobile application that integrates our artificial intelligence model capable of identifying plant diseases. The application's workflow follows several steps (Fig. 9) , from image acquisition to displaying the diagnosis. Users can provide an image in two ways: by taking a photo directly with their phone's camera or by selecting an image from their gallery. The verification module then analyzes the submitted image. If it corresponds to a tomato leaf, it is sent to the classification model for analysis. Otherwise, the process is stopped, and an error message informs the user that the image is not suitable. If the image is validated, the model compares its features with its training database and displays one or more labels corresponding to the detected diseases. The embedded model is lightweight and can be executed locally on the device, eliminating any dependence on a stable Internet connection.

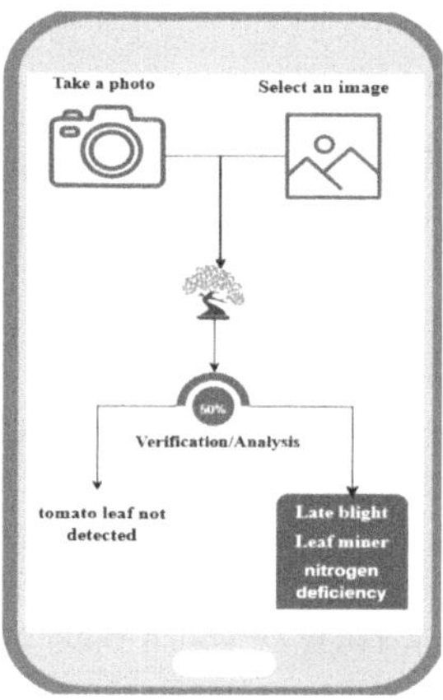

Fig. 9. Usage of the proposed solution.

5 Results

We evaluated our model using multiple metrics, including Accuracy, Precision, Recall, F1-score, Hamming Loss and AUC-ROC (Area Under the ROC Curve), to comprehensively and accurately measure its performance.These metrics are widely used in multi-label classification due to their ability to measure different aspects of a model's performance.

The Fig. 10 reveals that the MLP achieves the highest performance in terms of Accuracy, reaching 80.02%, followed closely by the Perceptron (77.15%) and the SVM (71.19%). The Random Forest achieves an accuracy of 49.12%, while the decision tree has the lowest performance with only 39.74%. In summary, neural networks (MLP and Perceptron) stand out as the most effective algorithms using the BR approach in terms of Accuracy, followed by SVM, which also provides satisfactory results. In contrast, RF and Decision Tree show weaker performance, with results below 50%.

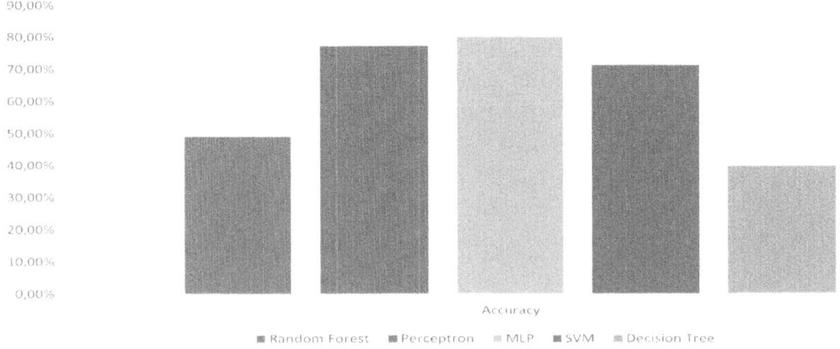

Fig. 10. Model performance in terms of Accuracy.

According to the graphs in Fig. 11, the MLP stands out with the highest precision, reaching 87.18%, followed by Perceptron at 85.58%. The SVM achieves a precision of 79.36%, close to that of the Perceptron, while the RF scores 54.53% and the Decision Tree records the lowest at 52.10%. In summary, MLP and Perceptron remain the most effective baseline algorithms using the BR approach in terms of Accuracy and Precision. The SVM also demonstrates satisfactory results, albeit slightly lower than the Perceptron. In contrast, RF and Decision Tree exhibit weaker performance. Although Precision measures the proportion of correct predictions among the predicted labels, it does not reflect the model's ability to detect all positive instances.

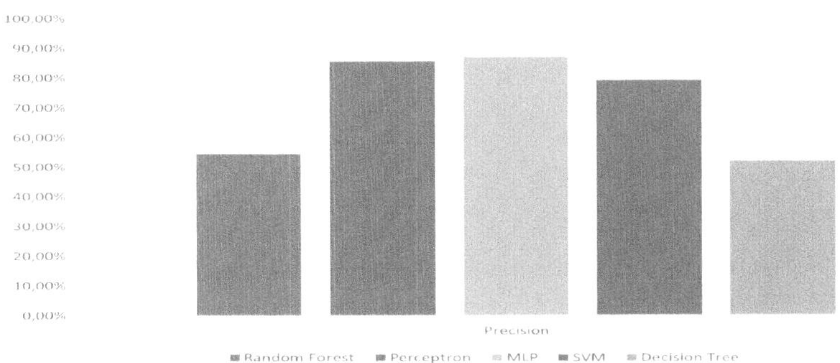

Fig. 11. Model performance in terms of Precision.

Figure 12 illustrates the recall rates of different baseline algorithms. The Perceptron stands out as the best performer with a recall of 86.33%, demonstrating its ability to correctly identify the majority of examples. It is followed by MLP at 86.22%, which is slightly less effective, and SVM, which shows a slightly lower recall (77.01%). In contrast, the Decision Tree and the Random Forest achieve the lowest scores, with 56.05% and 52.21%, respectively. Beyond accuracy and precision, neural networks (Perceptron and MLP) also exhibit strong performance in terms of recall, confirming their suitability for the Binary Relevance (BR) approach. The SVM maintains a satisfactory recall, though lower than that of neural networks, while RF and Decision Tree continue to show the least convincing results.

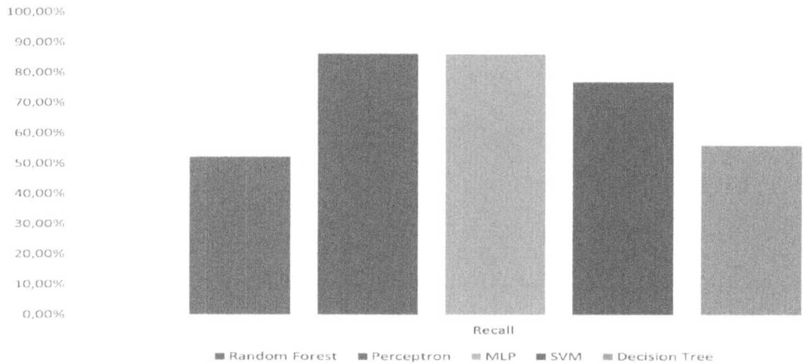

Fig. 12. Model performance in terms of Recall.

The Fig. 13 presents the F1-score for each baseline algorithm. The Multi-Layer Perceptron (MLP) achieves the highest score at 86.06%, demonstrating an optimal balance between recall and precision. It is followed by the Perceptron at 85.06%, which also maintains a well-balanced performance. As with other metrics, SVM (77.44%) shows slightly lower performance compared to neural networks. In contrast, Decision Tree (52.50%) and Random Forest (52.91%) yield the lowest results.

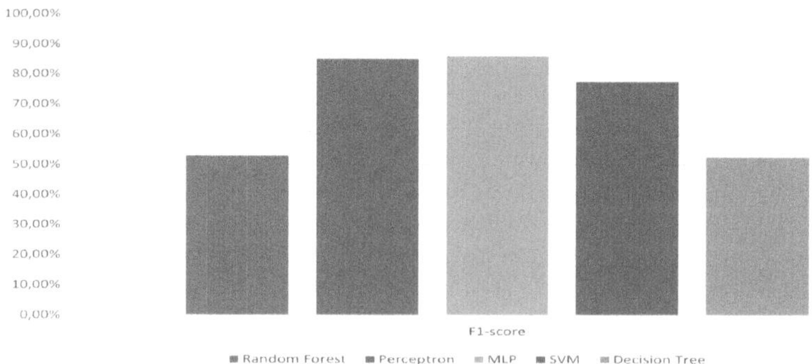

Fig. 13. Model performance in terms of F1-score.

Figure 14 illustrates the Hamming Loss (HL) rate of our baseline algorithms. The MLP (5.34%) exhibits the lowest error rate, confirming its strong performance, followed closely by the Perceptron (6.29%), which has a slightly higher

HL. The SVM (7.24%) follows, making more errors than neural networks, while the RF (12.23%) and Decision Tree (16.40%) record the highest HL rates, indicating less optimal performance.

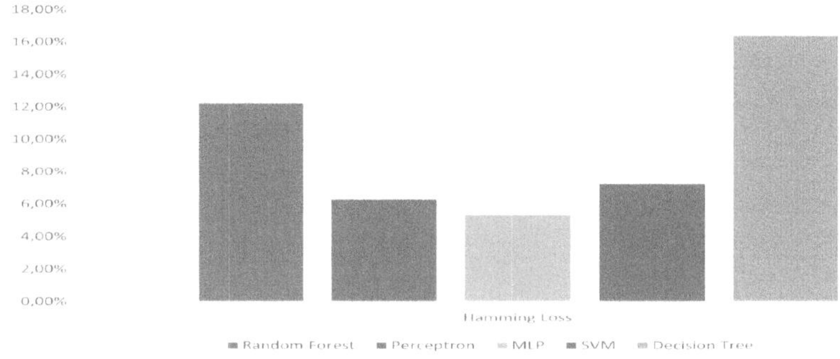

Fig. 14. Model performance in terms of Hamming Loss.

Table 1 present the performance of the five algorithms used for multi-label classification with the BR approach. The analysis of the results reveals that the MLP is the most performant model, with an F1-score of 86.06%, an accuracy of 80.02%, and a Hamming Loss of 5.34%. It is followed by the Perceptron, which displays similar performance with an F1-score of 85.06%, an accuracy of 77.15% and a Hamming Loss of 6.29%. The SVM comes next with an F1-score of 77.44%, an accuracy of 71.19% and a Hamming Loss of 7.24%. On the other hand, the RF shows more modest performance, with an F1-score of 52.91%, accuracy of 49.12%, and a Hamming Loss of 12.23%. Finally, the Decision Tree is the least performant, with an F1-score of 52.50%, accuracy of 39.74%, a Hamming Loss of 16.40%, precision of 52.10%, and recall of 56.05%. Given these results, the MLP, being the most performant. Finally, we will evaluate the models using the AUC-ROC metric, enabling robust visual comparison of their classification performance, independent of decision thresholds and class imbalance.

Table 1. Performance of the models

Metrics	RF	Perceptron	MLP	SVM	Decision Tree
Accuracy	49.12%	77.15%	80.02%	71.19%	39.74%
Precision	54.53%	85.58%	87.18%	79.36%	52.10%
Recall	52.21%	86.33%	86.22%	77.01%	56.05%
F1-score	52.91%	85.06%	86.06%	77.44%	52.50%
Hamming Loss	12.23%	6.29%	5.34%	7.24%	16.40%

ROC curves (Fig. 15) illustrate the performance of our five classification models on a multi-label task transformed into multiple binary classification tasks.

The neural network-based models (Perceptron and MLP) demonstrate the best overall performance with high AUC scores across all classes, reaching up to 0.97 for Perceptron (class 0). Random Forest and SVM show intermediate performance, although Random Forest performs significantly worse in class 4 (AUC = 0.68). The Decision Tree exhibits the weakest results with consistently low AUC values, particularly for class 1 (AUC = 0.67). To ensure accurate classification, MLP proves to be the ideal choice. Therefore, we prioritize it for the practical implementation of our solution in a real-world context.

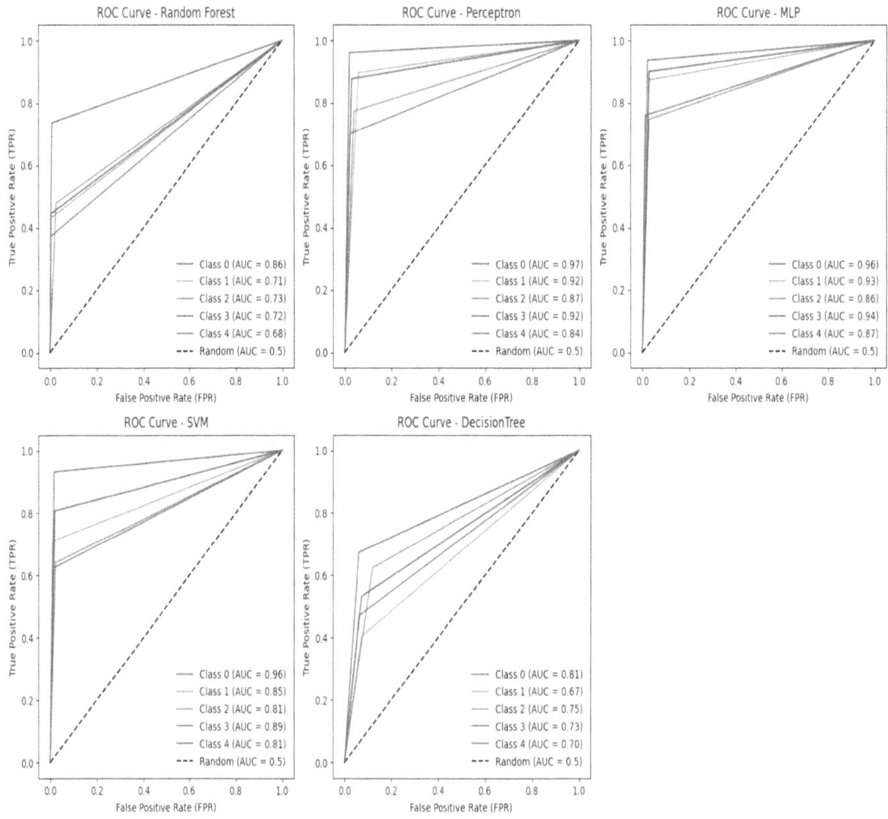

Fig. 15. ROC curves.

Figure 16, Fig. 17 and Fig. 18 illustrate the different stages of the automated diagnostic process implemented in our mobile application. They first present the image upload interface, where the user provides a photo—such as that of an infected tomato leaf—for symptom analysis. The image is then processed by the embedded artificial intelligence system, which is based on the Binary Relevance approach for multi-label classification. Finally, the application displays the diagnostic results, clearly indicating the detected diseases, if any. These screenshots provide a visual overview of the application's smooth operation while highlighting the simplicity of its user interface.

Fig. 16. Home interface.

Fig. 17. Processing phase.

Fig. 18. Results.

6 Discussion

Our final model, based on the multi-label classification approach using Binary Relevance, has demonstrated strong performance in detecting tomato diseases, highlighting the relevance of our method. Despite numerous studies [9,11–15] in this field, most focus on multi-class classification, which does not allow for the simultaneous detection of multiple diseases in a single image. Moreover, they do not always provide a mobile or web-based solution for broad and accessible dissemination of their results.

Despite promising results, our approach has some limitations. First, while BR has proven to be effective in our context, it does not account for relationships between different diseases. Other multi-label classification methods, such as Classifier Chains (CC), Label Powerset (LP), or RAKEL, could potentially improve performance by leveraging these relationships.

Second, ensuring the robustness of the model in real-world conditions remains a challenge. The images used for training were relatively homogeneous, but when farmers use the mobile application, blurry images, poor lighting, or distracting background elements can affect performance. Therefore, enhancing the robustness of the model is crucial to ensure reliable disease detection in various real-world environments.

7 Conclusion

In this paper, we addressed a major challenge for agriculture in Burkina Faso: detecting plant diseases using artificial intelligence and multi-label classification. We developed a model capable of simultaneously classifying multiple diseases, integrated into a mobile application to provide farmers with a fast and accurate diagnosis of tomato plant infections. Although the results obtained are promising, our approach has certain limitations. To improve the performance and effectiveness of the model, several avenues for improvement and further research are being considered. In general, this innovation represents a promising advancement for the agricultural sector, offering a technological tool to improve productivity and crop management.

References

1. Tan, M., Le, Q.: Efficientnet: Rethinking model scaling for convolutional neural networks. Int. Conf. Mach. Learn. PMLR. **97**, 6105–6114 (2019)
2. Zerbo, K.B.F., Yameogo, F., Zan, N., Hien, A., Bonzi, S., Wonni, I.: Impact des maladies sur le rendement du cotonnier au Burkina Faso. Afrique Sci. **24**(5), 80–92 (2024)
3. Stoppa, A., Dick, W.: Agricultural Insurance in Burkina Faso: Challenges and Perspectives (2018)
4. Ashtagi, R., Jaybhaye, S. M.: Fusion of AI techniques: A hybrid approach for precise plant leaf disease classification. J. Electr. Sys., **20**(1), 850-861 (2024). https://doi.org/10.52783/jes.836
5. Hamim, I., Sipes, B., Wang, Y.: Detection, characterization, and management of plant pathogens. Front. Plant Sci. **15**, 1354042 (2024). https://doi.org/10.3389/fpls.2024.1354042
6. Appiah, O., et al.: PlanteSaine: An artificial intelligent empowered mobile application for pests and disease management for maize, tomato, and onion farmers in Burkina Faso. Agric., **14**(8), 1252 (2024). https://doi.org/10.3390/agriculture14081252
7. Patil, Rutuja, R., Kumar, S., Rani, R.: Comparison of Artificial Intelligence Algorithms in Plant Disease Prediction. Revue d'Intelligence Artific., **36**(2), (2022). https://doi.org/10.18280/ria.360202
8. Ferentinos, K.P.: Deep learning models for plant disease detection and diagnosis. Comput. Electron. Agric. **145**, 311–318 (2018). https://doi.org/10.1016/j.compag.2018.01.009
9. Sharma, S., Mehrotra, D.: Comparative analysis of multi-label classification algorithms. In 2018 First International Conference on Secure Cyber Computing and Communication (ICSCCC), pp. 35–38, IEEE (2018). https://doi.org/10.1109/ICSCCC.2018.8703285
10. Nareshpalsingh, J.M., Modi, H.N.: Multi-label classification methods: A comparative study. Int. Res. J. Engg. Tech. (IRJET) **4**(12), 263–270 (2017)
11. Luaces, O., Díez, J., Barranquero, J., del Coz, J.J., Bahamonde, A.: Binary relevance efficacy for multilabel classification. Prog. Artif. Intell. **1**, 303–313 (2012). https://doi.org/10.1007/s13748-012-0030-x
12. Priyanka, K., Swaroopa, S.: Rice leaf diseases detection using machine learning. J. Sci. Res. Tech., **2**(1), 17–22 (2024). https://doi.org/10.61808/jsrt81

13. Zayani, H.M., et al.: Deep learning for tomato disease detection with yolov8. Engg. Technol. Appl. Sci. Res., **14**(2), 13584–13591 (2024). https://doi.org/10.48084/etasr.7064
14. David, H.E., Ramalakshmi, K., Venkatesan, R., Hemalatha, G.: Tomato leaf disease detection using hybrid CNN-RNN model. Adv. Parallel Comput. **38**, 593–597 (2021). https://doi.org/10.3233/APC210108
15. Bayram, H.Y., Bingol, H., Alatas, B.: Hybrid deep model for automated detection of tomato leaf diseases. Traitement du Sig., **39**(5), 1781 (2022). https://doi.org/10.18280/ts.390537
16. Poornima, S., Sripriya, N., Alrasheedi, A.F., Askar, S.S., Abouhawwash, M.: Hybrid convolutional neural network for plant diseases prediction. Intell. Autom. Soft Comput., **36**(2), (2023). https://doi.org/10.32604/iasc.2023.024820
17. Subhadra, K., Kavitha, N.: Multi label leaf disease classification using enhanced deep convolutional neural network. J. Adv. Res. Dyn. Cont. Sys. **12**, 97–108 (2020). https://doi.org/10.5373/JARDCS/V12SP4/20201470
18. Abou, S., Jean, S.D.O., Didier, B., Abdoulaye, S., Yaya, T.: Towards a plant pathologies detection solution. EAI. JRI (2022). https://doi.org/10.4108/eai.11-11-2021.2317975
19. Ji, M., Zhang, K., Wu, Q., Deng, Z.: Multi-label learning for crop leaf diseases recognition and severity estimation based on convolutional neural networks. Soft. Comput. **24**(20), 15327–15340 (2020). https://doi.org/10.1007/s00500-020-04866-z
20. Kaggle Homepage, https://www.kaggle.com/datasets/mamtag/tomato-village. Last accessed 3 Feb 2025

Prediction of Stroke Using Brain Computed Tomography (CT) Images

Seydou Nourou Sylla(✉), Sangoulé Ndao, and Adrien Bass

University Alioune Diop, Bambey, Senegal
seydounourou.sylla@uadb.edu.sn

Abstract. This paper presents an artificial intelligence (AI) model designed to predict strokes using computed tomography (CT) brain images. Stroke is one of the leading causes of mortality and disability in Senegal, where access to advanced diagnostic technologies is limited. The proposed AI system aims to assist radiologists by providing rapid, accurate stroke predictions and is integrated into a mobile application to support diagnosis in remote areas.

Keywords: Stroke · CT imaging · Deep learning · Medical AI · Classification

1 Introduction

Stroke, defined as the rapid development of clinical signs of localized or global brain dysfunction, is a major health concern worldwide [World Health Organization (2021)]. In Senegal, strokes are a leading cause of morbidity and mortality, accounting for over 30% of hospitalizations and two-thirds of deaths in the neurology department Tohme (2020). The country is currently undergoing an epidemiological transition, with an increasing prevalence of non-communicable diseases like hypertension and diabetes—key risk factors for stroke [World Health Organization (2021)]. The high incidence of stroke, combined with the scarcity of advanced diagnostic tools and the lack of trained medical professionals in remote regions, exacerbates the challenge of early and accurate diagnosis Tohme (2020). Brain Computed Tomography (CT) is a critical tool for diagnosing strokes, allowing for the visualization of brain abnormalities and assessing the extent of damage Xie et al. (2019). However, access to CT facilities is limited, especially outside urban areas, and patients often face long wait times. This issue underscores the need for a more efficient and accessible approach to stroke diagnosis [Diallo et al. (2020)]. One of the challenges in using Artificial Intelligence (AI) for stroke diagnosis is the high rate of false positives, where the model incorrectly identifies a stroke in patients without it. This issue can lead to unnecessary treatments and psychological distress for patients. False positives are particularly problematic in low-resource settings like Senegal, where medical facilities and trained professionals are limited, making follow-up testing and confirmation

D. Bassole et al. (Eds.): InterSol 2025, LNICST 671, pp. 32–40, 2026.
https://doi.org/10.1007/978-3-032-15154-4_3

of the diagnosis challenging [Williams et al. (2021)]. Artificial Intelligence (AI), specifically deep learning models, holds significant promise in addressing this challenge by providing quick, reliable, and remote stroke predictions from CT images. However, the implementation of AI models must be accompanied by rigorous validation to reduce the occurrence of false positives. High precision and recall rates, along with model calibration, are critical to minimize errors in diagnosis and ensure that only patients who truly need intervention are identified. This study aims to develop and implement an AI system capable of predicting strokes from CT images. The proposed AI model is designed to assist radiologists by reducing diagnosis time, enabling healthcare professionals to make faster and more informed decisions, particularly in areas where access to medical resources is limited [Williams et al. (2021)]. At the same time, the model incorporates strategies to reduce false positives, improving the reliability of the diagnosis and minimizing unnecessary treatments.

1.1 Problem Statement

The challenge of stroke diagnosis is compounded by the scarcity of advanced diagnostic tools such as CT machines in Senegal. The limited access to such resources, combined with the long wait times for CT scans, delays stroke detection and treatment. Additionally, human error in the interpretation of CT images, such as false positives, further complicates the process. The objective of this study is to develop a machine learning model capable of accurately predicting strokes from CT images to support clinicians in making timely and reliable diagnoses.

2 Stroke Typology and Diagnostic Approaches

Strokes can be classified into three primary categories based on their causes and mechanisms:

2.1 Ischemic Stroke

The most common type, accounting for approximately 85% of cases [Benjamin et al. (2019), Feigin et al. (2017)]. It occurs when a blockage in an artery supplying blood to the brain disrupts blood flow. This blockage may result from a thrombus (a blood clot formed locally) or an embolism (a clot that travels from another part of the body). The blockage prevents oxygen and nutrients from reaching brain cells, leading to cell death. Ischemic strokes can be further divided into two subtypes: thrombotic strokes and embolic strokes (Fig. 1).

2.2 Hemorrhagic Stroke

Hemorrhagic strokes occur when a blood vessel in the brain ruptures, leading to an intracerebral hemorrhage. These strokes account for approximately 15%

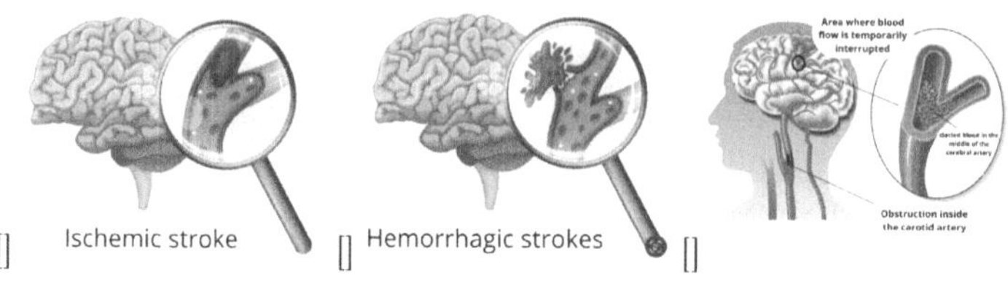

Fig. 1. (a) Ischemic Stroke (b) Hemorrhagic Stroke (c) Transient Ischemic Attack (TIA).

of stroke cases [Krishnamurthi et al. (2013), Sacco et al. (2013)] and are often more severe than ischemic strokes due to the direct damage caused by blood leakage into brain tissue. Uncontrolled hypertension is one of the leading causes, as it weakens the vessel walls, increasing the risk of rupture. Other contributing factors include aneurysms, arteriovenous malformations, and trauma to the head. Hemorrhagic strokes require prompt surgical intervention to stop the bleeding and relieve pressure on the brain. Prevention strategies focus on managing risk factors such as hypertension and addressing vascular abnormalities.

2.3 Transient Ischemic Attack (TIA)

A Transient Ischemic Attack (TIA) is a brief episode of neurological dysfunction caused by a temporary blockage of blood flow to the brain. Unlike a full stroke, the symptoms of a TIA typically resolve within 24 h and do not cause permanent damage. However, TIAs are strong predictors of future strokes, and their occurrence warrants immediate medical evaluation and intervention. TIAs are often caused by the same mechanisms as ischemic strokes, such as thrombus formation or embolism. Although the blockage is temporary, TIAs serve as a critical warning sign for potential long-term cerebrovascular issues.

3 Methodology

By leveraging machine learning techniques, we aim to develop a reliable tool capable of distinguishing a healthy brain (Normal) from a brain affected by a stroke (Stroke). To achieve this goal, we have chosen a neural network model with 12 layers, which we will then compare to other models to select the one that offers the best performance for our specific task. The development of our project is structured around several essential steps:

3.1 Data Collection and Preprocessing

The dataset used in this study consists of CT images of the brain from stroke patients, labeled as either indicating the presence of a stroke or being normal. The dataset was obtained from publicly available medical datasets on platforms such as Kaggle, which hosts a variety of brain CT image datasets, including the "Brain Stroke CT Image Dataset" used for training [Rahman (2021)]. The total dataset contains 1920 images, which were preprocessed to standardize their size to 224×224 pixels and to normalize pixel values.

3.2 Data Splitting and Normalization

We carefully split the data, using 90% of the images for training and 10% for testing. This distribution ensures that we have a representative sample to evaluate the robustness of our model. Additionally, we normalized the images by dividing pixel values by 255 [Nguyen et al. (2016)].

$$x_{\text{train\_s}} = \frac{x_{\text{train}}}{255}, \quad x_{\text{test\_s}} = \frac{x_{\text{test}}}{255}$$

Interpretation: This formula demonstrates how normalization is applied to the data to optimize model training. By scaling pixel values between 0 and 1, we enhance computational efficiency and reduce gradient variance during training [Chen et al. (2019)].

4 Models StrokeNet

We chose to develop a custom 12-layer neural network named **StrokeNet**, a model for brain image classification based on promising results from similar architectures in medical image processing. Instead of using pre-existing models like VGG16 [Simonyan and Zisserman (2015)], ResNet He (2016), and DenseNet [Huang et al. (2017)], we opted to create our own model to better adapt to the specific characteristics of brain CT data. While pre-trained models are general-purpose, our custom model allows for fine-tuning to capture the nuances of medical images. Additionally, by designing our own architecture, we can optimize for efficiency and resource use, ensuring a more lightweight solution. We also aim to compare our model's performance with these established architectures.

4.1 Architecture of StrokeNet

The proposed architecture has been carefully designed to capture relevant visual features at each level of abstraction. Below is the model representation (Fig. 2):

Interpretation: This figure presents the complete architecture of our model. Each convolutional layer extracts increasingly abstract features, while the fully connected layers make final classification decisions. Pooling layers reduce the dimensionality of images, improving the model's efficiency. This model consists of several key layers: Conv2D for feature extraction, MaxPooling2D for dimensionality reduction, and Flatten to prepare data for the Dense layers. The Dense layers are fully connected with ReLU activation to capture complex relationships, and Dropout is used to prevent overfitting. The final output layer uses a Sigmoid activation for binary classification. The model is compiled with the

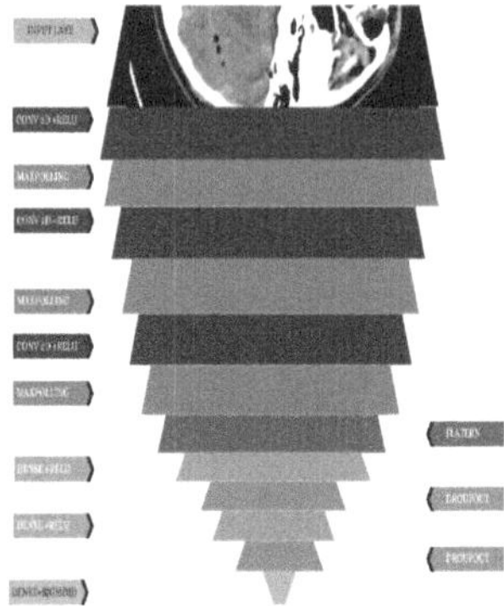

Fig. 2. Architecture of StrokeNet.

Adam optimizer, binary cross-entropy loss, and accuracy as the evaluation metric. This architecture is designed to process and classify images efficiently while preventing overfitting.

4.2 Model Training

The model was trained over 10 epochs using our normalized dataset. We used binary cross-entropy as the loss function and the Adam optimizer [Kingma and J. Ba (2015)] to adjust the model's weights.

$$\text{loss} = \frac{1}{m}\sum_{i=1}^{m}(-y_i \log(h_\theta(x_i)) - (1 - y_i)\log(1 - h_\theta(x_i)))$$

The model was trained with the following command: `hist= model.fit (x_train, y_train, epochs=10, validation_data=(x_test, y_test))`

- **x_train**: Input dataset containing images for training.
- **y_train**: Output labels corresponding to the images in **x_train**.
- **epochs=10**: The model iterates over the dataset `(x_train, y_train)` a total of 10 times. Each iteration is called an "epoch". During each epoch, the model adjusts its weights based on the errors it makes.
- **validation_data=(x_test, y_test)**: Specifies a separate dataset for evaluation. **x_test** contains test images, and **y_test** contains corresponding labels.

5 Results

To understand the model's behavior, we generated a series of visualizations. Even in difficult cases, the model correctly identified most strokes, demonstrating its robustness. However, misclassified images were analyzed using additional algorithms to understand the sources of error. **Interpretation:** This table shows that out of 110 examples from class 0 (Normal), 108 were correctly classified (true negatives) and 2 were misclassified (false positives). For class 1 (Stroke), 78 out of 82 were correctly classified (true positives) with 4 errors (false negatives). This indicates a strong predictive capability for both classes, with minimal errors. **Classification Report:** - **Precision**: 96% for class 0 and 97% for class 1, showing that the model makes very few errors when predicting these classes. - **Recall**: 98% for class 0 and 95% for class 1, indicating that the model effectively identifies real examples of each class. - **F1-score**: 0.97 for class 0 and 0.96 for class 1, demonstrating a good balance between precision and recall. - **Accuracy**: 97%, meaning the model correctly classifies 97% of test examples.

Table 1. Classification results of the model on Normal and Stroke classes.

Class	Precision	Recall	F1-Score	Examples
Class 0 (Normal)	96%	98%	0.97	110
Class 1 (Stroke)	97%	95%	0.96	82
Accuracy	97%			

5.1 Comparison with Other Models

To evaluate the effectiveness of our model, we compared its performance with VGG16, ResNet50, and DenseNet121 in the same dataset. The results are summarized in Table 1 (Table 2).

Table 2. Performance comparison of different models.

Model	Accuracy	Recall	Precision	F1-Score
StrokeNet	97%	95%	96%	0.96
VGG16	94%	91%	92%	0.92
ResNet50	96%	94%	95%	0.95
DenseNet121	95%	93%	94%	0.94

6 Model Evaluation

Although StokeNet demonstrated excellent performance on the test set, some predictions were incorrect. To better understand the causes of these errors, we applied additional analysis methods, such as the **Signal-to-Noise Ratio** (SNR) and **variance**. These methods help quantify image interference and measure pixel value dispersion, providing insights into the sources of classification errors [Nguyen et al. (2016), Chen et al. 2019)]. Specifically, we compared two correctly classified images with two misclassified images using SNR and variance as analysis metrics. The results show that misclassified images generally exhibit a lower signal-to-noise ratio (SNR) and a higher variance compared to correctly classified images. This suggests that a higher level of noise or greater pixel value dispersion makes the classification task more challenging for StokeNet. In other words, significant noise or strong local variations may obscure key discriminative features, leading to incorrect predictions. These findings highlight the importance of better image preprocessing or enhancing the model's robustness to noise (Figs. 3 and 4).

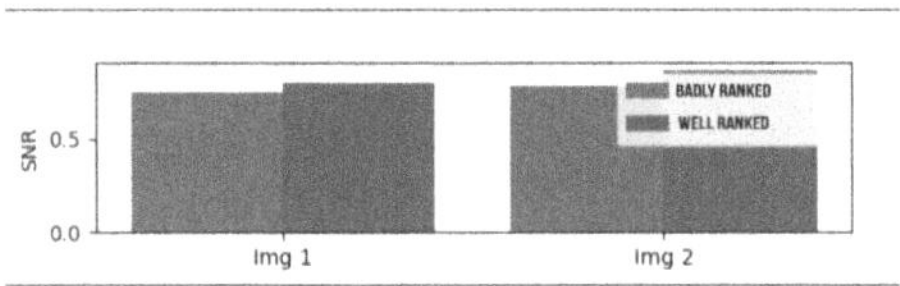

Fig. 3. SNR result.

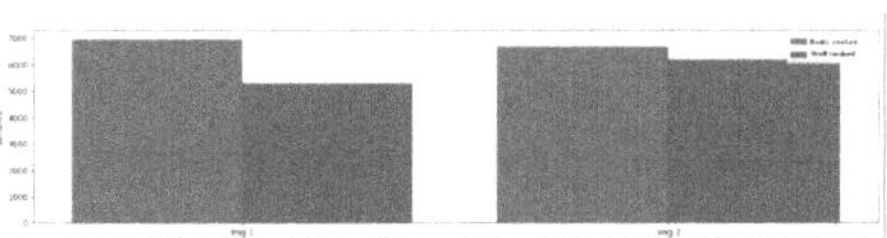

Fig. 4. Variance result.

7 Conclusion

This study demonstrates that our deep learning-based model, named StrokeNet, is a promising solution for stroke detection from CT images. StrokeNet achieved high accuracy (97%) and excellent sensitivity, making it a reliable tool to assist clinicians in stroke diagnosis, especially in areas with limited access to advanced diagnostic resources.

Notably, our dataset, composed of only 1,920 images, shows that it is possible to achieve very good results even with a relatively small amount of data, which is particularly promising in contexts like Senegal, where access to medical data is often limited.

However, despite these encouraging results, there are several areas for improvement. Future work should focus on increasing the dataset size and diversity to enhance the model's generalization ability. Incorporating additional imaging modalities could further improve diagnostic accuracy and robustness. Moreover, integrating explainable AI techniques would provide more transparency in decision-making, helping clinicians better understand the model's predictions. Deploying the model in real-world clinical settings and validating its performance on prospective patient data is another crucial step towards practical implementation. Finally, the development of a user-friendly interface for automated stroke detection could facilitate its adoption by healthcare professionals, particularly in resource-constrained environments. These advancements would significantly contribute to making AI-driven stroke detection a standard tool in modern medical diagnostics.

References

Benjamin, E.J., Muntner, P., Alonso. A., et al.: Heart Disease and Stroke Statistics—2019 Update: A Report From the American Heart Association. Circulation 139 10, e56–e528 (2019). https://doi.org/10.1161/CIR.0000000000000659

Wei, C., Hongyu, Z., Rui, Z.: A Survey on Image Preprocessing and Augmentation Techniques for Deep Learning in Medical Image Classification. Med. Image Anal. **58**, 101–119 (2019)

Diallo, S., et al.: Using Artificial Intelligence to Enhance Healthcare Delivery in Senegal: A Case Study. International Journal of Medical Informatics 138 (2020)

Feigin, V.L., Norrving, B., Mensah, G.A.: Global Burden of Stroke. Circulation Research 120, 3, 439–448 (2017). https://doi.org/10.1161/CIRCRESAHA.116.308413

He, K. et al.: Deep Residual Learning for Image Recognition. IEEE Conference on Computer Vision and Pattern Recognition (CVPR), 770– 778 (2016). https://doi.org/10.1109/CVPR.2016.90

Gao, H., Zhuang, L., Laurens, M., Kilian, Q.W.: Densely Connected Convolutional Networks. Proceedings of the IEEE Conference on Computer Vision and Pattern Recognition (CVPR), 4700–4708 (2017). https://doi.org/10.1109/CVPR.2017.24

Kingma D.P., Ba, J.: Adam: A Method for Stochastic Optimization. Proceedings of the International Conference on Learning Representations (ICLR) (2015). https://arxiv.org/abs/1412.6980

Krishnamurthi, R.V., Moran, A.E., Forouzanfar, M.H., et al.: The Global Burden of Hemorrhagic Stroke: A Summary of Findings From the GBD 2010 Study. Glob. Heart **8**(2), 101–106 (2013)

Trung, A.N., Minh, N., Tung, V., Thi, M.N.: Preprocessing techniques for image classification. International Journal of Image Processing **10**(2), 55–66 (2016)

Afridi, R.: Brain Stroke CT Image Dataset. https://www.kaggle.com/datasets/afridirahman/brain-stroke-ct-image-dataset/data. A dataset containing labeled brain stroke CT images, used for training machine learning models in stroke detection. Available on Drive (2021)

Sacco, R.L., Kasner, S.E., Broderick J.P. et al.: An Updated Definition of Stroke for the 21st Century. Stroke 44, 7, 2064–2089. (2013). https://doi.org/10.1161/STR.0b013e318296aeca

Karen, S., Andrew, Z.: Very Deep Convolutional Networks for Large-Scale Image Recognition. International Conference on Learning Representations (2015)

Tohme, S.M.K.: Health Infrastructure Challenges in Africa: MRI Access and Utilization. J. Glob. Health **12**, 4 (2020)

Williams, M.L., et al.: Mobile Health Applications for Stroke Detection in Low Resource Settings: A Systematic Review. Journal of Mobile Health **8**, 2 (2021)

World Health Organization. 2021. Stroke: A Global Overview. World Health Organization (2021)

Xie, J. et al.: Artificial Intelligence in Medical Imaging: A Review. Journal of Healthcare Engineering 2019 (2019)

The Contribution of Explainable AI Techniques in the Integration of AI in Education: An Application of the SHAP Method on a Machine Learning Model

Serigne Mbacke Gueye[1(✉)] and Babacar Mbaye[2]

[1] Université Laval, OBVIA, Quebec City, Canada
serigne.mbacke-gueye@cegepsi.ca

[2] Laboratoire de Sécurité Informatique (LSI), Université Laval, Quebec City, Canada
babacar.mbaye.6@ulaval.ca

Abstract. The integration of artificial intelligence (AI) in the field of education offers promising opportunities for personalized learning and the prediction of student performance. However, the adoption of these technologies is often hindered by the lack of transparency and explainability of AI models, particularly those considered as "black boxes." This article explores the use of explainable AI (XAI) techniques, specifically the SHAP (SHapley Additive exPlanations) method, to improve the interpretability of machine learning models in an educational context. We apply the XGBoost (eXtreme Gradient Boosting) algorithm to predict student performance in mathematics using the Student Performance dataset from the UCI Machine Learning Repository, and then use SHAP to explain the model's predictions. The results show that previous grades (G1 and G2, i.e., the first and second evaluations) are the most influential factors, while absences have a significant negative impact. Additionally, features such as study time and family relationships contribute positively, though to a modest extent. SHAP visualizations, such as Summary Plots, Waterfall Plots, and Dependence Plots, reveal complex and non-linear relationships between features, highlighting the importance of a multifactorial approach to improving student performance. This study demonstrates that explainable AI techniques, such as SHAP, can not only improve the transparency of predictive models but also provide valuable insights to guide targeted and equitable educational interventions.

Keywords: Explainable Artificial Intelligence (XAI) · SHAP (SHapley Additive exPlanations) · XGBoost (eXtreme Gradient Boosting) · AI Model Transparency · AI in Education

1 Introduction

Artificial intelligence (AI) has the potential to radically transform the education sector by offering personalized solutions for learning, assessment, and the management of educational resources [1,2]. Indeed, opaque machine learning models

D. Bassole et al. (Eds.): InterSol 2025, LNICST 671, pp. 41–51, 2026.
https://doi.org/10.1007/978-3-032-15154-4_4

"black boxes") are increasingly used to make important predictions in the field of education. However, the adoption of AI in education is hindered by several challenges, including the lack of transparency and explainability of AI models [3]. Decision-makers, teachers, and other stakeholders are often skeptical of systems whose decisions cannot be easily explained or understood [4]. His skepticism is particularly pronounced in the case of generative AI models, which are often perceived as "black boxes" [5]. In this context, explainable AI (XAI) techniques emerge as a promising solution and can serve to verify and certify the results of models, enriching them with desirable notions such as reliability, responsibility, transparency, and equity.

Among these techniques, the SHAP (SHapley Additive exPlanations) method stands out for its ability to provide local explanations, which clarify individual predictions by showing how each feature contributes to a specific outcome, as well as global explanations, which offer insights into the overall behavior of the model by summarizing the importance of features across the entire dataset. This article explores how the use of explainable AI techniques, particularly SHAP, can help overcome the barriers to the adoption of AI in education.

The remainder of the document will be organized as follows. In Sect. 2 will conduct a literature review examining the benefits and challenges of implementing AI in education, followed by an overview of explainable AI techniques and their applications in this domain. In Sect. 3, we will explore the use of SHAP with an XGBoost machine learning model to predict student performance. This section will begin with a description of the study context, followed by a discussion of the methodology and simulations. In Sect. 4, we will present and analyze the results. Finally, we will conclude this work with a summary and propose future perspectives.

2 Literature Review

2.1 AI in Education: Advantages and Challenges

AI has been widely studied in the educational context, with applications ranging from personalized learning to the prediction of student performance. Several studies have explored predictive models to identify key factors of academic performance. For example, the authors of [6] reviewed the applications of educational data mining (EDM) to predict academic success and identify at-risk students. Similarly, the authors of [7] compared several classification algorithms to predict student performance, concluding that ensemble methods such as boosting offer better accuracy.

However, as highlighted by [8], the adoption of AI in education is hindered by several challenges, including the lack of transparency of models and the difficulty in interpreting their decisions. Indeed, they emphasize the need for a remedial and ethical approach when deploying AI in education, highlighting the necessity of clear and transparent ethical principles, as well as a deep pedagogical reflection. [9] sheds light on several challenges related to the integration of generative AI (GenAI) technologies in higher education, particularly concerns regarding accuracy and transparency. The authors point out that the accuracy of GenAI responses cannot always be guaranteed, and the complex functioning of these systems can be difficult to understand, which may undermine public trust. According to [10], the use of AI models such as ChatGPT in higher education presents challenges related to transparency and explainability. Indeed, AI models can be biased due to insufficient training data, which can lead to biased models and results. These biases can perpetuate misconceptions among learners instead of helping them build accurate knowledge. Therefore, it is essential to verify the facts of all results from these models to identify potential biases or inaccuracies.

2.2 Explainable AI Techniques

Explainable AI techniques, such as LIME (Local Interpretable Model-agnostic Explanations) and SHAP, have been proposed to make AI models more interpretable. SHAP, in particular, is based on game theory and provides local and global explanations for the predictions of a model. According to [11], SHAP SHAP is particularly useful for explaining the decisions of complex models. XAI (Explainable AI) techniques, which are model-agnostic, are designed to be applied to any machine learning model after it has been trained [12]. The flexibility of these methods lies in their ability to explain any machine learning model [13]. In what follows, we will rely on [3] and [14] to explain the functioning of the SHAP (SHapley Additive exPlanations) method.

SHAP is grounded in a robust theoretical framework rooted in game theory, ensuring the validity of its explanations through adherence to mathematical axioms. It offers contrastive explanations by comparing individual predictions to the average prediction, making it particularly useful for users who require confidence that the explanations accurately reflect the model's behavior. By evaluating predictions through all possible combinations of feature presence and absence, SHAP enables a detailed understanding of how each feature contributes to the final prediction. Specifically, SHAP leverages Shapley values, a concept from cooperative game theory, which provides a fair and mathematically rigorous approach to attributing the contribution of each participant in a cooperative setting. This is achieved by averaging the marginal contributions of each feature across all possible sequences in which they could be added to the model [11]. SHAP decomposes the prediction of a model among all the features involved using an additive feature attribution analysis:

$$g(x') = \phi_0 + \sum_{i=1}^{M} \phi_i x'_i,$$

where :

- $g(x')$ is the explanation model that approximates the original model $f(x)$. It is used to explain the prediction of the original model.
- x' is a binary vector of size M (where M is the number of features).

- ϕ_0 represents the base value of the model, i.e., the average prediction of the model when all features are absent (or at their default value).
- ϕ_i is the SHAP value of feature i, i.e., its contribution to the model's prediction. It is expressed as follows:

$$\phi_i = \sum_{S \subseteq N \setminus \{i\}} \frac{|S|!(M - |S| - 1)!}{M!} \left[f_X(S \cup \{i\}) - f_X(S) \right],$$

where :

- N is the set of all features in the model.
- S is a subset of features not containing i (i.e., $S \subseteq N \setminus \{i\}$).
- M is the total number of features in N.
- $f_X(S)$ is the model's prediction using only the features in S.
- $f_X(S \cup \{i\})$ is the model's prediction using the features in S as well as feature i.
- $f_X(S \cup \{i\}) - f_X(S)$ is the marginal contribution of feature i when it is added to the subset S.
- $\frac{|S|!(M-|S|-1)!}{M!}$ is a weighting factor that ensures all feature combinations are considered fairly. It is derived from cooperative game theory (Shapley values).

In summary, this equation calculates the contribution of each feature i by averaging its marginal contributions over all possible subsets of features.

2.3 Applications of XAI in Education

The rapid rise of artificial intelligence (AI) has transformed various fields, including education. However, the inherent opacity of many AI models, such as deep neural networks, poses significant challenges in terms of transparency and trust. In education, the application of explainable AI is particularly crucial, as it allows teachers, students, and administrators to better understand the decisions and predictions of AI systems. Several studies have been proposed in this direction to explore the main approaches of explainable AI, their unique characteristics in the educational context, and the challenges and opportunities they present for improving the learning experience and decision-making in educational institutions. In this context, [15], provides an overview of XAI applications in the field of education, illustrated by examples of empirical studies. It addresses the main categories of XAI approaches used to interpret and explain AI models, the specific characteristics of XAI in education, and how these models can be leveraged by teachers, students, and researchers to inform their decisions. Finally, it explores the challenges and opportunities of XAI applications in the education sector. in [16], a comparative analysis of explainable AI (XAI) techniques for interpreting machine learning models on a dataset comprising 1205 instances was presented. The authors applied several algorithms, among which the random forest stood out with an accuracy of 91%. AI techniques such as SHAP, LIME, Anchors, ALE, and counterfactual explanations revealed the specific contributions of features to adaptability predictions. The results highlighted key factors such as

"Course Duration" and "Financial Condition," emphasizing the importance of a multifaceted approach to bridge the gap between model performance and educational relevance. This study provides clear and actionable explanations, offering a framework for more equitable and effective educational policies. In the context of exploring the impacts of artificial intelligence on education, research has shown that parental income significantly influences children's schooling [17]. This work examined how complex AI models make important decisions using explainable AI tools, revealing complexities related to parental income and providing reasonable explanations for these decisions. However, biases in AI have also been identified, contrary to the principles of transparency and fairness. These biases can affect families and children's schooling, highlighting the need for improved AI solutions that offer equitable opportunities for all. A recent study on advances in explainable artificial intelligence (XAI) addressing the interpretability challenges of complex AI models, aiming to enhance the trust and usability of AI systems, was proposed in [18]. The study examines various emerging XAI techniques to improve the transparency of AI models, using approaches such as post-hoc explanations, model transparency methods, and interactive visualization techniques. By highlighting the strengths and weaknesses of each method, the authors demonstrate promising advances in model interpretability, facilitating a better understanding of AI systems by humans.

3 Prediction of Student Performance Using XGBoost and Interpretation with SHAP

3.1 Study Context

In the field of education, predicting student performance is a crucial issue for identifying key factors influencing their academic success [19]. Thanks to machine learning techniques, it is possible to model these predictions, but relatively little attention has been paid to explaining their predictions, especially for tree-based machine learning models such as random forests, decision trees, and gradient boosting trees, which are non-linear and therefore difficult to interpret, yet very popular [20,21]. In this study, we use the XGBoost (eXtreme Gradient Boosting) algorithm to predict students' final grades in mathematics, and then apply the SHAP (SHapley Additive exPlanations) method [22] to explain this prediction by interpreting the contributions of the different features by using SHAP visualizations (Summary Plots, Waterfall Plots and Dependence Plots). Summary plot highlights the features that have the greatest impact on predicted performance. Waterfall plot provided a detailed interpretation of how individual features contributed to specific predictions. Dependence plots provide a detailed view of how key features influence predicted student performance.

3.2 Methodology and Simulation

The dataset used in this study is the Student Performance Dataset, available on the UCI Machine Learning Repository [23]. his dataset contains detailed information on 395 students, including various characteristics such as demographic data (age, gender, school), family context (parents' education level, family size), study habits (study time, school support), as well as other factors such as extracurricular activities and internet access. Categorical variables were encoded using a LabelEncoder to make them compatible with machine learning algorithms, and the data were divided into training (80%) and test (20%) sets to evaluate the model's performance.

For modeling, we chose XGBoost [24], a tree-based boosting algorithm known for its performance, robustness, and ability to capture complex relationships between features. The model was configured with the following hyperparameters: n_estimators = 100 (number of trees), learning_rate = 0.1 (learning rate), and random_state = 42 (to ensure the reproducibility of results). After training, the model was evaluated using the mean squared error (MSE), demonstrating satisfactory performance on the test set.

The simulations presented in this study were conducted on the Google Colab platform. The notebook used to run these simulations is available here.

4 Results and Discussion

4.1 Summary Plots and Waterfall Plots

SHAP visualizations, particularly Summary Plots and Waterfall Plots, provide a deep understanding of the factors influencing student performance and their individual contributions to the model's predictions.

The Summary Plot identified the most influential features on the predicted performance. Previous grades (G1 and G2) stood out as the most important predictors, confirming that past performance is a reliable indicator of future results. Absences showed a strong negative influence, highlighting the critical impact of attendance on academic success. Features such as family relationships (famel) and study time (studytime) also demonstrated a positive, albeit moderate, contribution, emphasizing the role of family support and study investment. On the other hand, variables such as school support (schoolsup) or internet access (internet) showed a lesser impact, suggesting that their influence is less significant in this context (Fig. 1).

The Waterfall Plot provided a detailed interpretation of the contributions of features for individual predictions. For example, for a specific student, we observed that absences strongly contributed to a decrease in the prediction, while features such as family relationships (famel) and study time (studytime) had a positive impact. These visualizations allow us to understand how different features interact to arrive at a final prediction, offering valuable insights for targeted interventions (Fig. 2).

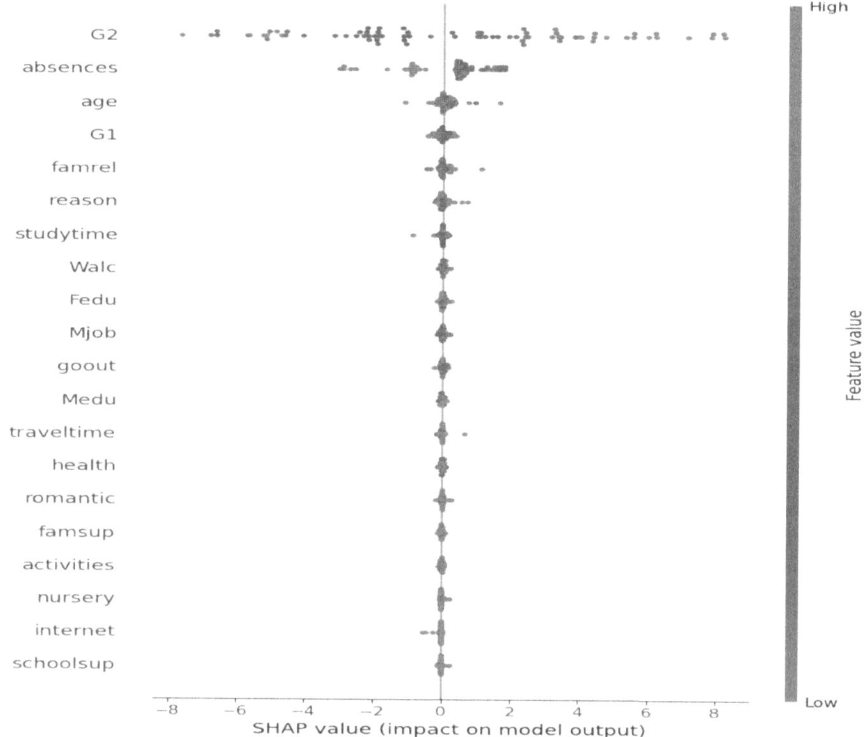

Fig. 1. Summary Plots.

By combining the insights from Summary Plots and Waterfall Plots, several conclusions emerge: (1) Previous Performance: Previous grades (G1 and G2) are powerful predictors, justifying continuous monitoring of students. (2) Attendance: Absences have a significant negative impact, highlighting the need for policies aimed at reducing absenteeism. (3) Family Support and Study Time: Features such as family relationships (famel) and study time (studytime) play a positive, albeit moderate, role, suggesting that interventions combining family support and study encouragement could be beneficial. (4) Complex Interactions: The variability of contributions in Waterfall Plots highlights the complex interactions between features, indicating that multifactorial approaches are necessary to improve student performance.

4.2 Dependence Plots

The Dependence Plots generated by SHAP allow for a detailed exploration of the relationships between key features and their impact on the predicted student performance. For study time (studytime), we observe a non-linear relationship where higher study time is associated with a gradual improvement in performance, although this relationship is modulated by other factors such as family

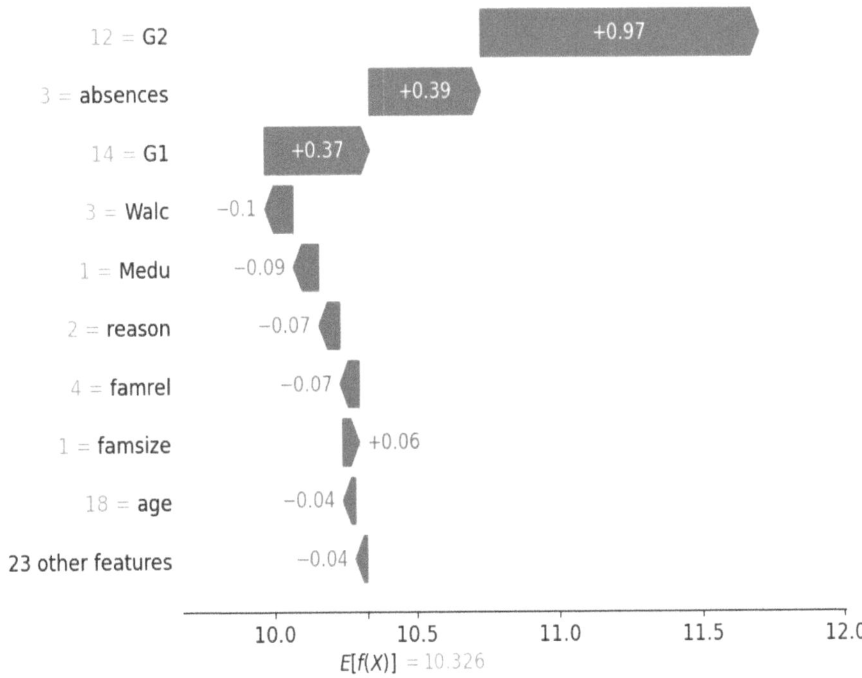

Fig. 2. Waterfall Plot.

support or motivation. This confirms the importance of encouraging students to devote more time to their studies, while taking into account individual contexts that may influence this relationship. For family relationships (famel), the plot reveals a significant positive contribution, indicating that a favorable family environment is a key factor for academic success. However, the variability of SHAP values suggests that this feature interacts with other variables, such as school support or available educational resources. This highlights the need for an integrated approach, combining family support and educational interventions, to maximize the impact on student performance (Fig. 3).

In summary, Dependence Plots highlight complex and often non-linear relationships between features and student performance. They emphasize the importance of considering both individual factors (such as study time or absences) and the interactions between these factors (such as family support and educational resources) to develop effective strategies for improving academic success.

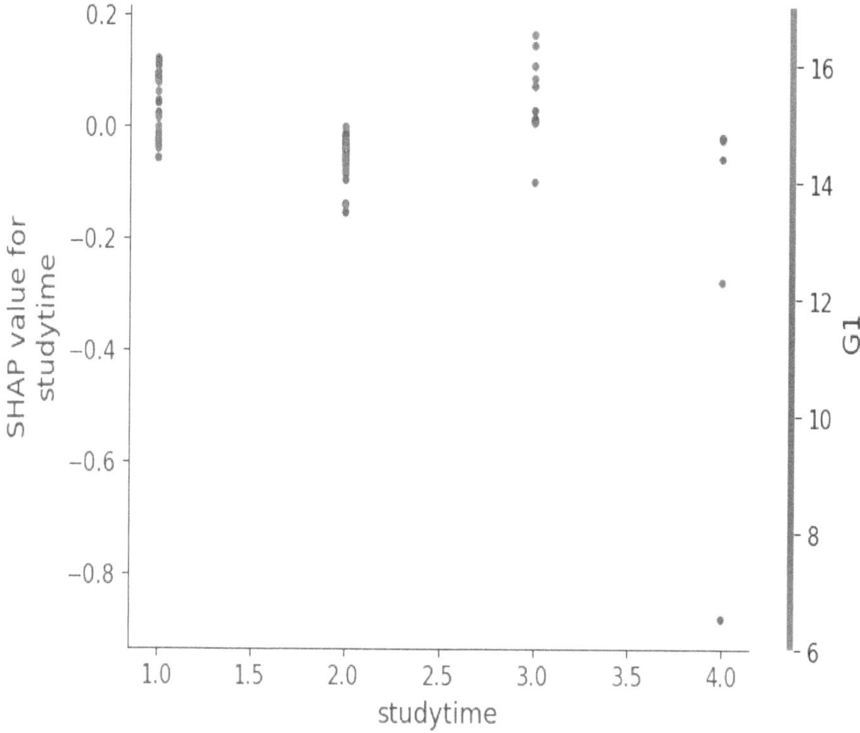

Fig. 3. Dependence Plots.

5 Conclusion and Perspectives

This study demonstrates the importance of explainable AI techniques, such as SHAP, for improving the transparency and interpretability of machine learning models in the field of education. The results show that previous grades (G1 and G2) are the most influential factors in predicting student performance, while absences have a significant negative impact. Other features, such as study time and family relationships, also play a positive, albeit moderate, role. SHAP visualizations, such as Summary Plots, Waterfall Plots, and Dependence Plots, have revealed complex and non-linear relationships between features, highlighting the importance of a multifactorial approach to improving student performance. The study emphasizes that explainable AI techniques can not only improve the transparency of predictive models but also provide valuable insights to guide targeted and equitable educational interventions. By making AI model decisions more understandable, these techniques can help teachers, administrators, and policymakers better understand the factors influencing student performance and implement more effective educational strategies.

For future work, several perspectives can be considered to deepen and expand the implications of this study. First, it would be interesting to extend this research to other educational domains beyond mathematics performance to verify whether the influential factors vary depending on the context and subject. Second, the integration of additional data, such as more detailed psychological or socio-economic variables, could enrich the model and provide even more precise insights into the determinants of student performance. Furthermore, although XGBoost has demonstrated good performance, exploring other machine learning algorithms, particularly hybrid models or deep learning approaches, could improve prediction accuracy. Additionally, the development of interactive tools based on SHAP for teachers and administrators could facilitate the interpretation of results and the implementation of targeted interventions in real time. A thorough analysis of potential biases in the data and models is also essential to ensure that predictions and interventions remain equitable and do not reinforce existing inequalities. Finally, the results of this study could be integrated into educational policies, particularly to reduce absenteeism and promote a family environment conducive to learning. These perspectives open the way for future research that could strengthen the impact of explainable AI techniques in the field of education.

References

1. Davy T.K.N., Jiahong, S., Jac, K.L.L., Samuel, K.W.C.: Artificial intelligence (ai) literacy education in secondary schools: a review. Interact. Learn. Environ., **32**(10), 6204–6224, (2024)
2. Peter, B.: Ai in education, learner control, and human-ai collaboration. Int. J. Artif. Intell. Educ. **34**(1), 122–135 (2024)
3. Adrien, B., et al.: A practical tutorial on explainable ai techniques. ACM Comput. Surv. **57**(2), 1–44 (2024)
4. Umar, A.B., Md Shohel, S., Siti Fatimah, A.R., Sumendra, Y., Radhwan, S.: Decision-making framework for the utilization of generative artificial intelligence in education: A case study of chatgpt. IEEE Access, (2024)
5. Yueqiao, J., Lixiang, Y., Vanessa, E., Dragan, G., Roberto, M.-M.: Generative ai in higher education: A global perspective of institutional adoption policies and guidelines. Comput. Edu. Artif. Intell. **8**, 100348 (2025)
6. Cristobal, R., Sebastian, V., Mykola, P., Ryan, S.B.: Handbook of Educational Data Mining. CRC press, (2010)
7. Sotiris, B.K., Ioannis, Z., Pintelas, P., et al.: Supervised machine learning: A review of classification techniques. Emerg. Artifi. Intell. Appl. Comput. Engg. **160**(1), 3–24 (2007)
8. Aïssa, M.: Les défis de l'ia dans l'éducation: de la protection des données aux biais algorithmiques. Médiations & médiatisations **18**, 148–160 (2024)
9. Cecilia, K., Yuk, C., Wenjie, H.: Students' voices on generative ai: Perceptions, benefits, and challenges in higher education. Int. J. Educ. Technol. High. Educ. **20**(1), 43 (2023)
10. Tareq, R., et al.: The role of chatgpt in higher education: Benefits, challenges, and future research directions. Journal of Applied Learning and Teaching **6**(1), 41–56 (2023)
11. Lloyd, S.S.: A value for n-person games. Contribution to the Theory of Games, 2, (1953)

12. Diogo, V.C., Eduardo, M.P., Jaime, S.C.: Machine learning interpretability: A survey on methods and metrics. Electr. **8**(8), 832 (2019)
13. Carl, O.R., et al.: Post-hoc vs ante-hoc explanations: xai design guidelines for data scientists. Cogn. Syst. Res. **86**, 101243 (2024)
14. Scott L.: A unified approach to interpreting model predictions. arXiv preprint http://arxiv.org/abs/1705.07874 (2017)
15. Qianhui, L., Juan, D.P., Luc, P.: Applications of explainable ai (xai) in education. In: Kourkoulou, D., Tzirides, AO.(., Cope, B., Kalantzis, M. (eds.) Trust and Inclusion in AI-Mediated Education: Where Human Learning Meets Learning Machines, p. 93–109. Springer, Cham (2024). https://doi.org/10.1007/978-3-031-64487-0_5
16. Leonard, C.N., Yutaka, W., Md Mostafizer, R., Adetokunbo Macgregor, J.O.: Prediction of students' adaptability using explainable ai in educational machine learning models. Appl. Sci. **14**(12), 5141 (2024)
17. Supriya, M., Niladri, S.: Need of ai in modern education: in the eyes of explainable ai (xai). arXiv preprint http://arxiv.org/abs/2408.00025, (2024)
18. Daniel, E.M., Deborah, U.E., Anayo, C.I., Pamela, E.U., Ngozi, F.D.: Recent emerging techniques in explainable artificial intelligence to enhance the interpretable and understanding of ai models for human. Neural Process. Lett. **57**(1), 16 (2025)
19. Kingsley, O., Julius, T.N., Jose, E., Samira, H.: Machine learning model (rg-dmml) and ensemble algorithm for prediction of students' retention and graduation in education. Comput. Edu. Artifi. Intell. **6**, 100205 (2024)
20. Sai Ram, A.P., Mayukha, P.: Enhancing trust and interpretability of complex machine learning models using local interpretable model agnostic shap explanations. Int. J. Data Sci. Anal. **18**(4), 457–466 (2024)
21. Scott, M.L., et al.: From local explanations to global understanding with explainable AI for trees. Nat. Mach. Intell., **2**(1), 56–67, (2020)
22. Scott, M.L., Su-In, L.: A unified approach to interpreting model predictions. In Guyon, I., et al. (eds.), Advances in Neural Information Processing Systems 30, pp. 4765–4774. Curran Associates, Inc., (2017)
23. Paulo, C.: Student Performance. UCI Machine Learning Repository, (2008) https://doi.org/10.24432/C5TG7T
24. Tianqi, C., et al.: Xgboost: extreme gradient boosting. R Package Version 0.4-2, **1**(4), 1–4 (2015)

AI-Based Early Diagnosis of Malaria in Blood Smear for Resource-Limited Settings in Africa

Ertony Basilwango[1(✉)] and Seydou Nourou Sylla[1,2]

[1] Dakar Institute of Technology, Dakar, Senegal
ertonylbasil@gmail.com, seydounourou.sylla@uadb.edu.sn
[2] Alioune Diop University, Bambey, Senegal

Abstract. Malaria is a deadly infectious disease, mainly affecting children and pregnant women in Africa, with hundreds of thousands of deaths each year. Rapid diagnosis is crucial, however, traditional methods such as microscopic examination of blood slides require resources and skilled technicians, which are often scarce in rural areas. The main challenge for doctors is decision-making, particularly due to the complexity and variability of symptoms. Therefore, computer-aided diagnosis systems assist to prioritize high-risk cases and reduce diagnostic errors. To overcome these situations, a computer-aided diagnosis system is developed to automatically identify trophozoite stages of *P. falciparum* Malaria as early identification species, white blood cell (WBC), and negative cells. A CNN was used as the backbone network for training the artificial intelligence algorithm model architecture to classify whether a cell is infected or not. To achieve high accuracy and recall, YoloV11m and DDQ-Detr (Deformable Dynamic Query DETR) were both combined through NMS ensemble learning techniques to detect and classify trophozoite and WBC. These algorithms were integrated into an end-to-end mobile application, specifically designed to meet diagnostic needs in low-resource settings in Africa.

The results showed that the proposed model is capable of detecting the trophozoite stage of Malaria with an accuracy of 0.927 and 0.99 to classify whether a cell is infected or uninfected. Our method outperforms existing approaches in terms of speed and validation on data from diverse fields. This makes it a promising tool for the diagnosis of malaria in resource-limited environments.

Keywords: AI · healthcare · computer vision · medical imaging · deep learning · Africa

1 Introduction

The introduction of AI in the medical field marks a decisive turning point. It goes far beyond traditional tools by enabling in-depth data analysis, diagnostic

D. Bassole et al. (Eds.): InterSol 2025, LNICST 671, pp. 52–66, 2026.
https://doi.org/10.1007/978-3-032-15154-4_5

assistance, and the ability to predict disease trajectories. These advanced technologies offer unprecedented perspectives: they make care more precise, faster and better adapted to the specific needs of patients. Among the most revolutionary technologies, deep learning [6]. Deep Learning is actually used in medical image analysis and in the detection of pathologies such as cancer with an accuracy comparable to, or even superior to, that of human experts [13]. It is also used in the diagnosis of diseases such as malaria [14].

Malaria diagnosis is a key component of patient management. It allows to quickly and accurately identify infected individuals to provide appropriate treatment and prevent the spread of the disease. However, It has always been quite problematic, the traditional methods of dignostic such as blood smear microscopy and rapid diagnostic tests present several challenges. In this context, artificial intelligence (AI) and machine learning have emerged as promising tools to improve malaria diagnosis. Malaria parasites can be classified into five species which are P. Falciparum, P. Vivax, P. Malariae, P. Ovale and P. Knowlesi. P. falciparum causes the most severe form of malaria, responsible for the majority of malaria-related deaths globally. Transmitted to humans through the bite of an infected female Anopheles mosquito, primarily in tropical and subtropical regions, Sub-Saharan Africa is the most heavily affected, especially children and pregnant woman due to their weaker immune defenses. [23]

Given the high mortality rate associated with P. falciparum, improving diagnostic accuracy is crucial. Automated image analysis systems are emerging as tools to assist in the detection and staging of malaria parasites. By analyzing quantitative phase images of unstained cells, these systems aim to reduce reliance on human expertise and increase diagnostic accuracy. However, their implementation is still under investigation and not yet widespread [6].

1.1 Problem Statement

Malaria is endemic in 85 countries, with 627,000 deaths and 246 million cases in 2023. The World Health Organization (WHO) reports that since 2000, 2.2 billion cases and 12.7 million deaths have been averted worldwide [21]. Traditionally, malaria is diagnosed by examining blood samples under a microscope for parasite-infected red blood cells. This method, however, faces several challenges, including a lack of trained parasitologists and poor facilities in malaria-endemic regions [4].

One of the major obstacles to effective malaria diagnosis is human error, as doctors must process large volumes of data [8], often leading to inconsistencies in diagnosis. The interpretation of test results is a cognitively demanding task requiring the highest precision. Without expert supervision, microscopy and traditional diagnostic methods can result in incorrect diagnoses, leading to inappropriate treatment. This challenge is particularly significant in regions with limited resources and non-professional involvement [2]. Therefore, this study focuses on a systematic review of how malaria diagnosis by light microscopy can effectively improve using artificial intelligence techniques, such as Deep Learning (DL) approaches.

2 Related Work

We begin by reviewing traditional image classification approaches for malaria diagnosis and their limitations, followed by a discussion on recent advancements using automated classification and object detection techniques. Early methods relied on hand-crafted features and statistical models for feature extraction [3, 19], which required manual tuning and were highly sensitive to data variations—often resulting in suboptimal diagnostic performance in real-world scenarios

CNNs have significantly advanced malaria diagnosis, with EfficientNet achieving 97.57 accuracy [12]. In this study, a deep learning-based tool was proposed to detect malaria from red blood cell images, outperforming several pre-trained models including EfficientNet-B2, VGG16, Inception, DenseNet121, MobileNet, and ResNet. Using batch normalization and expert-annotated data, the model achieved superior F1 scores, with 0.985 accuracy for infected cells and 100 accuracy for uninfected cells. Ten-fold cross-validation further confirmed high recall, AUC, and low test loss.

Faster R-CNN has been used to detect and classify developmental stages of Plasmodium vivax directly from thin blood smears, eliminating the need for prior segmentation [7]. Detected red blood cells were further classified by AlexNet, achieving 0.98 accuracy—significantly higher than the 0.72 average accuracy of human annotators for the same task

In [22], a cascaded YOLOv2 model with transferred AlexNet achieved a mean accuracy (mAP) of 0.792 for detecting P. vivax-infected cells in thin blood smear images. While improved over YOLOv2 and YOLOv3, its applicability remains limited due to reliance on a single species and dataset. In [9], Sukumarran evaluated YOLOv4, Faster R-CNN, and SSD-300 for infected cell detection, with YOLOv4 outperforming others at 0.938 accuracy. Validation on an independent dataset yielded 0.84 accuracy, demonstrating the model's strong generalization. Their smartphone-based system is promising for malaria detection in low-resource settings

In [18], scaled YOLOv4 and YOLOv5 models were applied to classify malaria parasite species from MP-IDB blood smear images—the only known study using object detectors for this task. However, the work lacked dataset cross-validation and model tuning, limiting its evaluation. In contrast, [11] proposed a hybrid model combining a capsule neural network with Inception for feature extraction, achieving over 95 accuracy in classifying infected versus healthy cells, and offering a more reliable alternative to traditional microscopy.

In [20], a YOLOv7-based deep learning model was developed to detect and classify malaria parasites in thin blood smears, achieving 0.902 average precision, with sensitivity and specificity above 0.968 and 0.993, respectively. The model processed 1,116 parasites in 13 s (0.01 s per parasite). However, its reliance on a relatively small dataset and lack of real-world validation raise concerns about generalizability. In [10], Li et al. introduced DTGCN, a hybrid model combining CNNs and Graph Convolutional Networks to recognize multiple malaria parasite stages. The model outperformed existing methods on public datasets and demonstrated robustness across unseen malaria and Babesia samples.

Semakula et al. [15] employed Bayesian belief networks using household data to predict malaria, achieving 0.91 accuracy. However, environmental factors influencing mosquito activity were not considered. Shambhu et al. [1] reviewed key steps in malaria image analysis, including data acquisition, preprocessing, RBC segmentation, feature extraction, and classification. Sora-Cardenas et al. [17] developed a CNN-based system to detect and classify malaria parasites and leukocytes in Romanowsky-stained smears, achieving high accuracy and robustness. Their model also automated image quality assessment and reported F1-scores of 0.85 for trophozoites, 0.8 for schizonts, and 0.83 for gametocytes, highlighting its potential in resource-limited settings.

[16] developed an intelligent classification system to differentiate trophozoite stages of Plasmodium knowlesi, P. falciparum, and P. vivax in thin blood smears. The system utilized image processing techniques, including contrast enhancement, segmentation, and feature extraction, followed by classification using a Multilayer Perceptron (MLP) trained with the Bayesian Regularization (BR) algorithm. This approach achieved an accuracy of 98.95, outperforming other training algorithms like Levenberg-Marquardt and Conjugate Gradient Backpropagation. The study's limitations include potential overfitting due to dataset dependence, reliance on handcrafted features, and limited species coverage (P. malariae, P. ovale not included). Additionally, the MLP model may lack efficiency for large-scale or real-time applications compared to deep learning approaches. The Detection Transformer (DETR) architecture [5], introduced by Facebook AI Research, has significantly influenced object detection tasks by integrating transformers with convolutional neural networks. In malaria detection, a notable adaptation is the Real-Time Detection Transformer (RT-DETR) algorithm. This model has been trained on a dataset comprising 24,720 images from 475 thin blood smears, totaling over 2 million labeled instances. When evaluated on a test set of 4,508 images from 170 smears, the RT-DETR achieved an overall accuracy of 0.794 at the patient level. Specifically, it demonstrated recall rates of 0.9 for Plasmodium falciparum, 0.818 for P. malariae, and 0.76 for P. ovale/vivax. These results correspond to a World Health Organization competence level 2 for species identification. The RT-DETR's capability to operate in real-time on low-cost devices, such as smartphones mounted on microscopes, underscores its potential for deployment in resource-limited settings lacking microscopy experts. The application of DETR and its variants in malaria detection is an emerging area of research. While initial studies like the RT-DETR have demonstrated encouraging results, further research and development are necessary to enhance accuracy and reliability.

3 Study Area, Data, and Methods

3.1 Study Area

The study focuses on the detection of trophozoites, the early stage of malaria parasites, in microscopic blood smear images obtained from patients in malaria-endemic regions, Central and East Africa. These regions are highly affected by malaria, therefore accurate, automated detection methods can help enhance diagnostic capabilities in resource-limited settings where expert microscopists are scarce.

3.2 Data

The dataset used in the study consists of microscopic blood smear images, collected from patients in malaria-endemic Central and East Africa regions. These images include both infected and healthy blood samples, focusing on the early-stage malaria parasites (trophozoites). The images in the dataset were captured by placing a smartphone over a microscope to capture the Field of View (FOV) of the blood slide through the eyepiece of the microscope. Along with the image, the slide from which the image was captured, the stage micrometer readings of the microscope, and the objective lens settings were recorded, and a maximum of 40 images were captured from each slide. The dataset is sourced from UGANDA, MAKERERE Artificial Intelligence Health Lab (Fig. 1)

Fig. 1. "Image Acquisition at AI LAB IN UGANDA"

There are 2 747 images in the train and 1 178 images in the test. The images were annotated by experts, using bounding boxes to label the life stages of each parasite. To our knowledge, no previous studies have used dataset of Malaria UGANDA (Fig. 2)

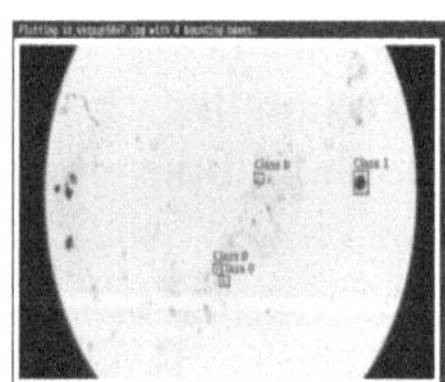

Fig. 2. Infected cells and their classes.

3.3 Methods

The data had a significant imbalance between infected WBC, Trophozoite, and uninfected cells, representing over 0.95 of all cells. For this research case, the above labels were simplified into two classes: Trophozoite and WBC. Many samples appear to have incomplete annotations, with about 0.8 of the trophozoites unlabeled according to our assessment. It was also noticed that some samples never contained WBC labels (especially those with a resolution of 3120×4160). This dataset, although imperfect, presents characteristics that are close to real conditions (noise, variable quality), offering a better opportunity to generalize the model, and it presents a novel character.

As part of this work, an important step was to transform the categorical labels into numerical values. As part of the data preparation for training the YOLO model, a key step was to filter out negative images. We removed duplicates images. The dataset is splitted into two separate subsets to allow for model training and validation. This division is done in a stratified manner using the class column to maintain the proportions of the classes in the two subsets, important when the classes are unbalanced.

We optimized detection results using Non-Maximum Suppression (NMS) to eliminate redundant bounding boxes. In our ensemble learning approach, NMS effectively combined outputs from two detection models, retaining only the highest-scoring boxes.

Model Training In this project, ResNet was used to perform binary classification, determining whether an observation is positive or negative. Data in the negative class exhibit significantly different characteristics, patterns compared to the positive class. Furthermore, the "NEG" class was extremely underrepresented (0.03). By limiting the model to the initial classification between benign and infected images, we reduced the processing load as well (Fig. 3)

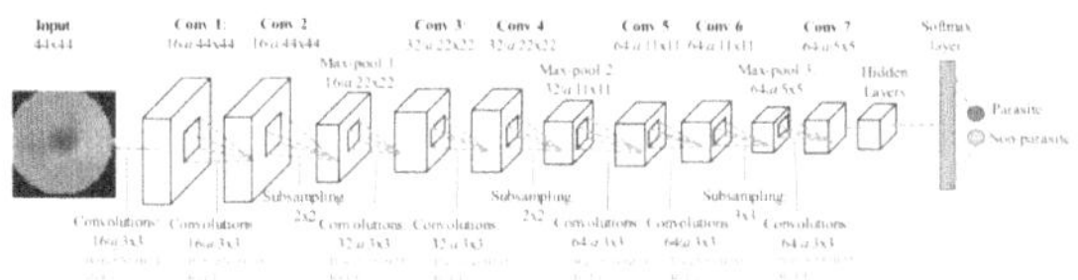

Fig. 3. Resnet50 architecture for parasites classification.

YOLO can be used for a variety of computer vision tasks, from real-time object detection to classification, making it a game changer for developers and researchers. The model employs a transformer-based backbone, capturing long-range dependencies to improve small object detection. A dynamic head design adapts to image complexity, optimizing resource allocation for efficient processing. The C3k2 (Cross Stage Partial with kernel size 2) block enhances feature extraction. It primarily enhances multi-scale feature representation while keeping computational costs lower, while the Spatial Pyramid Pooling - Fast (SPPF) module facilitates multi-scale feature integration. Additionally, the C2PSA (Convolutional block with Parallel Spatial Attention) component improves spatial attention, contributing to more accurate object detection and classification (Fig. 4)

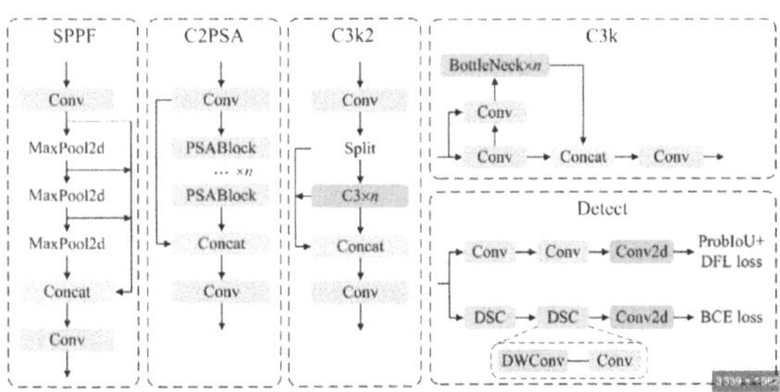

Fig. 4. LW-YOLO11: A Lightweight Arbitrary-Oriented Ship Detection.

Non-Maximum Suppression (NMS) is applied to remove redundant boxes by selecting the highest-confidence detections. The entire process is optimized using a loss function that combines classification, localization, and confidence loss.

Hyperparameter Settings, the initial learning rate was 1e-3, the weight-decay was 5.7e-05, and was 0.99. The batch-size was set to 16, dropout: 0.4. The images were preprocessed via the following steps auto-augment: false, copy-paste-mode: flip, degrees: 10.6, fliplr: 0.5, flipud: 0.5, hsv-h: 0.14, hsv-s: 0.87, hsv-v: 0.52, mixup: 0.33. Image resolution 2040pp, epoch 60, patience 5, and batch size 32.

Deformable Dynamic Query Detection Transformer(DDQ-DETR) enhances the DETR(Detection Transformer) model by introducing Dense Query Generation to improve object recall. It selects Distinct Queries from the dense set to reduce redundancy and optimize detection. The Transformer Encoder-Decoder processes these queries for refined object localization. The Detection Transformer (DETR) combines transformers and convolutional neural networks (CNNs) for end-to-end training. The input image is passed through a CNN backbone (such as ResNet) to extract feature maps. These feature maps represent the spatial structure and information of the image (Fig. 5).

Let $I \in \mathbb{R}^{H \times W \times C}$ be the input image, where H is the height, W is the width, and C is the number of channels. The CNN processes this image to generate feature maps $F \in \mathbb{R}^{H' \times W' \times C'}$. Positional encodings are added to the feature maps to retain the spatial information of the image. Let $P \in \mathbb{R}^{H' \times W' \times C'}$ be the positional encoding added to the feature map. Thus, the encoded feature map becomes:

$$\tilde{F} = F + P$$

The positional encoded feature maps $\tilde{F}$ are passed to a transformer encoder, which is composed of self-attention layers. The transformer encoder computes the attention mechanism:

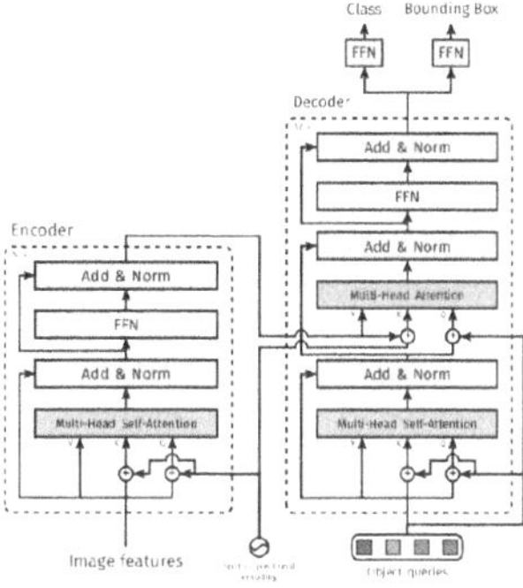

Fig. 5. Architecture-of-DETRs-transformer.

$$Q, K, V\& = \text{Linear Projections of Input},$$
$$\text{Attention}\& = \text{softmax}\left(\frac{QK^T}{\sqrt{d_k}}\right)V$$

where Q, K, and V are query, key, and value matrices, respectively, and d_k is the dimension of the query and key vectors.

The output of the encoder is fed into a transformer decoder, which processes a set of learned object queries. These queries are fixed-length vectors that represent different object proposals. The decoder attends to the encoded image features and produces a set of object predictions, one for each query. Each query is associated with a potential object class, bounding box, and confidence score.

The output from the transformer decoder is passed through two fully connected layers, classification output to predict the class label for each object in the image and the bounding to predict the coordinates of the bounding box (center (x, y), width w, and height h) for each detected object. Let $z_i = (c_i, b_i)$ be the output for query i, where: $c_i \in \mathbb{R}^C$ is the classification vector, with C being the number of possible classes, $b_i \in \mathbb{R}^4$ is the bounding box vector (center x, y and size w, h). The final output is compared with the ground truth labels to calculate the loss function. DETR uses cross-entropy loss between the predicted class and the true class and Bounding Box Loss: A combination of L1 loss and giou loss for measuring the quality of the predicted bounding boxes.

$$L_{\text{box}} = L_1(b, b^*) + \text{GIoU}(b, b^*)$$

where b is the predicted bounding box, and b^* is the ground truth bounding box. The total loss is a weighted sum of the classification and bounding box losses:

$$L_{\text{total}} = \lambda_{\text{class}} L_{\text{class}} + \lambda_{\text{box}} L_{\text{box}}$$

where λ_{class} and λ_{box} are hyperparameters controlling the weight of each term.

The model was trained using mmdetection framework, image resolution 2040pp, epoch 60, patience 5, and batch size 32. Both models were trained on an NVIDIA-SMI 535.104.05 GPU with 40 GB of memory in 6hrs hours (60 epochs) for the Yolo11m model. Overfitting was not observed during training of the models.

Model Evaluation. In our study, we used mean accuracy (mAP) as our evaluation metric, specifically mAP@0.5 that combines two essential aspects of object detection. Our ability to localize objects (bounding box accuracy) and our accuracy in classifying what we found (infected or healthy cells). Average Precision (AP): AP is a combined precision and recall metric, calculated as the area under the Precision-Recall curve (AUC) calculated for each object class. The Mean Average Precision (mAP) is the average of the AP values of all detected object classes.

We evaluated these models on the training and test set to check its generalization. In addition to quantitative metrics, we performed a visual evaluation of the results to demonstrate the effectiveness of the model in detecting parasites in medical images. Since we work with models like YOLO and DDQ-DETR, we compared their performances to demonstrate which architecture is the best suited for parasite detection in images, using metrics like mAP, precision and recall. Another important evaluation was to compare the inference time and resource usage (GPU memory, CPU, etc.).

4 Development Pipeline

The proposed pipeline preprocesses the dataset and converts it into a YOLO-compatible format. YOLO, DETR, and ResNet models are then trained in parallel to detect uninfected cells. After individual testing, ensemble learning combines their strengths to improve accuracy, followed by post-processing for final predictions.

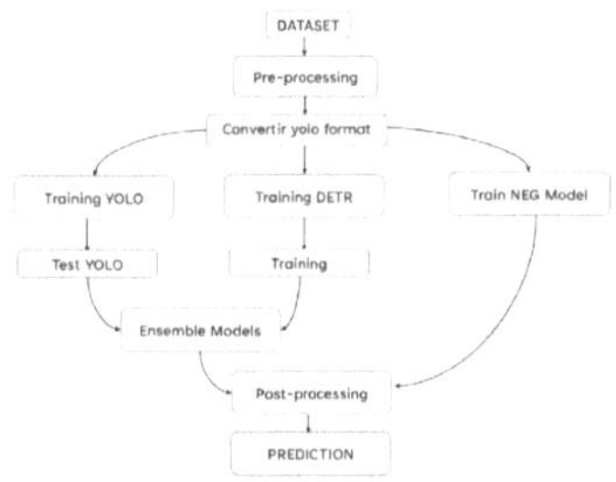

Fig. 6. Model pipeline.

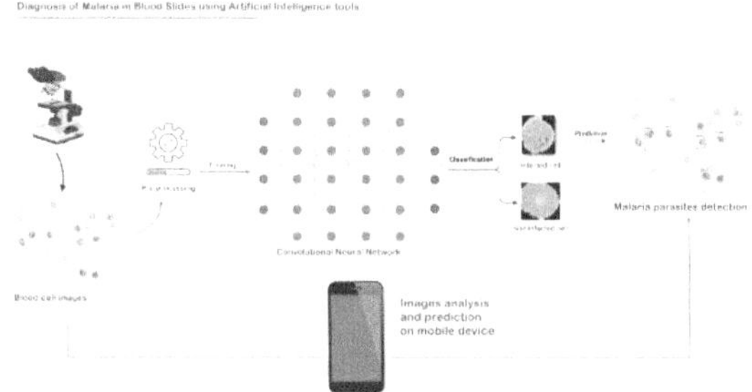

Fig. 7. Workflow of Automated Malaria Detection and Classification Using AI-Powered Mobile Application.

As illustrated in Fig. 6, the proposed system offers a user-friendly and intuitive interface. After collecting and preparing a patient's blood sample using a microscope, the user uploads the blood smear image to the dedicated mobile application. This application directly interacts with the integrated artificial intelligence model. The embedded image processing and analysis module examines the sample to determine if it is infected. In the case of a positive diagnosis, the model automatically performs a detailed analysis to identify whether the detected parasites are trophozoites or affected white blood cells (Fig. 7).

5 Experiments and Results

For this task, we experimented with different models, to find the one that generalized best with noisy data. We first tried a segmentation approach, then leveraged pre-trained models from the Hugging Face model library. Initially, we encountered a common limitation of models, poor performance in detecting small objects. We tried several different types of YOLO models, from YOLOv8 to YOLOv10. However, during the writing of this work, YOLO11 was released and was found to be the best performing model. We continuously improved Resnet, DDQ-DETR, and Ultrallytics-YOLO models, after we found that assembling them was promising.

5.1 Model Results

We used an Ensemble Learning approach to combine the predictions of two parasite detection models: YOLO and DDQ-DETR. The goal was to improve the accuracy by merging their results using the Non-Maximum Suppression (NMS) method, with an Intersection over Union (IoU) threshold set to 0.6 to eliminate redundant predictions.

The Resnet model has 0.99 accuracy in classifying both positive and negative cells. The DETR model has a slightly higher mAP@50-95 (0.92) compared to Yolo's (0.87), indicating better accuracy for easier IoU thresholds. The DQ-Detr can produce fewer false positives, making it more accurate in localizing objects with more relaxed requirements. Generalized accuracy DDQ-Detr: 0.49 and YOLO: 0.46 for (mAP@50-95), which indicates that DDQ-Detr has a slight advantage in terms of accuracy on IoU thresholds, potentially due to better localization handling. The recall rate represents the model's intolerance towards false negatives. The DETR model has a recall (0.71) and YOLO11m (0.87), suggesting that DETR detects more objects but may include more false positives (Tables 1, 2 and 3).

Table 1. Model Performance Results

Models	Image Size	mAP@0.5	mAP@[0.5;0.95]	Accuracy(%)	Recall(%)	Epochs/ Time
YOLO11m	1024	0.87	0.46	87.6	87.2	50/4.5 h
YOLO11s	2048	0.84	0.41	83.6	79.3	100/5.1 h
YOLO8m	2048	0.82	0.42	82.8	81.1	60/6h
YOLO8l	2048	0.85	0.44	84.6	82.9	100/8 h
YOLO9m	1024	0.86	0.45	85.2	83.1	50/4.8 h
YOLO8s	4080	0.79	0.39	78.4	77.1	50/6.5 h
DDQ-DETR	1280	0.92	0.49	92.6	71.1	50/9.9 h
Resnet	-	-	-	99.6	99.2	10/2hrs

Table 2. Table of Performance of YOLO Model Across Different Classes

Classes	mAP@0.5	mAP@[0.5;0.95]	Accuracy	Recall
Tous	0.87	46	87.6	87.2
WBC	0.96	60	95	95.9
Trophozoites	0.81	32	76.87	77.3

Table 3. Table of Performance Results of the DETR Model Across Different Object Sizes

Size object	mAP@0.5	mAP@75	mAP@[0.5:0.95]	Average Precision	Recall
Large	-	-	-	0.66	0.68
Middle	-	-	-	0.51	0.67
Small	-	-	-	0.39	0.63

5.2 Model Performance

The results of our study showed contrasting performances between YOLO and DETR models for parasite detection in medical images. While YOLO excels in its ability to detect many objects, especially smaller ones, DDQ-DETR, with its higher accuracy provides better localization and avoids some false positives (Fig. 8).

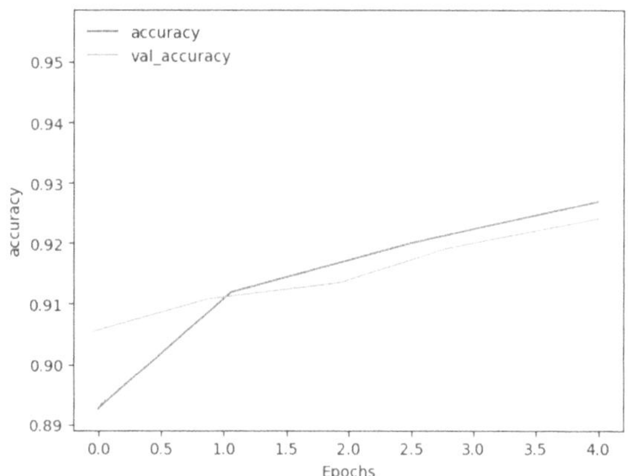

Fig. 8. Training and validation curve of the retained model(DETR).

The minimal gap between training and validation performance suggests that the model generalizes well to unseen data. By combining the predictions of the three models (binary classification + YOLO + DETR), we obtained a final output that takes advantage of the strengths of each, thus optimizing parasite detection (Fig. 9).

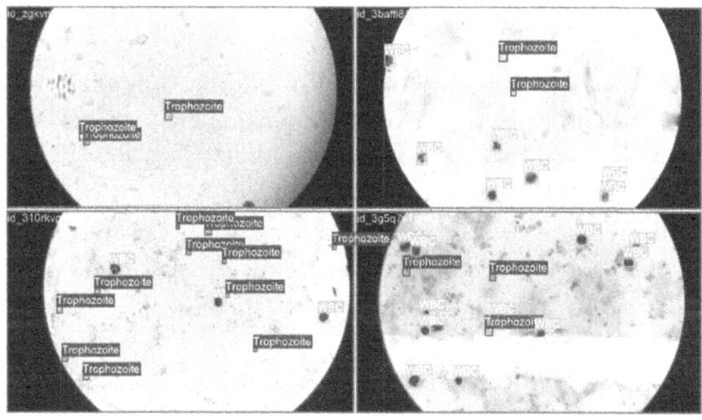

Fig. 9. Examples of image detection results of Trophozoites and White Blood Cell (WBC).

6 Conclusion

We focused our efforts on improving the state of the art, and to some extent, contributed to the ongoing paradigm shift in the field of automated malaria diagnosis from microscopic images of blood smears. This project explored and demonstrated the effectiveness of artificial intelligence in detecting malaria parasites from medical images, addressing a critical need in endemic regions where trained parasitologists are often lacking. Despite these constraints, the integration of innovative technologies has yielded promising results. The model was then deployed in an end-to-end mobile system, specifically designed to address local constraints in these regions. In the future work, the use of ensemble learning could boost overall performance by combining predictions from multiple models via adapted weights, outperforming approaches such as non-maximum suppression (NMS). Introducing a preliminary model to filter out irrelevant images would also optimize resources and improve the analysis of critical cases. Additionally, implementing test time augmentation methods, such as contrast variations or rotations, could increase the robustness of predictions to diverse data.

References

1. Abubakar, A., Ajuji, M., Yahya, I.U.: Deepfmd: Computational analysis for malaria detection in blood-smear images using deep-learning features. Appl. Syst. Innov. **4**(4) (2021). https://doi.org/10.3390/asi4040082
2. consultatif de la médecine tropicale et de la médecine des voyages (CCMTMV), C.: Diagnostic du paludisme. In: Recommandations canadiennes pour la prévention et le traitement du paludisme (malaria). Agence de la santé publique du Canada (2014). https://www.canada.ca/fr/sante-publique/services/ccmtmv/recommandations-canadienne-prevention-traitement-paludisme-malaria/chapitre-6-diagnostic-paludisme.html
3. Devi, S.S., Laskar, R.H., Sheikh, S.A.: Hybrid classifier based life cycle stages analysis for malaria-infected erythrocyte using thin blood smear images. Neural Comput. Appl. **29**(8), 217–235 (2017). https://doi.org/10.1007/s00521-017-2937-4
4. Fila-Fila, G.P.U., et al.: Quality control of microscopic diagnosis of malaria in healthcare facilities and submicroscopic infections in mossendjo, the department of Niari, the republic of the Congo. Pathogens **13**(8) (2024). https://doi.org/10.3390/pathogens13080709
5. Guemas, E., et al.: Automatic patient-level recognition of four Plasmodium species on thin blood smear by a real-time detection transformer (RT-DETR) object detection algorithm: a proof-of-concept and evaluation. Microbiol. Spectrum **12**(2), e0144023 (2024)
6. Gómez-González, E., et al.: Artificial intelligence in medicine and healthcare: a review and classification of current and near-future applications and their ethical and social impact. arXiv preprint arXiv:2001.09778 (2020). https://arxiv.org/abs/2001.09778

7. Hung, J., et al.: Applying faster r-CNN for object detection on malaria images (2019). https://arxiv.org/abs/1804.09548
8. Kilian, A., et al.: Reliability of malaria microscopy in epidemiological studies: results of quality control. Tropical medicine & international health : TM & IH **5**, 3–8 (02 2000). https://doi.org/10.1046/j.1365-3156.2000.00509.x
9. Koirala, A., et al.: Deep learning for real-time malaria parasite detection and counting using yolo-mp. IEEE Access **PP**, 1–1 (01 2022). https://doi.org/10.1109/ACCESS.2022.3208270
10. Li, S., Du, Z., Meng, X., Zhang, Y.: Multi-stage malaria parasite recognition by deep learning. GigaScience **10** (06 2021). https://doi.org/10.1093/gigascience/giab040
11. Mujahid, M.R.: Approche efficace basée sur l'apprentissage profond pour la détection du paludisme à l'aide de frottis de globules rouges. Rapports scientifiques **14**(1), 13249 (2024). https://doi.org/10.1038/s41598024638310
12. Mujahid, M., et al.: Efficient deep learning-based approach for malaria detection using red blood cell smears. Sci. Reports **14**, 13249 (06 2024). https://doi.org/10.1038/s41598-024-63831-0
13. Park, H.S., Rinehart, M.T., Walzer, K.A., Chi, J.T.A., Wax, A.: Automated detection of p. falciparum using machine learning algorithms with quantitative phase images of unstained cells. PLOS ONE **11**(9), 1–19 (09 2016). https://doi.org/10.1371/journal.pone.0163045
14. Sawant, S., Singh, A.: Malaria cell detection using deep neural networks (2024). https://arxiv.org/abs/2406.20005
15. Semakula, H., et al.: Bayesian belief network modelling approach for predicting and ranking risk factors for malaria infections among children under 5 years in refugee settlements in Uganda. Malaria J.**22** (10 2023). https://doi.org/10.1186/s12936-023-04735-8
16. Kanafiah, S.N.A.M., Mashor, M.Y., Mohamed, Z., Way, Y.C., Shukor, S.A.A., Jusman, Y.: An intelligent classification system for trophozoite stages in malaria species. Intell. Autom. Soft Comput. **34**(1), 687–697 (2022). https://doi.org/10.32604/iasc.2022.024361, http://www.techscience.com/iasc/v34n1/47349
17. Sora-Cardenas, J., et al.: Image-based detection and classification of malaria parasites and leukocytes with quality assessment of romanowsky-stained blood smears. Sensors **25**(2) (2025). https://doi.org/10.3390/s25020390
18. Sukumarran, W., Vythilingam, I., Divis, P.: An optimised yolov4 deep learning model for efficient malarial cell detection in thin blood smear images. Parasites & Vectors **17** (04 2024). https://doi.org/10.1186/s13071-024-06215-7
19. Tek, F., Dempster, A., Kale, I.: Parasite detection and identification for automated thin blood film malaria diagnosis. Comput. Vision Image Understand. **114**, 21–32 (01 2010). https://doi.org/10.1016/j.cviu.2009.08.003
20. Wang, G., Luo, G., Lian, H., Chen, L., Wu, W., Liu, H.: Application of deep learning in clinical settings for detecting and classifying malaria parasites in thin blood smears. Open Forum Infect. Diseases **10**(11), ofad469 (09 2023). https://doi.org/10.1093/ofid/ofad469
21. World Health Organization: World Malaria Report 2023. World Health Organization, Geneva, Switzerland (2023). https://www.who.int/publications/i/item/9789240086173

22. Yang, F., et al.: Cascading YOLO: automated malaria parasite detection for Plasmodium vivax in thin blood smears. In: Hahn, H.K., Mazurowski, M.A. (eds.) Medical Imaging 2020: Computer-Aided Diagnosis, vol. 11314, p. 113141Q. International Society for Optics and Photonics, SPIE (2020). https://doi.org/10.1117/12.2549701
23. Yimam, Y., Nateghpour, M., Mohebali, M., Abbaszadeh Afshar, M.J.: A systematic review and meta-analysis of asymptomatic malaria infection in pregnant women in sub-saharan africa: A challenge for malaria elimination efforts. PLOS ONE **16**(4), 1–15 (04 2021). https://doi.org/10.1371/journal.pone.0248245

A Machine Learning Model for Resurgence Prediction of Ten Infectious Diseases in Senegal

Cheikh Tidiane Seck(✉) and Abdourahmane Ndao

Alioune Diop University, BP 30, Bambey, Senegal
cheikhtidiane.seck@uadb.edu.sn

Abstract. Ongoing changes in our environment have favored the emergence and/or resurgence of numerous infectious diseases, posing a real public health problem. Our aim in this work is to predict the resurgence of such diseases in the Senegalese context, using an extract from the Ministry of Health's epidemiological surveillance database, comprising 68,698 observations. We propose a multi-output decision tree (MO-DT) model which, introduces an inertia criterion (calculated with the chi-squared distance) as the node impurity measure, and allows to simultaneously predict ten infectious diseases targeted by the surveillance program. The results show that these diseases have an average resurgence probability of 12.2%, with the exception of Poliomyelitis, which records a resurgence probability of 2.4%. Our study also reveals that during the period under consideration (January 2018 to November 2022), Covid-19 had a fairly high resurgence probability approaching 60%. In comparison with multi-class random forests (MC-RF) and multinomial logistic regression (MLR), we find that our model performs slightly better. For example, for Accuracy, we have: MO-DT (0.9945), MC-RF (0.9943), RLM (0.9162).

Keywords: Resurgence prediction · Multi-output decision tree · Inertia criterion

1 Introduction

In the last few decades, we have witnessed changes in almost all aspects of our existence: human habits and behaviors, activities, climate change, environmental modifications, evolution of pathogens, and so on. This is a real public health concern, as many infectious diseases have emerged or re-emerged due to ecosystem upheaval. For example, the spread of certain infectious diseases, such as those transmitted by tiger mosquitoes or ticks, is increasing worldwide, and we are seeing a resurgence of zoonoses in many regions of the globe.

To address this situation, the WHO (World Health Organization) has initiated a strategic plan to combat these emerging or re-emerging infections, advocating surveillance, alert and response, applied research, prevention, control and strengthening of public health structures. In Senegal, health authorities have adopted the Integrated Disease and Response Strategy (IDRS), as have done other country members of the WHO African

D. Bassole et al. (Eds.): InterSol 2025, LNICST 671, pp. 67–79, 2026.
https://doi.org/10.1007/978-3-032-15154-4_6

Region. This strategy aims to improve disease surveillance and enhance rapid response capacity to face epidemics and other health emergencies. In addition to the IDSR program, a network named "4S" (Syndromic Sentinel Surveillance Network in Senegal) has also been set in place since 2012, thanks to the collaboration between the Ministry of Health and the Pasteur Institute of Dakar.

A large number of diseases are included in the IDSR surveillance program, but in this work, we focus on ten of them, whose monitoring is particularly crucial for health authorities. Indeed, these latter are potentially epidemic infectious diseases and belong to the priority diseases for the national health system. Some of them are emerging and others, which were considered as eradicated a few decades ago, are reappeared. These ten pathologies are: Covid-19, Measles, Poliomyelitis (PFA), Dengue, Meningitis, Rift Valley Fever (Rift), Crimean-Congo Hemorrhagic Fever (CCHF), Chikungunya (CHIK), West Nile Fever (WN) and Yellow Fever (YF).

Predictive models allow the forecast of epidemic trends before they occur, facilitating thus an early and effective response from healthcare systems. In recent years, Machine Learning models have been largely applied in epidemiology, and have led to significant improvement in predictive performance. For example, Gonçalves et al. (2024) developed an LSTM-model to predict dengue cases, in Brazil, from climatic and spatial variables, and identified the most important climatic predictors by using SHAP method. While Santangelo et al. (2023) provided a systematic review of several machine learning techniques and showed the possibility to combine them in order to obtain accurate predictions for the incidence and trends of many infectious diseases.

Our goal in this paper is to develop a machine learning model for the resurgence prediction of the ten above mentioned infectious diseases. To this end, we'll use a multi-label classification approach, which present challenges in terms of accuracy and efficiency as the number of classes to be predicted is large; see Wang et al. (2020). When there are several tasks to learn, Evegeniou and Pontil (2004) suggest learning them simultaneously rather than separately if the tasks are correlated; improving thus predictive performance. Also, Linusson (2013) proposes a multi-output random forest model, that generalizes the tree induction algorithm of Glocker et al. (2012) and allows learning simultaneously multiple classification and regression tasks. This model is based on an impurity measure defined as a combination of Shannon and differential entropies.

Whenever there are multiple quantitative output variables that are covariant, multivariate regression trees studied in Segal (1992) generally provide good predictions. De'Ath (2002) applied this strategy to produce multivariate regression trees and solve classification problems for geographic and ecological data. Also, Segal and Xiao (2011) utilized multivariate regression trees to build a random forest model with multiple responses. While Zhang (1998) applied classification trees to analyze multiple binary responses. The common feature of all these models is that they employ an impurity measure based on covariance-weighted entropy or least square distance, which requires to determine the covariance structure of the output variables and then to ultimately work with quantitative data.

In this paper, we propose a predictive multi-output model that can directly deal with qualitative data and ignore the covariance structure required in the calculation of the impurity measure. This model is a Multi-Output Decision Tree (MODT) algorithm, which introduces an inertia criterion, inspired from Multiple Correspondence Analysis technique, as the node impurity measure and allows to jointly predict the occurrence of all ten diseases. It enables us to estimate resurgence probabilities for each of the ten targeted diseases, by taking the proportion of positives predictions of each disease in the sample test.

This paper is structured as follows: Sect. 2 describes the methodology, Sect. 3 presents and discusses the results, and Sect. 4 concludes the work.

2 Methodology

2.1 Data

Data are extracted from the global Ministry of Health surveillance database. They cover confirmed cases (patients) of ten infectious diseases recorded during the surveillance period from January 2018 to November 2022. The database comprises 68,698 instances or observations. Each instance is associated with a confirmed case (or patient) from a given health district and provides: the patient's age and sex, the diagnosed disease and its properties, as well as district characteristics such as: environmental, climatic, human behaviors and socioeconomic living conditions. The studied variables are presented in Table 1.

Table 1. Definition of the variables

Variable	Description	Nature	Type	Modalities
Disease	Disease type	Qualitative	Nominal non ordered	Covid-19, Measles, PFA, Dengue, Meningitis, Rift, CCHF, Chikungunya, WN, YF
ModTrans	Transmission mode	Qualitative	Binary	Direct, Indirect
Vaccine	Existence or not of vaccine	Qualitative	Binary	Yes, No
VitesProp	Propagation speed of the disease	Qualitative	Ordinal	Rapid, Moderate, slow
FactEnv	Environnemental factors	Qualitative	Nominal non ordered	Lack of hygiene and sanitation, Pollution, Presence of enclosures or parks
FactCompHum	Human behaviour factors	Qualitative	Nominal non ordered	Promiscuity, High demographic density, Social inter-relations

(continued)

Table 1. (*continued*)

Variable	Description	Nature	Type	Modalities
FactSocioEco	Socioeconomic factors	Qualitative	Nominal non ordered	Poverty, Existence of public meeting places, No-access to quality healthcare
FactClimat	Climatic factors	Qualitative	Nominal non ordered	Temperature, Wind and dust, rain, Humidity
Rcrudes	Recrudescence period of the disease	Qualitative	Nominal non ordered	Rainy season, Dry season
GrpAge	Patient age	Qualitative	categorial	[0,20[, [20,40[,[40,60[, [60,80[, [80, plus[
Gender	Patient sex	Qualitative	Nominal	Man, Woman

2.2 Proposed Model: A Multi-output Decision Tree Algorithm

The objective of this work is to simultaneously predict the resurgence of ten infectious diseases based on the spread risk factors (variables) identified in Table 1. We can consider this problem as a multi-label classification problem, i.e. where the output variable has more than two labels or classes. To solve such a problem, we can reduce it to a multi-output problem, where the output variable is a vector or set of several elements. For example, to simultaneously predict the positivity or not of a patient for all of ten diseases, we need a model that outputs a vector of 10 binary components (0/1) corresponding respectively to the 10 diseases. So, depending on whether the outputs are correlated or not, we can use either algorithms that make separate predictions with individual outputs, or algorithms that simultaneously make predictions for all the outputs.

A classic and simple approach to multi-label prediction problems is the "Binary Relevance" one. But, its drawback is that it does not take into account the dependencies between labels. To overcome this difficulty, others kind of approaches such as: Classifier Chains; see, e.g. Read et al. (2011) and Classifier Treillis; see, e.g. Read et al. (2015) have been proposed. But, the disadvantage of these latter methods is that they impose a dependency structure between labels, and then learning will only be possible with dependencies that respect this structure.

Generally, infectious diseases share common spread risk factors, which can lead to interdependencies between them. For example, in a recent paper, Ndao and Seck (2024) showed that the presence of enclosures or parks is a common spread risk factor for Crimean-Congo, Rift Valley fever and Dengue fever. Similarly, temperature variations are common spread risk factors for Covid-19, Meningitis and Measles. Thus, resurgence of one these diseases may increase the likelihood emergence or resurgence of others, particularly in the Senegalese context, where various propagation risk factors are present in health districts such as: winter season, wind and dust, promiscuity, humidity, temperature variations, gatherings in public places, etc.

In this paper, we develop a multi-class prediction model that takes account of interdependencies, without fixing any particular dependence structure between labels. This model, which is described below, enables us to simultaneously predict the resurgence probabilities of ten potentially epidemic infectious diseases within the Senegal's health districts.

Multi-output Decision Tree (MO-DT) Model: It is an adaptation of the tree induction algorithm proposed by Linusson (2013); see Appendix for algorithm code and tree visualization. But, instead of entropy, our algorithm utilizes the inertia criterion as a node impurity measure. The information gain is then replaced by the inertia gain, which is calculated with the chi-square distance, as in the calculation of inertia in Multiple Correspondence Analysis technique.

Let us assume that the output variable Y has K modalities (here $K = 10$) and that the frequency of a modality j, $j = 1,\ldots,K$ in a node t is denoted by p_{jt}. Then, the inertia of a node t is given by:

$$I(t) = \Sigma_{i\in t}\frac{1}{n_t}d^2(i, g_t), \tag{1}$$

where n_t is the node size, $g_t = (p_{1t}, \ldots, p_{Kt})$ is the center of gravity of node t, i represents an instance in node t, i.e. an observation or individual, and

$$d^2(i, g_t) = \sum_{j=1}^{K}\frac{1}{p_{jt}}\left(y_{ij} - p_{jt}\right)^2, \tag{2}$$

where y_{ij}= 1 if individual i takes modality j, and 0 elsewhere.

The inertia $I(t)$ may be interpreted as a measure of the homogeneity of the node t.

2.3 Performance Measures

To assess the predictive performance of our model, we define adequate metrics from the confusion matrix which provides the following categories:

	Observed classes	
Predicted classes	TP	FP
	FN	TN

- True Positive (TP): The number of instances that are predicted positive for a disease, and which are actually positive for that disease.
- True Negative (TN): The number of instances that are predicted negative for a disease, and which are actually negative for that disease.
- False Positive (FP): The number of instances that are predicted positive for a disease, and which are actually negative for that disease.

- False Negative (FN): The number of instances that are predicted negative for a disease, and which are actually positive for that disease.

Accuracy: It gives the probability of correct predictions among all predictions.
$Accuracy = \frac{TP+TN}{TP+TN+FP+FN}$

Kappa Coefficient: It measures the agreement between model predictions and actual classes.
$Kappa = \frac{P_o-P_e}{1-P_e}$ where P_o is the observed Accuracy and P_e is the expected Accuracy.

Precision: It measures the probability of true positives among all instances that are predicted positive.
$Precision = \frac{TP}{TP+FP}$

Recall/Sensitivity: It measures the probability of true positives among all instances that are actually positive.
$Recall = \frac{TP}{TP+FN}$

F1-Score: It is the harmonic mean of precision and recall

$$F1\_score = 2*\left(\frac{(Pre'cision*Rappel)}{(Pre'cision + Rapell)}\right).$$

In case of multi-label classification problem, these different metrics are aggregated. Two aggregation methods are generally used:

-**Macro-averaging:** This calculates the arithmetic mean of the different classes for each of these metrics, giving a balanced measure that does not take into account the relative frequency of the classes. For example

$$Precision\_macro = \frac{1}{K}\sum_{i=1}^{K} Precision\_i$$

where *Precision_i* is the Precision evaluated for class *i*.

-**Micro-averaging:** Here, true positives, false positives, true negatives and false negatives are respectively aggregated over all classes to obtain an overall metric. For example,

$$Precision\_micro = \frac{\sum_{i=1}^{K} TP\_i}{\sum_{i=1}^{K}(TP_i + FP_i)}$$

where *TP_i* is the number of true positive and *FP_i* the number of false positive in class *i*.

3 Results and Discussion

We split the database into two parts: a training sample (90%) and a test sample (10%). We evaluate the resurgence probabilities by taking the proportion of positive predictions of each disease in the test sample. The results are displayed in Table 2.

Before analyzing the results, we test for relationship between the ten infectious diseases. A Chi-square test yields the p-value matrix in Fig. 1, and indicates the significance degree of associations between the ten diseases. A low p-value (generally $< = 0.05$) suggests a significant association, whereas a high p-value (> 0.05) indicates no association between diseases.

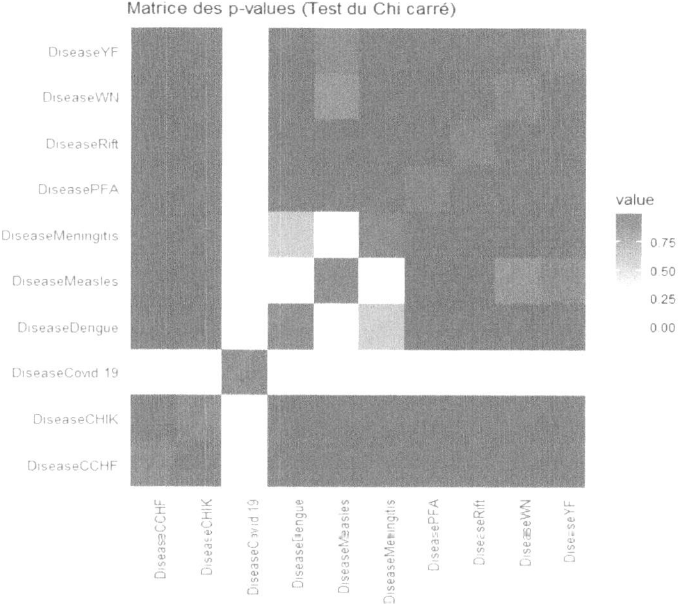

Fig. 1. p-values matrix of Chi square test for associations between infectious diseases.

Figure 1 reveals that there are significant associations between certain diseases, indicating that there exist interdependencies between them, i.e. they share common propagation risk factors. For example, Covid-19 is significantly associated with almost all the other diseases (the white color indicates a low p-value).

As Covid-19 is over-represented in the database, to avoid its possible influence on the predictions of the other diseases, we present results in two cases: with Covid-19 and without Covid-19 in the following table:

Table 2. Resurgence probability of the ten diseases

Infectious diseases	MO-DT	
	With Covid-19	Without Covid-19
CCHF	0,051785046	0,13573521
CHIK	0,050535339	0,12694722
Covid-19	0,606208411	XXXXXXX

(continued)

Table 2. *(continued)*

Infectious diseases	MO-DT	
	With Covid-19	Without Covid-19
Dengue	0,050591703	0,12589665
Measles	0,036245018	0,09044603
Meningitis	0,047580506	0,11302989
PFA	0,009227454	0,02392803
Rift	0,049016127	0,13505944
WN	0,048928176	0,13036992
YF	0,049882221	0,11858761

From Table 2, we can say on one hand that without Covid-19, the infectious diseases have an average resurgence probability of 12.2%, with the exception of Poliomyelitis, which recorded a lower resurgence probability of 2.39%. These results are in line with those of Barry et al. (2023) who found that, out of 24,296 fever cases, 11.0% were related to arboviruses/hemorrhagic fevers. Moreover, Barry et al. (2023) observed that during the period under consideration, Senegal experienced a high incidence of infectious diseases epidemics, some of which had already been eradicated (Poliomyelitis, Measles); and others are emerging due to climate change and pathogens evolution (Chikungunya, Rift Valley Fever, Crimean Congo Hemorrhagic Fever, Covid-19).

On the other hand, in the presence of Covid-19 we noted a decrease on the resurgence probability value for all of these diseases, hovering around 5%. This could be explained by the fact that during the Covid-19 pandemic, surveillance was much more focused on the latter, pushing other existing pathologies into the background. This fact was confirmed by Dieng et al. (2020) who recommended that efforts deployed against Covid-19 should be redirected towards the treatment of other priority pathologies affecting Senegalese people. The fairly high resurgence probability of 60% observed for Covid-19 disease reinforces the results of Diouf et al. (2020), who showed an upward evolution of this disease during the study period January 2018 to November 2022.

In Table 3, we compare our model (MO-DT) with two standard models: multi-class random forest (MC-RF) and multinomial logistic regression (MLR), by using the aggregated (macro-averaging) versions of the performance metrics mentioned in Subsect. 2.3.

Table 3. Performance comparison

Performance metrics	MO-DT	MC-RF	MLR
Accuracy	0.9945	0.9943	0.9162
Kappa	0.8952	0.8264	0.8952
Precision	0.8277	0.7970	0.7716
Recall	0.7863	0.7954	0.7578

(continued)

Table 3. (*continued*)

Performance metrics	MO-DT	MC-RF	MLR
F1-Score	0.8751	0.8558	0.8332

We can observe that our proposed model MO-DT displays good performance metrics. It has the best accuracy, compared to MC-RF and MLR models. We also note that our model performs better for almost all other metrics (Kappa, Precision and F1-score), and the multinomial logistic regression model (MLR) is less performant, see also Fig. 2 for model ranking by performance visualization.

By taking account of interdependencies between the ten diseases, our proposed Machine Learning model, MO-DT, shows some advantages, compared to MC-RF and RLM models. First, MO-DT outputs simultaneous predictions for all ten diseases, whereas MC-RF outputs one single disease, only. Second, the Chi-square distance used in the calculation of the inertia, as impurity measure, is more adequate than entropy for qualitative data which are frequent in epidemiologic studies.

The fairly good performance and advantages of our model lead us to its validation, and to recommend it as a decision-making tool for monitoring infectious diseases. This highlights again the relevance of Machine Learning approach to improve accuracy of predictions in epidemiology.

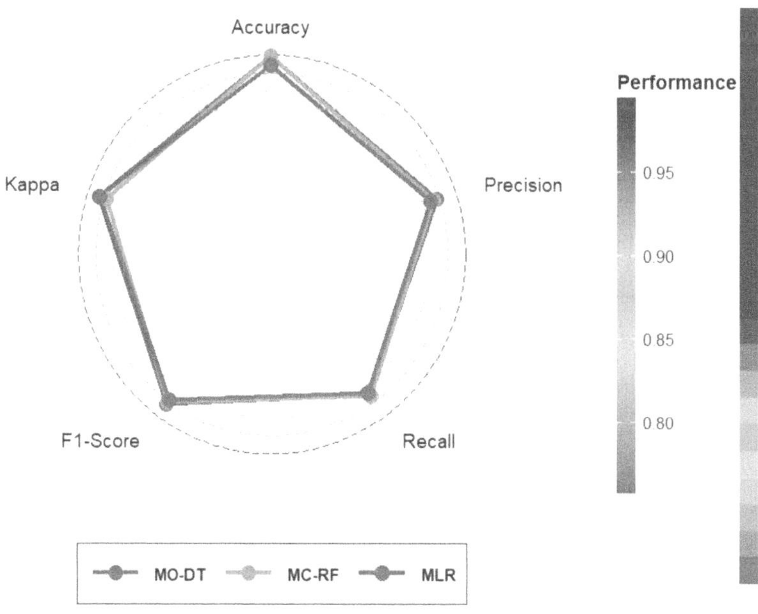

Fig. 2. Model ranking

4 Conclusion

This paper proposed a new multi-class prediction model to simultaneously predict the resurgence of ten infectious diseases under surveillance in Senegal. This model consists of multi-output decision tree algorithm (MO-DT) which is based on an impurity measure defined by the inertia criterion calculated with the chi-squared distance. The model shows good predictive performance compared to standard competitors, and allows to estimate the resurgence probabilities of ten potentially epidemic infectious diseases in Senegal. Moreover, our findings corroborate existing results on the incidence rate of these diseases, suggesting that our model MO-DT might be recommendable for the monitoring of infectious diseases in Senegal.

However, this study has some limitations. Indeed, predictions are based on a specific data set and at a fixed period, then it may not be generalizable to other geographical or temporal contexts. Furthermore, the proposed model does not take into account all the propagation risk factors that likely influence the resurgence of infectious diseases such as: population movements, trade, air traffic, and so on.

Appendix

- **Algorithm for constructing the model MO-DT**

```
> ## ----------- Fonction pour calculer l'inertie (critere d'impurete) -------- ##
> inertie=function(x)
+ { N = length(x$Disease)
+ X = as.factor(x$Disease)
+ class = levels(X)
+
+ K = length(class)
+ Y = matrix(data = NA, N, K)
+ for(j in 1:K)
+ { v = rep(NA, N)
+ for (i in 1:N) { if(X[i]== class[j]) v[i] = 1 else v[i] = 0 }
+ Y[,j] = v
+ }
+ Pt = rep(NA, K) ## Vecteur des proportions des  classes
+ for (j in 1:K) { Pt[j] = sum(Y[,j])/ N }
+ G = diag(Pt)
+ if (any(is.na(G)) || det(G, tol = 1e-9) == 0) G <- G + diag(1e-9, K)
+ H = rep(NA, N)
+ for(i in 1:N) { H[i] = t(Y[i,]-Pt)%*%solve(G)%*%(Y[i,]-Pt)}
+ sum(H)/N
+ }
> ## ------------- Fonction pour calculer le gain d'inertie ------------------- ##
> calc_inertia_gain <- function(parent, left, right) {
+   if (nrow(left) == 0 || nrow(right) == 0) return(0)
+
+   parent_inertia <- inertie(parent)
+   left_inertia <- inertie(left)
+   right_inertia <- inertie(right)
+
+   N <- nrow(parent)
+   N_left <- nrow(left)
+   N_right <- nrow(right)
+
+   gain <- parent_inertia - (N_left / N) * left_inertia - (N_right / N) * right_inertia
+   return(gain)
+ }
> ## ----------------- Definition de la classe Node --------------------------- ##
> Node <- function(dataset) {
+   node <- list(
+     dataset = dataset,
+     left_child = NULL,
+     right_child = NULL,
+     split_feature = NULL,
+     split_value = NULL
+   )
+   return(node)
+ }
> ## ------------------ Fonction pour faire croitre l'arbre ------------------- ##
> grow_tree <- function(node) {
+   zs <- node$dataset
+   if (nrow(zs) <= 1 || all(is.na(zs))) return(node)  # Arret si trop peu d'observations
+
+   best_gain <- -Inf
+   best_split <- NULL
+   best_split_val <- NULL
+   for (feature in names(zs)[-ncol(zs)]) {  # Ne pas inclure la colonne cible
+     if (is.numeric(zs[[feature]])) {
+       unique_vals <- unique(zs[[feature]])
+       for (val in unique_vals) {
+         left <- zs[zs[[feature]] <= val, ]
+         right <- zs[zs[[feature]] > val, ]
+
+         if (nrow(left) == 0 || nrow(right) == 0) next
+
+         gain <- calc_inertia_gain(zs, left, right)
+         if (gain > best_gain) {
+           best_gain <- gain
+           best_split <- feature
+           best_split_val <- val
+         }
+       }
+
+       } else if (is.factor(zs[[feature]])) {
+         levels_list <- levels(zs[[feature]])
+         for (level in levels_list) {
+           left <- zs[zs[[feature]] == level, ]
+           right <- zs[zs[[feature]] != level, ]
+
+           if (nrow(left) == 0 || nrow(right) == 0) next
+
+           gain <- calc_inertia_gain(zs, left, right)
+           if (gain > best_gain) {
+             best_gain <- gain
+             best_split <- feature
+             best_split_val <- level
+           }
+         }
+       }
+     }
+
+     if (best_gain == -Inf) return(node)
+   node$split_feature <- best_split
+   node$split_value <- best_split_val
+
+   if (is.numeric(zs[[best_split]])) {
+     left_node <- Node(zs[zs[[best_split]] <= best_split_val, ])
+     right_node <- Node(zs[zs[[best_split]] > best_split_val, ])
+   } else {
+     left_node <- Node(zs[zs[[best_split]] == best_split_val, ])
+     right_node <- Node(zs[zs[[best_split]] != best_split_val, ])
+   }
+
+   node$left_child <- grow_tree(left_node)
+   node$right_child <- grow_tree(right_node)
+
+   return(node)
+ }
```

- **Tree visualization**

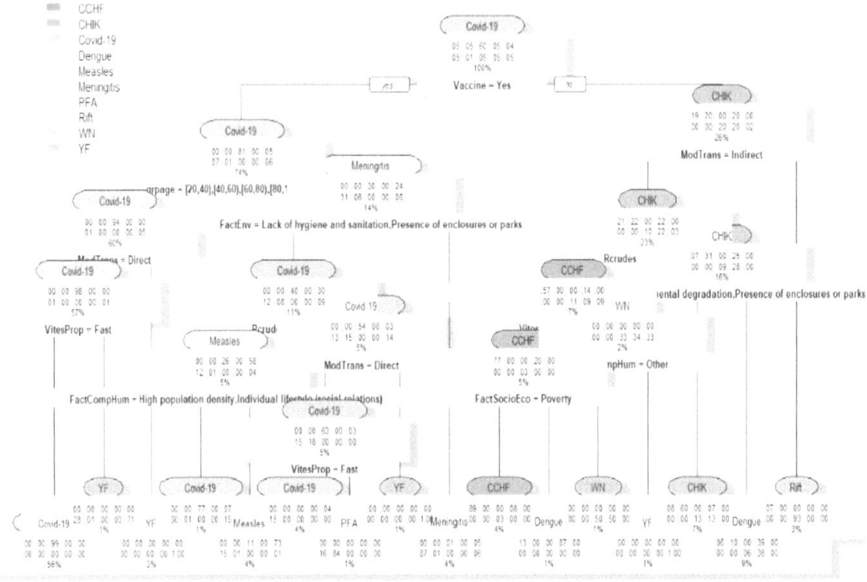

References

OMS-MSAS. Bulletin hebdomadaire des urgences infectieuses de sante publique au Sénégal, semaine n°32. Rapport OMS_Sénégal/MSAS_DP_DSRV (2024)

Barry A., et al.: Surveillance sentinelle des maladies à potentiel épidémique au Sénégal, Revue d'Épidémiologie et de Santé Publique, Volume 71, Supplement 3, 101872 (2023). ISSN 0398-7620, https://doi.org/10.1016/j.respe.2023.101872

Dieng A., Diouf J.B.N., Ndiaye S.M.L.: COVID-19 au Sénégal: réflexion d´un microbiologiste. Pan Afr Med J. **35**(Suppl 2), 31 (2020). https://doi.org/10.11604/pamj.supp.2020.35.2.22860. PMID: 33623556; PMCID: PMC7875736

Diouf I., Bousso A., Sonko I.: Gestion de la pandémie COVID-19 au Sénégal [COVID-19 pandemic management in Senegal]. Médecine De Catastrophe, Urgences Collectives. Sep;4(3):217–22. French (2020). https://doi.org/10.1016/j.pxur.2020.08.009. Epub 2020 Aug 24. PMCID: PMC7445002

De'Ath, G.: Multivariate regression trees: a new technique for modeling species-environment relationships. Ecology **83**(4), 1105–1117 (2002)

Evgeniou, T., Pontil, M.: Regularized multi-task learning. In: Proceedings of the Tenth ACM SIGKDD International Conference on Knowledge Discovery and Data Mining, pp. 109–117. ACM (2004)

Glocker, B., Pauly, O., Konukoglu, E., Criminisi, A.: Joint classification-regression forests for spatially structured multi-object segmentation. In: Computer Vision ECCV 2012, pp. 870–881. Springer (2012)

Gonçalves, R.M., et al.: Forecasting dengue across Brazil with LSTM neural networks and SHAP-driven lagged climate and spatial effects. medRxiv (2024). https://doi.org/10.1101/2024.12.11.24318832

Linusson, H.: Multi-Output Random Forests. Dissertation. University of Borås/School of Business and IT (2013). https://urn.kb.se/resolve?urn=urn:nbn:se:hb:diva-17167

Ndao A., Seck C.T.: Identification of propagation risk factors for ten infectious disesases under surveillance in Senegal. Afr. J. Appl. Stat. **11**(1), 1535–1551 (2024). https://doi.org/10.16929/ajas/2024.1535.281

Read, J., Martino, L., Olmos, P.M., Luengo, D.: Scalable multi-output label prediction: from classifier chains to classifier trellises. Pattern Recogn. **48**(6), 2096–2109 (2015)

Read, J., Pfahringer, B., Holmes, G., Frank, E.: Classifier chains for multi-label classification. Mach. Learn. **85**(3), 333–359 (2011)

Santangelo, O.E., Gianfredi, V., Provenzano, S., Cedrone, F.: Machine learning and prediction of infectious diseases: a systematic review. Mach. Learn. Knowl. Extr. **5**(1), 175–198 (2023). https://doi.org/10.3390/make5010013

Segal, M., Xiao, Y.: Multivariate random forests. Wiley Interdisc. Rev. Data Mining Knowl. Discov. **1**(1), 80–87 (2011)

Segal, M.R.: Tree-structured methods for longitudinal data. J. Am. Stat. Assoc. **87**(418), 407–418 (1992)

Wang C., Zhou J., Huang H., Shen, H.: Classification Algorithms for Unbalanced High-Dimensional Data with Hyperbox Vertex Over-Sampling Iterative Support Vector Machine Approach. Chinese Control and Decision Conference (CCDC), Hefei, China, pp. 2294–2299 (2020). https://doi.org/10.1109/CCDC49329.2020.9164585

Zhang, H.: Classification trees for multiple binary responses. J. Am. Stat. Assoc. **93**(441), 180–193 (1998)

Short-Term Hourly Rainfall Prediction: A Hybrid Approach with LSTM and TimeGAN

Paul Diokine Batista[1(✉)], Daouda Diouf[1], François Kaly[2], and Samuel Ouya[1]

[1] Université Cheikh Anta Diop de Dakar, LITA-ESP, Dakar, Senegal
batigaol17@gmail.com
[2] Université Iba Der Thiam, Thies, Senegal

Abstract. Short-term rainfall prediction is crucial in regions like West Africa, where unpredictable climate fluctuations between droughts and heavy rainfall complicate water and resource management. Accurate hourly forecasts can enhance water allocation for agriculture, drinking water, and irrigation, while improving disaster preparedness for floods and droughts. This study introduces a hybrid approach using LSTM networks and TimeGAN to address traditional forecasting limitations. By generating synthetic data with TimeGAN, the model tackles data scarcity and improves prediction robustness. Results show that models trained on synthetic data perform as well as or better than those trained on real data, demonstrating the value of synthetic data augmentation. This approach has significant potential for water management, agriculture, and disaster mitigation, offering scalable solutions to build resilience against extreme weather. The study highlights the effectiveness of combining generative models with recurrent neural networks for accurate, adaptive forecasting systems tailored to local needs.

Keywords: LSTM · TimeGAN · Rainfall

1 Introduction

Short-term rainfall prediction is essential in regions with variable climates like West Africa, where sudden climatic changes complicate water management [1]. Accurate forecasts enhance water allocation for agriculture and drinking supply while supporting disaster management through timely preventive actions [2, 3], particularly crucial in developing countries with limited infrastructure [4]. Reliable forecasts strengthen food security by helping farmers make informed decisions [5], with hourly rainfall predictions enabling better planning to reduce agricultural losses [6] and improve infrastructure management of reservoirs and dams [7].

This paper explores hourly rainfall prediction using LSTM neural networks combined with generative models like TimeGAN to create additional data, improving prediction accuracy for high-frequency climatic events [8, 9]. While traditional models like ARIMA have been used for short-term forecasting, they struggle with complex meteorological data [10]. LSTM and GRU offer enhanced predictive capabilities by

D. Bassole et al. (Eds.): InterSol 2025, LNICST 671, pp. 80–93, 2026.
https://doi.org/10.1007/978-3-032-15154-4_7

capturing temporal relationships [11] but face challenges including overfitting and difficulty generalizing to extreme weather [12]. Integrating TimGAN addresses these issues by generating synthetic data that increases dataset diversity and improves robustness [13, 14], particularly beneficial in data-limited regions like West Africa.

2 Data

Our study focuses on the West African region, which encompasses three major climatic zones: the Guinean zone (approximately 6°–8°N), the Sudanian zone (approximately 8°–12°N), and the Sahelian zone (approximately 12°–16°N). The weather parameters examined are categorized as: geographical coordinates spanning longitude [−20W; 10E] and latitude [17N; 5S]; temporal data in year-month-day and hour format; and six pressure levels [100hpa, 200hpa, 600hpa, 700hpa, 825hpa, 1000hpa] corresponding to precipitation formation. The key variables analyzed include relative humidity, specific humidity, eastward and northward wind components (measured at different precipitation levels), total precipitation, sea surface temperature, temperature at 2 m above ground, and pressure level.

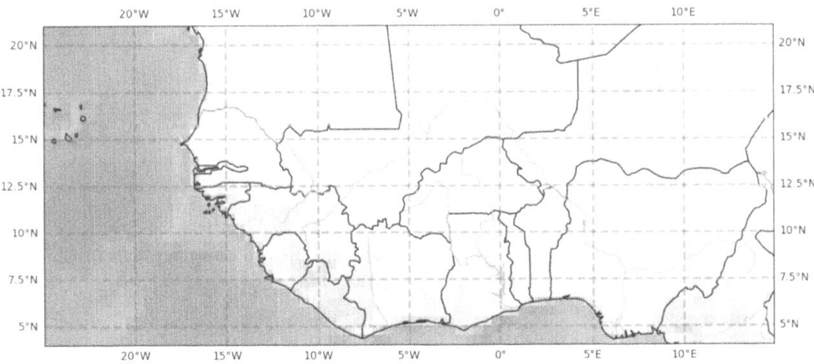

Fig. 1. Map of West Africa, the studied area

3 Methodology

The methodology of this project is based on the use of deep learning algorithms, particularly recurrent neural networks (RNN) and their advanced variants such as Long Short-Term Memory (LSTM) networks, Gated Recurrent Unit (GRU) networks, and Bidirectional LSTM (BiLSTM) networks.

Deep learning models were chosen because of their ability to handle sequential data and capture long-term dependencies. RNNs are particularly suited for sequence modeling as they can take previous information into account during their prediction process.

3.1 RNN, LSTM, BiLSTM, and GRU

3.1.1 Recurrent Neural Networks (RNN)

Before introducing LSTM and GRU networks, it is helpful to review the basic RNN architecture, as both LSTM and GRU are extensions built upon this fundamental structure. The standard RNN, illustrated in Fig. 2, processes an input vector $\boldsymbol{x_t}$ at each time step $\boldsymbol{t}$ and produces a corresponding hidden state $\boldsymbol{h_t}$ as output.

In a traditional RNN, the hidden state $\boldsymbol{h_t}$ is computed using a combination of the previous hidden state $\boldsymbol{h_{t-1}}$ and the current input $\boldsymbol{x_t}$. This update is formally defined as:

$$h_t = \tanh\left(U_{x_t} + W_{h_{t-1}} + b\right) \tag{1}$$

where ***tanh*** is the hyperbolic tangent activation function, $\boldsymbol{b}$ is a bias vector, and $\boldsymbol{U}$ and $\boldsymbol{W}$ are weight matrices associated with the input and hidden state, respectively [15]. These parameters ($\boldsymbol{U}$, $\boldsymbol{W}$, and $\boldsymbol{b}$) are shared across all time steps in the sequence, ensuring consistent computation throughout the network.

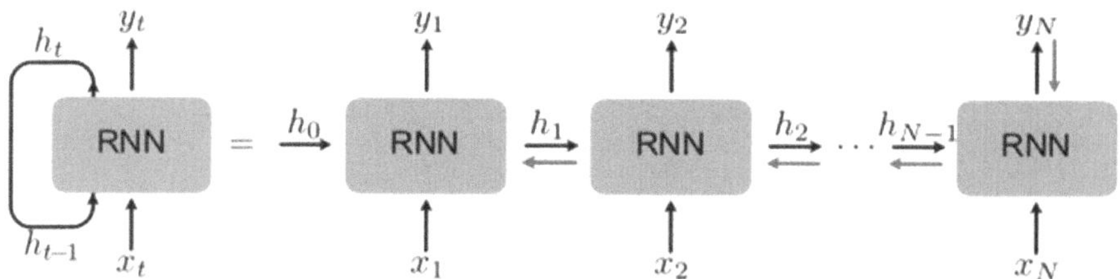

Fig. 2. The traditional RNN structure: Basic compressed RNN (left) and unfolded (right)

The final output of an RNN depends on both the current input and the hidden state from the previous time step [12]. Although RNNs are theoretically capable of capturing dependencies over sequences of arbitrary length, they often encounter vanishing and exploding gradient issues, which impair their ability to learn long-term dependencies. To address these limitations, LSTM and GRU architectures were specifically designed [16].

3.1.2 Long Short-Term Memory (LSTM)

The Long Short-Term Memory (LSTM) network, proposed by Hochreiter and Schmidhuber in 1997 [17], was developed as a powerful alternative to conventional recurrent neural networks (RNNs). Its key innovation lies in the introduction of a cell state, which acts as a memory unit capable of retaining information over extended time intervals. An LSTM cell processes an input vector $\boldsymbol{x_t}$, along with the hidden states $\boldsymbol{h_t}$ and $\boldsymbol{h_{t-1}}$, and the cell states $\boldsymbol{c_t}$ and $\boldsymbol{c_{t-1}}$, which are propagated through time. The flow of information within the cell is governed by three main gates:

- the forget gate ($\boldsymbol{f_t}$), which decides what information should be discarded,
- the input gate ($\boldsymbol{i_t}$), which regulates which new information to store, and
- the output gate ($\boldsymbol{o_t}$), which determines what information is emitted as output [18].

Thanks to this gating mechanism, LSTM networks effectively capture both short-term dependencies and long-term temporal relationships, offering a major advancement over traditional RNN architectures [12].

In Fig. 3, the cell state $\boldsymbol{c_t}$ and hidden state $\boldsymbol{h_t}$ of the LSTM unit are computed according to the following equations:

$$f_t = \sigma\left(W_{xf}x_t + W_{hf}h_{t-1} + b_f\right) \tag{2}$$

$$i_t = \sigma\left(W_{xi}x_t + W_{hi}h_{t-1} + b_i\right) \tag{3}$$

$$\tilde{C}_t = \tanh(W_{xc}x_t + W_{hc}h_{t-1} + b_c) \tag{4}$$

$$c_t = f_t \otimes c_{t-1} + i_t \otimes \hat{c}_t \tag{5}$$

$$o_t = \sigma\left(W_{xo}x_t + W_{ho}h_{t-1} + b_o\right) \tag{6}$$

$$h_t = o_t \tanh \otimes c_t \tag{7}$$

where $\boldsymbol{\sigma}$ is the logistic sigmoid function, $\otimes$ represents the element-wise multiplication of two vectors, and W_{xf}, $W_{xi}, W_{hi}, W_{hf}, W_{xo}, W_{ho}, W_{xc},$ and W_{hc} are the weight matrices of the network. Similarly, $\boldsymbol{b_i}$, $\boldsymbol{b_f}$, $\boldsymbol{b_o}$ and $\boldsymbol{b_c}$ are bias vectors. Finally, $\boldsymbol{f_t}$, $\boldsymbol{i_t}$ and $\boldsymbol{o_t}$ are vectors corresponding to the activation values of the forget gate, input gate, and output gate, respectively.

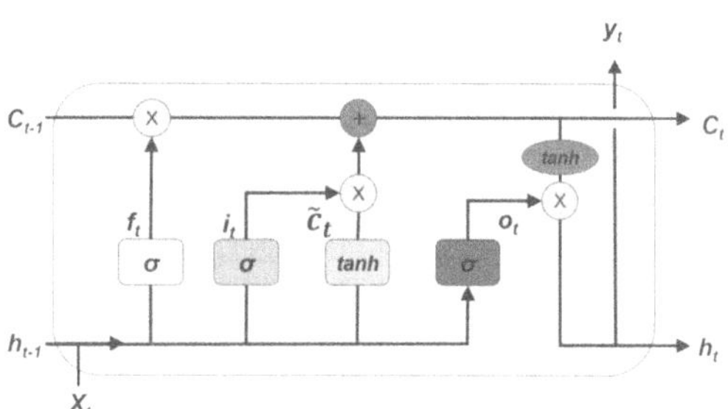

Fig. 3. Description of an LSTM Cell

3.1.3 Bidirectional Long Short-Term Memory (BiLSTM)

In standard time series modeling, unidirectional LSTM networks typically utilize only past information, ignoring future context. To address this limitation, Bidirectional LSTM (BiLSTM) employs two separate hidden layers that process the sequence in forward and backward directions, connecting both to a common output layer [19]. This allows the network to incorporate both past and future information as the temporal representation for each time step [20].

Consequently, BiLSTM networks generally achieve better predictive performance compared to unidirectional LSTMs. The hidden layer output in BiLSTM combines the activation outputs from the forward ($\overrightarrow{h_t}$) and backward ($\overleftarrow{h_t}$) layers. The mathematical formulation of BiLSTM is expressed in formulas (8), (9), and (10), where σ\sigmaσ denotes the activation function and $\boldsymbol{H_t}$ represents the input to the hidden layer. The overall architecture of BiLSTM is depicted in Fig. 4.

$$\overrightarrow{h_t} = \sigma\left(W_{x\overrightarrow{h_t}}x_t + W_{\overrightarrow{h_t}\overrightarrow{h_t}}\overrightarrow{h_{t-1}} + b_{\overrightarrow{h_t}}\right) \tag{8}$$

$$\overleftarrow{h_t} = \sigma\left(W_{x\overleftarrow{h_t}}x_t + W_{\overleftarrow{h_t}\overleftarrow{h_t}}\overleftarrow{h_{t-1}} + b_{\overleftarrow{h_t}}\right) \tag{9}$$

$$H_t = W_{x\vec{h}}\vec{h} + W_{\overleftarrow{h}y}\vec{h} + b_y \tag{10}$$

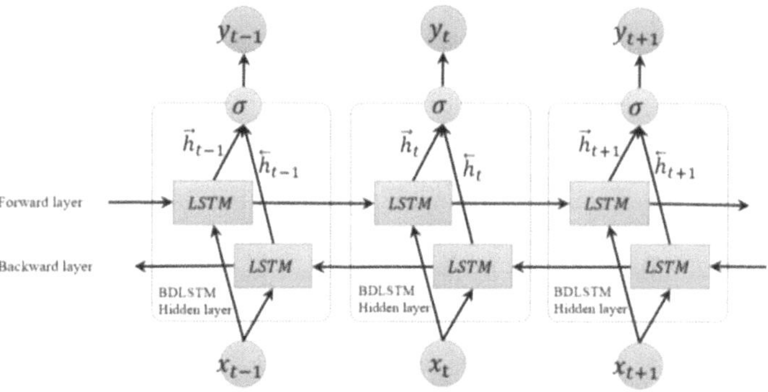

Fig. 4. Description of a BiLSTM Cell

3.1.4 Gated Recurrent Unit (GRU)

The Gated Recurrent Unit (GRU), proposed by Kyunghyun Cho and collaborators in 2014 [21], represents a streamlined variant of the LSTM architecture, designed to speed up training and reduce model complexity. The main structural difference between GRUs and LSTMs is that GRUs combine the hidden state ($\boldsymbol{h_t}$) and the cell state ($\boldsymbol{c_t}$) into a single unified representation. A GRU cell operates with only two gating mechanisms:

- the update gate (z_t), which determines how much of the previous hidden state ($\boldsymbol{h_{t-1}}$) is preserved and carried forward, and
- the reset gate ($\boldsymbol{r_t}$), which decides how much of the past information contributes to generating the new candidate activation.

This simplified gating structure allows GRUs to maintain performance comparable to LSTMs while being computationally more efficient. In Fig. 5, the update rules governing the GRU cell are expressed as follows:

$$r_t = \sigma(W_{xr}x_t + W_{hr}h_{t-1} + b_r) \tag{11}$$

$$z_t = \sigma(W_{xz}x_t + W_{hz}h_{t-1} + b_z) \tag{12}$$

$$\hat{c}_t = \tanh(W_{xc}x_t + W_{hc}(r_t \otimes h_{t-1}) + b_c) \tag{13}$$

$$c_t = (1 - z_t) \otimes c_{t-1} + z_t \otimes \hat{c}_t \tag{14}$$

$$h_t = c_t \tag{15}$$

where W_{xr}, W_{hr}, W_{xz}, and W_{hz} are the weight matrices of the network. $\boldsymbol{b_r}$ and $\boldsymbol{b_z}$ are the bias vectors, and $\boldsymbol{r_t}$ and z_t are the vectors of the activation values of the update gate and the reset gate.

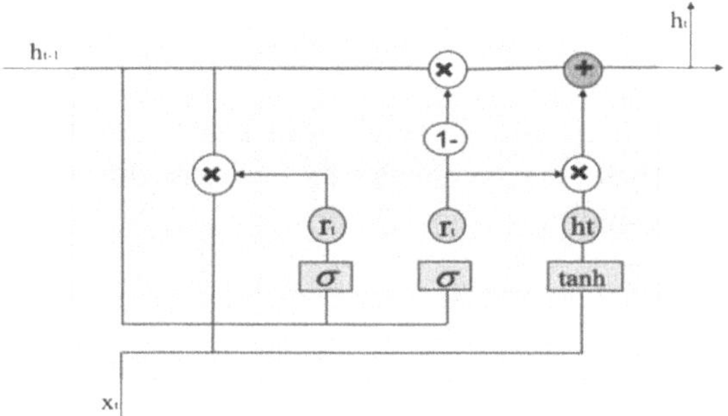

Fig. 5. Description of a GRU Cell

3.2 Generative Adversarial Networks for Time Series (TimeGAN)

Introduced by Jinsung Yoon and colleagues at the 33rd Conference on Neural Information Processing Systems (NeurIPS 2019) held in Vancouver, Canada [22], TimeGAN was designed to address the challenge of modeling complex temporal dependencies in sequential data. In particular, when dealing with multivariate time series $\boldsymbol{X_{1:T}} = \boldsymbol{(X_1,\ldots,X_T)}$, the objective is to accurately learn the conditional distribution $\boldsymbol{p(X_t \mid X_{1:t-1})}$, which describes how variables evolve over time.

Generally, data can be divided into two components: a static part, consisting of attributes that remain constant (e.g., name, gender), and a dynamic part, which includes variables that change over time (e.g., age, health condition). Let $\boldsymbol{S}$ denote the vector space of static features and $\boldsymbol{X}$ the vector space of dynamic features. Thus, $\boldsymbol{S}$ and $\boldsymbol{X}$ are random vectors whose specific realizations are represented by $\boldsymbol{s}$ and $\boldsymbol{x}$, respectively.

Over a given time interval $\boldsymbol{T}$, the dataset can be expressed as $\boldsymbol{(S, X_{1:T})}$, associated with a joint probability distribution p that also accounts for the temporal dimension T. The training dataset is therefore defined as

$$D = (s_n, x_n)_1^{T_n}$$

and the aim is to generate from this data a distribution $\hat{p}(\mathrm{S}, X_{1:T})$ that approximates as closely as possible the true distribution $p(\mathrm{S}, X_{1:T})$.

Achieving this directly through a conventional GAN framework is challenging. To overcome this, TimeGAN employs an autoregressive decomposition of the joint distribution:

$$p(\mathrm{S}, X_{1:T}) = p(S)\prod_t p(X_t|S, X_{1:t-1})$$

This approach emphasizes learning conditional probabilities, allowing for the simplified task of estimating the conditional density $\hat{p}(X_t|\,\mathrm{S}, X_{1:t-1})$ at each time step $\boldsymbol{t}$.

From this formulation, two learning objectives arise. The first, global, minimizes the divergence between the real and generated joint distributions:

$$\min_{\hat{p}} D\big(p(\mathrm{S}, X_{T-1})\hat{p}(S, X_{T-1})\big) \tag{16}$$

where D measures the overall distance between the two distributions.

The second, local, focuses on minimizing the pointwise difference between true and generated temporal transitions:

$$\min_{\hat{p}} D\big(p(X_t|\mathrm{S}, X_{1:t-1})\hat{p}(X_t|S, X_{1:t-1})\big) \tag{17}$$

This local formulation connects the generative adversarial component from the first objective with a supervised learning term based on maximum likelihood estimation from the second. Together, they form the core learning principle behind TimeGAN.

3.2.1 Architecture of the TimeGAN Model

The TimeGAN architecture comprises four network components: embedding function, recovery function, sequence generator, and sequence discriminator. Its innovation lies in jointly training auto-encoding components (the first two) with adversarial components (the last two), enabling TimeGAN to simultaneously learn feature encoding, representation generation, and temporal iteration. The embedding network establishes the latent space where the adversarial network operates, while a supervised loss synchronizes the latent dynamics of real and synthetic data. The embedding and recovery components function as autoencoders that map the latent space, facilitating the adversarial network's ability to learn temporal relationships through dimensionality reduction. With static characteristics denoted as $\boldsymbol{s}$, dynamic characteristics as $\boldsymbol{x}$, and latent space components as $\boldsymbol{h}_S$ and $\boldsymbol{h}_t$ (static and temporal), the embedding network operates as a recurrent network performing specific operations:

$\boldsymbol{h}_S = \boldsymbol{e}_S(s); \boldsymbol{h}_t = \boldsymbol{e}_{\mathcal{X}}(\boldsymbol{h}_S, \boldsymbol{h}_{t-1}, \boldsymbol{x}_t)$.

Where $\boldsymbol{e}_S$ and $\boldsymbol{e}_X$ are two networks, the first for static functions, the second for temporal functions. The recovery network will need to reconstruct the static characteristics $\bar{s}$ and temporal characteristics $\bar{\boldsymbol{x}}_{1:T}$ implemented with two networks $\boldsymbol{r}_S$ and $\boldsymbol{r}_X$:

$$\bar{s} = \boldsymbol{r}_S(\boldsymbol{h}_S); \bar{\boldsymbol{x}}_t = \boldsymbol{r}_{\mathcal{X}}(\boldsymbol{h}_t)$$

implemented by feedforward networks.

3.2.2 Sequence Generator and Discriminator

Here too, the generator and discriminator operate on static and dynamic data. For the generator: $\hat{\boldsymbol{h}}_S = \boldsymbol{g}_S(z_S)$; $\hat{\boldsymbol{h}}_t = \boldsymbol{g}_{\mathcal{X}}(\hat{\boldsymbol{h}}_S, \hat{\boldsymbol{h}}_{t-1}, z_t)$.

where $\boldsymbol{g}_S$ is a generator network for static functions and $\boldsymbol{g}_X$ is a recurrent network for temporal functions. The random vector z_S can be sampled from a distribution of choice, and $\boldsymbol{zt}$ follows a stochastic process; here we use the Gaussian distribution and the Wiener process.

For the discriminator: $\tilde{\boldsymbol{y}}_S = \boldsymbol{d}_S(\hat{\boldsymbol{h}}_S)$; $\tilde{\boldsymbol{y}}_t = \boldsymbol{d}_{\mathcal{X}}\left(\overleftarrow{\boldsymbol{u}}_t, \vec{\boldsymbol{u}}_t\right)$.

Where $\vec{u}_t = \vec{c}_{\mathcal{X}}(\hat{h}_S, \hat{h}_t, \vec{u}_{t-1})$ and $\overleftarrow{u}_t = \overleftarrow{c}_{\mathcal{X}}\left(\hat{h}_S, \hat{h}_t, \overleftarrow{u}_{t+1}\right)$ represent the forward and backward hidden state sequences, respectively the recurrent functions, $\vec{c}_{\mathcal{X}}$, $\overleftarrow{c}_{\mathcal{X}}$ and the output layer classification functions $\boldsymbol{d}_S, \boldsymbol{d}_{\mathcal{X}}$.

3.2.3 Training Scheme

During training, the first component is the reconstruction loss, used to train the integration and reconstruction networks. This loss measures the discrepancy between the original data $\boldsymbol{s}, \boldsymbol{X}_{1:T}$ and their reconstructions $\tilde{s}, \overline{\boldsymbol{X}}_{1:T}$ obtained from the latent representations $\boldsymbol{h}_S, \boldsymbol{h}_{1:T}$:

$$\mathcal{L}_{\boldsymbol{R}} = \mathbb{E}_{s.\boldsymbol{X}_{1:T}\sim p}\left[\|s-\tilde{s}\|_2+\Sigma\|X_t-\tilde{X}_t\|_2\right] \tag{18}$$

The second component is the unsupervised GAN loss, which encourages the discriminator to correctly classify real and synthetic sequences, while the generator is trained to fool the discriminator:

$$\mathcal{L}_U = \mathbb{E}_{S.X_{1:T}\sim p}[\mathbf{log}ys+\Sigma_t\mathbf{log}yt] + \mathbb{E}_{S.X_{1:T}\sim p}[\mathbf{log}(\mathbf{1}-\hat{y}_S)+\Sigma_t\mathbf{log}(\mathbf{1}-\hat{y}_t)] \tag{19}$$

To better align with the conditional distributions of the data, an additional supervised loss $\boldsymbol{L}_S$ is introduced to train the generator using sequences derived from real data. This loss captures the difference between the latent vector predicted by the generator and the corresponding latent vector from the integration network:

$$\mathcal{L}_S = \mathbb{E}_{s.X_{1:T}\sim p}\left[\Sigma_t\|h_t-g_{\mathcal{X}}(h_S,h_{t-1},z_t)\|\right] \tag{20}$$

In practice, during training, $\boldsymbol{L}_U$ ensures that the generator produces realistic sequences acceptable to the discriminator, while $\boldsymbol{L}_S$ enforces temporal consistency by making sure that generated latent transitions align progressively with the real sequences.

3.2.4 Optimization

For the recovery network parameters, $\boldsymbol{\theta}_{\mathbf{g}}$ for the generator parameters, and $\boldsymbol{\theta}_{\mathbf{d}}$ for the discriminator parameters.

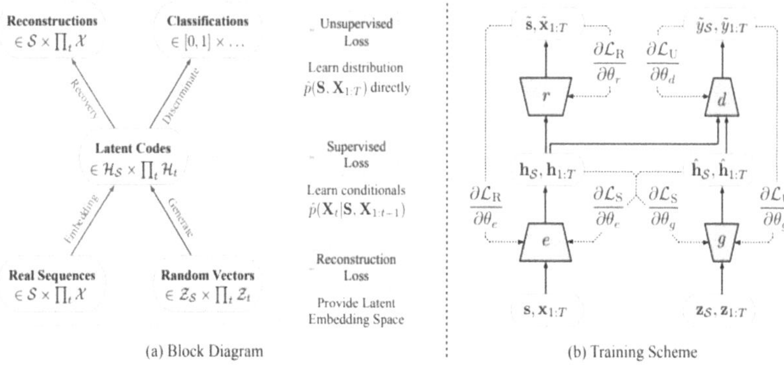

Fig. 6. TimeGAN Training Scheme

In the model architecture, solid arrows represent the forward flow of data, while dotted arrows illustrate the backward propagation of gradients during training.

For the first two subnetworks, the objective function combines both reconstruction loss and supervised loss, balanced by a positive hyperparameter λ > 0 that determines their relative contribution:

$$\min_{\theta_e,\theta_r} (\lambda \mathcal{L}_S + \mathcal{L}_R) \tag{21}$$

Similarly, for the generator and discriminator components, the training objective integrates an adversarial loss with an inverted supervised term, regulated by another hyperparameter η ≥ 0 to control the trade-off between the two losses:

$$\min_{\theta_g} \left(\eta \mathcal{L}_S + \max_{\theta_d} \mathcal{L}_U \right) \tag{22}$$

In practical implementations, TimeGAN exhibits limited sensitivity to these hyperparameters. Across all experimental configurations, the values were kept constant at λ = 1 and η = 10.

4 Implementation of the Hybrid Prediction Model with TimeGAN

Our hybrid approach integrate TimeGAN to create synthetic datasets for training three time series prediction models: LSTM, BiLSTM, and GRU, with optimized parameters and architectures. This method enhances predictive performance by combining data augmentation with the strengths of RNN variants (LSTM, BiLSTM, and GRU). The goal is to determine the most efficient model for hourly precipitation forecasting, evaluated using specific performance metrics.

- Mean Squared Error (MSE): $MSE = \frac{1}{n}\sum_{i=1}^{n}\left(Y_i - \overline{Y}_i\right)^2$
- Mean Absolute Error (MAE): $MAE = \frac{1}{n}\sum_{i=1}^{n}\left|Y_i - \widehat{Y}_i\right|$
- -Root Mean Squared Error (RMSE): $RMSE = \sqrt{\frac{1}{n}\sum_{i=1}^{n}\left(Y_i - \hat{Y}_i\right)^2}$

4.1 Preprocessing ERA5 Data

Since ERA5 data are reanalysis data derived from various meteorological sources, they are already preprocessed and do not contain missing values. The preprocessing methods applied here are specific to the requirements of deep learning models. To facilitate network learning, we scaled the data to a range between 0 and 1 using Min-Max normalization.

4.2 TimeGAN Training Data

We use a sliding window of size 24 applied across the dataset, shifting one position at a time. In the ERA5 dataset, there are 4,368 rows. By sampling every 24 rows, we obtain 4,368 entries, each consisting of 24 rows and 11 features. These entries can be randomly shuffled to make them independent and identically distributed.

As a result, we created a dataset with dimensions [4368, (24, 11)], where each of the 4,368 instances contains 24 rows (also referred to as time steps) and 11 features.

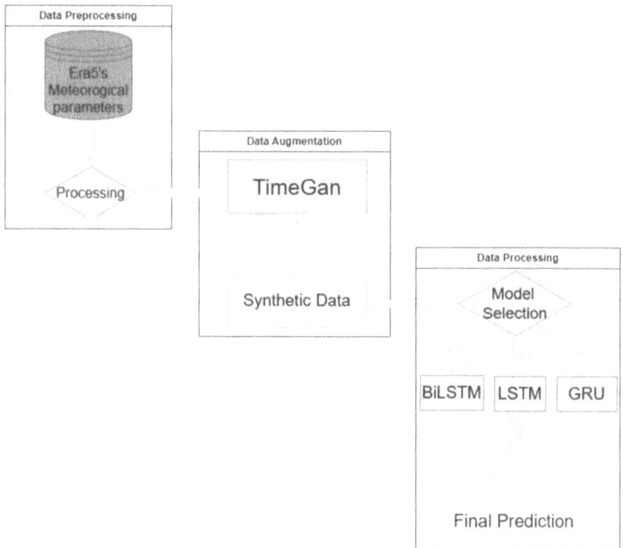

Fig. 7. Hybrid Prediction Model with TimeGAN Scheme

5 Results

5.1 Presentation of TimeGAN Training Results

5.1.1 2D Visualization: A Qualitative Evaluation of Diversity

To enable visualization of both the real and generated time series, each comprising 24 time steps and 11 features, we first perform dimensionality reduction to project the data into a two-dimensional space. Specifically, we randomly select 250 normalized sequences, each containing 11 features, and reshape them to form a dataset with dimensions 2750×24 for subsequent analysis and visualization.

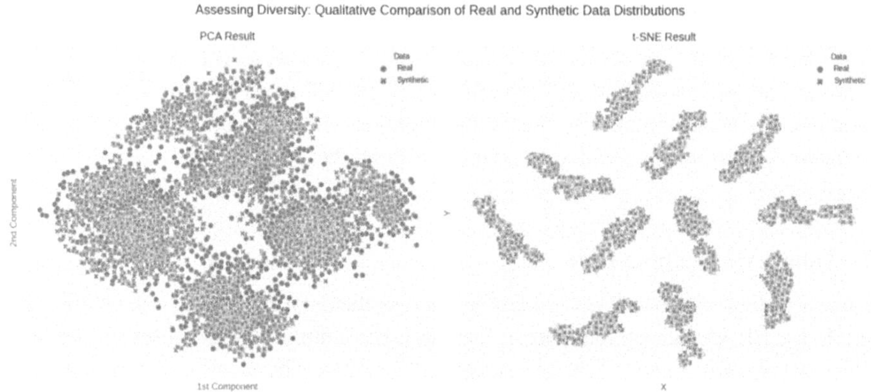

Fig. 8. PCA and t-SNE Visualization

5.1.2 Time Series Classification: A Quantitative Evaluation of Fidelity

While visualization provides only a qualitative understanding, a quantitative assessment of the synthetic data's fidelity requires training a time series classifier to distinguish between real and generated sequences. To do this, we split the sliding sequences into a training set (the first 80%) and a test set (the remaining 20%). We then construct a simple RNN with six hidden units, which processes mini-batches of time series with shape 24 × 1124 \times 1124 × 11 and employs a sigmoid activation function. The network is trained using binary cross-entropy loss and the Adam optimizer, while monitoring AUC and precision metrics to evaluate classification performance.

5.2 Training on Synthetic Data, Testing on Real Data: Evaluating Utility

Finally, we evaluated the utility of synthetic data for prediction tasks by comparing a time series model trained on synthetic data versus real data, assessing performance on a real data test set. We implemented a single-layer RNN with 12 GRU units to predict the next time step for all 11 features, using Adam optimizer to minimize mean absolute error (MAE).

The model was trained twice—once with synthetic data and once with real data while maintaining consistent evaluation on the real test set. Training utilized cross-validation with a rolling/sliding window split and daily time windows.

Figure 9 displays the evolution of actual versus predicted precipitation across months in the test dataset, demonstrating that monthly predictions closely track actual values and highlighting the prediction quality of our hybrid TimeGAN-LSTM model.

Figure 10 presents a scatter plot comparing actual precipitation against predicted precipitation, with a red line representing perfect prediction. This visualization, based on test data from 07/10/2021 at 12 PM, provides a realistic assessment of model performance under real-world conditions and illustrates how closely predictions align with actual values.

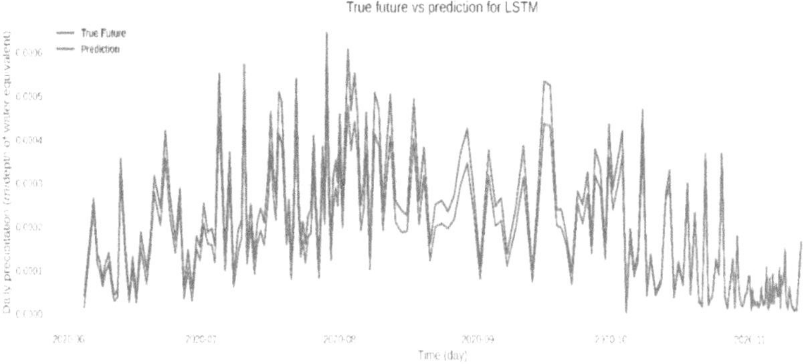

Fig. 9. Evolution of Actual and Predicted Precipitation on the Test Dataset with the Hybrid TimeGAN-LSTM Model

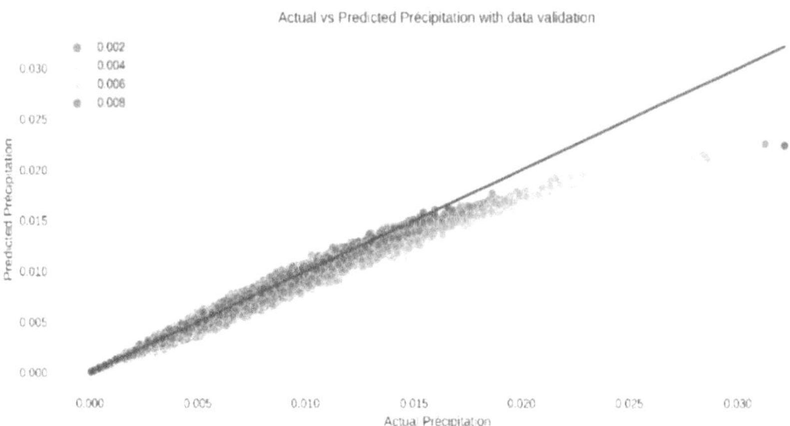

Fig. 10. Scatter Plot of Actual vs. Predicted Precipitation with Ideal Reference Line for LSTM Model Evaluation

The model demonstrates exceptional performance, with a Mean Squared Error (MSE) of 2.099×10^{-9}, a Mean Absolute Error (MAE) of $3.500 \times 10^{-}5$, and a Root Mean Squared Error (RMSE) of $4.582 \times 10^{-}5$, collectively validating the high precision of the TimeGAN-LSTM hybrid approach across both monthly trends and hourly precipitation forecasts.

6 Conclusion

This study demonstrates that TimeGAN-generated synthetic data successfully reproduces real time series patterns, enabling effective data augmentation. Integrating TimeGAN with advanced RNNs like LSTM, BiLSTM, and GRU yields accurate short-term rainfall forecasts, with synthetic data performing as well as or better than real data.

This approach helps mitigate data scarcity and overfitting, offering significant benefits for water resource management, agriculture, and disaster prevention in regions like West Africa. The study shows that generative models can enhance forecasting in data-limited contexts.

References

1. Henderson, M., Thompson, S., James, A.: Climate variability and its impact on water resources in West Africa. Environ. Monit. Assess. **190**(3), 178 (2018)
2. Harrington, M., Mahfouf, J.: Short-term precipitation forecasting: a case study from West Africa. Atmos. Res. **240**, 104907 (2020)
3. McCarty, D., Zhao, Y., Zhang, H.: Advancements in short-term weather prediction for disaster mitigation. Environ. Hazards **18**(2), 210–225 (2019)
4. Diouf, D., Ndiaye, A.: Challenges of weather prediction in West Africa: application of machine learning models. Climate Change Dev. **32**(2), 109–122 (2021)
5. Pérez, E., López, A., García, A.: Short-term precipitation prediction: benefits for agricultural planning. Agric. Meteorol. **23**(4), 211–220 (2017)
6. Patel, R., Sharma, K.: Impact of weather prediction on agriculture: a case study of West Africa. Agric. Syst. **178**, 102758 (2020)
7. Srinivasan, R., Nair, A., Sharma, T.: Management of water reservoirs using weather forecasting models. Water Resour. Manage **32**(7), 2357–2369 (2018)
8. Chouhan, P., Sharma, R.: Improved rainfall prediction using generative adversarial networks for synthetic data augmentation. Environ Model Softw. **116**, 37–45 (2019)
9. Li, F., Li, J., Zhao, W.: Data augmentation using TimGAN for time series forecasting. J. Mach. Learn. Res. **21**(125), 1–16 (2020)
10. Wang, X., Zhang, S., Zhao, M.: Time series forecasting of precipitation using deep learning models: a comparative study. Water Resour. Manage **33**(10), 3399–3412 (2019)
11. Shi, Y., Sun, Q., Wang, J.: Precipitation prediction using a hybrid LSTM-GRU model: a case study of East Asia. J. Hydrol. **590**, 125679 (2021)
12. Zhao, Y., Liu, D., Wu, X.: A hybrid LSTM and GAN model for precipitation prediction under changing climate conditions. Environ Model Softw. **132**, 104766 (2020)
13. Yoon, J., Kim, S., Choi, Y.: Improved short-term weather forecasting using a hybrid model of LSTM and TimGAN. J. Clim. **33**(14), 4876–4893 (2020)
14. Dai, J., Zhang, Z., Li, B.: A hybrid model combining LSTM and GAN for short-term precipitation forecasting. Atmos. Res. **246**, 105128 (2021)
15. Zhang, J., et al.: Developing a long short-term memory (LSTM) based model for predicting water table depth in agricultural areas. J. Hydrol. **561**, 918–929 (2018)
16. Sak, H., Senior, A., Beaufays, F.: Long short-term memory recurrent neural network architectures for large scale acoustic modeling. In: Proceedings of the Annual Conference of the International Speech Communication Association, INTERSPEECH, pp. 338–342 (2014)
17. Hochreiter, S., Schmidhuber, J.: Long short-term memory. Neural Comput. **9**(8), 1735–1780 (1997)
18. Fischer, T., Krauss, C.: Deep learning with long short-term memory networks for financial market predictions. Eur. J. Oper. Res. **270**(2), 654–669 (2018)
19. Cui, Z., Ke, R., Pu, Z., et al.: Deep bidirectional and unidirectional LSTM recurrent neural network for network-wide traffic speed prediction (2018). arXiv preprint arXiv:1801.02143
20. Kim, J., Moon, N.: BiLSTM model based on multivariate time series data in multiple field for forecasting trading area. J. Ambient Intell. Humanized Comput. 1–10 (2019)

21. Cho, K., et al.: Learning phrase representations using RNN encoder-decoder for statistical machine translation (2014). arXiv preprint arXiv:1406.1078
22. Yoon, J., Jarrett, D., van der Schaar, M.: Time-series Generative Adversarial Networks. Neural Information Processing Systems (NeurIPS) (2019)

On the Power of Deep Learning for Pest Bird Detection in Agriculture

Osias Noël N. F. Tossou[1(✉)], Yawoa Makafui Sandra Atopia[2], Mouhamadou Lamine Ba[1], Idy Diop[1], and Arlindo Veiga[3]

[1] Université Cheikh Anta Diop, Dakar, Senegal
osias.tossou@aims-senegal.org, {mouhamadoulamine.ba,idy.diop}@esp.sn
[2] African Institute for Mathematical Sciences, Mbour, Senegal
yawoa.m.s.atopia@aims-senegal.org
[3] University of Cape Verde, Praia, Cape Verde

Abstract. Pest birds represent significant threats to agricultural productivity and cause substantial economic losses around the world. Traditional pest control methods and tracking models are often laborious, harmful to the environment, and ineffective in practice. This paper explores the potential of deep learning models to improve pest bird detection and classification in agricultural settings. We evaluated the performance of three robust state-of-the-art object detection models, which are YoLOv8, Faster R-CNN, and C3Det, using various dataset configurations comprising high-resolution bird images, low-resolution bird images, and a mixed configuration. Our results show that while YOLOv8 excels in real-time detection of high-resolution bird images with a precision of 96.15%, C3Det is better detecting low-resolution bird images with a precision of 97.48%. These findings highlight the power of deep learning models to revolutionize pest-bird management.

Keywords: Pest Bird · YOLO · Faster R-CNN · C3Det · Object Detection · Precision Agriculture

1 Introduction

Bird pests represent a serious and growing threat to agricultural production around the world, leading to devastating economic consequences. As an example, a study conducted in Sweden between 2000 and 2015 [28] examined the estimated and actual losses caused by various bird species, recording 2,194 complaints of crop damage estimated around 34,500 t of different crops. Similarly, according to [10], it was reported that between 2003 and 2007, the average annual economic loss associated with bird damage to rice crops amounted to approximately 4.7 billion FCFA (7.1 million euros) in Senegal. These significant economic losses highlight the urgent need for innovative and sustainable strategies to mitigate bird-induced crop damage. Traditional approaches for bird deterrent, such as scarecrows, netting, and chemical repellents [27], are often tedious, ineffective, and harmful to the environment [29]. Amongst the challenges, we can note the

D. Bassole et al. (Eds.): InterSol 2025, LNICST 671, pp. 94–106, 2026.
https://doi.org/10.1007/978-3-032-15154-4_8

early detection of the pest birds in realtime with automated systems that respect the environment within a very noisy setting.

Deep learning, a major advancement in artificial intelligence (AI), offers promising potential to overcome the limitations of conventional methods and revolutionize bird pest management, as shown in [11]. Models such as YOLOv8 and Faster R-CNN have now proven high effectiveness for general object detection tasks, making them promising candidates for adaptation to bird pest management [31]. We hypothesize that these models should be able to thoroughly analyze, identify, and classify birds in both images and video streams. However, despite their potential, current AI-based bird detection systems still face several limitations. These include accuracy challenges, where existing systems fail to achieve sufficiently reliable detection rates, leading to missed or incorrect identifications; a lack of species-level identification, which hampers targeted control operations; and the high computational cost of complex models, which can limit their applicability in resource-constrained environments such as African rural farms. To address these challenges, this work investigates first steps toward an AI-based pest bird detection system using deep learning models. We rely on generic models with the aim at enhancing the detection accuracy for specific classes of agriculturally important bird species. This approach has the potential to offer farmers a more targeted, efficient, and cost-effective solution to control pest birds. To this end, we evaluated the performance of three robust state-of-the-art object detection models, which are YoLOv8, Faster R-CNN, and C3Det, using various dataset configurations comprising high-resolution bird images, low-resolution bird images, and a mixed configuration. Preliminary results show that while YOLOv8 excels in real-time detection of high-resolution bird images with a precision of 96.15%, C3Det is more accurate to detect low-resolution bird images with a precision of 97.48%.

The sequel of this paper is structured as follows. Firstly, Sect. 2 provides a review of the current literature. Secondly, Sect. 3 details the methods and materials used in this study. Then, Sect. 4 presents and discusses the results of our experiments. Finally, Sect. 5 concludes the study and outlines future research directions.

2 Related Work

Several research directions have been explored for the control of pest birds. Conventional techniques have been used to minimize bird-related damage to agricultural fields, including scare tactics [3], physical barriers [3], and habitat modification [32]. Some of these methods have shown partial success in specific contexts, while many face persistent challenges in terms of precision, sustainability, and long-term effectiveness [3]. In addition, bio-acoustic and visual deterrent systems like distress calls and laser tools, have been used [6,9]. Their effectiveness decreases during the time, particularly if the devices are not relocated regularly [9]. An interesting traditional approach used for bird monitoring is the point count method, which involves observing and recording birds within a defined radius around a fixed point for a specified time period [5,33]. This method allows researchers to directly observe bird behavior and is adaptable to various habitats and environmental conditions [1,35]. However, observers often face difficulty estimating distances or the position of birds accurately [2,39], leading to potential errors in counting birds. Detection rates also vary by species, leading to bias in biodiversity estimates [2,41]. Moreover, bird visibility and activity can fluctuate depending on the day or season time period [13], and human presence itself can alter bird behavior [19]. Recent efforts have focused on automated alternatives such as autonomous sound recording [38]. Widely used in ecological research and population monitoring [12], this approach captures bird calls and songs using sound recorders placed in the field for extended durations. It enables systematic and unbiased sampling across time and space, reduces the need for human presence, and can provide a more continuous record of vocal activity [38]. However, this method is limited to vocally active species, as silent birds can only be detected visually. Vocalization rates also vary by species, season, and time of day [16,18]. In the sequel of this section, we survey mathematical modeling of pest-bird management and existing deep learning approaches for bird detection.

2.1 Mathematical Models for Pest Bird Management

Mathematical modeling approaches have been introduced in order to understand population dynamics, spatial distribution, behavioral adaptations, and the effectiveness of control strategies for pest birds. These models provide a rigorous framework for evaluating management interventions and supporting informed, sustainable decision-making process. An important tool is the *logistic growth model*, which captures how bird populations evolve over time in response to environmental constraints. This model is useful for analyzing migration patterns and understanding how pest birds spread across agricultural landscapes. Since control measures often need to address both local presence and large-scale movement, incorporating spatial effects into population models is essential to design impactful strategies. Beyond population dynamics, managing pest birds also requires optimizing intervention efforts to minimize crop losses while preserving ecological balance. *Optimal control theory* offers a mathematical framework for identifying the most cost-effective and ecologically sound control measures by minimizing the combined costs of bird damage and mitigation efforts. However, birds are not passive actors; their behavior adapts in response to control tactics and environmental changes. *Game theory* is well-suited to modeling this dynamic, treating the interaction between pest birds and control mechanisms as a strategic game. This approach helps to anticipate how birds might adapt to deterrents, enabling the development of more robust and resilient control techniques [8,26]. Because real-world bird behavior is subject to random environmental fluctuations and migration uncertainties, *stochastic models*, such as Markov chains, are used to incorporate probabilistic elements into predictions. These models provide a more realistic representation of bird behavior by accounting for randomness in transitions between different populations or behavioral states.

To assess the impact of control methods, these mathematical models often integrate real-world effectiveness data. This integration enhances their predictive power and helps refine the deployment of control technologies. Ultimately, the development of sustainable pest bird control solutions benefits from a holistic modeling approach, combining deterministic, stochastic, behavioral, and spatial aspects as proposed in [15, 40]

2.2 Deep Learning Approaches for Pest Bird Detection

Saliency methods, combined with convolutional neural networks (CNNs), have been employed to categorize insect pests. Saliency techniques, which highlight the most crucial regions of an image by mimicking human attention mechanisms, achieved an impressive accuracy of 92.43% on a small dataset [30]. Other researchers have explored a combination of Super-Resolution (SR) technique to enhance the quality of the input images and CNNs for classification purposes to identify birds in vineyards [4]. In [24], YOLOv5, based on the CSP-DarkNet architecture, achieved an accuracy of 95.36% and a mAP of 91.28%, making it highly suitable for real-time detection tasks. Faster R-CNN, using ResNet50 as the backbone, is recognized for its robust performance, although it is generally slower compared to single-shot detectors [24]. RetinaNet, also based on ResNet50, stands out as a strong candidate for real-time applications due to its balance between speed and accuracy [24]. Other models like RepPoints (with ResNet50), SSD300 (based on VGG16), and CenterNet (with ResDCN18) also contribute to the growing arsenal of efficient bird detection techniques [24]. Although there are numerous deep learning models available, this study focuses specifically on YOLOv8, Faster R-CNN, and C3Det. YOLOv8 is one of the most popular one-stage detection models, renowned for its speed and efficiency in real-time object detection. Faster R-CNN, despite its slower inference time, offers high detection accuracy given its two-stage architecture. Lastly, C3Det has been specifically designed to improve the detection of small objects, addressing challenges often encountered in real-world pest bird monitoring scenarios.

3 Methods and Materials

We first proceed to the collection of the needed real dataset. We then select the proper models to compare and finally we do experimental evaluation.

3.1 Real World Datasets

For this study, we compiled three distinct datasets to evaluate the performance of the models under different conditions. The datasets were designed to include a variety of bird species, focusing on both pest and non-pest birds, as well as large and small birds (Fig. 1).

D1 contains 2,631 images of high resolution birds, with 1,338 images representing pest birds and 1,293 images representing non-pest birds. The images were collected using web scraping tools such as Beautiful Soup and manually annotated to ensure accuracy (Fig. 2).

Fig. 1. Exemple of images in our D1.

D2 comprises 2,631 images of small resolution bird images, including 1,338 images of pest birds and 1,293 images of non-pest birds. The small bird data was specifically designed to test the models' ability to detect smaller objects, which is a common challenge in agricultural settings.

Fig. 2. Example of images in our D2.

D3 is the merge of D1 and D2, resulting in 5,262 mixed images of both high and small resolution birds. The mixed dataset was used to evaluate the performances of the detection models in more complex and realistic scenarios.

3.2 Pre-processing

Before training the models, the datasets underwent a rigorous pre-processing phase to ensure data quality and consistency. First, irrelevant images, such as those unrelated to birds or of poor quality (e.g., blurry or overly dark), were removed. Duplicate images were then identified and eliminated to prevent overfitting and maintain a balanced dataset. To standardize the input data and improve computational efficiency during training, all images were resized to a uniform dimension of 416 × 416 pixels. Finally, each image was manually annotated using bounding boxes and class labels (pest bird or non-pest bird), a critical step to enable the models to accurately detect and classify birds.

3.3 Baseline Models

We considered the three following models for pest bird detection based on criteria such as accuracy, speed and type of supported image resolution.

(i) **YOLOv8** (You Only Look Once) is a widely used object detection algorithm, originally introduced in 2015 by Joseph Redmon et al. [34]. It is renowned for its ability to process an entire image in a single pass, simultaneously predicting bounding boxes and classifying objects, thus enabling real-time detection with high accuracy. Since its inception, YOLO has evolved through multiple versions, each bringing significant improvements. Developed by Ultralytics, YOLOv8 represents a major leap in both accuracy and efficiency, building on the success of YOLOv5. Designed to be versatile across different applications and hardware platforms, YOLOv8's architecture is composed of two main components: the backbone and the head, both built using fully convolutional neural networks. The backbone, inspired by CSPDarknet53, incorporates 53 convolutional layers and multi-level partial connections through the C2f module, enhancing information flow and detection precision. Additionally, the SPPF (Spatial Pyramid Pooling Fast) module further processes features at multiple scales [20,21]. The head autonomously handles objectivity scoring, classification, and bounding box regression, utilizing upsampling layers (U-layers) to refine feature map resolution for precise and rapid detection [21].

(ii) **Faster R-CNN** is a two-stage object detection architecture proposed by Ren et al. in 2015 [37], designed to improve both accuracy and efficiency over earlier R-CNN methods. It introduces the Region Proposal Network (RPN) to replace selective search, enabling end-to-end training for region proposal and object detection tasks [14,36]. The architecture consists of a backbone CNN (e.g., ResNet or VGG) for feature extraction [7,17], the RPN for generating region proposals using anchor boxes, and the Fast R-CNN detector for classification and bounding box refinement [22,25]. By sharing convolutional features between the RPN and detector, Faster R-CNN reduces redundancy and improves speed without sacrificing accuracy. Its high precision makes it ideal for complex detection tasks. However, due to its two-stage nature, it requires greater computational resources compared to single-stage models like YOLO, which may hinder real-time or resource-constrained applications [14,36].

(iii) **C3Det** [23] is an interactive annotation framework optimized for multi-class tiny object detection. It significantly reduces annotation time and cost by enabling users to annotate multiple small objects across various classes with minimal interaction. The system transforms user clicks into heatmaps and incorporates two key modules: (i) **Late Fusion Module (LF)**, which captures local contextual information from user input, and (ii) **Class-wise Collated Correlation (C3)**, which propagates the influence of user inputs across the entire image to detect distant or unspecified objects. Additionally, it applies a User-input Enforcing Loss (UEL) to ensure alignment between user guidance and model predictions. Evaluations on Tiny-DOTA and LCell datasets demonstrate that C3Det achieves higher mean Average Precision (mAP) with fewer interactions, reducing annotation time by approximately twice compared to manual annotation.

4 Experimental Evaluation

In this section, we detail the experiments conducted on real datasets as well as the results obtained.

4.1 Experiment Set up End Evaluation Metrics

The tests were carried out on Google Colab cloud environment. OpenCV, NumPy, TensorFlow, and PyTorch Python libraries were used for image processing, model training and testing. For all of our tests, we considered 80% of the data for training, 10% for validation, and 10% for testing. We evaluated *precision*, *recall*, *F1 score*, and *mean Average Precision (mAP)* of all models considered. We refer to [11] for more details on these metrics.

4.2 Description of the Results

Tables 1, 2, and 3 summarized the performances of the tested models on datasets D1, D2 and D3 respectively. A comparative view is given by Figs. 3, 4 and 5.

Table 1. Results of the evaluation of the models on D1

Metric	YOLOv8	Faster R-CNN	C3Det
Precision	**0.9615**	0.90	0.88
mAP@50	**0.9907**	0.80	0.78
mAP@50:95	**0.8661**	0.70	0.68
F1 Score	**0.9651**	0.85	0.83
Recall	**0.9688**	0.82	0.80

Table 1 reflects that YOLOv8 achieved the best performance among the three models. It showed a very low false positive rate of 3.85% and a high precision of 96.15%, effectively recognizing pest birds with few errors. Its mAP at IoU = 50 reached 99.07%, demonstrating excellent detection capability under loose match conditions, while its mAP at IoU = 50:95 was 86.61%, reflecting robustness under stricter evaluation criteria. Furthermore, its F1 score of 96.51% indicates an outstanding balance between precision and recall, and its recall rate of 96.88% ensures that most pest birds were correctly detected, supporting efficient pest population management. Faster R-CNN also achieved decent results but underperformed compared to YOLOv8. It detected approximately 90% of the birds but produced more false positives. Its mAP at IoU = 50 was 80%, and it dropped to 70% at IoU = 50:95, revealing difficulties with stricter overlap thresholds. The F1 score of 85% and recall rate of 82% suggest a higher risk of missing pest birds, potentially limiting its effectiveness for pest management. Finally, C3Det performed less effectively than both YOLOv8 and Faster R-CNN. It attained an accuracy of 88%, with a

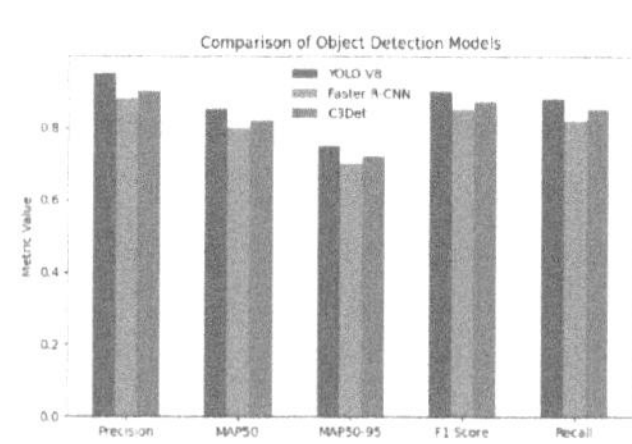

Fig. 3. Comparison on D1

mAP at IoU = 50 of 78% and a lower mAP at IoU = 50:95 of 68%. Its F1 score of 83% and recall rate of 80% indicate an increased risk of missing pest birds and reduced reliability under strict detection conditions, which could compromise its use for pest management. In conclusion, YOLOv8 emerges as the most effective model for detecting pest birds in D1 with high resolution images.

Table 2. Results of the evaluation of the models on D2

Metric	YOLOv8	Faster R-CNN	C3Det
Precision	0.7365	0.5210	**0.9748**
mAP@50	0.7373	0.6572	**0.9840**
mAP@50:95	0.6290	0.7000	**0.8425**
F1 Score	0.7356	0.4758	**0.9553**
Recall	0.7347	0.4974	**0.9370**

The results in Table 2 show that YOLOv8 demonstrated a precision of 73.65% and a recall of 73.47% which indicate a good compromise between correctly identifying small sized pest birds and minimizing missed detections. However, these values are lower than those obtained with C3Det, suggesting that YOLOv8 may be less suited to detecting small objects. Faster R-CNN achieved the least convincing results in D2 with a relatively low precision of 52.10%. In contrast, C3Det performed exceptionally well, achieving a precision of 97.48% and a recall of 93.70%. It demonstrated a remarkable ability to correctly identify small-sized pest birds while minimizing false negatives. Its mAP50 value of 98.40% and mAP50-95 of 84.25% confirm the robustness of the model. C3Det is the most effective model for detecting small-sized pest birds, offering the highest accuracy and strongest overall performance. Conversely, Faster R-CNN and YOLOv8 exhibit limitations when it comes to completely and accurately detecting small pest birds.

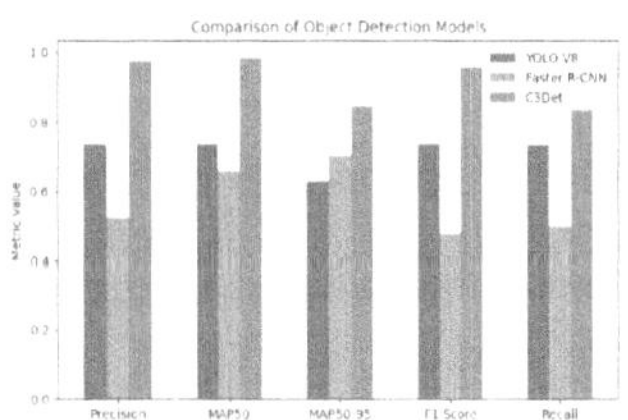

Fig. 4. Comparison on D2

Table 3. Results of the evaluation of the models on D3

Metric	YOLOv8	Faster R-CNN	C3Det
Precision	0.8490	0.7105	**0.9274**
mAP@50	0.8639	0.7286	**0.8810**
mAP@50:95	0.7476	0.70	**0.7603**
F1 Score	0.8504	0.6629	**0.8942**
Recall	0.8517	0.6587	**0.8685**

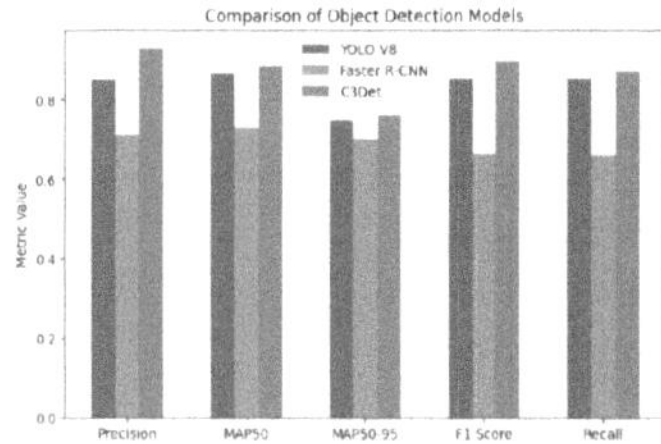

Fig. 5. Comparison on D3

Finally, Table 3 shows that YOLOv8 demonstrates strong overall performance, particularly in terms of accuracy, with a low tendency to generate false positives. Its results on the mAP50 suggest robust detection capabilities, especially for medium to large objects. However, a slight performance degradation observed on the mAP50-95 indicates potential limitations in detecting very small objects. Faster R-CNN shows less convincing performance, especially regarding accuracy, resulting in a higher risk of false positives. Its mAP50 and mAP50-95 scores highlight difficulties in accurately locating objects, particularly smaller ones, and the F1 score reflects a less favorable balance between precision and recall, confirming these limitations. In contrast, C3Det stands out with particularly high precision, effectively minimizing the risk of false positives. Although its mAP50 and mAP50-95 scores are slightly lower than those of YOLOv8, C3Det shows remarkable ability to detect small objects, making it particularly suitable for the detection of pest birds, where targets are often small. Its balanced F1 score and satisfactory recall further confirm the strong overall performance of the model.

4.3 Analysis of the Results

YOLOv8 demonstrated exceptional performance across datasets, excelling in detecting large pest birds with high precision (96.15%) and recall (96.88%) in Dataset 1, while also balanced performance for mixed datasets with a precision of 84.90%. C3Det, on the other hand, proved superior for small object detection, achieving the highest precision (97.48%) and recall (93.70%) on Dataset 2, highlighting its specialization for small pest birds. Faster R-CNN consistently underperformed compared to YOLOv8 and C3Det, making it less suitable for these scenarios. For practical applications, YOLOv8 is best suited for real-time detection tasks involving large or mixed datasets due to its speed and adaptability, while C3Det is ideal for specialized tasks focused on detecting small objects. These results underscore YOLOv8's general versatility, C3Det's effectiveness for smaller objects, and Faster R-CNN's limitations in handling diverse datasets.

4.4 Limitations of the Study

The performance of AI models for detecting pest birds depends very much on the quality and annotation of the training data. Inconsistent or poorly annotated datasets can lead to sub-optimal detection results. This affects the model's ability to generalise to different agricultural contexts. Furthermore, the C3Det model has higher computational requirements, which could limit its use in resource-poor locations, such as rural farms. This makes access to advanced AI tools difficult for small farmers.

Although C3Det is designed to improve the detection of small objects, there are still challenges in identifying small bird species, especially when they are far away or partially hidden by environmental features. To solve these problems, it is very important to collect and annotate consistent and good quality data. This can be achieved through rigorous validation processes and community involvement.

In addition, exploring optimization techniques for the model, such as quantification or pruning, could help to reduce C3Det's resource requirements without losing too much precision. This would make it easier to use on less powerful equipment. For future improvements, we should also think about creating a hybrid model that combines the strengths of YOLO v8 and C3Det. We could take advantage of YOLO's speed for real-time detection while using C3Det's precision to find small objects.

Carrying out field tests in various conditions would provide valuable information for making improvements. At the same time, organising training sessions for farmers could increase user involvement and ensure effective use of these AI tools in their pest management. If we can address these limitations and implement these suggestions, the effectiveness of AI-based pest bird detection systems could really improve, helping farmers to better protect their crops.

5 Conclusion

This study highlights the transformative potential of deep learning models in revolutionizing pest-bird detection in agriculture. YOLO v8 excels in real-time detection of large birds, while C3Det demonstrates superior precision in detecting small objects, addressing a critical limitation in tiny-object detection. By integrating these technologies into agricultural practices, farmers can significantly reduce crop losses and adopt more sustainable pest management strategies. However, challenges remain, particularly in computational efficiency and the detection of partially hidden or distant small birds. Future research should focus on developing hybrid models that combine the strengths of YOLO v8 and C3Det, leveraging YOLO v8's speed for real-time detection and C3Det's precision for small objects. Field testing in diverse agricultural contexts will provide valuable information on the practical applicability of these models, while optimization techniques such as model pruning and quantification could reduce computational costs, making these technologies more accessible to small-scale farmers.

By addressing these limitations and exploring these future directions, deep learning models can further enhance their impact on agricultural pest management, contributing to improved food security and sustainable farming practices.

Acknowledgments. This work is supported by the KNUST hosted RAIL project funded by IDRC within the AI4D Africa Initiative.

References

1. Alexander, J.D., et al.: Using regional bird density distribution models to evaluate protected area networks and inform conservation planning. Ecosphere **8**(5), e01799 (2017)
2. Alldredge, M.W., Simons, T.R., Pollock, K.H.: A field evaluation of distance measurement error in auditory avian point count surveys. J. Wildl. Manag. **71**(8), 2759–2766 (2007)
3. Augustina, P., Nicoleta, V., Dan, C., Mihaela, N., Iuliana, G.: Review of effectiveness of visual and auditory bird scaring techniques in agriculture. In: Proceedings of the 22nd International Scientific Conference on Engineering for Rural Development, 24–26 May 2023, Jelgava, Latvia, pp. 275–281 (2023)
4. Bhusal, S., Bhattarai, U., Karkee, M.: Improving pest bird detection in a vineyard environment using super-resolution and deep learning. IFAC-PapersOnLine **52**(30), 18–23 (2019)
5. Bibby, C.J.: Bird Census Techniques. Elsevier (2000)
6. Bishop, J., McKay, H., Parrott, D., Allan, J.: Review of international research literature regarding the effectiveness of auditory bird scaring techniques and potential alternatives, pp. 1–53. Food and Rural Affairs, London (2003)
7. Boesch, G.: The fundamental guide to faster R-CNN (2025). https://viso.ai/deep-learning/faster-r-cnn-2/
8. Broom, M., Rychtář, J.: Game-Theoretical Models in Biology. CRC Press (2013)
9. Clarke, T.L.: An autonomous bird deterrent system (2004)
10. De Mey, Y., Demont, M., Diagne, M.: Estimating bird damage to rice in Africa: evidence from the Senegal river valley. J. Agric. Econ. **63**(1), 175–200 (2012)
11. Diakhaby, I., Ba, M.L., Gueye, A.D.: Pest birds detection approach in rice crops using pre-trained yolov4 model. In: Mambo, A.D., Gueye, A., Bassioni, G. (eds.) Innovations and Interdisciplinary Solutions for Underserved Areas. LNCS, vol. 449, pp. 223–234. Springer, Cham (2022). https://doi.org/10.1007/978-3-031-23116-2_19
12. Digby, A., Towsey, M., Bell, B.D., Teal, P.D.: A practical comparison of manual and autonomous methods for acoustic monitoring. Meth. Ecol. Evol. **4**(7), 675–683 (2013)
13. Ehnes, M., Dech, J., Foote, J.: Seasonal changes in acoustic detection of forest birds. J. Ecoacoustics **2**(1), 7 (2018)
14. CloudFactory Limited: Faster R-CNN (2023). https://wiki.cloudfactory.com/docs/mp-wiki/model-architectures/faster-r-cnn
15. Flint, M.L., van den Bosch, R.: Introduction to Integrated Pest Management. Springer, Boston (1981). https://doi.org/10.1007/978-1-4615-9212-9
16. Fuller, R., Glue, D.: Seasonal activity of birds at a sewage-works. British Birds J. **71**(6), 235–244 (1978)

17. Geek: Faster R-CNN | ML (2023). https://www.geeksforgeeks.org/faster-r-cnn-ml/
18. Gwinner, E.: Circannual rhythms in birds: their interaction with circadian rhythms and environmental photoperiod. J. Reprod. Fertil. (Suppl.) **19**, 51–65 (1973)
19. Harris, J.B.C., Haskell, D.G.: Simulated birdwatchers' playback affects the behavior of two tropical birds. PLoS ONE **8**(10), e77902 (2013)
20. He, K., Zhang, X., Ren, S., Sun, J.: Spatial pyramid pooling in deep convolutional networks for visual recognition. IEEE Trans. Pattern Anal. Mach. Intell. **37**(9), 1904–1916 (2015)
21. Jocher, G., Chaurasia, A., Qiu, J.: YOLO by Ultralytics (2023). https://github.com/ultralytics/ultralytics
22. Khazri, A.: Faster R-CNN object detection (2019). https://towardsdatascience.com/faster-rcnn-object-detection-f865e5ed7fc4
23. Lee, C., et al.: Interactive multi-class tiny-object detection (2022). https://arxiv.org/abs/2203.15266
24. Liao, Z., Tian, M.: A bird species detection method based on YOLO-v5. In: 2021 International Conference on Neural Networks, Information and Communication Engineering, vol. 11933, pp. 65–75. SPIE (2021)
25. Martinez, H.: Faster R-CNNs (2023). https://pyimagesearch.com/2023/11/13/faster-r-cnns/
26. Maynard Smith, J.: Evolution and the Theory of Games. Cambridge University Press (1982)
27. Micaelo, E.B., Lourenço, L.G., Gaspar, P.D., Caldeira, J.M., Soares, V.N.: Bird deterrent solutions for crop protection: approaches, challenges, and opportunities. Agriculture **13**(4), 774 (2023)
28. Montràs-Janer, T., Knape, J., Nilsson, L., Tombre, I., Pärt, T., Månsson, J.: Relating national levels of crop damage to the abundance of large grazing birds: implications for management. J. Appl. Ecol. **56**(10), 2286–2297 (2019)
29. Naggiar, M.: Man vs. birds. Florida Wild **27**(12), 2–5 (1974)
30. Nanni, L., Maguolo, G., Pancino, F.: Insect pest image detection and recognition based on bio-inspired methods. Ecol. Inform. **57**, 101089 (2020)
31. Orchi, H., Sadik, M., Khaldoun, M., Sabir, E.: Real-time detection of crop leaf diseases using enhanced YOLOv8 algorithm. In: 2023 International Wireless Communications and Mobile Computing (IWCMC), pp. 1690–1696 (2023)
32. Pruteanu, A., Vanghele, N., Cujbescu, D., Nitu, M., Gageanu, I.: Review of effectiveness of visual and auditory bird scaring techniques in agriculture, pp. 24–26 (2023)
33. Ralph, C.J., Sauer, J.R., Droege, S.: Monitoring bird populations by point counts. Pacific Southwest Research Station (1995)
34. Redmon, J.: You only look once: unified, real-time object detection. In: Proceedings of the IEEE Conference on Computer Vision and Pattern Recognition (2016)
35. Reif, J.: Unusual abundance-range size relationship in an Afromontane bird community: the effect of geographical isolation? J. Biogeogr. **33**(11), 1959–1968 (2006)
36. Ren, S.: Faster R-CNN: towards real-time object detection with region proposal networks. arXiv preprint arXiv:1506.01497 (2015)
37. Ren, S., He, K., Girshick, R., Sun, J.: Faster R-CNN: towards real-time object detection with region proposal networks. IEEE Trans. Pattern Anal. Mach. Intell. **39**(6), 1137–1149 (2016)
38. Shonfield, J., Bayne, E.M.: Autonomous recording units in avian ecological research: current use and future applications. Avian Conserv. Ecol. **12**(1) (2017)

39. Siegel, R.B., Desante, D.F., Nott, M.P.: Using point counts to establish conservation priorities: how many visits are optimal? J. Field Ornithol. **72**(2), 228–235 (2001)
40. Stern, V.M., Smith, R.F., van den Bosch, R., Hagen, K.S.: The integrated control concept. Hilgardia (1959)
41. Tomiałojć, L.: Accuracy of the mapping technique for a dense breeding population of the Hawfinch Coccothraustes coccothraustes in a deciduous forest. Acta Ornithologica **39**(1), 67–74 (2004)

Feature Encoding for Automatic Multi-criteria Determination from Clinical Records

Bamfa Ceesay(✉), Mbemba Hydara, and Aminu Adamu

Department of Computer Science, University of The Gambia, MDI Rd, Kanifing, PO Box 3530, Serrekunda, Gambia
{bamfa,hmbemba,aadamu}@utg.edu.gm

Abstract. Finding patients who meet certain medical criteria in a clinical trial for qualification is an important aspect of reliable medical research. However, this can be challenging because of complexity of medical research and the difficulty of translating medical criteria into a database query. An efficient alternative approach would be to examine the clinical narratives in the patient's medical history. In this study, we proposed an automated multi-criteria classification model for identification of clinical criteria met by candidate patients for a clinical trial. The model leverages Convolutional Neural Network (CNN) and sentiment embedding features in solving the problem of identification criteria met by a patient's medical narrative. We adopted an encoding approach for extraction of features. Our results show significant improvement in the use of deep-learning and feature embedding for training. The original result submitted to Track 1 of n2c2 used one-level encoding features with a micro F1 score of 0.7526. In the two-two-levels encoding model, the distance between input and encoding features has reduced. This significantly improved the classification rating of our model with a micro F1 score of 0.8718. The outcome of the study have shown that Automating identification of patients for clinical trials using natural language processing and machine learning techniques saves the time required to recruit patients as well as the benefit of moving unwanted bias.

Keywords: Feature Encoding · Auto-encoders · Multi-criteria · Clinical Records · Deep Learning · Neural Network

1 Introduction

Finding patients who are qualified for certain criteria to be selected for placement in clinical trials is not only an important part of medical research but also represents the biggest hurdle for finding patients for clinical trials. Biomedical text is complicated, and medical criteria are hard to translate into a standard database query. These difficulties arise because database queries cannot be used to retrieve information. In addition, a thorough examination of the patient's medical narrative or history is a requirement. This process is time consuming and prone to bias. Instead, it requires examining the clinical narratives in the patients' records, which results in two fundamental problems:

D. Bassole et al. (Eds.): InterSol 2025, LNICST 671, pp. 107–120, 2026.
https://doi.org/10.1007/978-3-032-15154-4_9

1. Medical researchers need lot of time to recruit patients and such selection of patients is limited to patients who are willing to participate themselves or are selected by their doctors.
2. Recruiting from a specified place or group of patients can lead to a selection bias and consequently a biased research result.

The development of a natural language processing (NLP) system has capability to automatically assess whether a patient's narrative fits a given criterion with its significant benefits. However, such a system would equally need to deal with the complex nature of biomedical text to efficiently perform this task with a meaningful result. One approach could be the use of a corpus with linguistic annotations for learning purposes. Track 1 of the National NLP Clinical Challenges (n2c2) 2018 [1] entitled Cohort selection for clinical trials, challenged participants to develop a method of identifying if a patient meets, does not meet, or possibly meets a collection of eligibility criteria based on their history of medical records. In recent studies, traditional NLP approaches consider words as the basic unit for assigning labels or classes. These words are further processed to extract a rich set of features to that can be fed into standard classification algorithms such as a support vector machine (SVM) [2]. Krizheysky et al. [3] used a deep convolutional neural network 60 million parameters and 500,000 neurons, to classify the 1.3 million high-resolution images in the LSVRC-2010 ImageNet training set into 1,000 different classes. For the test data, they achieved top-1 and top-5 error rates of 39.7% and 18.9%, respectively. That neural network comprises five convolutional layers, some of which are followed by max-pooling layers, and two fully connected layers with a final 1000-way softmax. With respect to sequential data, recurrent neural networks (RNNs) have been highly successful. With these networks, it is possible to include end-to-end training methods such as connectionist temporal classification for sequential labeling proposed by Graves et al. [4] for speech recognition. They investigated deep RNNs, combining many layers that proved effective with long ranging context to empower the RNN model. When subjected to end-to-end training with suitable regularization, a test-set error of 17.7% on the TIMIT phoneme recognition benchmark is obtained with deep long short-term memory RNNs [5].

NLP techniques such as ruled based framework to analyze and predicted acceptable results in several NLP problems [6]. It provides a mechanism for querying non-structured data using non-structured query language. Long et al. [7] proposes an integrated rule-based clinical NLP system which employs a generic rule-based framework plugged in with lexical-, syntactic- and meta-level, task-specific knowledge inputs. In addition, the authors also implemented and evaluated a general clinical NLP (cNLP) system which is built with the Unified Medical Language System and Unstructured Information Management Architecture.

Another significant technique used in NLP is the deep learning architectures. This technique requires domain knowledge to efficiently learn parameters. Isabel et al. [8] present a comparative study of various popular deep learning architectures applied to the challenging task of cohort selection, posed as a multilabel text classification problem. These techniques emphasis the adoption of learning criteria to produce acceptable results. Several machine learning techniques learned from features to perform specific task efficiently. There is need to develop models that best extract for learning algorithms.

In this study the key objective is to apply natural language processing and machine learning techniques to extract feature and implement an automatic multi-criteria classification model for identification of clinical criteria met by candidate patients for a clinical trial. Several studies that are based on deep-learning methods involve learning word vector representations using neural language models. The work of LeCun et al. [9, p. 6] applied gradient-based learning to document recognition by reviewing various methods for handwritten character recognition and comparing their performance in a standard handwritten-digit–recognition task. The result shows that Convolutional Neural Networks (CNNs), which are specifically designed to deal with the variability in two–dimensional shapes, perform better than all other techniques and can eliminate the need for finding features manually. Yeh et al. [7] ventured a new projection learning framework that finds the optimal matrix for minimizing the loss of the preselected similarity function (e.g., cosine) of the projected vectors. The authors were able to efficiently handle a great volume of training examples in a high dimensional space. The proposed system discriminatively learns conceptual vector representations of input text objects, adopting the general Siamese neural network architecture [8] and using an algorithm to verify signatures written on a pen –input tablet.

A recent study [10] demonstrate techniques that can be used for learning high-quality word vectors from datasets containing billions of words and can efficiently estimate word representations in a vector space. This method is called the skip-gram model [11] and is efficient for learning high-quality vector representations of words from large amounts of textual data. CNN models have yielded state-of-the-art results in NLP especially for question and answering (QA) tasks, Yih et al. [12] developed a semantic parsing framework based on the semantic similarity between open-domain QA tasks [13]. They used single-relation questions and decomposed each question into an entity mention and a relation pattern. Using CNN models, they assessed the similarity of entity mentions to entities in the knowledge base (KB) and the similarity of relation patterns to relations in the KB. In NLP, many works using deep learning are centered around vector models [10, 14, 15]. Word2vec [16] has seen wide usage in NLP and achieved state-of-the-art results in many NLP tasks. Patients with serious diseases may wish to participate in trials of unapproved drugs. Online patient communities may provide a potential environment to monitor drug usage and their consequences. Paul et al. [17] analyze data on the website Patients Like Me [18], by patients with amyotrophic lateral sclerosis (ALS) receiving lithium carbonate treatment. To reduce potential bias from selection of patients, an approach to match 149 treated patients with multiple controls (447 total) based on the progression of their disease was proposed. After one-year treatment, no lithium effect was found on disease progression. Brennan et al. [19] compared the patients with lower back pain and received treatments matched or unmatched in their subgroups based on initial clinical presentation. Patients that had certain physical condition for a period and were referred to physical therapy were classified into three subgroups. Patients were randomly selected for three treatment groups to receive treatment for a period. Comparisons were drawn from patients receiving treatment that matched their assigned subgroup and those that did not match the treatment to their subgroup. After the short-term assessment, the difference between the matched and unmatched groups was 6.6 points in favor of the matched group (95% CI, 0.70–12.5), and for the long-term follow-up, the difference was 8.3 points (95% CI, 2.5–14.1). In this study, we propose a multi-criterion labeling system using a CNN model trained on sentence vectors. The study uses a slight variation on the skip-thought model proposed by Kiros et al. [20]. The variation uses convolution and feature mapping for encoding-decoding feature parameters from sentence vector. The sentence vector representation used in this approach is the encoder result from the skip-thought model. The model architecture used in this study is presented in Fig. 1. Our study provides an incentive for studies into automatic feature extraction using machine learning. The contribution of this work will help to limit the requirement, bias and influence of human curators in annotating features for machine learning algorithms. The rest of the paper is organized as follows: Sect. 2 design and methods, Sect. 3, experimental result and Sect. 4, conclusion.

2 Design and Methods

We illustrate in this section Fig. 1, CNN architecture for sentence classification. We depict two filter regions of size 6. Using the sentence matrix and the filter, feature maps were generated. We then apply A1-max pooling to each map (i.e., selecting the largest number from each feature map). The results are then concatenated to generate a feature vector [21], of size 1×6, for weight optimization. Finally, we used Softmax to classify feature vectors for sentence criteria prediction. We used binary classification with two possible output states (met criteria and unmet criteria). The sentence used as example "He has a history of diabetes and sleep apnea," which contains nine words. We chose 6 to be the dimension of the word vectors. Hence, we now get a sentence matrix of the shape 9×6. To obtain the feature map, we apply a ReLU [22] activation function and add a bias term (a scalar, i.e., shape 1×1).

One of the advantages of CNN as applied in other research field is the preservation of 2D spatial orientation [23]. Texts, like pictures, also have an orientation. In contrast, texts only have one dimensional structure. Word sequence is important in the structure of texts. By extension, each word in [20] is represented by a six-dimensional word vector; and a filter of one dimension is used to match the word vectors [23]. In this study, we adapt this method to perform automatic feature extraction and classification of patients' records, and made the following contributions to the field:

- Use of sentence-level feature extraction to effectively train the machine learning system, which allows us to take advantage of word order and sentence semantics; and
- Understanding of the importance of encoding-level feature extraction for training the models.

In **Error! Reference source not found.**, feature vectors are generated using two-levels encoding. As an illustration filter operation, consider the first word "He" from Fig. 1 with a vector $V = [v_1, v_2, \ldots, v_6]$ and using a filter h where

$$h = \begin{bmatrix} a_{11} & \cdots & a_{16} \\ \vdots & \ddots & \vdots \\ a_{61} & \cdots & a_{66} \end{bmatrix} \tag{1}$$

will yield a value of $\sum_{i=1}^{6} \sum_{j=1}^{6} v_i a_{ij}$ on the feature map.

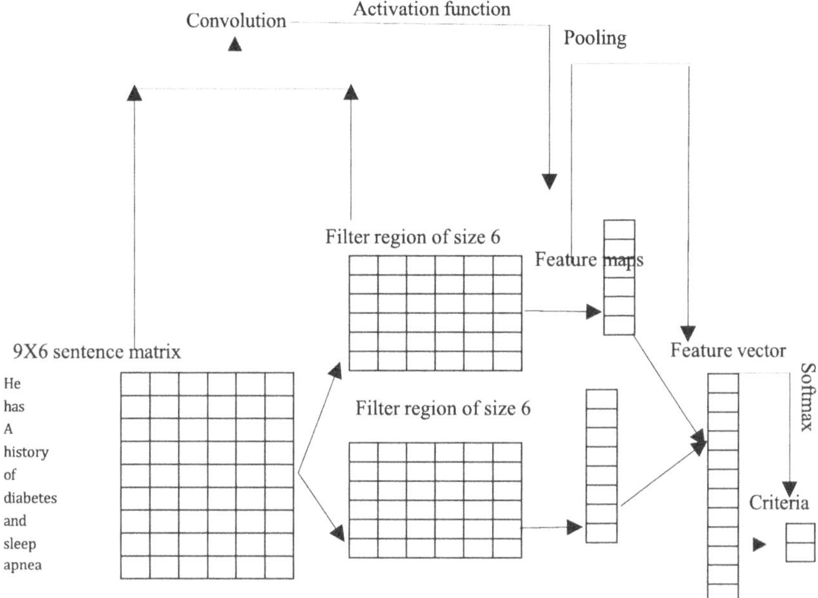

Fig. 1. Model architecture, with channels for an input document with n sentences.

2.1 Experimental Data and Problem Definition

The dataset obtained for this task contained records of 296 patients, with 2–5 records per patient. There were 202 training files and 86 files for testing. From the training data, 152 files were used for preliminary training and 50 were used as development data for fine tuning the training data. The training data were annotated at document level to indicate whether a patient met a set of 13 selection criteria. A limited number of gold standard span annotations were also given. For evaluation, participating results were evaluated against predicted category for each patient in test data. Table 1 shows the set of selection criteria used. The test data consisted of unannotated documents for the annotating system to assess and determine whether the conditions were met for each criterion. If they were, the annotators were supposed to annotate the part (or parts) of the text that provided evidence for their assertion. As an illustration, consider this excerpt from a patient's record:

> *"Past medical history is notable for no previous ankle injuries. He has a history of diabetes and sleep apnea. He takes Prozac, Cardizem, Glucophage, and Amaryl. He is also followed by Dr. X for an arrhythmia. He does not smoke. He drinks minimally. He is a set designer at Columbia Pictures."*

The annotation system would be expected to annotate "He does not smoke" as evidence that the criterion DRUG-ABUSE was not met, and "He drinks minimally" as evidence that the criterion ALCOHOL-ABUSE was not met. If it seemed that one record in a patient's history confirmed a criterion but another refuted it, this evidence should have been annotated and marked with the "possible" attribute. However, this is only useful if the evidence is truly unclear. The only tag that required multiple annotations was ADVANCED-CAD. For a patient to meet that criterion, they had to have any two of the listed symptoms/diseases. Both pieces of evidence had to be marked. For other tags, if there was more than one piece of evidence for a criterion being met, those pieces could be annotated, but it was not required. If there was no evidence of a criterion in the document at all, a "non-consuming tag" was created, which indicated whether the criterion was met or not. In most cases, no mention of a criterion would indicate that it was not met (e.g., if the person's "HBA1C" was never measured, we could not say whether they met that criterion). However, in some cases the system assumed the opposite; for instance, if it was not mentioned whether a person could speak English or make their own medical decisions, this was probably because they could, so we could make annotations that those criteria were met.

Table 1. List of Criteria

Tag	Criteria
DRUG-ABUSE	Drug abuse, current or past
ALCOHOL-ABUSE	Current alcohol use above weekly recommended limits
ENGLISH	Patient must speak English
MAKES-DECISIONS	Patient must make their own medical decisions
ABDOMINAL	History of intra-abdominal surgery, small or large intestine resection, or small bowel obstruction
MAJOR-DIABETES	Major diabetes-related complications. For annotation purposes "*major complication*" (as opposed to "*minor complication*") is defined as any of the following that are a result of (or strongly correlated with) uncontrolled diabetes: • Amputation • Kidney damage • Skin conditions • Retinopathy • Nephropathy • Neuropathy
ADVANCED-CAD	Advanced cardiovascular disease. For annotation purposes "*advanced*" is defined as including two or more of the following: • Taking two or more medications to treat CAD • History of myocardial infarction • Currently experiencing angina • Ischemia, past or present
MI-6MOS	Myocardial infarction in the past six months
KETO-1YR	Diagnosis of ketoacidosis in the past year
DIETSUPP-2MOS	Taken a dietary supplement (excluding Vitamin D) in the past two months
ASP-FOR-MI	Use of aspirin to prevent myocardial infarction
HBA1C	Any HbA1c value between 6.5% and 9.5%
CREATININE	Serum creatinine above upper limit of normal

This document can be represented as a set of sentence vectors. Each sentence is represented by a vector derived from the skip-thought encoder [18]. The document can thus be represented as:

$$D = \{s_1\ , s_2, s_3, s_4, s_5, s_6, s_7\}. \tag{2}$$

Let s_i^l ....s_i^N be the sentences in document Di where N is the number of sentences in the document. At each time step, the encoder produces a hidden state h_i^t, which can be interpreted as a representation of the sequence s_i^1 ....s_i^t. The hidden state h_i^N consequently describes the full document. Our sentence-encoding model is an adaptation of the skip-thought model [20] in which sentences are encoded with gated recurrent units (GRUs), with the objective of using the current sentence representation to predict the immediately preceding and following sentences. Given $h^t{}_{i+1}$, the probability of sentence $s^t{}_{i+1}$, given the previous $t - 1$ sentences and the encoder vector, is

$$P\left(s_{i+1}^t | s_{i+1}^{<t} h_i\right). \tag{3}$$

This is directly proportional to the distribution $e^{(v_{s_{i+1}^t} + h_{i+1})}$ where $v_{s_{i+1}^t}$ denotes vector V corresponding to the sentence s_{i+1}^t. Given a tuple $(s_{i-1,} s_i, s_{i+1})$, the optimized objective is the total of the log-probabilities for the forward and backward sentences conditioned on the encoder and it is represented as

$$\sum\nolimits_t \log P(s_{i+1}^t | s_{i+1}^{<t} h_i) + \sum\nolimits_t \log P(s_{i-1}^t | s_{i-1}^{<t} h_i) \tag{4}$$

The whole objective is the above summation over all training tuples for a given document. These encoded parameters are used as a sentence vector representation of the document for training purposes. A convolution operation involves a filter $F \in R^{NK}$, which is applied to a window of N sentences to generate a new feature. For example, a feature c_i is produced from a window of sentences $s_{i:i+N-1}$

$$c_i = f(F.s_{i:i+N-1} + b). \tag{5}$$

Here $b \in R$ is a bias term and f is a non-linear function such as a hyperbolic tangent. In this way, the filter is applied to each possible window of words in the sentence, and then generates a feature map.

$$c = \left[c_1, c_2, c_3, \ldots\ldots\ldots, c_{N-1}\right]. \tag{6}$$

The results from this approach had a micro F1 of 0.7526. Further investigation revealed that improving the features could help to improve the learning and yield better results. To improve feature learning, we can set an objective of minimizing the loss from decoding and encoding this result to get the sentence vectors. The solution utilizes two levels of two-levels in the encoding to extract sentence representation. Given any sentence, it is difficult even for a human to predict the sentences, word for word, that might occur before or after it. Take, for example, the sentence "He drinks minimally." The possibilities that could precede and succeed this sentence are enormous. In addition, sentences similar in meaning are not treated as the same sentence; the skip-thought decoder is tasked with predicting the exact sentence word for word. To minimize the loss function, we consider the sentence neighborhood to not only include the preceding and succeeding sentences but also the sentence itself. The objective to be optimized in the encoding from Eq. (5) is now

$$\sum_t \log P(s_{i+1}^t | s_{i+1}^{<t} h_i) + \sum_t \log P(s_{i-1}^t | s_{i-1}^{<t} h_i) + \sum_t \log P\left(s_i^t | s_i^{<t} h_i\right). \quad (7)$$

Figure 2 represents the two-two-levels encoding used to generate sentence vectors.

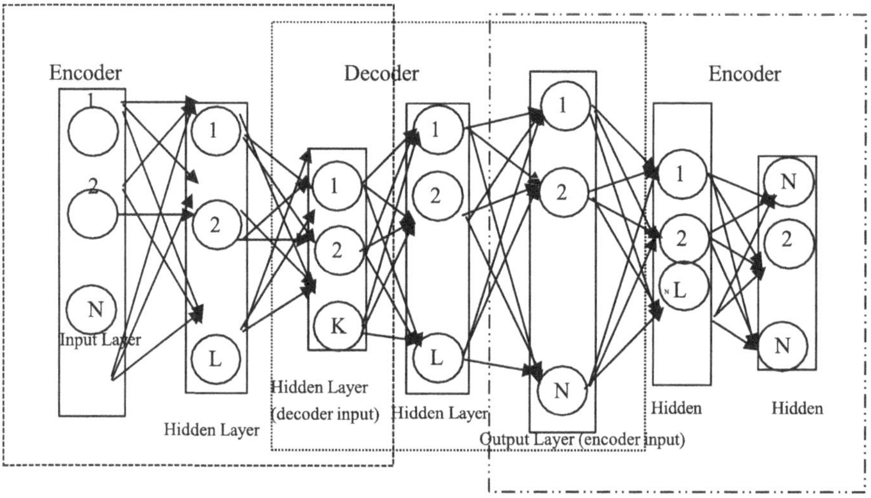

Fig. 2. Two-two-levels encoding for the embedding of sentence vectors.

Figure 2 presents the skip-thought model. Given a tuple $(s_i - 1, s_i, s_i + 1)$ of contiguous sentences, with s_i representing the ith sentence, sentence s_i is encoded and the system tries to reproduce the previous sentence, s_{1-1} and next sentence, s_{i+1}. Given the same tuple $(s_{i-1,} s_i, s_{i+1})$, the optimized objective is the total of the log-probabilities for the forward and backward sentences conditioned on the encoder representation. In Fig. 2, the general objective is to extract feature vectors for the model presented in Fig. 1. Using an input sentence s, with the encoder, a representation can be defined as h = f(s) where f is the encoder function. In our hyper-parameter, we adapted a masking of the input for optimization. For masking the function f, we used a sigmoid function $Sig(s) = \frac{1}{1+e^{-s}}$. Hence the encoder is represented as $h = Sig(Ws + b)$, where W is the input weight, b is the bias, and $f(s) = Ws + b$. With the decoder, a presentation is defined as $d = g(h)$, where g is the decoder function. To subsequently reconstruct input features of s at decoder levels, we use $d = Sig(W^T h + b)$ for $g(h) = W^T h + b$. Masking or corrupting the input resulted in significant reductions in the error relative to the basic feature extractor we used for our submission to n2c2. This loss can be computed using the expressions in Eq. (8). As shown in Table 2, the loss with two-levels encoding is lower than that with basic encoding. This implies that the two-levels encoding approach produces feature properties closer to the input.

Table 2. Training losses.

Time (seconds)	Loss	
	Basic encoding	Two-level encoding
10	0.170	0.124
20	0.130	0.110
30	0.115	0.108
40	0.110	0.101
50	0.100	0.082

2.2 Encoder and Decoder Model

Whenever we want to represent or understand a sentence, we pay attention to the words. With a machine, similar behavior can be adopted using neural network. Neural networks can mimic this behavior by giving attention to a subset of the information they are given. One neural network can accept output of another neural network and paying focus on different detail in the other neural network. The Recurrent Neural Network (RNN) can be used to focus on specific information in the output of another neural network. In this study, we use RNN-RNN architecture to create an attention interface. In this architecture, the second RNN will focus on specific parts of the information generated by the first RNN to refine it and improve the quality of the knowledge.

Figure 3 below represents neural model used in encoder and decoder models. In this model, two LSTM models (A and B) are used. Model A serves as an attending RNN and generates a query representing what it wants to focus on. The input to the softmax is a dot product score describing how best the focus item from A best matches the context in B. The softmax creates attention distribution from these scores. In this figure, two symbols are shown, the X and cross symbol s. The X is an element-by-element multiplication operation. This operation serves as a gate to control how much information will be allowed to pass. The cross symbol is an element-by-element addition to yield an attention distribution.

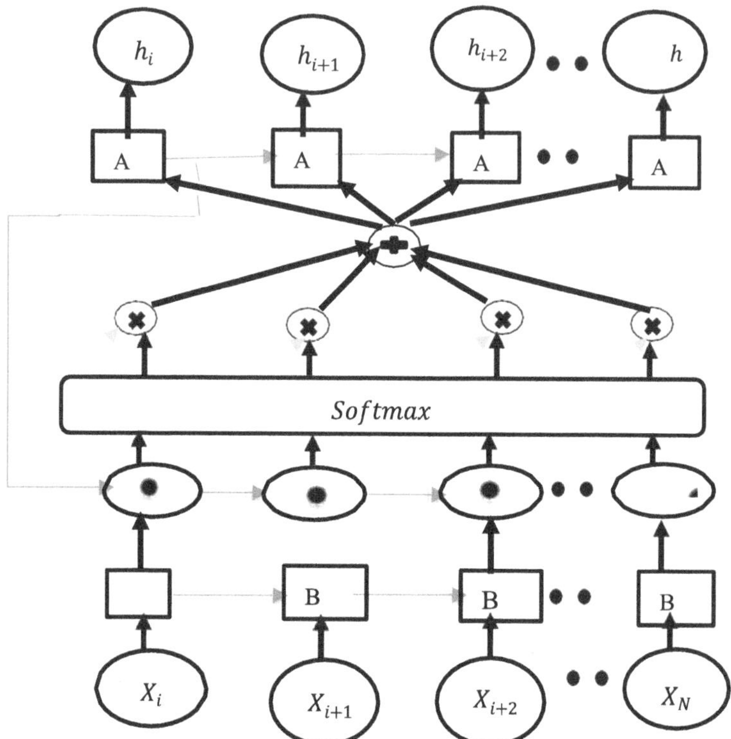

Fig. 3. The attending RNN. First outputs are fed into a softmax to create the attention

Figure 4 represents components of an LSTM model. The key important component in this figure is shown below (Table 3).

Table 3. LSTM module's key components.

Component	Representation	Expression
f_t	Forget gate	$f_t = \sigma(W_f.[h_{t-1}, x_t] + b_f)$
$i_t + \widehat{C}_t$	Update gate	$i_t = \sigma(W_f.[h_{t-1}, x_t] + b_f), \widehat{C}_t = tanh(W_C.[h_{t-1}, x_t] + b_C)$
C_t	Output gate	$C_t = f_t * C_{t-1} + i_t * \widehat{C}_t$

3 Experimental Result

The evaluation results are based on the standard Precision/Recall/F-score metrics:

Precision. This is the percentage of correctly labeled records found by the learning system. That is, precision is the ratio of the number of records correctly labeled (true positives) to the total number of record labels that were found by the system (true positives (TP) + false positives (FP)).

$$p = \frac{TP}{TP + FP}. \tag{8}$$

Recall. This is the percentage of record labels present in the corpus that are found by the system. In other words, recall is the ratio of the number of records correctly labeled (true positives (TP)) to the total number of gold standard annotation records (true positives (TP) + false negatives (FN)).

$$R = \frac{TP}{TP + FN}. \tag{9}$$

F-score. This is the harmonic means of precision and recall.

$$F = \frac{2 * R * P}{P + R}. \tag{10}$$

System results are evaluated for individual criteria using the precision, recall, and F-score metrics, and micro and macro precision, recall, and F-scores are determined to evaluate the general performance of the system in the task. Micro F1 is the primary evaluation metric. Table 4 shows the metrics of the aggregate micro F1 score for the participating systems in n2c2 Track 1. Our original system, which had one level of encoding, had a micro F1 of 0.7526, which was lower than the average score.

Table 4. Aggregate metrics—Micro F1 for all systems participating in Track 1.

	Micro F1
Minimum	0.2117
Maximum	0.91
Average	0.799
Standard deviation	0.116
Median	0.8227

Using two-two-levels encoding can enable the system to predict values not only for s_{i-1} and s_{i+1}, but also for s_i. This implies that, by inferring si as a neighborhood of itself, we are also considering a neighborhood set of $\{s_{i-1}, s_i, s_{i+1}\}$. . This has enabled us to achieve an improvement in the micro F1 score (0.8718), as shown in Table 5. Out of the top ten systems shown in Table 5, four (numbers 1, 4, 7, and 9) utilized rule-based approaches and the other six were based on hybrid methods; in other words, none were exclusively based on machine learning methods [24]. Rule-based methods have been shown to yield high-quality results in this task. In contrast to these systems, our method uses a machine learning approach with sentence embedding and deep learning techniques. The advantages of machine learning approaches include automatically discovering formerly unknown knowledge and identifying implicit relationships in datasets.

This facilitates the objective quantification of uncertain knowledge, and this approach is suitable for the handling of both large and small datasets. Thus, with machine learning techniques a competitive result can be obtained with no requirement to manually generate rules for training the system. A rule-based system is used for the two components: (1) a set of facts about a situation, and (2) a set of rules for how to make inference with these facts. The most important benefit of rule-based methods is that it is easy to trace for identifying situations of interest. However, significant effort is necessary to account for any special cases. Therefore, rule-based systems are deterministic in nature.

Table 5. Top 10 teams (best run only) in n2c2 Track 1, and our system's results.

Rank	Team	Micro F1
1	MedUniGraz	0.91
2	University of Michigan	0.9075
3	Sorbonne Université	0.9069
4	Med Data Quest	0.9028
5	Cincinnati Children's Hospital Medical Center	0.9026
6	Arizona State University	0.9003
7	University of New South Wales / National Cancer Institute	0.8913
8	Harbin Institute of Technology	0.8855
9	University of Utah	0.8837
10	NTTMUNSW	0.8765
	Our system, one-level encoding	**0.7526**
	Our system, two level encoding	**0.9434**

4 Conclusion

In this study we employ NLP techniques to learn the extraction of lexical features for training machine learning models. Embedding features in solving the problem of identification criteria met by a patient's medical narrative. We adopted an encoding approach for extraction of features. Feature elements are an essential part of training machine learning systems. A system's performance depends strongly on the features that can be extracted for learning. Sentence embedding thus helps to enhance features such as the order of words or sentences. In this study, we were able to demonstrate the importance of using encoding features for learning. Our original system, which was submitted to Track 1 of n2c2, used one-level encoding features and had a micro F1 score of 0.7526. With two-two-levels encoding, the distance between the input and encoding features has been minimized. This significantly improved the classification performance of our system, which then scored a micro F1 of 0.8718 rating. Since sentences are made up of words, it is reasonable to argue that simply considering the constituent word vectors should result in a reasonable sentence representation. This concept suffers from some significant limitations; for example, it ignores the order of words and sentence semantics completely. A system of rules can be relatively simple initially, but it can become complicated as changes are made to rules. While a simple rule can be easily understood by non-experts, the complex interactions of a set of rules may be more difficult to follow [25]. Another challenge faced by rule-based systems is that the data and associated information that may change faster than the rules can be updated. A point may be reached at which it is difficult to keep track of changes in scenarios and update of the rules. The system will become useless when rules are changed beyond the reality of input data. This can increase the false positives and false negatives [25]. This study have shown that rules can be replaced with engineering features for machine learning adaptation. Future research work will consider the used of feature extraction in multi-level classification of gene and gene regulatory network.

References

1. D. o. B. I. Harvard Medical School: National NLP Clinical Challenges (n2c2). 2018 n2c2 Shared-Task and Workshop, Track 1: Cohort selection for clinical trials, 2018. [Online]. https://n2c2.dbmi.hms.harvard.edu/track1.php
2. Collobert, R., Weston, J., Bottou, L., Karlen, M., Kavukcuoglu, K., Kuksa, P.: Natural language processing (almost) from scratch. J. Mach. Learn. Res. **12**, 2493–2537 (2011)
3. Krizhevsky, A., Sutskever, I., Hinton, G.E.: ImageNet classification with deep convolutional neural networks. In: Advances in Neural Information Processing Systems, pp. 1097–1105 (2012)
4. Graves, A., Mohamed, A., Hinton, G.: Speech recognition with deep recurrent neural networks. In: 2013 IEEE International Conference on Acoustics, Speech and Signal Processing (ICASSP), pp. 6645–6649. IEEE (2013)
5. Garofolo, J.S., et al.: TIMIT acoustic-phonetic continuous speech corpus, LDC93S1. Web Download. Philadelphia: Linguistic Data Consortium, 199 (1992). https://catalog.ldc.upenn.edu/LDC93S1. Accessed 2018
6. Mahmud, T., Hasan, K.M.A., Ahmed, M., Chak, T.H.C.: A rule based approach for NLP based query processing. In: 2015 2nd International Conference on Electrical Information and Communication Technologies (EICT), pp. 78–82. IEEE (2015)
7. Chen, L., et al.: Clinical trial cohort selection based on multi-level rule-based natural language processing system. J. Am. Med. Inform. Assoc. **26**, 1218–1226 (2019)
8. Segura-Bedmar, I., Raez, P.: Cohort selection for clinical trials using deep learning models. J. Am. Med. Inform. Assoc. **26**, 1181–1188 (2019)
9. LeCun, Y., Bottou, L., Bengio, Y., Haffner, P.: Gradient-based learning applied to document recognition. Proc. IEEE **86**, 2278–2324 (1998)
10. Mikolov, T., Chen, K., Corrado, G., Dean, J.: Efficient estimation of word representations in vector space. arXiv preprint arXiv:1301.3781 (2013)
11. Mikolov, T., Sutskever, I., Chen, K., Corrado, G.S., Dean, J.: Distributed representations of words and phrases and their compositionality. In: Advances in Neural Information Processing Systems, pp. 3111–3119 (2013)
12. Yih, W., He, X., Meek, C.: Semantic parsing for single-relation question answering. In: Proceedings of the 52nd Annual Meeting of the Association for Computational Linguistics (Volume 2: Short Papers), vol. 2, pp. 643–648 (2014)

13. Prager, J., et al.: Open-domain question–answering. In: Foundations and Trends in Information Retrieval, vol. 1, pp. 91–231
14. Yih, W., Toutanova, K., Platt, J.C., Meek, C.: Learning discriminative projections for text similarity measures. In: Proceedings of the Fifteenth Conference on Computational Natural Language Learning, pp. 247–256. Association for Computational Linguistics (2011)
15. Bengio, Y., Ducharme, R., Vincent, P., Jauvin, C.: A neural probabilistic language model. J. Mach. Learn. Res. **2**, 1137–1155 (2003)
16. Goldberg, Y., Levy, O.: word2vec explained: deriving Mikolov et al.'s negative-sampling word-embedding method. arXiv preprint arXiv:1402.3722 (2014)
17. Wicks, P., Vaughan, T.E., Massagli, M.P., Heywood, J.: Accelerated clinical discovery using self-reported patient data collected online and a patient-matching algorithm. Nat. Biotechnol. **29**, 411 (2011)
18. Smith, C.A., Wicks, P.J.: PatientsLikeMe: consumer health vocabulary as a folksonomy. In: AMIA Annual Symposium Proceedings, p. 682. American Medical Informatics Association (2008)
19. Brennan, G.P., Fritz, J.M., Hunter, S.J., Thackeray, A., Delitto, A., Erhard, R.E.: Identifying subgroups of patients with acute/subacute "nonspecific" low back pain: results of a randomized clinical trial. Spine **31**, 623–631 (2006)
20. Kiros, R., et al.: Skip-thought vectors. In: Advances in Neural Information Processing Systems, pp. 3294–3302 (2015)
21. Kim, Y.: Convolutional neural networks for sentence classification. arXiv preprint arXiv: 1408.5882 (2014)
22. Li, Y., Yuan, Y.: Convergence analysis of two-layer neural networks with ReLU activation. In: Advances in Neural Information Processing Systems, pp. 597–607 (2017)
23. Kim, J.: Understanding how Convolutional Neural Network (CNN) perform text classification with word embeddings, 02 December 2017. https://joshuakyh.wordpress.com/
24. N. N. C. C (n2c2): Track 1: Cohort selection for clinical trials. In: 2018 n2c2 Shared-Task and Workshop (2018). https://n2c2.dbmi.hms.harvard.edu/track1
25. deparkes: Machine Learning vs Rules Systems. deparkes.co.uk, 24 November 2017. https://deparkes.co.uk/2017/11/24/machine-learning-vs-rules-systems/
26. Bromley, J., Guyon, I., LeCun, Y., Sackinger, E., Shah, R.: Signature verification using a "siamese" time delay neural network. In: Advances in Neural Information Processing Systems, pp. 737–744 (1994)

Deep Learning for Quranic Reciter Recognition and Audio Content Identification

Mohamet Tall[1,2(✉)], Thierno Ibrahima Diop[1], Ndeye Fatou Ngom[2], and El hadj Abdoulaye Thiam[1]

[1] Baamtu, Dakar, Senegal
[2] LTISI Laboratory, Ecole Polytechnique de Thiès, Thiès, Senegal
tmohamet@ept.sn

Abstract. This paper presents a novel approach for identifying the reciter, sura, and verse of a given Quranic passage using pre-trained embedding models and transfer learning. Our approach involves training a deep learning model on a large Quranic recitation audio recordings dataset and using the resulting embeddings to compare and classify different reciters. We also present a workflow for identifying the specific sura and verse of a Quranic passage using a speech-to-text model and elastic-search for the query. We evaluate our approach using a variety of metrics and demonstrate its effectiveness in accurately identifying the reciter, sura, and verse of a given passage. We discuss the potential applications of this approach in the fields of Quranic studies and Islamic education and outline directions for future work in this area.

Keywords: Speaker identification · Speaker recognition · Deep learning · Transfer learning · Audio embedding

1 Introduction

Researchers in various fields continue to show interest in the automatic identification and verification of speakers using representative audio [11]. The two categories of speaker recognition are speaker identification and speaker verification. In speaker verification, the system automatically confirms whether a speaker claimed identity is genuine, without human intervention. Speaker identification aims to determine a speaker identity by comparing an unknown voice sample against a database of known speakers. Given the availability of existing audio datasets, substantial research is focused on speech and speaker recognition, as well as the identification of imitation sound clips of speakers. Speech processing is inherently more complex than other pattern recognition tasks, such as text classification and image recognition, because it involves the analysis of spoken language, which is a more complex form of communication. It is a multidisciplinary field encompassing statistics, signal processing, phonetics, linguistics

D. Bassole et al. (Eds.): InterSol 2025, LNICST 671, pp. 121–131, 2026.
https://doi.org/10.1007/978-3-032-15154-4_10

and deep learning. Compared to the significant research efforts dedicated to English speech recognition and to developing emotion recognition systems based on speech signals, [4,5,16], comparatively less focus has been paid to Arabic speech recognition [1].

This study presents a new, deep learning-based approach to accurately identifying the reciter, sura and verse of Quranic passages. The study's key contribution is the use of pre-trained embedding models for speaker classification, which have been demonstrated to be highly accurate in distinguishing between different speakers. The proposed workflow uses speech-to-text and an elastic search to identify the sura and verse of a given passage and has several advantages. This method could be used to study the Quran and in Islamic education. For instance, it could be employed to develop digital Quranic libraries or educational resources. The study suggests some ideas for future research, such as experimenting with different audio embedding models and using larger or more diverse data sets. It also suggests that this approach could be applied to other languages or text-based datasets.

The results show that deep learning techniques can be used to accurately identify the reciter, sura, and verse of Quranic passages. This could make a significant contribution. It could contribute to the fields of Quranic studies and Islamic education. This approach has the potential to advance Quranic studies and enhance Islamic education. The development of digital Quranic libraries, intelligent tutoring systems and educational tools to support students in learning and improving their Quranic recitation are just some of the possible applications. For example, real-time feedback could be received by learners on their recitation or references could be accessed by them based on specific reciters or verses.
The rest of the paper is organized as follows. Section 2 discuss previous research and identifies gaps in the literature. Section 3 describes the research design and data collection methods, as well as the techniques used for reciter classification and sura and verse identification. Section 4 describes the process of identifying the sura, verse and challenges encountered. Section 5 presents the results of the reciter classification experiments and discusses notable trends or patterns, summarize the main findings, and discusses the implications and applications of the results. Section 6 summarizes the key contributions and suggests directions for future research.

2 Related Work

Around 1.6 billion Muslims worldwide consider the Holy Quran to be their primary source of reference [13]. Recitation and listening to the Holy Quran are essential activities of a Muslim. There are many known Quranic recitations or reading methods. Tajweed is a set of rules to read the Quran in a correct Pronunciation of the letters with all its Qualities while Reciting the Quran [2]. Two well-known narrations (Rewayah) exist in each recitation, which has been authenticated and passed down by qualified and experienced scholars (Sheikhs) to their students. The most popular recitation is that of Hafs Bin Suleiman, on the authority of Asim Al-Koufi, which is being recited in Arabia, Egypt, India, Pakistan, a Turkey [11]. The sacred Arabic text is the Holy Quran, which has 114 chapters (suras) and 78,000 words. A word can be associated with numerous concepts (polysemy) and a concept can be associated with many words (synonyms). There are challenging points regarding the structure of the Holy Quran. These arise when searching for certain information on Quran reciters or verses.

A system for factoid questions specialized in Islamic sciences such as prophetic tradition (Hadith), Hadith narrator, and Quran interpretation (Tafsir) is proposed in [12]. The proposed QA System follows a symbolic approach composed of query formulation, information search, and answer extraction and treatment. In [17], automatic identification of Arabic speakers was performed using Continuous Hidden Markov Models (CHMMs), with speech signals represented by Mel-Frequency Cepstral Coefficients (MFCCs). In text-independent experiments, the system achieved an identification rate of 80%. An automated system can assist in identifying the specific voice of a Qari from numerous available offline and online recitations. In [19], In [19], the author utilized a Support Vector Machine (SVM) classifier to detect and recognize narrator name entities within Hadith texts. In [8], the authors analyzed the recitation of the Twelve Qari, reciting the last ten Surah of the Quran, thus representing a 12-class problem. The Mel-frequency Cepstral Coefficient (MFCC) and pitch were used as the features for model learning. The features were learned with the naive Bayes and random forest, being selected due to their overall excellent performance in the state of the art.

Transformer-based speech representations align more closely with human perception than earlier approaches using phonetic transcriptions or MFCC acoustic features as shown in [6]. They also found that features extracted from the middle hidden layers of the models are generally more effective than those from the final layer. In [14], the authors propose a simplified deep-learning approach to accomplish the speaker identification task using as little training data. To represent the feature vectors of over 4,000 speakers using approximately 343 h of speech signals, the MFCC method was utilized. Bidirectional LSTM neural networks provided up to 76.9% accuracy rate for individual voice segments, and 99.5% when considering the segments of each speaker as a bundle. In [3], the authors introduce an isolated word speaker identification system based on a new feature extractor and using an artificial neural network. The classification of the features, extracted MFCC, is done using Multi-layer perceptron with back-propagation algorithm.

This study presents a novel approach for accurately identifying the reciter, sura, and verse of Quranic passages using deep learning techniques. One key contribution of this study is the use of pre-trained embedding models to classify different reciters, which demonstrates high accuracy in identifying both the Quran reciter and audio content.

3 Methodology

3.1 System Design

The proposed workflow (Fig. 1) is mainly based on a fine-tuned deep audio embedding model that extracts the acoustic characteristics of the input audio and a part represented by the classification layer whose purpose is to classify the reciter. Fine-tuning a network is a procedure based on the concept of transfer learning.

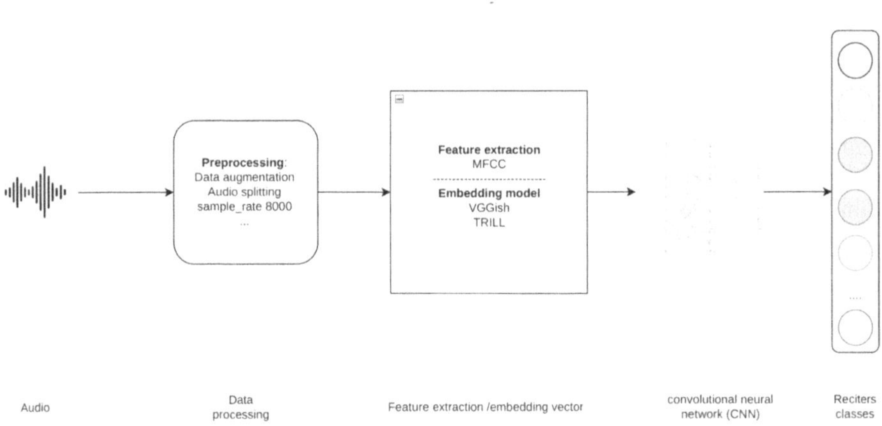

Fig. 1. Classification of Quran reciters using a fine-tuned deep audio embedding model.

The fine-tuning consists of implementing first a transfer learning by configuring the pre-trained model layer with the parameter *trainable=False*. We train our model by adding some layers and the classification layer. Once convergence is reached, we change the previous parameter to *True* and then re-train the model with a low learning rate. It is important to note that it is possible to have overfitting. Fine-tuning a network is a huge advantage because it allows initializing the parameters of our neural network with those of a pre-trained model. We can expect a fast convergence and an increase in the learning precision of our classification model for our downstream task, reciter identification. For some types of problems, it can be difficult to find a large volume of data to implement our deep learning model. Transfer learning can be used to train our deep learning model with a low volume of data. Deep audio embedding methods allow us to efficiently capture high-dimensional features into a compact representation. The power of deep audio embedding is to automatically identify predominant aspects in the data at scale [10].

3.2 Dataset

The dataset is obtained by downloading audio from sheiks through several open-source platforms. The raw data used are mainly in mp3 format of variable length, divided into folders for each sheik (a reciter of the Quran). Each folder contains the audio files of the different suras recited by the sheik. The global dataset contains 169 sheiks, i.e. 169 folders representing our model's classes. For each sheik and each of his suras, the sound is cut according to the silence. Indeed, the psalmodist makes momentary pauses to mark the end of a verse or to apply the rules of the stop during the recitation.

We also added the last class composed of random sounds (music, discussion, ambient noise, etc.) to allow our model not to classify a random song as a sheik. So in total, we will have 170 sheiks for our experiment.

3.3 Data Preprocessing

For audio samples, we use a sample rate of *8000 Hz*. The audio sample rate is a measurement of the samples per second taken by the system from a continuous digital signal.

There are several ways of reciting the Quran. These different readings are methods of vocalization that arise from the addition of diacritical marks on the consonantal Quranic skeleton. We distinguish several riwayat [18]. In the dataset, we have only two of them. However, there are some sheiks who have two classes with different riwayats. These classes are grouped into one since we do not predict the riwayat but the sheik in person. This increases the number of classes from 169 to 170.

Data augmentation is a common strategy adopted to increase the quantity of training data, avoid over fitting and improve the robustness of the models [9]. We added different random noises in the audios of our data-set to not allow our model to learn with too perfect data. Indeed, the audios in our data-set were recorded in a studio, and wanting to train our classifier with these data can create a high bias. Adding noise to our training dataset can have a regularizing effect and reduce over-fitting.

3.4 Pre-trained Embedding Models

In this section, we will introduce the pre-trained embedding models that we used in our experiments. Embedding models are machine learning algorithms that transform input data, such as audio recordings, into a fixed-length vector representation. These vectors, known as embedding, capture the important characteristics of the input data and can be used for a variety of tasks, such as classification and comparison. The embedding models we used have been trained on large data-sets of audio recordings, which allows them to effectively extract the key features of an input sound. As a result, they are an efficient and effective way to represent and analyze audio data.**TRILL** is an embedding model trained in a semi-supervised way on audio clips of the audio-set [7,15] data-set proposed in the article *Towards Learning a Universal Non-Semantic Representation of Speech* [15]. *TRILL* transforms audio into a fixed-size vector with the principle that sounds that are close in time are also close in embedding space. In the original paper [15], the authors show that this definition of the loss function (*triplet loss*) is very efficient to learn a robust representation for several non-semantic tasks. *TRILL* was evaluated on the *Non-Semantic Speech Benchmark (NOSS)* [15], designed by the same authors, by training several small models and comparing their performances. By performing transfer learning for several sub-tasks, the models obtained give good results on the proposed benchmark. With transfer learning, the authors have proposed a new state-of-the-art for several tasks, thus outperforming several previously proposed methods.

VGGish is a pre-trained audio embedding model developed by researchers at Google. It is designed to extract features from short (1-second) segments of audio and has been trained on a data-set of approximately 2 million YouTube audio recordings. The VGGish model converts the raw audio waveform into a spectrogram representation using a short-time Fourier transform (STFT) and then applies a series of convolutional and fully connected layers to the spectrogram to generate embeddings. These embeddings capture the key characteristics of the input audio. They can be used for tasks such as music classification, speaker identification, and sound event recognition. The VGGish architecture consists of a series of convolutional layers, which apply filters to the spectrogram and extract relevant features, followed by fully connected (dense) layers, which refine the features and generate the final embeddings. The embeddings are then passed through a layer with a softmax activation function, which converts the embeddings into a probability distribution over a set of classes. Overall, the VGGish model is effective at extracting meaningful features from audio data and generating embeddings that can be used for a variety of tasks.

3.5 Features Extraction with Mel Frequency Cepstral Coefficients (MFCC)

The MFCC (Mel Frequency Cepstral Coefficients) is a method of extracting characteristics of the signal developed around the Fast Fourier Transform (FFT) and the Discrete Fourier Transform (DCT) on a Mel scale. The Mel scale is a logarithmic transformation of a signal's frequency. The fundamental principle of this transformation is that sounds of equal distance on the Mel scale are perceived as being of equal distance to humans. The transformation from the Hertz to Mel scale is given by the following formula:

$$m = 1127.log(1 + \frac{f}{700})$$

The calculation of the MFCC is done through the following steps:

1. Split the signal between several overlapping windows (windowing),
2. To reduce the spectral distortion created by the overlap, apply a Hamming window on the signal,
3. apply the Fast Fourier transform to the window (which gives the spectrum),
4. move on to the previously explained Mel scale,
5. finishes with the conversion of Mel's logarithmic spectrum into time using the Discrete Cosine Transform. This reduces the number of data characterizing

the signal and we obtain a limited number of cepstral coefficients (13 for our experiment) per window.

The MFCC is used for automatic speech recognition or for audio denoising. The number of coefficients used is a hyper-parameter of the model. It can vary according to the problem to be solved. To implement the MFCC with speaker identification, we can feed a neural network with the extracted features (MFCC) as input and the number of speakers to identify as the classification layer.

4 Verses and Sura Identification

To identify the sura and the verse using the audio file as input, we follow different steps of preprocessing, content extraction, and database query (Fig. 2). Indeed, first, we apply different layers of pre-processing by adapting the format and the different intrinsic characteristics such as the *sample rate*, etc. Then, we use a *Speech-To-Text model*[1] specifically trained with the Quran data which returns a textual output. However, the Quran is a sacred text so we have to make sure that we have consistent and correct results. The last step is to return the correct part of the Quran extracted from the audio file. This step consists in querying an *elasticsearch*[2] instance which contains all the verses of the Quran and is extracted according to a defined format. For each verse, we have the verse number, the textual content in Arabic, the transcription in Latin, the translation in several languages, and the information of the concerned sura. In summary, the workflow presented in Fig. 2 consists of extracting an audio file's textual content with a *speech-to-text* model and then querying an *elasticsearch* instance to obtain the results.

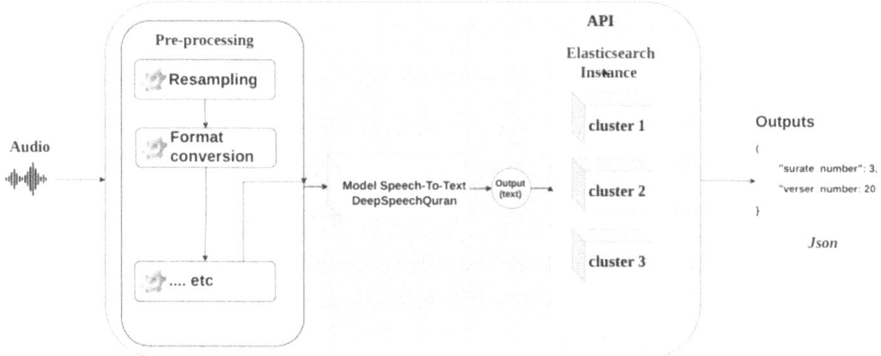

Fig. 2. Sura and verse identification workflow.

[1] https://github.com/tarekeldeeb/DeepSpeech-Quran.
[2] https://www.elastic.co/fr/elasticsearch/.

5 Experimental Results

5.1 Experimentation

With the above-mentioned models, we trained a neural network with as output the classification layer i.e. the reciters of the Quran to classify. With the feature extraction methods, we trained a convolutional neural network and for the embedding models an extraction mode where we will use the model, extract the embedding vector, and then ingest it into our convolutional neural network.

For the experiments, we used a computer equipped with an Intel Core i7-7700HQ CPU (2.80 GHz, 8 cores) and an NVIDIA GeForce GTX 1050 Mobile GPU (GP107M).

	Name	Runtime	accuracy	best_epoch	best_val_loss	epoch	loss	val_accuracy	val_loss
0	VGGish	47097	0.684158	97	0.935010	99	1.124289	0.744445	0.946231
1	MFCC	5178	0.881004	88	0.336364	99	0.445884	0.903174	0.373936
2	TRILL	25821	0.975997	70	0.126861	99	0.115250	0.974353	0.136676
3	TRILL	30864	0.980501	162	0.125846	11	0.096234	0.975837	0.133122
4	VGGish	37980	0.689695	80	0.963028	99	1.101851	0.738093	0.975881

Fig. 3. Model performance.

Figure 3 gives detailed information on the performance of the models. Figure 4a shows that *Trill* model performs better than the other models in terms of accuracy and loss.

5.2 Model Performance Analysis

An analysis of the previous experimental results helps determine the optimal model for sheiks classification. Indeed, after convergence, the Trill model has an accuracy of 98% while the *MFCC* and the *VGGish* have respectively 88% and 68%. The validation accuracy is 97.58% for the *TRILL* model, 90% for the *MFCC*, and 73% for the *VGGish*. For the loss *(Sparse Categorical Cross-entropy)*, the Trill model has a value of 0.096, the *MFCC* 0.44, and the *VGGish* model 1.11. For the validation loss, Trill has a value of 0.13, 0.37 for the *MFCC*, and 0.99 for the *VGGish*. On the other hand, Trill has a much higher training time with a time equal to 2h 5 m 15 s than *MFCC* which is 1h 14 m 22 s. *VGGish* takes much longer with 4h 6 m 57 s. The Trill model converges faster followed by *MFCC*. In sum, the results obtained show that the *Trill* model performs better than the other models in terms of accuracy, loss, validation accuracy, and validation loss with sufficient training time and graphics card usage.

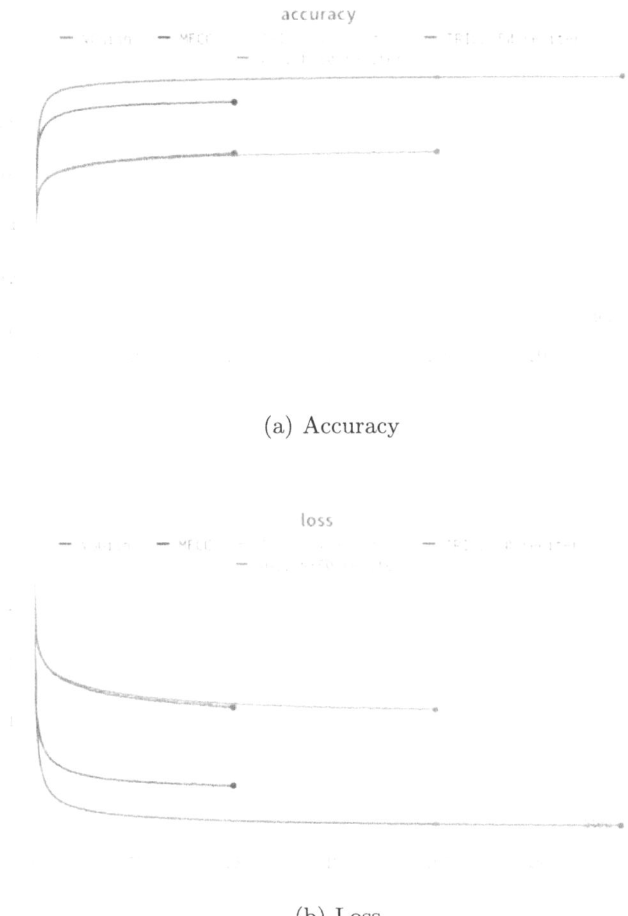

(a) Accuracy

(b) Loss

Fig. 4. Analysis of the performance.

5.3 Discussion

One of the key contributions of this study is the use of pre-trained embedding models to classify Quranic reciters. These models have been shown to be effective at extracting meaningful features from audio data and generating embeddings that can be used for a variety of tasks. Training the model on a large corpus of Quranic recitation audio enabled highly accurate identification of the reciter for each passage, confirming the robustness and efficiency of the proposed method.

In addition to the use of embedding models, the proposed workflow for identifying the sura and verse of a Quranic passage using a speech-to-text model and elasticsearch offers a number of benefits. Speech-to-text models are able to accurately transcribe spoken language into written text, making it possible to search for specific passages within the Quran. By combining this transcription with the use of elasticsearch, we were able to quickly and efficiently identify the sura and verse of a given passage.

The proposed method can be used to create digital Quranic libraries, allowing users to easily search and identify specific reciters, suras, and verses. It also can be used to create educational tools that help students and scholars learn more about the Quran and the various styles of recitation.

The experimental results elastic search feasibility of using deep learning techniques to accurately identify the reciter, sura, and verse of Quranic passages. We believe that our approach has the potential to make a significant contribution to the fields of Quranic studies and Islamic education and to provide a foundation for future research in this area.

5.4 Application

The proposed method of Quranic reciter recognition using deep learning can be applied to the development of a platform like *Shazam*[3], but for the Quran, to identify the reciter and specific verse being recited. The platform can improve the understanding of the Quranic text and recitation, provide personalized learning experiences for students to learn from their favorite reciters, and enhance recitation skills with feedback from the algorithm. Ultimately, such a platform has the potential to revolutionize the way people engage with the Quran and its recitation.

6 Conclusion

In this study, we presented a novel approach to accurately identifying the reciter, sura and verse of a Quranic passage, based on deep learning techniques. We demonstrated that pre-trained embedding models are highly effective for speaker discrimination and can accurately identify the speaker of a given passage. Additionally, we described a workflow for using a speech-to-text model in conjunction with elasticsearch to identify the specific sura and verse of a Quranic passage. Our results have the potential to be applied in a variety of settings, including Quranic studies and Islamic education, and provide a foundation for future research in this area. Our approach offers a promising solution to accurately and efficiently identify the receiver, sura, and verse of Quranic passages.

Future research could improve this study by exploring alternative deep learning architectures and embedding models to improve receiver classification. Investigating the detection of specific riwayat (recitation traditions) through additional data and specialized models is another promising direction. Broader extensions include the use of larger and more diverse datasets, the application of the method to other languages, and the expansion to various text-audio tasks. These developments would increase the method's utility in Quranic studies and Islamic education, highlighting the potential of deep learning to support the preservation and teaching of Quranic recitation.

---

[3] an application that can identify music.

References

1. Al-Anzi, F., Abuzeyna, D.: Synopsis on Arabic speech recognition. Ain Shams Eng. J. **13**, 101534 (2022)
2. Alagrami, A., Eljazzar, M.: Automatic recognition of Arabic Quranic recitation rules
3. Antony, A., Gopikakumari, R.: Speaker identification based on combination of MFCC and UMRT based features. Procedia Comput. Sci. **143**, 250–257 (2018)
4. Aouani, H., Ayed, Y.: Speech emotion recognition with deep learning. Procedia Comput. Sci. **178**, 251–260 (2020)
5. Atmaja, B., Sasou, A., Akagi, M.: Survey on bimodal speech emotion recognition from acoustic and linguistic information fusion. Speech Commun. **140**, 11–28 (2022)
6. Bartelds, M., De Vries, W., Sanal, F., Richter, C., Liberman, M., Wieiling, M.: Neural representations for modeling variation in speech. J. Phoneticc **92**, 101137 (2020)
7. Gemmeke, J.F., et al.: Audio set: an ontology and human-labeled dataset for audio events. In: 2017 IEEE International Conference on Acoustics, Speech and Signal Processing (ICASSP), pp. 776–780. IEEE (2017)
8. Khan, R., Qamar, A., Hadwan, M.: Quranic reciter recognition: a machine learning approach. ASTESJ **4**, 173–176 (2019)
9. Ko, T., Peddinti, V., Povey, D., Khudanpur, S.: Audio augmentation for speech recognition. In: Sixteenth Annual Conference of the International Speech Communication Association (2015)
10. Koh, E., Dubnov, S.: Comparison and analysis of deep audio embeddings for music emotion recognition. arXiv preprint arXiv.2104.06517 (2021)
11. Lataifeh, M., Elnagar, A.: Arabic diversified audio dataset. Data Brief **33**, 106503 (2020)
12. Maraoui, H., Hadar, K., Roomary, L.: Arabic factoid questions-answering system for Islamic sciences using normalized corpora. In: Procedia computer science, 25th International Conference on Knowledge Based and Intelligent Information and Engineering System, vol. 192, pp. 69–79 (2021)
13. Mohamed, E., Shokry, E.: QSST: a Quranic semantic search tool based on word embedding. J. King Saud Univ. Comput. Inform. Sci. **34**, 934–945 (2022)
14. Nammous, M., Saeed, K., Kobojek, P.: Using a small amount of text-independent speech data for a BiLSTM large scale speaker identification approach. J. King Saud Univ. Comput. Inf. Sci. 764–770 (2022)
15. Shor, J., et al.: Towards learning a universal non-semantic representation of speech. arXiv preprint arXiv:2002.12764 (2020)
16. Singkul, S., Woraratpanya, K.: Vector learning representation for generalized speech emotion recognition. Heliyon **8**, e09196 (2022)
17. Tolba, H.: A high-performance text-independent speaker identification of Arabic speakers using a CHMM-based approach. Alex. Eng. J. **50**, 43–47 (2011)
18. wikipedia: Lectures du Coran (2022). https://fr.wikipedia.org/wiki/Lectures_du_Coran
19. Yusup, F., Bijaksana, M., Huda, A.: Narratorś name recognition with support vector machine for indexing Indonesian hadith translation. In: Procedia Computer Science, 4th International Conference on Computer Science and Computational Intelligence, vol. 157, pp. 191–198 (2019)

Networks, Security, Blockchain and Applications

Millimeter Wave Transmitter Model Based on an Optical Phase-Locked Loop (OPLL) for High Bit Rate and Low Cost in Next Generation Networks

Wilfried Albert Duniwangda Kiélem, Mamadou Diallo Diouf(✉), and Moumouni Sawadogo

Laboratory of Information Processing and Intelligent Systems (LTISI), Thies Polytechnic School (EPT), Thies, Senegal
waduniwangda.kielem@univ-thies.sn, mddiouf@ept.edu.sn
http://www.ept.sn

Abstract. The convergence of optical and wireless technologies is pivotal for enhancing digital communication systems and is foundational to future millimeter-wave networks. While electronic RF generation systems are well-established, optical methods are gaining traction due to their simplicity, scalability, and compatibility with existing silicon technology. Among these, optical heterodyning stands out as an efficient approach for generating millimeter waves, leveraging commercially available components and streamlined architectures. However, this method is hindered by the phase noise inherited from laser sources, which can impair signal quality.

This paper explores a millimeter-wave transmitter model based on an Optical Phase-Locked Loop (OPLL), designed to mitigate phase noise and support high data-rate, cost-efficient applications in next-generation networks. Using OptiSystem software, the open-loop transfer function and characteristics of the resulting RF millimeter-wave signals are evaluated. The transmitter achieves millimeter-wave frequency generation by leveraging the frequency difference between two laser sources. The insights presented underline the potential of OPLL architectures in bridging optical and wireless technologies for emerging 5G and 6G networks.

Keywords: Millimeter wave · optical phase-locked loop (OPLL) · Radio Over Fiber (RoF) · coherent communications

1 Introduction

The rapid evolution of telecommunications is driven by advancements in technologies such as the Internet of Things (IoT), Artificial Intelligence (AI), and massive real-time data processing. Modern networks must deliver ultra-fast connectivity to support the increasing demand for reliable, high-capacity communication, even in remote regions [8]. Next-generation networks, such as 5G and 6G, address these challenges by leveraging frequencies above 6 GHz, including the millimeter-wave band. Although offering

D. Bassole et al. (Eds.): InterSol 2025, LNICST 671, pp. 135–148, 2026.
https://doi.org/10.1007/978-3-032-15154-4_11

unparalleled data rates and low latency, millimeter-wave systems face inherent limitations in propagation distance due to atmospheric absorption, which requires a higher density of base stations for widespread coverage [7,8].

To make this advanced networks transition economically viable, especially for deployment in rural environment, telecommunication infrastructure must be designed with a primary focus on both affordability and robust reliability [11]. A low-cost transmitter capable of supporting high bit rates is essential for applications such as Radio-over-Fiber (RoF) transmission. Optical techniques, which leverage the shared silicon technology underlying both optical and electronic systems, present an opportunity to reduce costs while maintaining performance. Specifically, optical heterodyning is emerging as a promising approach for millimeter wave generation due to its simplicity, scalability, and compatibility with standard semiconductor lasers [11].

This study proposes a millimeter wave transmitter based on an Optical Phase-Locked Loop (OPLL), designed to enable high-data-rate communications in 5G and 6G networks. By incorporating balanced photodetection and leveraging tunable semiconductor lasers, the proposed architecture ensures precision, stability, and cost efficiency. The work explores the feasibility of using OptiSystem software to model and simulate the open-loop behavior of the OPLL while addressing challenges in phase noise suppression and coherent transmission.

2 Related Works

The rapid evolution of mobile networks aligns with the International Mobile Telecommunications (IMT-2020) performance indicators, which aim to deliver user-experience data rate of 100 Mbps and support mmWave technologies capable of reaching up to 10 Gbps [6]. This represents a significant improvement over previous generations (2G, 3G, and 4G), where user data rates peaked at 100 Mbps. The inclusion of the 24 GHz to 100 GHz mmWave bands, as defined in Release 15 and beyond, demonstrates the critical role of the spectrum in achieving reliable and high-speed communication [6,7]. The licensed 5G 1 GHz–7 GHz mid-band spectrum is specific for the mobile industry. The 7 GHz–24 GHz unlicensed shared spectrum band provides no QoS guarantee and is being studied for specification. The 24 GHz–100 GHz mmWave bands are shared spectrum for more reliable operations, with the supported mmWave 24.25 GHz–52.6 GHz band in Release 15, prioritized expansion of mmWave at the 52.6 GHz–71 GHz band in Release-17, and the 71 GHz–114.25 GHz expansion band beyond Release 17. The Release 16 has defined a maximum 100 MHz uplink (UL) bandwidth (BW) and a maximum 400 MHz downlink (DL) BW for anchored and standalone unlicensed New Radio (NR-U) [7].

2.1 OPLL Implementation

Since its introduction in 1965 [4], the optical phase locked loop (OPLL) has undergone various innovations to improve phase tracking, frequency locking, and noise suppression. Steed et al. [12] highlighted the importance of Photonic Integrated Chips (PICs) for OPLL implementation, significantly reducing propagation delays and power consumption. Compact PIC-based OPLL designs, such as those integrating Semiconductor Gain Distributed Bragg Reflector (SGDBR) lasers, have achieved loop propagation delays as low as 1 ns, marking a milestone for coherent detection systems [12]. A short delay of 50 ps in the integrated OPLL between lasers and photodetector, combined with 1 ns for loop propagation delay in electronics, has also been carried out [13].

2.2 Laser Sources

For laser sources with low-frequency and direct modulation, the response of the semiconductor laser is out of phase with the modulation signal. This red shift arises from thermal effects. At high modulation frequency, the change of the frequency of the semiconductor laser is in phase with the input signal. The so-called electronic blue shift is due to carrier injection in the gain section [1]. Phase reversal occurs between the two regimes. The distributed feedback laser (DFB) is a three-section laser. The tuning occurs by current injection in the laser gain section, and the direct current (DC) frequency modulation (FM) sensitivity is approximately 1–3 GHz/mA and limits the loop bandwidth to $\leq$10 MHz [9]. The SGDBR is a four sections component. The frequency tuning occurs by current injection in a separate phase section, with a sensitivity of 20 GHz/mA, a large gain in the feedback loop, and no phase reversal in the FM response [9]. SGDBR laser has more than 40 nm quasi-continuous tuning range than the DFB laser, enabling the OPLL-Photonic Integrated Circuit (PIC) to generate a beat frequency from DC to 5 THz [9]. For fiber laser, the near diffraction-limited narrow linewidth is suitable for coherent and long-haul links [5]. However, its rare-earth doped core need optical pumping and its footprint is larger for PIC integration than semiconductor laser's.

2.3 Loop Bandwidth Characteristics

The loop bandwidth determines the speed of the OPLL response to phase or frequency deviations. A higher bandwidth provides a faster tracking, but is associated with increased noise and jitter. The loop bandwidth is limited by the loop propagation delay and the semiconductor laser frequency modulation phase reversal [10]. To keep the residual phase noise variance as small as possible, the loop bandwidth must be larger than the summed linewidth of the master and slave lasers. The multisection laser can help overcome the phase reversal in the FM response [14]. However, the integrated OPLL PIC that implements the SGDBR laser and external electronics, achieved a record of 247.8 MHZ in [9] and 300 MHz by Ristic et al. [10].

2.4 Loop Delay

Loop delay is crucial in coherent systems. It introduces phase shift and reduces the phase margin. The loop delay also limits the maximum bandwidth and compromises the stability of the loop. A short loop delay is necessary to track high-speed phase changes and suppress phase noise effectively. The loop delay affects the lock acquisition time and the response time and slows the dynamics of the loop. Photonic integrated chip is gaining more importance due to its ability to reduce propagation delay in the loop. The compact structure of PIC OPLL allows for packaging and lower power consumption compared to discrete space optics components [12]. A delay of 50 ps in integrated OPLL between lasers and photodetector, combined with 1 ns for loop propagation delay in electronics has been carried out by Steed et al. [12]. The trend solution is the combination of PIC and electronic integrated chip (EIC) on the same chip.

2.5 Loop Filter Characteristics

The role of the loop filter is to shape the response of the resulting error signal to apply to the laser modulation. It is based on phase error and determines loop stability, settling time, and rejection of frequency components. Parameters such as filter gain, bandwidth, and phase margin are used to design the optimal loop. OPLL loops are classified. Type I OPLL contains an integrator in the entire loop, which is the voltage controlled oscillator (VCO) or current controlled oscillator (CCO) in the case of the laser as the loop's actuator. This kind of OPLL can only track phase differences and is suitable for systems where the input signal frequency is constant or varies very slowly. Type II OPLL has a CCO as an integrator and a loop filer as a second integrator. It can track phase and frequency differences, particularly in systems where the input frequency varies. Type III OPLL has three integrators in the loop to track frequency change acceleration in highly dynamical systems. The order of the OPLL loop refers to the number of integrators used to process the error signal, except the CCO. A first-order OPLL loop does not include a filter at the output of the CCO. It is convenient for systems with fast response and minimal noise. A second-order OPLL uses a single pole low-pass filter to process the output of the CCO to achieve a balanced response between speed and noise suppression. It is suitable for systems requiring stability and noise performance. A third order OPLL loop includes a second order filter and multiple poles which results in lower response time and better noise suppression.

2.6 Noise Suppression

Phase noise suppression is the ability of the OPLL to reduce the noise from the inputs of the reference and slave lasers. Phase noise suppression is essential for optical coherent communications. Residual phase noise and residual phase noise variance depend on four parameters: loop gain, loop delay, lasers linewidth and power. A record residual phase noise of $0.012\,\text{rad}^2$ has been demonstrated in [14].

2.7 Power Consumption

Power consumption in OPLL can be significantly reduced with system-on-chip PIC OPLL (SoC-PIC). SoC-PIC allows for savings in size, weight, power injection, cost, and high data rate. For heterodyning OPLL, a dissipated power of 1.12 W has been demonstrated, 0.66 W for PIC with SGDBR laser and semiconductor optical amplifier (SOA) for 10 mW output power versus 0.18 W for 10 mW output power without SOA [2]. [14] has reached a −54 dBm for master laser (ML) power and residual phase noise variance of $0.02\,\text{rad}^2$, with a possible −56 dBm ML power for residual phase noise variance of $0.02\,\text{rad}^2$ if the summed linewidth is 10 kHz.

3 Optical Phase-Locked Loop Description

An optical phase-locked loop is a control system that is used to synchronize an optical source with a reference laser to stabilize the beating frequency between the two. It uses a highly tunable optical source like a semiconductor laser. Optical frequencies are many orders above radio frequencies. It is more easy to generate a carrier in the millimeter band $[30,300]$ GHz using photonic devices than electronics. The drawback is the spectral purity of the wave generated, which inherits phase noise from different components in the system architecture. Among photonic-assisted millimeter wave carrier generation, optical heterodyning is drawing more attention because of the simplicity of the architecture and flexibility in frequency tuning. In order to mitigate phase noise effects for coherent transmission, optical injection locking, optical phase-locked loop, or a combination of both techniques can be used. OPLL principle consists of mixing two optical waves. The beat signal is detected with a frequency that equals the difference between the two optical signals. To stabilize the millimeter wave frequency, an OPLL is used to extract the phase difference variations between the two incident lights as an error signal. This error signal is then processed and feed back to control the emission of one of the sources to keep a constant phase difference between the two optical waves. In homodyne OPLL, the two optical sources (the master laser and the slave laser) have the same frequency ($f_M = f_S$). The beating signal generated inherits the phase noise of the two lasers. In heterodyne OPLL, the central frequencies are different ($f_M \neq f_S$). The second laser is first modulated by and RF source f_{RF} to produce sidebands. The mixing process uses one sideband $f_M = \omega_S \pm f_{RF}$ to produce the beating signal which contains the relative phase difference information.

4 OPLL Basic Components Models

For a heterodyne loop, two different laser sources are needed. Due to their availability and compactness, semiconductor lasers with a great tunable range are used. A photodiode acts as a mixer and detects the incident light power. It outputs an electrical signal with a frequency equal to the difference frequency of the optical signals.

4.1 Semiconductor Laser

The semiconductor laser is a current-controlled device. It is commercially available, and it has a frequency response that can be controlled by the modulating current over a wide range of frequencies. The ideal laser output signal can be represented by a monochromatic electrical field with amplitude E_0 and instantaneous phase φ such as $E(t) = E_0(t)cos(\Phi(t))$ or:

$$E(t) = E_0(1+\alpha(t))\cdot cos(2\pi\nu_0 t + \varphi(t) + \varphi_0) \tag{1}$$

$\varphi(t)$ is called phase noise and is a critical parameter in advanced optical modulation formats and link capacity improvement. OPLL aims to control the phase error of the resulting mmWave for advanced coherent transmission applications. The frequency of this sinusoidal function $\nu(t) = \frac{1}{2\pi}\frac{d\Phi(t)}{dt}$, is the time derivative of the instantaneous phase

$\Phi(t)$. The phase varies around a central frequency ν_0 according to the laser linewidth $\delta\nu(t)$:

$$\nu(t) = \frac{1}{2\pi}\frac{d\Phi(t)}{dt} = \nu_0 + \frac{1}{2\pi}\frac{d\varphi(t)}{dt} = \nu_0 + \delta\nu(t) \tag{2}$$

4.2 Electro-optical Modulator

The role of the electro-optical modulator is to facilitate frequency conversion. The radio frequency (RF) electrical signal applied to the modulator has the following form:

$$V_m(t) = V_0 \cdot \cos\left(\Omega_{RF}t + \varphi_{RF}(t)\right) \tag{3}$$

This electrical signal modulates the incoming carrier field by changing the refractive index of the waveguide. From Eq. 1, the resulting field has the expression:

$$E_{out}(t) = E_0 e^{j(2\pi\nu_0 t + \varphi(t) + \varphi_0)} \cdot e^{j\beta\cos(\Omega_{RF}t + \varphi_{RF}(t)} \tag{4}$$

The coefficient β represents the modulation index, and $\varphi_{RF}(t)$ is the RF source phase noise. The modulated signal phase noise $\varphi(t) + \varphi_{RF}$ can be approximated by $\varphi(t)$ due to the negligible phase noise of radio sources [3]. The modulation process creates multiple optical side bands with frequencies related to $\omega_0 \pm n\Omega$. In heterodyne OPLL, the master laser frequency and the slave laser frequency are separated by $f_M - f_s = n\Omega$. One side-band of the modulated electrical field of the slave laser is used to lock the master laser.

4.3 Phase Detector

The phase detector element in an OPLL is a photodiode. The photodiode can detect the average power of the incident light and is said to have a quadratic response. The photodiode produces an electrical beat signal when it receives two carriers and acts as a signal mixer. The difference between the two carriers must be in the photodiode bandwidth. The electrical field of the master laser can be written as $E_M = E_{M,0}e^{j(\omega_M + \varphi_M(t))}$. The same expression is used for the output of the slave laser $E_S = E_{S,0}e^{j(\omega_S + \varphi_S(t))}$. These signals are combined in a 3 dB coupler to produce the output signals E_1 and E_2. The 3 dB coupler mixed the incident lights and the coupling matrix:

$$\begin{bmatrix} E_1(t) \\ E_2(t) \end{bmatrix} = \frac{1}{\sqrt{2}} \begin{bmatrix} 1 & j \\ j & 1 \end{bmatrix} \begin{bmatrix} E_M(t) \\ E_S(t) \end{bmatrix} \tag{5}$$

creates the output expressions $E_1 = \frac{E_M + jE_S}{\sqrt{2}}$ and $E_2 = \frac{jE_M + E_S}{\sqrt{2}}$. A photodiode placed on one output of the coupler will detect a combination of E_1 and E_2, and will perform the mixing operation of the two output optical signals which are 90° apart. The photocurrent can be written as:

$$I_{PD} = \eta(E_M^2 + E_S^2 + 2\sqrt{E_M^2 + E_S^2}cos(\Delta\omega t + \Delta\varphi(t) + \Delta\Phi_0) \tag{6}$$

The photodiode efficiency is η. $\Delta\omega = \omega_M - \omega_S$, and $\Delta\varphi(t) = \Delta\varphi_M(t) - \Delta\varphi_s(t)$ is the accumulated phase. In locked condition with $\Delta\omega = 0$, the signal at the output of the photodiode with charge resistance R_{PD} is:

$$I_{PD} \approx \frac{1}{2\pi} 2\eta\sqrt{E_M{}^2 + E_s^2} \cdot \varphi_e(t) + i_{in}(t) \tag{7}$$

$\varphi_e(t) = \Delta\phi(t) - \varphi_c$ is the phase error. $i_{in}(t)$ is the internal photodiode current noise. The current I_{PD} is proportional to the voltage $V_{PD}(t) = R_{PD}I_{PD}$. The voltage V_{PD} is adjusted with a filter to obtain a feedback voltage $V_c(t) = V_{PD} * f_{filtre}(t)$ that is used to synchronize the phase of the slave laser with the phase of the master laser. The desired effect of this corrective signal on the laser response is given by the current $i_c(t) = \frac{V_c}{R_{laser}}$. R_{laser} is the charge resistance of the laser. The phase response of the laser subjected to a current $i_c(t)$ is given by:

$$\nu_c = i_c(t) * h_{laser}(t) = \frac{V_c}{R_{laser}} * h_{laser} \tag{8}$$

The control signal must be superimposed on the slave laser modulation current. Before feedback, the control current must be processed to suppress high-frequency components and noise from different sources with a loop filter. We have the following expression for the controlling signal:

$$\frac{1}{2\pi}\frac{d\varphi_c(t)}{dt} = \frac{R_{PD}}{R_{laser}}\left(\frac{2\eta\sqrt{E_M^2 + E_S^2}}{2\pi}\varphi_e(t) + i_{in}(t)\right) * f_{filtre}(t) * h_{laser}(t) \tag{9}$$

h_{laser} is the slave laser frequency modulation response. f_{filtre} is the filter transfer function. In order to account for feedback delay in the loop, a Dirac distribution is added to get the open-loop function $g(t)$ as:

$$\varphi_c(t) = g_{OL}(t) * \varphi_e(t) * e^{t/\tau} \tag{10}$$

4.4 OPLL Open Loop Transfer Function

The reference signal is the phase difference $\Delta\varphi(t) = \varphi_M(t) - \varphi_S(t)$ between the master laser and the slave laser. The objective of OPLL is to maintain this phase difference constant over time. This will result in a stable millimeter carrier. The error signal $\varphi_e(t) = \Delta\varphi(t) - \varphi_c(t)$ is the deviation between the correction applied to settle the slave laser phase and the reference signal. In the time domain, this corrective term depends on the loop components: the laser and filter transfer functions:

$$\varphi_c(t) = \varphi_e(t) * f_{filtre}(t) * h_{laser}(t) \tag{11}$$

For small deviations of the phase difference in the lock condition, the current at the photodetector can be linearized as (7). To study the loop properties, we need to move to the frequency-domain analysis or Laplace transform of the time-domain transfer function. With $p = 2\pi jf$, the expression of the open loop function is:

$$p \cdot \varphi_c(p) = \frac{R_{PD}}{R_{laser}}[2\eta\sqrt{E_M^2 + E_S^2} \cdot \varphi_e(p) + 2\pi i_{in}(p)] \cdot F_{filtre}(p) \cdot H_{laser}(p) \cdot e^{-\tau_D p} \tag{12}$$

This can be rewritten as

$$\varphi_c(p) = G_{OL}(p) \cdot \varphi_e(p) + 2\pi\frac{G_{OL}(p)}{2\eta\sqrt{E_M^2 + E_S^2}} i_{in}(p) \tag{13}$$

with the term:

$$G_{OL}(p) = \frac{R_{PD}}{R_{laser}}\frac{F_{filtre}(p) \cdot H_{laser}(p)}{p} e^{\tau_D p}$$

5 Optisystem Model

In this work, we designed a mmWave transmitter with optisystem software, as shown in Fig. 1. We use an ideal laser source as the master laser and a Distributed Feedback Laser (DFB) as the slave laser.

5.1 Transmitter Architecture

The system utilizes two lase sources: a reference laser and a secondary laser to generate a millimeter wave signal through heterodyne detection. It employs balanced photodetection to enhance the signal-to-noise ratio for signal processing and stability.

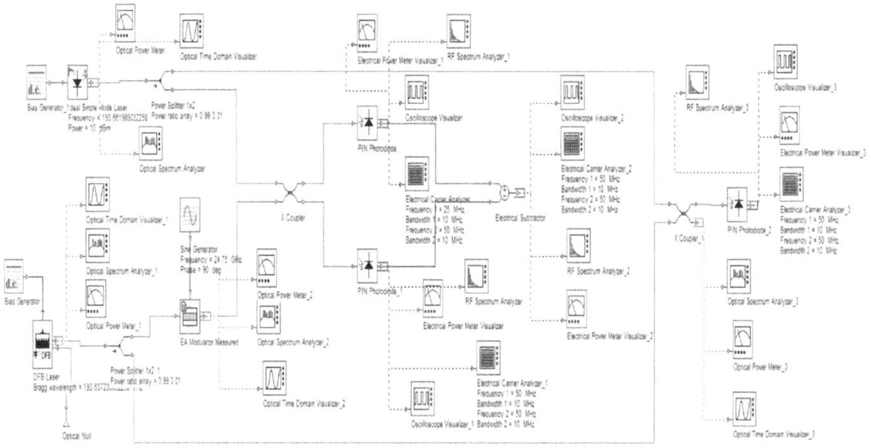

Fig. 1. Architecture of the millimeter-wave transmitter model designed in OptiSystem

5.2 Simulation and Results

The 5G core network demands high capacity, low network latency, and ultra-reliability of transmission. In addition, dense wavelength division multiplexing is widely adopted. To satisfy these requirements, the relevant and main optical transmission band for long-haul and high capacity is the C band (1530–1565 nm) (Table 1).

Simulation Parameters: The simulation covers a time window of 3.27 µs at a bit rate of 10 Gbps. A pseudo-random bit sequence of length 32,768 bits is employed, with 64 samples per bit to ensure signal fidelity. The resolution bandwidths are set to 0.01 nm for the optical spectrum analyser and 10 MHz for the RF spectrum analyser.

Table 1. Laser Parameters

Parameters	Reference Laser	DFB Laser
Frequency	193.661989 THz	193.637239 THz
Power	10 mW	-
Bias current	38.46 mA	5 mA
Modulation peak current	-	10 mA
Quantum efficiency	40%	40%
Noise	enabled	enabled
Phase noise	enabled	-
Linewidth enhancement factor	5	5

Reference Laser: Figure 2 illustrates the optical spectrum of the master laser highlighting its narrow linewidth centered around 1.5475 μm. This precision in wavelength ensures high spectral purity, which is critical for maintaining the stability of the loop and coherence of the system's reference frequency in the OPLL.

The corresponding operating frequency is 193.661989 THz. For the simulation, the single-mode laser model is used. Its properties include high purity emission and low phase noise Fig. 2.

Secondary Laser: Figure 3 presents the optical spectrum of DFB as secondary laser. It shows its broader linewidth compared to the master laser. Centered at 1.549 μm, the slave laser's tunability is essential for generating the required millimeter-wave frequencies through optical heterodyning despite its higher phase noise.

This kind of laser has a high output power and is more affordable but has a higher phase noise and shorter coherence time. The difference frequency between the sources $|f_M - f_S|$ lies in the primary n258 band [24.25, 27.5] GHz globally adopted [3].

Electro-Absorption Modulator (EAM): The electro-absorption modulator allows the creation of spectral components at $f_S \pm 24.75\,\text{GHz}$. Homodyne detection will be performed between the master laser beam and one harmonic generated by the modulation of the slave laser. The electrical RF source is used to modulate the output of the secondary laser to generate optical components at $f_{mmWave} = f_s \pm 24.75\,\text{GHz}$ (see Fig. 4). Its frequency is set to $\Omega = f_m - f_s = f_{mWave}$. Each spectral component has the same phase noise as the secondary laser.

Balanced Photodetection: Balanced photodetection is employed to characterize the signal resulting from the mixing of the two laser sources. This technique reduces intensity noise and enhances the signal-to-noise ratio. The phase noise of the resulting baseband signal is influenced by the phase noise of both the reference and slave lasers. These independent components are crucial for stabilizing phase fluctuations between the two sources. Figure 5 illustrates the output current from the balanced photodetection process. The balanced configuration significantly reduces intensity noise and enhances the

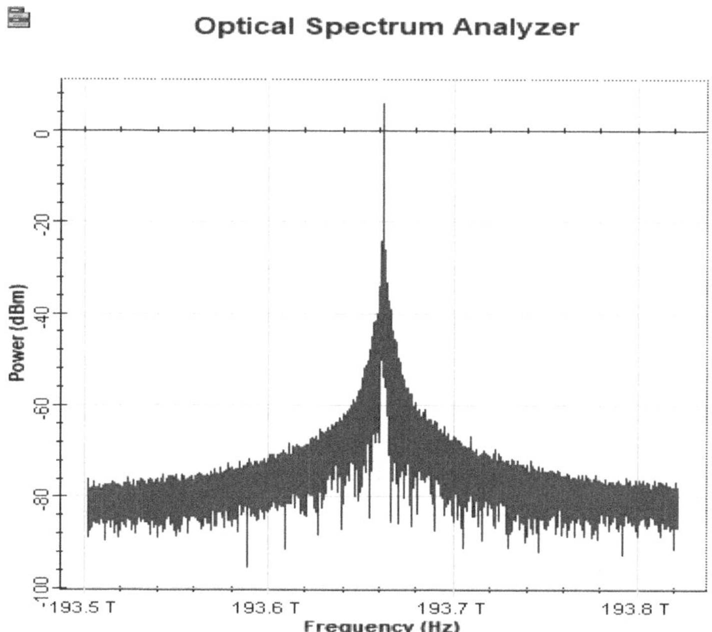

Fig. 2. Optical spectrum of the master laser

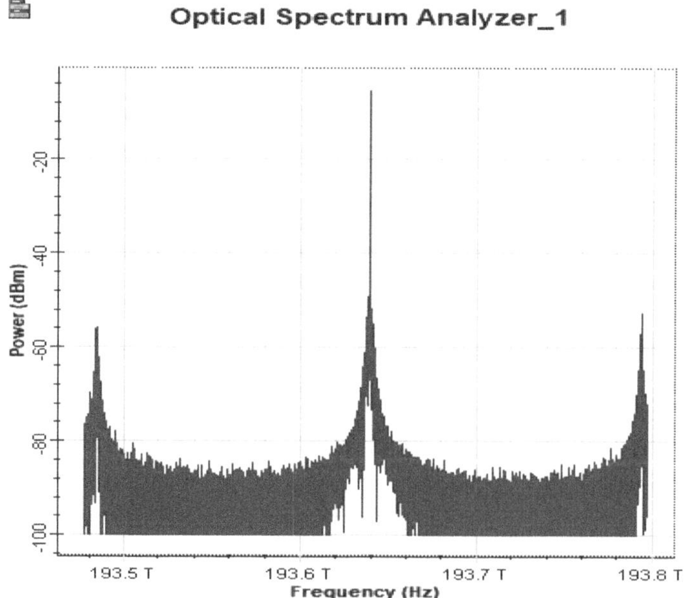

Fig. 3. Optical spectrum of the slave laser

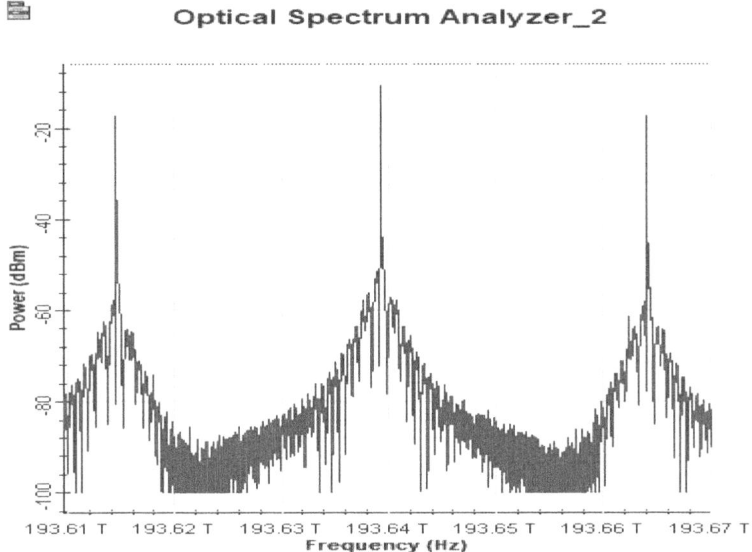

Fig. 4. Harmonics generation by EAM

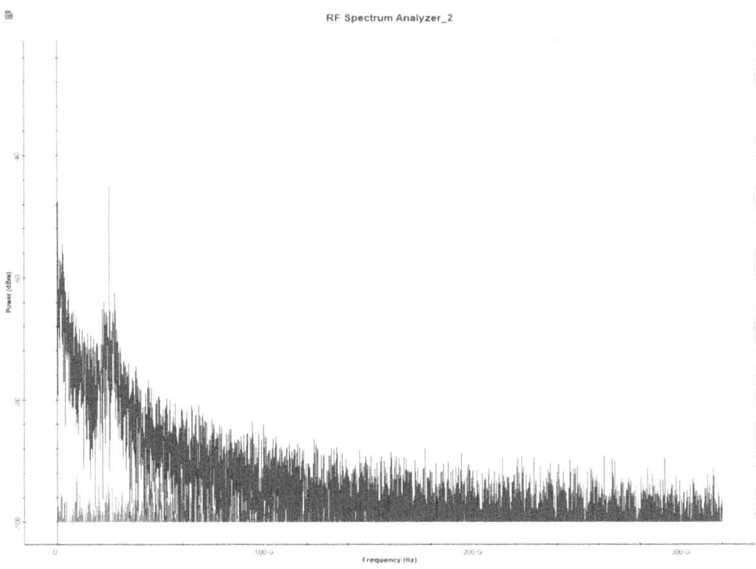

Fig. 5. Electrical spectrum of the balanced photodetection current

signal-to-noise ratio, making it possible to detect the mmWave carrier signal with minimized phase fluctuations. The electrical signal detected is a DC signal. Its amplitude is proportional to the phase difference between the two laser sources. This is the signal to

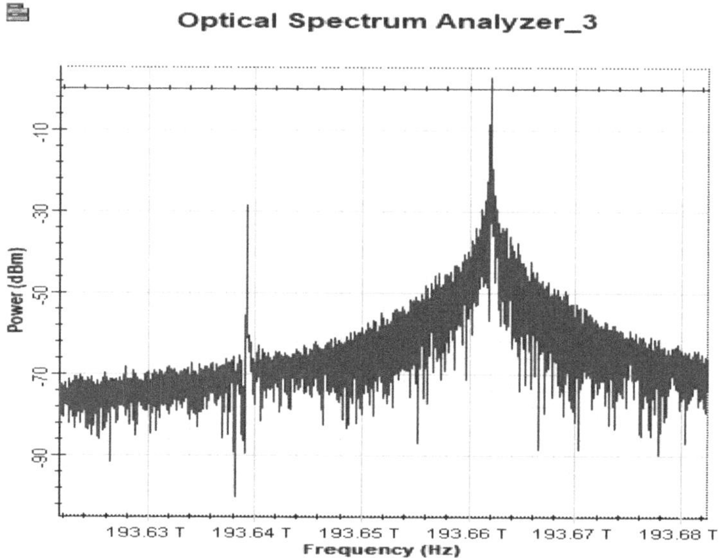

Fig. 6. Optical spectrum of the millimeter wave

process in order to feedback the loop oscillator (slave laser). The balanced configuration suppresses common noise.

Heterodyne Photodetection and Signal Transmission: The two optical signals mix in a photodetector to produce a mmWave. The detected signal includes a component at baseband spectrum and multiple harmonics of the form $nf_{ML} \pm mf_{SL}$. However, the detection range is limited to $f_{ML} - f_{SL}$ for the current available photodetectors.

The Optical Spectrum Analyzer (OSA) output shows two optical tones with a difference equal to the mmWave frequency $f_{mmWave} = 24.75$ GHz. Figure 6 depicts the optical spectrum resulting from the heterodyne mixing of the master and slave laser outputs. The two dominant tones represent the optical carriers, with a frequency difference precisely matching the desired millimeter-wave frequency (24.75 GHz). This demonstrates the system's ability to generate stable mmWave signals suitable for RoF applications.

The incident optical carriers at the photodetector generate an electrical signal. Figure 7 presents the electrical spectrum from the Electrical Spectrum Analyzer (ESA) obtained at the photodetector output. The dominant peak at 24.75 GHz confirms the successful generation of the desired mmWave frequency, making the transmitter suitable for high-speed, low-cost applications in the next generation networks. This compact transmittter with moderate phase noise can help overcome higher cost of proposed architecture [5].

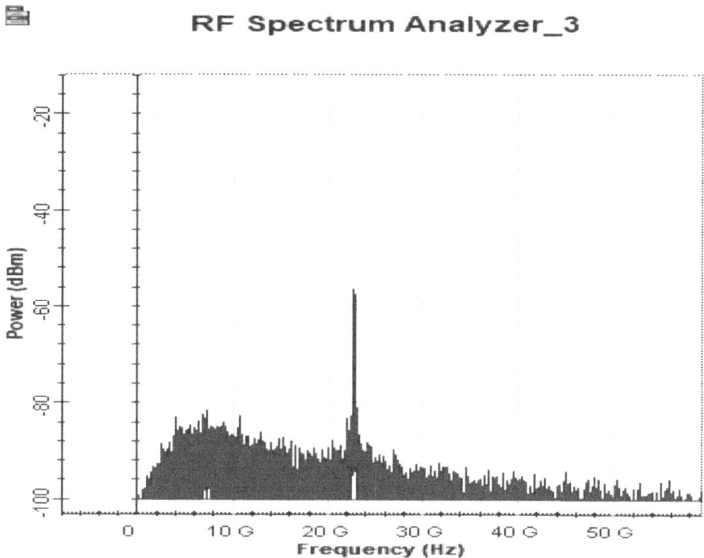

Fig. 7. Electrical spectrum of the millimeter wave

6 Conclusion and Futures Works

This study explored the design and simulation of a millimeter-wave transmitter model based on an Optical Phase-Locked Loop (OPLL) using OptiSystem software. The open-loop transmitter architecture successfully demonstrated stable millimeter-wave frequency generation through optical heterodyning, validating the feasibility of photonic-assisted millimeter-wave sources for high-speed, cost-efficient communication in next-generation 5G and 6G networks. While the closed-loop OPLL design remains a challenge, particularly in crafting a filter that balances phase noise suppression with loop stability. This limitation highlights opportunities for further optimization of integrated photonic and electronic feedback systems. Integrating Free Space Optical (FSO) technologies with the OPLL-based transmitter architecture opens new horizons for long-range, high-throughput communication. FSO links offer the potential to extend optical backhaul across challenging terrains where fiber is impractical, enabling rapid deployment in remote or underserved regions. This hybrid mmWave-over-FSO approach not only enhances spectral efficiency and physical layer security but also aligns with sustainable networking goals by reducing infrastructure demands. Future work will focus on completing the closed-loop implementation and experimentally evaluating the system under realistic environmental conditions. The integration of FSO transmission modules and dynamic beam-steering capabilities is also envisioned, supporting resilient and adaptive architectures for rural and edge network scenarios.

References

1. Ashtiani, F., Sanjari, P., Idjadi, M.H., Aflatouni, F.: High-resolution optical frequency synthesis using an integrated electro-optical phase-locked loop. IEEE Trans. Microwave Theor. Tech. **66** (2018). https://doi.org/10.1109/TMTT.2018.2878567
2. Coldren, L.A., Verrinder, P.A., Klamkin, J.: A review of photonic systems-on-chip enabled by widely tunable lasers. IEEE J. Quantum Electron. **58**(4), 1–10 (2022). https://doi.org/10.1109/JQE.2022.3168041
3. Dodane, D., et al.: Optical phase-locked loop phase noise in 5G mm-wave OFDM ARoF systems. Opt. Commun. **526**, 128872 (2023)
4. Enloe, L., Rodda, J.: Laser phase-locked loop. Proc. IEEE **53**(2), 165–166 (1965). https://doi.org/10.1109/PROC.1965.3585
5. Hyodo, M., Saito, S., Kasai, Y.: Optical phase-locked loop with fibre lasers for low phase noise millimetre-wave signal generation. Electron. Lett. **45**(17), 905–906 (2009). https://doi.org/10.1049/el.2009.1533
6. Qualcomm: What is 5G? October 2019. https://www.qualcomm.com/5g/what-is-5g. Accessed Oct 2024
7. Qualcomm: Global 5G spectrum update and innovations for future wireless systems, May 2023. https://www.qualcomm.com/content/dam/qcomm-martech/dm-assets/documents/global-5g-spectrum-status-and-innovations-for-future-wireless-systems.pdf
8. Rappaport, T.S., et al.: Millimeter wave mobile communications for 5G cellular: it will work! IEEE Access **1**, 335–349 (2013)
9. Ristic, S., Bhardwaj, A., Rodwell, M.J., Johansson, L.A., Coldren, L.A.: An optical phase-locked loop photonic integrated circuit. J. Lightwave Technol. **28** (2010). https://doi.org/10.1109/JLT.2009.2030341
10. Satyan, N., Liang, W., Kewitsch, A., Rakuljic, G., Yariv, A.: Coherent power combination of semiconductor lasers using optical phase-lock loops. IEEE J. Sel. Top. Quant. Electron. **15** (2009). https://doi.org/10.1109/JSTQE.2008.2011490
11. Seeds, A.J.: Microwave photonics. IEEE Trans. Microw. Theor. Tech. **50**(3), 877–887 (2002)
12. Steed, R.J., et al.: Hybrid integrated optical phase-lock loops for photonic terahertz sources. IEEE J. Sel. Top. Q. Electron. **17** (2011). https://doi.org/10.1109/JSTQE.2010.2049003
13. Xiao, M., et al.: Millimeter wave communications for future mobile networks. IEEE J. Sel. Areas Commun. **35**(9), 1909–1935 (2017). https://doi.org/10.1109/JSAC.2017.2719924
14. Yang, X., Luo, C., Zhang, B., Qiu, B., Zhang, R.: Simulation and design of a pic-based heterodyne optical phase locked loop. Photonics **10** (2023). https://doi.org/10.3390/photonics10030336

Enhancing Vehicle Fitness Recording and Integrity Through Blockchain-Based Decentralised Application in Mauritius

Ashley Ujoodah, Visham Ramsurrun, Parvesh Seeburrun(✉), Karel Veerabudren, Mrinal Sharma, and Amar Seeam

Middlesex University, Uniciti, Flic-en-Flac, Mauritius
AU239@live.mdx.ac.uk, {v.ramsurrun,p.seeburrun,k.veerabudren, m.sharma,a.seeam}@mdx.ac.mu

Abstract. Vehicle inspection is required in Mauritius to ensure roadworthiness and passenger safety. During visits to vehicle fitness centres, various inspection flaws were identified, indicating potential collusion between staff and vehicle owners. Certain tests were omitted or not recorded in the centralised database, potentially favouring vehicle owners. Furthermore, manual entry of test results into the software introduced human errors and compromised data integrity, posing risks to the information's confidentiality, integrity, and availability. To address these issues and combat corruption, this project proposes a smart blockchain-based vehicle fitness recording decentralised application (DApp). Through in-depth analysis, a technologically secure blockchain platform was selected for storing fitness data while leveraging the Firebase Cloud backend-as-a-service infrastructure to enhance security and mitigate threats such as Man-in-the-Middle attacks. The DApp consists of two secure web applications: an examiner portal for conducting vehicle inspections and a supervisor portal for monitoring vehicle counts and reviewing blockchain transactions. The DApp successfully stored recorded values on the Ethereum Goerli Test Network using the Proof of Stake (PoS) consensus algorithm. Evaluation by programming experts yielded an overall QXScore of 85%, indicating positive user interface and user experience functionalities.

Keywords: Blockchain · Vehicle Fitness · Corruption · DApp

1 Introduction

In most countries, the vehicle examination exercise is a compulsory inspection procedure mandated by respective legislations, whereby the vehicle is closely inspected to conform to safety regulations and emissions and detects cases of forgery. Vehicle checks are often conducted periodically, for instance, every two years, depending on the age of the vehicle, before being issued with a certificate of fitness by an authorised examination body. Based on a quantitative survey by Cuerden et al. [1], car accidents attributed to technical flaws in vehicles vary from 19% in developed countries to as high

D. Bassole et al. (Eds.): InterSol 2025, LNICST 671, pp. 149–164, 2026.
https://doi.org/10.1007/978-3-032-15154-4_12

as 27% of reported cases in developing countries. Due to inherent business risks such as greed and financial problems, frauds are more likely to occur owing to technological deficiencies, whereby shortcomings in data confidentiality, integrity and availability are adversely exploited. For instance, examiners at fitness centres may deliberately omit critical checkpoints or modify internal database records in exchange for illegal gratuity. Within the Mauritian context, inappropriate tools and equipment at fitness centres like Autocheck Motor Vehicle Test Centre may potentially engender corruption cases. According to Le Défi Media Group [2], the NTA (now NLTA) claims to have obtained information whereby employees at private vehicle fitness centres were involved in cases of bribery. As such, the Blockchain technology along with a wallet-incorporated system, would enable immediate upload of inspection data captured by IoT sensors to a secure, immutable database for analysis and benchmarking.

2 Literature Review

The Literature Review section comprehensively analyses and compares existing research in vehicle fitness recording systems. It was observed that many studies focusing on enhancing current vehicle examination techniques had overlooked the crucial aspect of cybersecurity. In response, this research project aims to address this gap by employing a Blockchain-based approach to enhance data transparency, security, and traceability of recorded vehicle fitness information at examination centres in Mauritius. Additionally, this approach serves as a deterrent against potential corruption and bribery within these institutions. Through a thorough examination of reputable research journals such as IEEE Explore, ACM Digital Library, and Research Gate, various vehicle fitness recording systems have been identified and critically evaluated in terms of their data security, leveraging the principles of the CIA triad.

2.1 Vehicle Fitness Recording Systems in Mauritius

The National Land Transport Authority (NLTA) - Road Transport Division in Mauritius holds the responsibility for overseeing and inspecting a wide range of motor vehicles, including heavy motor vehicles, motor cars, autocycles, motor tractors, buses, locomotives, trailers, goods vehicles, and heavy vehicles. The vehicle inspections are conducted at designated centres such as the Autocheck Vehicle Test Centre (Port Louis), SGS Fitness Centre (Curepipe), and Eastern Vehicle Examination Station (Laventure). These inspections are categorised based on the specific vehicle types, and each category is associated with a dedicated payment price list. There is a higher cost associated with heavy vehicles, motor tractors, and locomotives because of the increased number of inspection checkpoints. These checkpoints include additional requirements like speed limiters for heavy vehicles, which necessitate a more thorough examination by inspectors when compared to autocycles and motor cars. As a result, the pricing structure reflects the comprehensive nature of the inspections and the specific requirements for different vehicle types.

Various tests are conducted to ensure that the inspected vehicle complies with the regulations enforced by the laws. These tests include the Identification of the Vehicle,

Test for Brake Efficiency, Visual Inspection, Verification of Chassis No. And Engine No., Test for Exhaust Emission, Side-Slip, Test for Suspension Efficiency, and Axle Play Detector. Each test has specific procedures and criteria as described below.

- Identification of Vehicle: Visual verification of registration number and detection of plate tampering to ensure compliance.
- Test for Brake Efficiency: Measure braking effort using mechanical rollers, checking front handle, rear pedal, and brake binding thresholds.
- Visual Inspection: Inspect various components of motorcycles/auto cycles and motor vehicles to ensure compliance with legal standards and design requirements.
- Verification of Chassis No. and Engine No.: Verify chassis number, engine number, engine capacity, and vehicle color against registration book.
- Test for Exhaust Emission: Determine hydrocarbon and carbon monoxide emissions under controlled conditions, with specific threshold values for petrol engines.
- Sideslip: Measure excessive toe in and toe out deviation from the vehicle's center line using a side slip plate assembly.
- Test for Suspension Efficiency: Evaluate spring oscillation and shock absorber resistance, with the damping rate falling within an acceptable range

The evaluation process for vehicle fitness at the three fitness centres in Mauritius was consistent, as they followed similar tests before issuing a certificate of fitness. A thorough examination of procedures used in two centres (Autocheck Vehicle Test Centre and Eastern Vehicle Examination Station) was conducted, noting the specific steps in evaluating a vehicle. Subsequently, a critical analysis was conducted to identify potential issues, such as delays, errors, and loopholes that may arise due to the current evaluation methods employed by the centres (Table 1).

The assessment reveals several noteworthy issues in the current examination process for vehicle fitness recording. These issues encompass the omission of examination tests, the vulnerability of a single-point-of-failure in the centralised database, incomplete uploading of test results, manual entry of comments for failed tests, concerns regarding data integrity, limited data transparency for vehicle owners, and the potential for data censorship. Consequently, the adoption of blockchain technology in the fitness recording system in Mauritius presents a promising solution to address these identified technological loopholes and mitigate potential malpractices. Blockchain integration can effectively enhance the reliability, security, and transparency of the vehicle fitness recording process, providing an improved and more trustworthy system.

2.2 Blockchain Background

Blockchain, a ground-breaking technology introduced by Nakamoto [3], brings a paradigm shift from traditional centralised systems. Unlike centralised systems, where a central authority, such as a bank or government institution, controls and verifies transactions and data, blockchain operates in a decentralised manner, enabling direct peer-to-peer transactions without intermediaries.

Varma [4] explained that blockchain is a decentralised, replicated, tamper-resistant (immutable), and append-only ledger of transactions. This means that transactions are recorded sequentially and permanently, and once recorded, they cannot be altered or

Table 1. Assessment of Examination Performed at Mauritian Fitness Centres

Tests	Autocheck Vehicle Test Centre	Eastern Vehicle Examination Station
Test for Exhaust Emission	Recorded values pertaining to hydrocarbons and carbon monoxide are automatically validated within the software before results are displayed. However, in case of test failure, i.e. excessive concentrations of gases are detected, Autocheck Vehicle Test Centre claims that the examiner manually enters meaningful comments against the failed results within the software. Such practice could potentially influence the final decision of the supervisor, on whether to grant or revoke the vehicle's certificate of fitness	• Evidence of visual tampering is only subjective to the intelligence of the examiner, i.e. result of test may vary from one examiner to another • No image processing algorithm, such as Optical Character Recognition (OCR) is being used to detect cases of forgery or to identify the vehicle • Without image processing capabilities, the visual inspection process is subject to potential bribery and moral hazards
Side-Slip	Test results are automatically validated within the software Similar to the case of exhaust emission test, comments are entered manually against failed test results, which may lead to wrongly approving a vehicle exam by the supervisor	Recorded value for side slip is uploaded to the central database when test is done
Test for Suspension Efficiency	The software automatically validates test results recorded based on the suspension efficiency and damping rate obtained. However, comments added manually against failed results can negatively influence the final decision of the supervisor in approving the vehicle examination test	Recorded values are uploaded to the central database upon completion

(continued)

Table 1. (*continued*)

Tests	Autocheck Vehicle Test Centre	Eastern Vehicle Examination Station
Test for Brake Efficiency	Brake test efficiency values are automatically validated based on the threshold values in the software However, comments added manually against failed results can negatively influence the final decision of the supervisor in approving the vehicle examination test	Test results are uploaded to a dedicated central database located on premise
Visual inspection of vehicle	Visual inspection results are subjective to the intelligence of the examiner. For instance, an examiner may be more lenient and notify the vehicle owner if he detects a minimal degree of body rusts. The owner shall take responsibility to effect necessary repairs before the next vehicle fitness appointment or in the shortest delay	Inspections of steering system (poor alignment) and speedometer for auto cycles and motor cycles cannot be performed visually. To verify for wheel alignment, it is recommended to use an electronic wheel alignment tester that measures any misalignment detected with respect to the motorcycle wheels
Test for Noise Emission	Noise Emission Test is performed with a standalone sound level meter. The data recorded is not transmitted to any database or dedicated repository. Thus, decibel values obtained may be potentially altered so that the vehicle conforms as per Section 114 (3) of the Road Traffic Act	N/A

deleted. This immutability ensures the integrity and transparency of the transaction history. Table 2 below shows the key differences between a centralised and a decentralised system.

In a blockchain network, transactions are organised into blocks and linked together using cryptography to form an immutable chain. Once a block is added to the chain, the data it contains becomes highly resistant to alteration or tampering. The decentralised nature of blockchain removes the need for intermediaries, allowing participants to engage in direct transactions. This eliminates traditional intermediaries' costs, delays, and complexities, increasing efficiency and faster transactions. The system's security is maintained as long as at least 51% of the participating nodes are honest and in control of the network.

Table 2. Key Comparisons between Centralised and Decentralised Systems [5]

Aspect	Centralised System	Decentralised System
Maintained by	Single trusted third party	Multiple participating nodes
Transaction Ledger	Singular copy maintained	Exact copy maintained by all nodes
Forgery of Transactions	Possible through modification	Transactions are irreversible
Data Repository Vulnerability	Vulnerable to cyberattacks and corruption	Maintains confidentiality and security
Transparency and Trust	Limited transparency	Provides transparency and trust
Control and Ownership	Controlled by central authority	Distributed control and ownership

According to the research by Huang et al. [5], Blockchain technologies can be classified into three categories: public, private, and consortium. These categories exhibit distinct characteristics and serve different purposes depending on their specific applications, as shown in Table 3.

Public Blockchain. The public blockchain is a distributed ledger that operates openly, allowing any peer-to-peer protocol used to access and modify it anonymously [6]. The immutability of the blockchain is achieved through synchronising a complete copy of the ledger across all nodes [7].

One key advantage of the blockchain is its ability to function without the need for mutual trust among nodes, as each node possesses unique private and public keys. Consequently, transactions can be validated and verified without relying on a trusted third party. Furthermore, the transparency of the blockchain enables public access to all transactions for verification purposes [8]. However, it is essential to note that the blockchain may exhibit performance limitations when processing a large volume of transactional requests due to the periodic stages involved in transaction verification, as highlighted by Falazi et al. [9].

Private Blockchain. According to Zheng et al. [10], a private Blockchain is a fully controlled centralised network where individuals seeking participation in the blockchain network must obtain specific authorisation from the governing organisation [11].

Once authorised, nodes collaborate to establish a decentralised network, where each node maintains a copy of the blockchain and collectively reaches a consensus on updates. However, unlike public blockchains, private blockchains impose limitations on writing access [7].

Consortium Blockchain. The consortium blockchain, as described [11], shares similarities with a private blockchain, with the distinction being that it is controlled by a consortium or a group of organisations. As a result, it exhibits a partially decentralised nature. Consensus and block validation within the consortium blockchain are handled by a predetermined set of nodes, employing a multi-signature approach for block confirmation [7].

Compared to public blockchains, consortium blockchains demonstrate superior performance in terms of transaction processing speed, transaction and maintenance costs, as well as data security [11].

Table 3. Blockchain Taxonomy [12]

	Public Blockchain	Private Blockchain	Consortium Blockchain
Participants	Anyone	Individuals/companies	Consortium members
Consensus Mechanism	PoW/PoS/DPoS	Distributed consistent alg	Distributed consistent alg
Bookkeeper	Anyone	Custom	Consortium negotiation
Validation Speed	Slow	Fast	Medium
Transaction Data	Public	Semi-public	Private
Network	P2P network	Fast network	Fast network
Typical Applications	Cryptocurrency	Audit	Payment

2.3 Related Works

Many studies have been conducted within vehicle inspections, albeit with limited emphasis on comprehensive assessments of a vehicle's roadworthiness before obtaining a certificate of fitness. They are elaborate below.

Pan et al. [13] introduced an innovative approach for evaluating and enhancing the braking performance dynamics of vehicles. By utilising IoT sensors or intelligent sensor units, they aimed to address the limitations of conventional methods in accurately measuring brake performance parameters for each wheel independently and providing comprehensive brake health status. To achieve this, sensor modules were strategically positioned on the vehicle body and wheels to capture real-time three-dimensional acceleration data and timestamps. These data were wirelessly transmitted via Zigbee to a central processing module for signal conditioning. However, it is essential to note that a research paper by Olawumi et al. [14] uncovered various vulnerabilities and potential attacks from the Zigbee technology. These attacks include reconnaissance and scanning techniques to gather information about Zigbee-enabled devices and configurations, passive eavesdropping to intercept encrypted/unencrypted network traffic, and replay attacks involving capturing and retransmitting data to deceive the sender. Furthermore, it should be highlighted that the research did not establish benchmarks based on relevant regulations or threshold parameters to conclusively assess the vehicle's braking performance and determine its roadworthiness.

In their study, Vong et al. [15] proposed a method for actively monitoring and evaluating the air ratio of harmful engine emissions to assess the engine health status of vehicles. This approach utilised wireless sensor networks (WSN) or RFIDs, with lambda sensors capturing the air-ratio signal of exhaust emissions. The captured data were wirelessly transmitted from the RFID tag on the vehicle to the RFID interrogator (a red traffic light) and backend server for analysis and benchmarking. However, it should be noted that the proposed network architecture presented particular security vulnerabilities that could compromise critical security services, particularly confidentiality and integrity. The transmission of unencrypted data, including the values for the RFID tag and lambda, over an untrusted public domain could make the system susceptible to potential attacks such as Man-In-The-Middle attacks, where unauthorised entities could intercept and manipulate the data. Additionally, WSNs have been identified as vulnerable to various attacks, including jamming and replay attacks [16]. Furthermore, the study did not address database security measures, leaving room for potential data tampering and unauthorised access.

In their research paper, Tao et al. [17] presented a double-station mechanism aimed at segregating vehicles that could disrupt the flow of the inspection line and cause blockages and vehicle queues. The proposed method involved four dedicated workstations that performed different inspections, including exhaust fume and decibel level checks, as per the Chinese Government's Safety Specifications. The system followed a client-server model, where data collected by control computers at the workstations were transmitted to a central server over 10/100MB Ethernet cables via TCP/IP. However, despite its functional prototype status, the authors' paper highlighted several security and system resiliency flaws. These included centralising core databases on a single server, which created a single point of failure (SPOF) scenario where system unavailability could disrupt the entire inspection process. The proposed network design lacked a High Availability (HA) mechanism, multi-factor authentication (MFA) for enhanced security, and data protection against illegal tampering.

Tapak et al. [18] proposed using a dedicated Android application called MSTK to enable authorised technicians to perform periodic vehicle inspections in compliance with the regulations of the Slovak Republic. The app implemented a validation process to authenticate the identity of technicians before conducting inspections. During the examination, the app required technicians to capture images of the vehicle's identification number (VIN), odometer readings, and Onboard Diagnostics (OBD) data, which were instantly transmitted to a national server for analysis. Although the inspection results depended on the accuracy of the smartphone device, the authors claimed that the outcome was sufficient for periodic vehicle technical inspections. However, it is essential to note that the OBD interface is connected via Bluetooth serial port, making it vulnerable to potential Man-in-the-Middle attacks, such as the Blue Borne attack, which could alter the collected inspection data.

In their qualitative and quantitative study, Hermawan and Suhardi [19] thoroughly assessed the transparency level in the current business process model of technical vehicle inspections in Bontang City, Indonesia. Through the application of SWOT analysis and the Six Sigma methodology, the authors identified significant shortcomings in the inspection procedure, leading to a slow and ineffective data inspection process and fostering opportunities for corruption and illegal gratuities. The study highlighted instances where certain inspection areas were unknown to higher management, resulting in a lack of system comprehension and creating room for the manipulation of collected data. Overall, the findings revealed a non-transparent vehicle fitness system plagued by corruption.

In their work, Jiang and Sun [20] presented a novel solution for decentralising the second-hand vehicle market in Taiwan by implementing a private blockchain-based recording system. The objective was to enhance transparency and authenticity in the business, as the current market is dominated by second-hand dealers, raising concerns about the potential tampering of vehicle data provided to customers. To address these issues, the authors developed an Ethereum private blockchain infrastructure in collaboration with trusted government entities and integrated a user-friendly front-end interface. This enabled customers to access the blockchain-based database system, ensuring the retrieval of tamper-proof and highly reliable information about specific vehicles. Furthermore, the proposed method's processing capacity was evaluated, demonstrating sufficient scalability to support day-to-day transactions.

Existing research primarily focuses on specific technical aspects of vehicles to improve conventional inspection methods. However, there is a significant gap in the literature regarding comprehensive examinations encompassing the overall vehicle roadworthiness assessment using blockchain technology. Therefore, further investigation is necessary to fill this research gap and devise innovative approaches that enhance the efficiency and precision of the certification process. This study aims to serve as a foundation for addressing this gap and advancing the field in this direction.

3 Development

This section will explore the interconnected entities facilitating seamless communication within the context of a blockchain-based vehicle fitness recording Decentralised Application (DApp). The discussion will focus on the system's inherent versatility, simplicity, and functionality, highlighting the various components and their interactions.

3.1 Methodology

The development methodology for creating the blockchain-based vehicle fitness recording DApp followed a prototyping approach. The preliminary design was initially conceptualised based on a thorough analysis of the functional requirements. Subsequently, an iterative development process was adopted, which involved building successive versions of the DApp and conducting rigorous testing to identify any shortcomings or deviations from the desired functionality. Issues and challenges encountered during the testing phase were promptly addressed, allowing for quick resolution and improvement of the application. This iterative process, coupled with continuous feedback and collaboration with stakeholders, facilitated the refinement of the DApp to ensure that it met their specific needs and expectations. Throughout the development lifecycle, a strong emphasis was placed on maintaining transparency, traceability, and security by leveraging the inherent benefits of blockchain technology.

3.2 Requirements

The functional requirements for the system include a login feature for supervisors/examiners via Firebase Google Cloud authentication, vehicle search by category from the Firebase Google Cloud real-time database, display of valid vehicle details, connection to the blockchain using Metamask crypto-wallet, storage of test results on the blockchain, retrieval of test results from the blockchain, generation of unique transaction hash values, display of total tested vehicles per category, invoice/printout generation for tested vehicles, submission of details and results to the supervisor, access to Etherscan Blockchain Explorer, and DApp monitoring from the supervisor dashboard. These requirements ensure secure access, accurate data retrieval, transparent and immutable storage of test results, and effective system performance monitoring.

The non-functional requirements for the system include security, privacy, usability, scalability, consistency, and robustness. The blockchain's inherent security ensures that data tampering is impracticable due to the consensus mechanism, cryptographic encryption, and data decentralisation. Privacy and confidentiality are maintained by storing only test results on the blockchain without personal information. At the same time, vehicle and client details are kept on a Cloud database with data protection policies. The interface is user-friendly, ensuring ease of use and clear instructions. The system is scalable, allowing for more tests without performance impact. Consistency is achieved through the unique transaction hash, and the system is robust in handling erroneous input by providing appropriate feedback to the user.

3.3 Implementation

The selection of the MetaMask crypto wallet for the blockchain-based vehicle fitness recording DApp was based on several factors. MetaMask demonstrated scalability by offering interoperability across various blockchain solutions, allowing seamless integration with different networks. Additionally, its robust security standards, validated through comprehensive independent audits, ensured the safe transfer of funds and facilitated the retrieval of stored values from the designated smart contract address on the test network (Fig. 1).

Ethereum was chosen as the core blockchain technology for recording vehicle fitness data due to its unique features and benefits. Ethereum's implementation of gas fees for transactions helps prevent issues like infinite loops, denial of service attacks, and spamming. The extensive network of Ethereum nodes ensures high availability and minimises downtime, providing reliable service for the DApp.

The Hardhat Blockchain Development Framework was employed to develop and test smart contract functionalities. Hardhat's flexibility, comprehensive console log functionality, and support for the JavaScript language made it an ideal choice. The Ethers.js

Fig. 1. Proposed Architecture Overview

library, integrated with Hardhat, provided concise and efficient code snippets for easy reference and streamlined development.

To connect the DApp with the Ethereum network, the Alchemy API was utilised. Alchemy utilises a remote procedure call (RPC) URL, enabling efficient interaction with the Ethereum Virtual Machine (EVM) network. The scalability and ease of use offered by Alchemy were key factors in its selection, as it required no additional setup to enhance DApp functionalities. Moreover, Alchemy boasts high reliability, with an impressive claimed uptime of 99.9% and widespread adoption powering over 70% of Ethereum DApps worldwide.

4 Evaluation

Software evaluation in computer science engineering constitutes a critical stage within the product development lifecycle, facilitating the systematic collection of quantitative and qualitative data from a specific user cohort. The primary objective of this evaluation is to validate customer requirements and enhance the final product iteratively. In this context, the developed blockchain application necessitates a thorough evaluation from a user-centric standpoint to ascertain its conformity with the intended requirements and identify areas that may require further refinement and optimisation.

When assessing the extent of a software's integration into users' daily work routines, the Technology Acceptance Model (TAM) introduced by Fred Davis in 1985 has emerged as the predominant framework for scientifically evaluating the product's perceived usability and actual usage. The TAM revolves around two key determinants: perceived usefulness and perceived ease of use. However, an alternative evaluation methodology was adopted due to the unavailability of consent from vehicle examination centres to engage examiners and supervisors in evaluating the Vehicle Fitness DApp using TAM. This methodology incorporates the well-established techniques of Heuristics and Cognitive Walkthroughs, integrating them into a unified metric system that quantifies user attitudes towards the application and DApp functionalities, culminating in a comprehensive QXscore [21]. The QXscore represents a consolidated User Interface (UI) and User Experience (UX) measure for the Vehicle Fitness DApp, providing insights into the overall performance and identifying strengths and weaknesses from the user's perspective.

4.1 Hypothesis

The two outlined evaluation methods for user interface (UI) and user experience (UX) are presented below to calculate the final QXscore value. These methods are employed to thoroughly analyse the UI design and overall UX of the Vehicle Fitness DApp, facilitating a comprehensive assessment of its user-centred performance.

Heuristics Evaluation: Under the study of Schmidt et al. (2020), the heuristic evaluation method, initially introduced by Jakob Nielsen and Rolf Molich in 1990, involves a comprehensive examination conducted by usability experts to assess the UI/UX design of the interface. These experts utilise a set of ten salient heuristic checklists, as proposed by Nielsen and Molich [22], to identify areas for improvement and enhance the overall user experience. They are illustrated in the table below (Table 4).

Table 4. Heuristic Checklists

Heuristic No	Heuristics Checklist
H1	System Status is clearly visible
H2	There is a match between the actual system and the real world
H3	User Control and Freedom
H4	Consistency and Standards
H5	Error Prevention Control
H6	Recognition rather than Recall
H7	Flexibility and Efficiency of Use
H8	System is aesthetic, with minimalist design
H9	System can help its Users to recognise, diagnose and recover from potential errors
H10	Help and Documentation

Cognitive Walkthrough (CW) Evaluation: The evaluation method developed by Lewis and Wharton in 1997, as mentioned in the study by Schmidt et al. [23], involves evaluators performing a series of specific tasks on the user interface while considering the thought processes of a typical user. Feedback obtained through this method is based on the following criteria described in the table below (Table 5).

Table 5. Cognitive Walkthroughs Checklists

CW No	Cognitive Walkthrough Checklist
CW1	UI's first look and Impression
CW2	Ease with which user can navigate across UI and determine his/her next steps with minimal errors
CW3	Extent to which buttons and input forms function the manner the user thinks they would
CW4	To what extent the process workflow meets the user's expectation
CW5	How far the terminologies used are familiar to the user
CW6	To what extent are information present on the UI useful to the user to accomplish tasks

4.2 Results and Discussion

Data to perform the QXscore was collected through a questionnaire which was divided into two sections: Heuristics and Cognitive Walkthroughs. The participants were aged from 18 to 40 years old, and their years of experience in the industry ranged from 1 up to 15. The data was collected for each Heuristics and Cognitive Walkthrough discussed earlier. The QXscore was then calculated, summarising the results in the figure below (Fig. 2).

Participants	H1	H2	H3	H4	H5	H6	H7	H8	H9	H10	CW1	CW2	CW3	CW4	CW5	CW6	Final Av. QXscore (%)
P1	9.8	10	10	10	10	9.8	10	10	9.9	10	10	10	10	10	10	10	
P2	9	7.8	8	8.5	9.5	7	8.1	8.5	9	6	7.2	7.3	9	7	8	8.5	
P3	8	6.5	6.5	9	5	9	9	7.6	8	8.1	6.5	8	6	8	5.9	8	
P4	8	8	7.5	8	9	8	8	7.5	7.5	7.5	8	8	8	8	9	9	
P5	8.2	8.5	8.7	8	9.1	8.8	8.5	9	8.5	7	9	8.5	8.7	7.5	8.7	8.8	
P6	9.5	9.5	9.8	9	9.2	9.9	10	9.7	9.8	9.8	9.8	10	10	9	10	9.9	
P7	8.3	8.4	8.2	8.8	8.7	8.6	9.1	7	8.4	8.8	8.4	8.8	9.2	9.4	9	9	
P8	8.2	7.8	8.1	7.7	7.8	7.9	8.1	8.5	8.4	7.7	7.7	7.9	7.8	7.9	8	8.4	
P9	8	9	7	9	9	8	8	7	8	6	6	5	8	8	10	8	
P10	8	8	8.6	7.4	8.5	8.1	7.6	7.4	7.5	8.3	8	7.6	8.5	7.8	9.2	8.2	
P11	9.2	9.3	9.2	9.3	9.5	9.3	9.1	9.3	9.2	9.1	9.2	9.2	9.3	9.3	9.3	9.2	
Average Qxscore	**8.56**	**8.57**	**8.33**	**8.38**	**9.03**	**8.22**	**8.68**	**8.45**	**8.53**	**8.02**	**8.31**	**8.06**	**8.77**	**8.17**	**9.02**	**8.62**	**84.8**

Fig. 2. Finding the final QXscore for the Vehicle Fitness DApp

Based on the final QXscore obtained from the heuristics and cognitive walkthrough evaluations conducted by expert users, it can be concluded that the vehicle fitness DApp has had a positive impact. The highest scores were observed for error prevention (9.03)

and familiarity with UI terminologies (9.02) on the UserZoom scorecard. This can be attributed to the implementation of various controls to prevent accidental or intentional data entry errors. The application also applied the principles of the five-plane model for UI Design Optimization proposed by Garrett [24] to enhance the UI terminologies.

By further analysing the QXscore table, it becomes evident that a consistently low score (around 6.0) was obtained for the heuristics category, specifically for H10 - Help and Documentation. This weakness in providing adequate help and contextual material for user interaction was identified as a significant area for improvement, as it was consistently highlighted in the evaluation. To enhance the overall user experience, it is crucial to address this issue by implementing an easily accessible search box with meaningful suggestions for vehicles, thus improving the performance of heuristics H10.

5 Conclusion

This paper implements a blockchain-based vehicle fitness recording DApp for examination centres in Mauritius. The DApp aims to enhance data transparency and traceability of vehicle test results by leveraging the security features of blockchain technology. Integrating a public Ethereum network into a user-friendly web application, the DApp provides a secure and efficient interface to mitigate potential corruption risks. Smart contracts serve as self-executing programs that execute the business logic. Surveys were conducted at local vehicle examination centers to analyse current examination practices. A comparative analysis of different blockchain architectures was performed to propose the most technologically-secure design for the DApp. The DApp was implemented based on recommended best practices and evaluated using the QXscore system, as permission was not granted for the TAM evaluation. The QXscore system incorporated heuristics and cognitive walkthroughs to gather quantitative and qualitative data. Analysis reveals that the proposed blockchain-based vehicle fitness DApp is a novel and pioneering technological solution for Mauritius.

Future work for this project involves enhancing the DApp by incorporating automated data input and processing. The sensor output values are manually entered into the DApp for storage on the Ethereum blockchain. However, to improve efficiency and eliminate human errors, future development should focus on programmatically binding the recorded values from actual sensors directly to the DApp. This would involve establishing seamless integration between the sensors and the DApp, ensuring that the data is automatically fed as input variables and submitted to the blockchain without any human intervention. Furthermore, the integration of Optical Character Recognition (OCR) technology can be explored to extract vehicle registration numbers from the NLTA database automatically. By converting image-to-text files, the DApp can search for registered vehicles, ensuring that only authorised vehicles undergo the examination procedure.

Additionally, the combination of Machine Learning (ML) and Machine Vision (MV) techniques, such as the C4.5 classifier proposed by Ravikumar et al. [25], can be implemented to improve defect detection under the vehicle. Defects identified can be logically classified as true (pass) or false (fail), and this information can be fed back to the DApp for storage on the blockchain. These future enhancements will further streamline the vehicle examination process, increase automation, and enhance the overall functionality and effectiveness of the DApp.

References

1. Cuerden, R.W., Edwards, M.J., Pittman, M.B.: Effects of vehicle defects in road accidents (2011)
2. Le Defi Media Group. Le Defi Media Group. Le Defi Media Group. http://defimedia.info/defimedia-home. Accessed 29 July 2023
3. Nakamoto, N.: Centralised Bitcoin: A Secure and High Performance Electronic Cash System. SSRN Journal (2017). https://doi.org/10.2139/ssrn.3065723
4. Varma, J.R.: Blockchain in finance. Vikalpa **44**(1), 1–11 (2019). https://doi.org/10.1177/0256090919839897
5. Rejeb, A., Rejeb, K., Keogh, J.G.: Centralized vs. decentralized ledgers in the money supply process: a SWOT analysis. Quant. Finance Econ. **5**(1), 40–66 (2021). https://doi.org/10.3934/QFE.2021003
6. Viriyasitavat, W., Hoonsopon, D.: Blockchain characteristics and consensus in modern business processes. J. Ind. Inf. Integr. **13**, 32–39 (2019). https://doi.org/10.1016/j.jii.2018.07.004
7. Puthal, D., Malik, N., Mohanty, S.P., Kougianos, E., Das, G.: Everything you Wanted to Know about the Blockchain (2018)
8. Yang, R., et al.: Public and private blockchain in construction business process and information integration. Autom. Constr. **118**, 103276 (2020). https://doi.org/10.1016/j.autcon.2020.103276
9. Falazi, G., Hahn, M., Breitenbucher, U., Leymann, F., Yussupov, V.: Process-based composition of permissioned and permissionless blockchain smart contracts. In: 2019 IEEE 23rd International Enterprise Distributed Object Computing Conference (EDOC), Paris, France: IEEE, pp. 77–87 (2019). https://doi.org/10.1109/EDOC.2019.00019
10. Zheng, Z., et al.: An overview of blockchain technology: architecture, consensus, and future trends. In: 2017 IEEE International Congress on Big Data (BigData Congress), Honolulu, HI, USA, pp. 557–564. IEEE (2017). https://doi.org/10.1109/BigDataCongress.2017.85
11. Atlam, H.F., Alenezi, A., Alassafi, M.O., Wills, G.B.: Blockchain with Internet of Things: benefits, challenges, and future directions. IJISA **10**(6), 40–48 (2018). https://doi.org/10.5815/ijisa.2018.06.05
12. Huang, J., et al.: The application of the blockchain technology in voting systems: a review. ACM Comput. Surv. **54**(3), 1–28 (2022). https://doi.org/10.1145/3439725
13. Pan, M., et al.: Research on the parameters measurement of vehicle brake performance in driving. In: 2021 2nd International Conference on Artificial Intelligence and Information Systems, Chongqing China: ACM, pp. 1–9 (2021). https://doi.org/10.1145/3469213.3469226
14. Olawumi, O., et al.: Three practical attacks against ZigBee security: attack scenario definitions, practical experiments, countermeasures, and lessons learned. In: 2014 14th International Conference on Hybrid Intelligent Systems, Kuwait, Kuwait, pp. 199–206. IEEE (2014). https://doi.org/10.1109/HIS.2014.7086198
15. Vong, C.-M., Wong, P.-K., Ip, W.-F.: Framework of vehicle emission inspection and control through RFID and traffic lights. In: Proceedings 2011 International Conference on System Science and Engineering, Macao, pp. 597–600. IEEE (2011). https://doi.org/10.1109/ICSSE.2011.5961973
16. Bhushan, B., Sahoo, G.: Recent advances in attacks, technical challenges, vulnerabilities and their countermeasures in wireless sensor networks. Wireless Pers. Commun. **98**(2), 2037–2077 (2018). https://doi.org/10.1007/s11277-017-4962-0
17. Tao, L., Xu, H., Zhang, Z.: Distributed inspecting and control system for motor vehicle safety performance. In: 2009 International Conference on Intelligent Human-Machine Systems and Cybernetics, Hangzhou, Zhejiang, China, pp. 384–387. IEEE (2009). https://doi.org/10.1109/IHMSC.2009.219

18. Tapak, P., et al.: Android application for periodical vehicle inspection. In: 2020 Cybernetics & Informatics (K&I), Velke Karlovice, Czech Republic, pp. 1–6. IEEE (2020). https://doi.org/10.1109/KI48306.2020.9039805
19. Hermawan, W., Suhardi.: Business process transparency in Vehicle Inspection unit, Department of Transportation, Information and Communication Technology, Bontang, East Kalimantan, Indonesia. In: 2013 Joint International Conference on Rural Information & Communication Technology and Electric-Vehicle Technology (rICT & ICeVT), Bandung, Indonesia, pp. 1–4. IEEE (2013). https://doi.org/10.1109/rICT-ICeVT.2013.6741490
20. Jiang, Y.-T., Sun, H.-M.: A blockchain-based vehicle condition recording system for second-hand vehicle market. Wireless Commun. Mob. Comput. **2021**, 1–10 (2021). https://doi.org/10.1155/2021/6623251
21. Ratcliff, C.: Introducing our holistic score for measuring user experience: QXscore|UserZoom (2021). https://www.userzoom.com/ux-blog/what-is-qxscore-single-ux-metric-for-measuring-ux/. Accessed 11 June 2023
22. Nielsen, J., Molich, R.: Heuristic evaluation of user interfaces. In: Proceedings of the SIGCHI conference on Human factors in computing systems Empowering people - CHI '90, Seattle, Washington, United States: ACM Press, pp. 249–256 (1990). https://doi.org/10.1145/97243.97281
23. Schmidt, M., Earnshaw, Y., Tawfik, A.A., Jahnke, I.: Methods of User Centered Design and Evaluation for Learning Designers (2020)
24. Garrett, J.J.: The Elements of User Experience: User-Centered Design for the Web and Beyond, 2nd edn. New Riders Publishing, USA (2010)
25. Ravikumar, S., Ramachandran, K.I., Sugumaran, V.: Machine learning approach for automated visual inspection of machine components. Expert Syst. Appl. **38**(4), 3260–3266 (2011). https://doi.org/10.1016/j.eswa.2010.09.012

A Comparative Study of CDL/TDL Channel Models in 5G-mmWave Networks

Mahamadi Sogoba[1], Désiré Guel[1](✉), and Boureima Zerbo[2]

[1] Université Joseph KI-ZERBO (U-JKZ), Ouagadougou, Burkina Faso
{mahamadi_sogoba,desire.guel}@ujkz.bf
[2] Université Thomas SANKARA (UTS), Saaba, Burkina Faso
boureima.zerbo@uts.bf

Abstract. Millimeter-wave (mmWave) bands play a key role in 5G New Radio (5G-NR). They provide wider bandwidth and support much higher data rates. However, these bands also bring serious challenges. Signal propagation is more complex and affects system performance. This study fills an important gap. It compares two standard 3GPP channel models: Clustered Delay Line (CDL) and Tapped Delay Line (TDL). While many studies have looked at these models separately, few have compared them in realistic settings. We run simulations using CDL and TDL models defined by 3GPP. These models include both Line-of-Sight (LOS) and Non-Line-of-Sight (NLOS) conditions. We analyze key parameters like delay profile, delay spread, maximum Doppler shift, carrier frequency, and antenna setup. Performance is measured using Signal-to-Noise Ratio (SNR) and Block Error Rate (BLER). The results are clear. In NLOS, CDL models perform better than TDL. At 25 dB SNR, CDL-C achieves a BLER of 0.02%, compared to 0.3% for TDL-C. In LOS, CDL-D shows a BLER of 0.06%, while TDL-E reaches 6.495×10^{-5}%. These results highlight the need to choose the right channel model. Accurate modeling improves performance evaluation and network optimization. Finally, the study shows how advanced signal processing can reduce mmWave transmission issues.

Keywords: 5G-NR · NR-PDSCH · CDL/TDL channels · mmWave bands · BLER · SNR

1 Introduction

5G mobile networks in the mmWave spectrum promise high data rates, increased capacity, and new applications for IoT, virtual reality, and augmented reality. However, mmWave frequencies bring challenges such as higher path loss, multipath propagation, Doppler spread, and blockage and interference [1]. To evaluate the performance of 5G-NR systems under realistic propagation condi-

D. Bassole et al. (Eds.): InterSol 2025, LNICST 671, pp. 165–179, 2026.
https://doi.org/10.1007/978-3-032-15154-4_13

tions, standardized channel models—namely the Clustered Delay Line (CDL) and Tapped Delay Line (TDL) models—have been developed by the 3rd Generation Partnership Project (3GPP) [2]. CDL captures spatial effects better, while TDL is simpler and faster for simulations [3]. However, a direct comparison of these models in terms of BLER and SNR in real scenarios remains underexplored. This paper aims to fill this gap. We compare CDL and TDL models under real 5G-NR mmWave conditions. Unlike previous studies, we consider realistic 3GPP-defined parameters, such as delay profiles and Doppler effects. We evaluate BLER and SNR in both LOS and NLOS conditions. Our findings provide practical insights for improving 5G-NR deployments. The paper is structured as follows: Sect. 2 covers related work, Sect. 3 details the methodology, Sect. 4 presents the results, and Sect. 5 offers conclusions and future directions.

2 Background and Related Work

2.1 5G MmWave Technology

5G networks operate across three primary frequency ranges: low bands (below 1 GHz), mid bands (1–6 GHz), and high bands (above 24 GHz), including millimeter-wave (mmWave) frequencies [2,4]. Among these, mmWave technology has emerged as a key enabler for 5G networks due to its large bandwidth availability and the potential for high data rates [5]. The advantages and challenges of mmWave technology are summarized in Table 1.

Table 1. Advantages and Challenges of mmWave Technology in 5G Networks

Category	Details
Advantages of mmWave Technology	
High data rates	Enables multi-Gbps rates for VR, AR, and video streaming [1,5].
Low latency	Supports URLLC for autonomous driving and industrial automation [6,7].
Massive connectivity	Connects many devices in small areas with high spectrum efficiency [4].
Limitations and Challenges	
Limited range	High path loss limits range to a few hundred meters [8].
Susceptibility to obstacles	Sensitive to blockage from buildings, trees, and human bodies [6].
Mobility and Doppler shift	Doppler shift affects connectivity in high-mobility scenarios [7].

2.2 Characteristics of CDL/TDL Models

The CDL/TDL channel models are two fundamental approaches used to model the propagation characteristics in wireless communication systems, particularly in 5G mmWave networks [2,3]. These models enable the representation of complex interactions between multipath components while adapting to a variety of scenarios, ranging from stationary to highly dynamic and high-mobility environments.

The TDL (Tapped Delay Line) model is designed to represent multipath propagation environments using a set of paths (*taps*) characterized by specific delays, powers, and Doppler shifts. This model is mainly used for fast and straightforward network performance evaluations, particularly in non-MIMO scenarios. The TDL profiles include:

- TDL-A, TDL-B, TDL-C: Designed for Non-Line-of-Sight (NLOS) scenarios.
- TDL-D, TDL-E: Suitable for Line-of-Sight (LOS) scenarios, considering specific fading distributions (Barb et al., 2019) [2,3].

The TDL model is widely used for its simplicity and flexibility, as it allows realistic channel simulations under various conditions (3GPP, 2018; Barb et al., 2019; Moltchanov et al., 2022) [1–3]. It is defined by the following equations (3GPP, 2018) [9]:

- Channel Impulse Response:

$$h(t,\tau) = \sum_{m=1}^{M} \alpha_m e^{j\psi_m} \delta(\tau - \tau_m) e^{j2\pi f_{D_m} t}, \tag{1}$$

  where:
  - M: Number of *taps* or multipath components.
  - α_m: Complex amplitude of tap m.
  - ψ_m: Phase of tap m.
  - τ_m: Delay of tap m.
  - f_{D_m}: Doppler shift of tap m.
- Doppler Spectrum per Tap:

$$S(f) \propto \frac{1}{\sqrt{1 - \left(\frac{f}{f_{D_m}}\right)^2}}, \quad \text{for } |f| \leq f_{D_m}, \tag{2}$$

  where f_{D_m} is the maximum Doppler frequency.
- Tap Power:

$$P_m = P_0 e^{-\frac{\tau_m}{\tau_{\text{rms}}}}, \tag{3}$$

  where:
  - P_0: Total channel power.
  - τ_m: Delay of tap m.
  - τ_{rms}: RMS delay spread.

– Ricean or Rayleigh Fading (for LOS or NLOS):

$$f(\alpha) = \begin{cases} \frac{\alpha}{\sigma^2} e^{-\frac{\alpha^2}{2\sigma^2}}, & \text{(Rayleigh, NLOS)} \\ \frac{\alpha}{\sigma^2} e^{-\frac{\alpha^2+K}{2\sigma^2}} I_0\left(\frac{\alpha\sqrt{2K}}{\sigma^2}\right), & \text{(Ricean, LOS)} \end{cases} \tag{4}$$

where:

- σ^2: Fading variance.
- K: Rice factor (LOS).
- I_0: Modified Bessel function of the first kind and order zero.

The TDL model is widely used for fast evaluations in both NLOS and LOS scenarios by adjusting tap parameters. It facilitates the study of temporal and Doppler diversity through tap delays and Doppler spectra, enabling realistic multipath effect simulations in both indoor and outdoor environments. The CDL model, an advanced 3D extension of TDL, organizes paths into clusters and incorporates angular information (AoA, AoD, ZoA and ZoD), making it ideal for Massive MIMO and dynamic environments (Moltchanov et al., 2022) [1]. CDL-A to CDL-C target various indoor and suburban scenarios, while CDL-D and CDL-E are suited for high mobility, complex settings.
The CDL model is defined by the following equations (3GPP, 2018) [9]:

– General Channel Expression:

$$h(t, \tau, \theta, \phi) = \sum_{n=1}^{N} \sum_{m=1}^{M} \alpha_{n,m} e^{j\psi_{n,m}} \delta(\tau - \tau_{n,m}) e^{j2\pi f_{D_{n,m}} t}, \tag{5}$$

where:

- N: Number of *clusters*.
- M: Number of sub-paths per cluster.
- $\alpha_{n,m}$: Complex amplitude of sub-path (n, m).
- $\psi_{n,m}$: Phase of sub-path (n, m).
- $\tau_{n,m}$: Delay of sub-path (n, m).
- $f_{D_{n,m}}$: Doppler shift of sub-path (n, m).

– Angular Distribution (AoA, AoD, ZoA and ZoD):

$$\begin{aligned} \theta_{n,m} &\sim \mathcal{N}(\theta_n, \sigma_\theta), \\ \phi_{n,m} &\sim \mathcal{N}(\phi_n, \sigma_\phi), \end{aligned} \tag{6}$$

where:

- $\theta_{n,m}$ and $\phi_{n,m}$: Angle/Zenith of arrival and departure for sub-path (n, m).
- $\mathcal{N}$: Gaussian distribution with mean θ_n or ϕ_n and standard deviation σ_θ or σ_ϕ.

– Power per Cluster:

$$\mathrm{P}_n = \frac{\mathrm{P}_0}{\mathrm{N}} e^{-\frac{\tau_n}{\tau_{\mathrm{rms}}}}, \tag{7}$$

where:

- P_0: Total power.
- τ_n: Mean delay of cluster n.
- τ_{rms}: RMS delay spread.

Table 2. Existing Channel Models and CDL/TDL in 5G Standardization

Category	Details
Existing Models and Limitations	
Ray-based models	Simulates LOS/NLOS using ray tracing; high computational cost in complex environments [1,6].
Stochastic models	Uses fading distributions (Rayleigh, Rice); fast but inaccurate in spatial correlation [3].
Hybrid models	Combines ray-based and stochastic models; complex to implement at large scale [1].
Role of CDL/TDL in 5G Standardization	
Clustered Delay Line (CDL)	Models spatial features (AoD, AoA); used in Massive MIMO and beamforming [3,9].
Tapped Delay Line (TDL)	Represents multipath components; simpler, used for single-antenna systems [2].

2.3 Channel Modeling for 5G MmWave

Channel modeling plays a crucial role in the design and performance evaluation of 5G mmWave networks. An accurate channel model allows for the simulation of realistic propagation conditions, enabling the development and optimization of key technologies such as beamforming, MIMO, and equalization [2,3] (Table 2).

2.4 Previous Research

Prior studies in 5G-NR mmWave networks span three key areas: (i) Channel modeling and performance, (ii) Phase noise mitigation, and (iii) Machine learning applications.

(i) **Channel Modeling and Performance:** Channel characteristics such as delay spread, Doppler, and antenna configuration critically impact mmWave performance. Naqvi et al. [7] emphasized the role of delay profiles in indoor coverage. Barb and Otesteanu [3] compared TDL/CDL models, while Tsoulos et al. [5] highlighted interference and antenna effects in field trials. Xu et al. [10] examined energy efficiency variability, and Alkhateeb et al. [11] proposed hybrid precoding to improve robustness. Kim et al. [6] explored sidelink reliability, and Moltchanov et al. [1] advanced channel modeling techniques.

(ii) **Phase Noise Estimation and Compensation:** High-frequency phase noise impairs mmWave signals. Dikarev et al. [12] used PT-RS for uplink enhancement, Guel et al. [13] demonstrated ZF/MMSE methods for QoS gains, and Park et al. [14] proposed MMSE-based CPE estimation to boost reliability.

(iii) **Machine and Deep Learning:** ML/DL approaches improve channel estimation and interference handling. Zehra et al. [8] improved PRACH detection via supervised learning. Dahal and Vaezi [15] applied multi-agent RL for interference management, and Weragama et al. [16] achieved high-accuracy CNN-based detection in 6G MIMO networks.

The Table 3 summarizes a selection of key studies, highlighting the methods used, application areas, and targeted performance. This analysis identifies current trends and innovative approaches while pointing out potential areas for improvement.

(i) **Channel Modeling and Performance in 5G mmWave:** Propagation characteristics like delay spread, Doppler effects, and antenna setup significantly affect mmWave performance. Naqvi et al. [7] improved indoor coverage using MMSE-based CPE in massive MIMO. Barb and Otesteanu [3] showed delay spread impacts BER and throughput. Tsoulos et al. [5] and Xu et al. [10] emphasized antenna configuration and energy efficiency. Alkhateeb et al. [11] proposed hybrid precoding to mitigate interference. Kim et al. [6] applied Gaussian filtering for V2X reliability, while Moltchanov et al. [1] advanced channel sounding for mmWave and THz bands.

(ii) **Phase Noise Estimation and Compensation:** Phase noise degrades mmWave signals. Dikarev et al. [12] used PT-RS for uplink improvement. Guel et al. [13] tested ZF/MMSE algorithms and ML for QoS enhancement. Park et al. [14] proposed MMSE-based CPE estimation. Waidhuba et al. [17] suggested dual-frequency MIMO backhaul to reduce interference.

(iii) **ML/DL for Channel Processing:** ML/DL methods address PRACH detection, interference, and decoding. Zehra et al. [8] improved PRACH with supervised learning and cognitive radio. Dahal and Vaezi [15] used multi-agent RL for interference. CNN-based models by Weragama [16] and Robinson [19] achieved high RF detection accuracy. Thompson [18] used DNNs to optimize NOMA multi-user detection.

2.5 Limitations of Existing Research

Despite notable advancements, current studies exhibit several persistent limitations. First, while ray-based approaches (e.g., ray tracing) provide accurate modeling [1], their computational complexity hinders real-time implementation. Second, conventional stochastic models (Rayleigh/Rice distributions) inadequately represent urban propagation characteristics, particularly complex spatial correlations and multipath components [3]. Furthermore, high-mobility scenarios present unresolved challenges, including significant Doppler shifts and frequent signal blockages [6,7]. Finally, existing phase noise compensation (CPE) techniques demonstrate both high computational overhead and environmental sensitivity [14].

Table 3. Main contributions in 5G-NR mmWave networks

References	Contributions	Application Domain	Techniques Used	Targeted Performance
Kim et al. (2021) [6]	Methodology and simulation	5G-NR mmWave networks	Gaussian filtering for phase noise	Phase error estimation and compensation
Barb et al. (2019) [3]	Simulation	CDL/TDL models for 5G	Delay Spread analysis	BER and user throughput
Dikarev et al. (2022) [12]	Theoretical review and simulation	5G mmWave	Phase noise models and channel simulation	Network performance optimization
Naqvi et al. (2021) [7]	Methodology and experimentation	CPE algorithms for 5G-NR	MMSE approach	Phase error reduction
Xu et al. (2020) [10]	Empirical study	Deployed 5G networks	Real-world performance analysis	Coverage, throughput, and energy consumption
Waidhuba et al. (2019) [17]	Architecture proposal	Wireless backhaul for 5G-NR	Dual-frequency Massive MIMO (sub-6GHz, mmWave)	Interference and latency reduction
Guel et al. (2024) [13]	Methodology and simulation	mmWave and IoT networks	Supervised learning algorithms	Network performance improvement
Moltchanov et al. (2022) [1]	Theoretical review	5G/6G at mmWave and THz bands	Mathematical channel modeling	Reliability and spectral efficiency
Zehra et al. (2022) [8]	Methodology and experimentation	5G PRACH networks	Reinforcement learning and cognitive radio	PRACH performance optimization
Thompson (2019) [18]	Methodology	NOMA for dense networks	Deep Neural Networks (DNN)	Multi-user detection improvement
Dahal et al. (2023) [15]	Simulation	Multi-cell mmWave networks	Multi-agent reinforcement learning	Interference reduction
Weragama et al. (2024) [16]	Methodology and simulation	MIMO systems for 6G	Convolutional Neural Networks (CNN)	Complex interference detection
Robinson et al. (2023) [19]	Methodology and experimentation	Dense wireless networks	CNN for RF detection	Improved interference management accuracy
Barb et al. (2019) [3]	Simulation and analysis	5G with CDL/TDL models	Comparative study of TDL/CDL profiles	Throughput and BER improvement

3 Methodology and Implementation

This section outlines the methodological framework and simulation protocol used to evaluate the performance of 5G-NR mmWave networks under CDL and TDL channel models. It details the key processing stages, simulation parameters, and performance evaluation metrics, highlighting the impact of channel and phase noise characteristics on system performance.

3.1 Framework Overview

The modeling of 5G-NR mmWave systems requires a complex processing chain that integrates several key stages, from channel coding to signal reception. This section describes the methodological framework used to simulate CDL/TDL channel models, estimate phase noise, and assess network performance. The goal is to analyze the influence of channel parameters on system performance in a realistic environment.

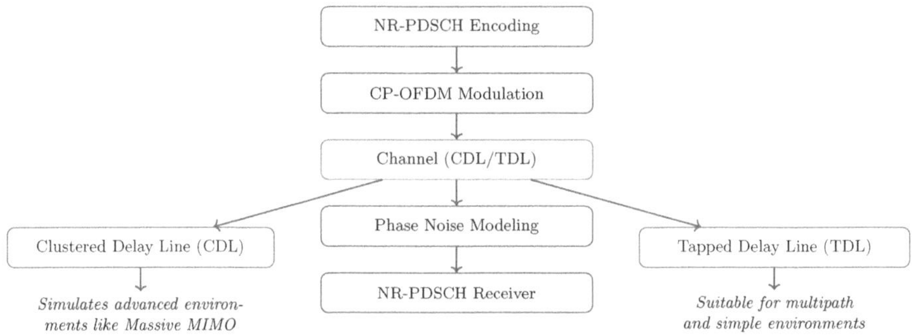

Fig. 1. NR-PDSCH processing chain including CDL/TDL channel models.

Figure 1 illustrates the processing chain used to evaluate phase noise models in 5G-NR mmWave systems. Accurate phase noise modeling enables identification and mitigation of phase errors, ensuring robust communication links and optimizing the overall precision of 5G-NR mmWave systems.

The various stages for NR-PDSCH (Physical Downlink Shared Channel) transmission and reception are described below:

(a) *NR-PDSCH Encoding*: Downlink data is encoded using LDPC or polar codes to ensure robustness through error correction.
(b) *CP-OFDM Modulation*: Encoded data is modulated via CP-OFDM, mapped to resource blocks, IFFT-transformed, and prefixed to combat multipath interference.
(c) *Phase Noise Modeling*: Phase noise is applied to reflect oscillator imperfections affecting signal integrity.

(d) *Channel (CDL/TDL)*: The signal traverses a CDL or TDL model to emulate real-world multipath propagation.
(e) *NR-PDSCH Receiver*: The receiver performs synchronization, demodulation, and MMSE-based CPE correction to recover the transmitted signal.

3.2 Simulation Parameters

The simulation considers various key parameters to evaluate the impact of propagation channels on the performance of 5G-NR mmWave networks (Table 4).

Table 4. Simulation parameters for CDL/TDL channel analysis

Category	Parameters	Values
Modulation and Signaling		
Modulation	Modulation Scheme	64-QAM
	Subcarrier Spacing	60 kHz
	Number of RBs (Resource Blocks)	66
	Number of OFDM Symbols per Slot	14
	Bandwidth	50 MHz
	User Identification Number (RNTI)	2
Channel Configuration		
Propagation Channel	Models Used	CDL/TDL
	Delay Spread	300 ns
	Maximum Doppler Shift	5 Hz
MIMO Antenna Configuration		
Antennas	Number of Transmit Antennas (N_{Tx})	2
	Number of Receive Antennas (N_{Rx})	2, 4
Phase Noise Modeling		
Phase Noise	Model Used	A
	Carrier Frequency (f_c)	30 GHz
SNR and Thermal Noise		
Signal-to-Noise Ratio	Tested SNR Range	-5 dB to 25 dB (2.5 dB step)
	Thermal Noise Added	Yes
Phase Error Compensation (CPE)		
CPE Compensation	Method Used	PT-RS
	Equalization Type	MMSE
	Compensation Test	Yes
Simulation Configuration		
Number of Frames	Simulation Duration	1 frame (10 ms)
Export Results	Format	Excel

- *(1) Phase Noise Configuration:* The code provides different phase noise models *(Phase Noise Models A, B, C)* as specified by 3GPP. For this simulation, the parameter `PNModel = 'A'` is used, corresponding to a carrier around `Fc = 30 GHz`. Similar conclusions are expected for other phase noise models.
- *(2) MIMO Architecture and Propagation Channels:* $N_{\mathrm{Tx}} \times N_{\mathrm{Rx}}$, where $N_{\mathrm{Tx}} = 2$ transmit antennas and $N_{\mathrm{Rx}} \in \{2, 4\}$ receive antennas.

- *(3) Simulation and Iteration Configuration:* The simulation is performed over an SNR range of -5 dB to 25 dB, with a step of 2.5 dB. To evaluate the impact of Common Phase Error (CPE), two configurations are tested: one without any phase compensation and another with compensation using the Phase Tracking Reference Signal (PT-RS) combined with an MMSE equalizer. To ensure a representative analysis, the simulation is conducted over a single transmission frame, but this parameter can be adjusted to enhance test realism.

3.3 Performance Evaluation Metrics

The performance evaluation of 5G-NR mmWave networks is primarily based on two key metrics: the Signal-to-Noise Ratio (SNR) and the Block Error Rate (BLER). These indicators quantify the quality of the received signal and the reliability of the transmission.

The SNR measures the quality of the received signal relative to the noise. It is defined as the ratio between the average power of the useful signal P_s and the average power of the noise P_n in the communication channel:

$$\mathrm{SNR\ (dB)} = 10\log_{10}\frac{\mathrm{P_s}}{\mathrm{P_n}} \tag{8}$$

where $\mathrm{P_s}$ is the received signal power and $\mathrm{P_n}$ of the noise power in the channel. The BLER measures the rate of erroneous blocks in the received signal relative to the total number of transmitted blocks. It is defined as:

$$\mathrm{BLER} = \frac{\mathrm{N_{errors}}}{\mathrm{N_{total}}} \tag{9}$$

where $\mathrm{N_{errors}}$ is the number of blocks containing at least one error and $\mathrm{N_{total}}$ is the total number of transmitted blocks.

4 Results and Discussion

This section presents the simulation results and performance analysis of NR-PDSCH under different CDL/TDL channel models. The analysis focuses on the impact of the number of reception antennas (RxAnt = 2 and 4) on the Bit Error Rate (BLER) as a function of the Signal-to-Noise Ratio (SNR), highlighting key differences between CDL and TDL models in terms of propagation characteristics and performance outcomes.

4.1 Results Analysis

In this section, we analyze the performance of NR-PDSCH under different CDL/TDL channel models, focusing on the impact of the number of reception antennas (RxAnt = 2 and 4) on the Block Error Rate (BLER) as a function of the Signal-to-Noise Ratio (SNR).

Fig. 2 and Fig. 3 compare the impact of various CDL channels on BLER for the RxAnt=2 and RxAnt=4 configurations. The CDL-C and CDL-D channels generally provide the best performance, whereas the CDL-E channel exhibits poorer performance, likely due to high inter-antenna correlation. Indeed, superior performance of CDL-C and CDL-D channels stems from their optimized delay profile, lower delay spread, moderate maximum Doppler shift, and suitable carrier frequency, which enhance signal robustness and reduce interference, whereas the poorer performance of the CDL-E channel is likely due to high inter-antenna correlation, leading to reduced spatial diversity and increased signal degradation. Increasing the number of reception antennas (RxAnt=4) reduces overall BLER; however, the effectiveness of this gain depends significantly on the specific characteristics of each channel.

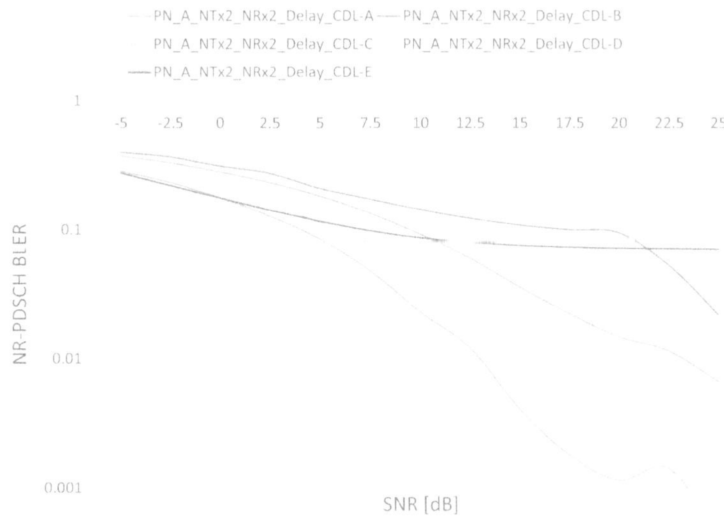

Fig. 2. Impact of CDL channels on NR-PDSCH performance for RxAnt=2.

Figure 4 and Fig. 5 illustrate the impact of TDL-A, TDL-B, TDL-C, TDL-D, and TDL-E channels on NR-PDSCH performance for reception antenna configurations of RxAnt=2 and RxAnt=4. In general, the BLER decreases progressively as the SNR increases, regardless of the channel. However, significant differences emerge between the channels:

TDL-D and TDL-E exhibit the best performance, with consistently lower BLER across the entire SNR range. This is because TDL-D and TDL-E model environments with multiple line-of-sight (LOS) paths that are less complex, have shorter delays, and offer a more balanced power distribution across paths. These characteristics reduce interference and enhance signal robustness.

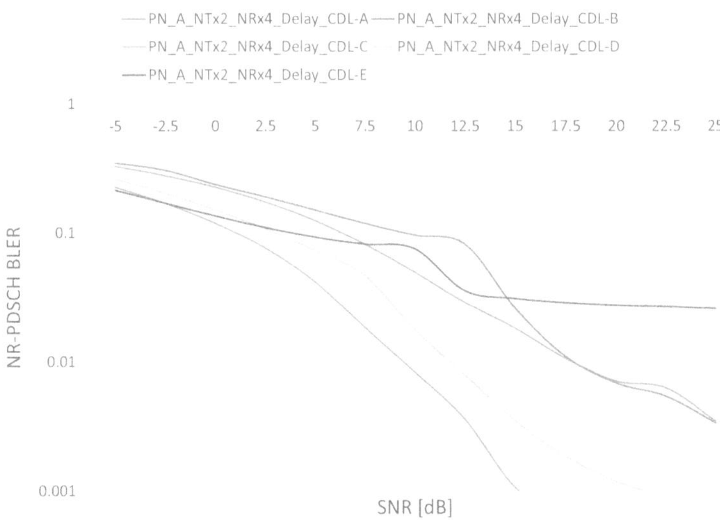

Fig. 3. Impact of CDL channels on NR-PDSCH performance for RxAnt=4.

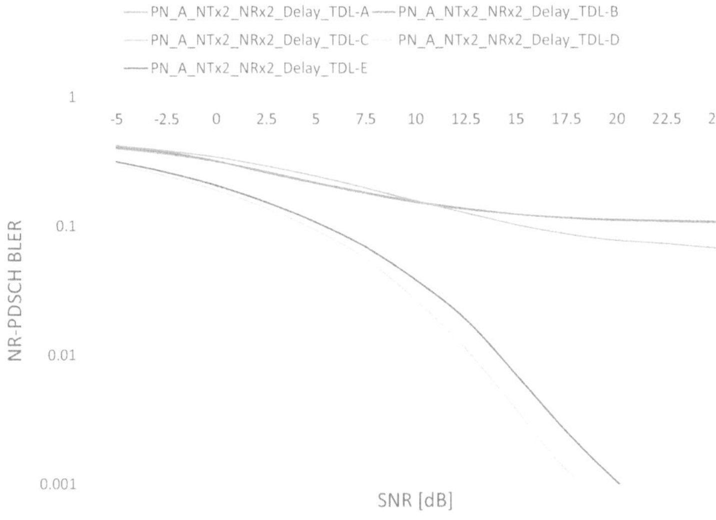

Fig. 4. Impact of TDL channels on NR-PDSCH performance for RxAnt=2.

TDL-A, TDL-B, and TDL-C exhibit higher BLER values, indicating lower robustness to propagation conditions. These channels model dense urban environments with complex multipath propagation, including both line-of-sight (LOS) and non-line-of-sight (NLOS) conditions, longer delays, and greater power dispersion across paths. These factors increase interference and degrade performance.

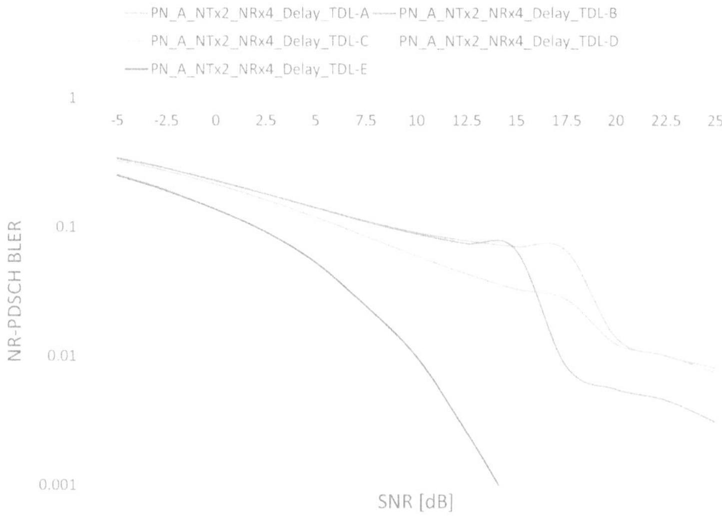

Fig. 5. Impact of TDL channels on NR-PDSCH performance for RxAnt=4.

The superior performance of TDL-D and TDL-E channels results from their shorter delay spread, lower complexity in multipath propagation, and more balanced power distribution, which enhance signal robustness and reduce interference, whereas the poorer performance of TDL-A, TDL-B, and TDL-C is primarily due to longer delay spreads, higher multipath complexity in dense urban environments, and increased interference from both Line-of-Sight (LOS) and Non-Line-of-Sight (NLOS) components.

4.2 Limitations of This Work

Despite promising results, this study has several limitations that affect generalizability. The CDL model, while accurate, is computationally intensive compared to TDL. Simulations were limited to a single frame and used only one phase noise model (PNModel A), which constrains statistical robustness and general applicability.

Mobility scenarios such as vehicular or high-speed conditions were not explored, and phase noise modeling excluded noisy phase errors (NPE). Additionally, the setup did not account for inter-cell interference, a critical factor in dense 5G deployments.

Future work should include high-mobility environments, alternative phase noise models (e.g., PNModel B, C), and interference-aware simulations. Integrating ML/DL approaches could further enhance adaptability through intelligent tuning of transmission parameters.

5 Conclusion

This study compared 3GPP-standardized CDL and TDL channel models in 5G-NR mmWave systems using a 3GPP-compliant simulation framework to evaluate BLER and SNR under LOS and NLOS conditions. CDL models outperformed TDL, especially in NLOS, with CDL-C achieving 0.02% BLER versus TDL-C's 0.3%, and CDL-D showing 0.06% BLER compared to TDL-E's $6.495\times10^{-5}\%$ in LOS. Accurate channel modeling is vital for optimizing 5G networks, with CDL's spatial resolution supporting applications like beamforming. Furthermore, MMSE-based phase noise mitigation enhanced reliability. Future work should explore deep learning, hybrid CDL-TDL models, and real-world trials to validate these findings in self-optimizing radio access networks.

References

1. Moltchanov, D., Andreev, S., Koucheryavy, Y.: "Metrology of the millimeter-wave band: channel sounding and modeling". In: IEEE Communications Magazine 60.2 (2022), pp. 38–44. https://doi.org/10.1109/MCOM.001.2100643. https://ieeexplore.ieee.org/document/9724546
2. 3rd Generation Partnership Project (3GPP). Study on channel model for frequencies from 0.5 GHz to 100 GHz. Technical report TR 38.901. Technical Report. 3GPP, June 2018. url: https://www.3gpp.org/ftp/Specs/archive/38_series/38.901/38901-f00.zip
3. Barb, G., Otesteanu, M.: On the Influence of Delay Spread in TDL and CDL Channel Models for Downlink 5G MIMO Systems (2019). https://doi.org/10.1109/uemcon47517.2019.8992982
4. GSMA. 5G mmWave Guide: A Resource for Operators. Copyright2022 GSMA. Feb. 2022. url: https://www.gsma.com/5GmmWave
5. Tsoulos, G., Athanasiadou, G., Zarbouti, D.: "5G and 4G in the field: performance assessment through trials". In: IEEE Transactions on Electronics & Telecommunications (2024). https://doi.org/10.1109/pacet60398.2024.10497064
6. Kim, J., Noh, G., Kim, T., Chung, H., Kim, I.: "Link-level performance evaluation of mmWave 5G NR sidelink communications". In: Jeju Island, Korea, Republic of (Oct. 20–22, 2021). Jeju Island, Korea, Republic of: IEEE, Oct. 20–22, 2021, pp. 1482–1485. isbn: 978-1-6654-2384-7. https://doi.org/10.1109/ICTC52510.2021.9621128
7. Naqvi, S.H.R., Ho, P.H., Peng, L.: "5G NR mmWave indoor coverage with massive antenna system". J. Commun. Netw. **23**(1)(Feb. 2021), pp. 1–11. issn: 1976-5541. https://doi.org/10.23919/jcn.2020.000031
8. Zehra, S.S., Magarini, M., Qureshi, R., Mustafa, S.M.N., Farooq, F.: Proactive approach for preamble detection in 5G-NR PRACH using supervised machine learning and ensemble model. Sci. Reports **12**(1), 8378 (2022). https://doi.org/10.1038/s41598-022-12349-4
9. 3rd Generation Partnership Project (3GPP). Study on channel model for frequencies from 0.5 to 100 GHz. Technical Report TR 38.901. Version V18.0.0. 3rd Generation Partnership Project (3GPP), Mar. 2024. url: https://www.3gpp.org/ftp/Specs/archive/38_series/38.901/

10. Xu, D., Zhou, A., Zhang, X., Wang, G., Liu, X., An., C.: Understanding operational 5G: A first measurement study on its coverage, performance and energy consumption. In: Proceedings of the ACM. 2020, pp. 2371–2378. https://doi.org/10.1145/3400806.3400832
11. Alkhateeb, A., El Ayach, O., Leus, G., Heath, R.W.: "Channel Estimation and Hybrid Precoding for Millimeter Wave Cellular Systems". IEEE J. Select. Topics Signal Process. **8**(5), 831–846 (Oct. 2014). pp.. issn: 1941-0484. https://doi.org/10.1109/jstsp.2014.2334278. eprint: 1401.7426
12. Dikarev, D., Davydov, A., Lee, D.W., Rane, P.: "Phase Noise Compensation for 5G NR System with DFT-s-OFDM in the Presence of Timing Errors". In: Seoul, Korea, Republic of. Seoul, Korea, Republic of: IEEE, 2022, pp. 2423–2428. isbn: 978-1-5386-8348-4 (2022). https://doi.org/10.1109/ICC45855.2022.9838979
13. Guel, D., Somda, F.H., Zerbo, B., Sie, O.: Evaluating Phase noise models with zero-forcing/MMSE algorithms for cpe estimation and compensation in 5G-NR mmWave systems. J. Commun. (2024)
14. Park, J., Lee, J., Lee, M.S.: "A common phase error estimation scheme with mmse equalizer". In: 2023 14th International Conference on Information and Communication Technology Convergence (ICTC). IEEE, Oct. 2023, pp. 1595–1597. https://doi.org/10.1109/ictc58733.2023.10393796. https://ieeexplore.ieee.org/abstract/document/10393796/
15. Dahal , M., Vaezi, M.: Multi-agent deep reinforcement learning for multi-cell interference mitigation". In: 2023 57th Annual Conference on Information Sciences and Systems (CISS). IEEE (2023). https://doi.org/10.1109/CISS56502.2023.10089622
16. Weragama, C., Ali, S., Rajatheva, N., Latva-Aho, M.: "Interference Detection of 6G MIMO LANs using Deep Learning". In: 2024 IEEE International Conference on Machine Learning for Communication and Networking (ICMLCN). 2024, pp. 354–359. https://doi.org/10.1109/ICMLCN59089.2024.10624949
17. Waidhuba, M.K., Tiang, S.S., Manzoor, S., Hong, M.V.: "A wireless backhaul using a massive mimo - 5g nr het-net design; at sub-6ghz and millimetrewave frequencies". In: Sarawak, Malaysia, Malaysia (June 28–30, 2019). Sarawak, Malaysia, Malaysia: IEEE, June 28–30, 2019, pp. 1–5. isbn: 978-1-7281-1558-0. https://doi.org/10.1109/ICSCC.2019.8843589
18. Narengerile, Thompson, J.: "Deep Learning for Signal Detection in Non-Orthogonal Multiple Access Wireless Systems". In: 2019 UK/ China Emerging Technologies (UCET), pp. 1–4 (Aug 2019). https://doi.org/10.1109/UCET.2019.8881888
19. Carmack, J., Bhatia, A., Robinson, J., Majewski, J., Kuzdeba, S., et al.: "Neural network generative models for radio frequency data". In: 2021 IEEE 12th Annual Ubiquitous Computing, Electronics & Mobile Communication Conference (UEMCON). IEEE (2021). https://doi.org/10.1109/UEMCON53757.2021.9666725

New Design and Efficient Implementation of the McEliece Cryptosystem from Quasi-Centrosymetric Goppa Code

Ousmane Ndiaye(✉), Massamba Sow, and Brice Odilon Boidje

Université Cheikh Anta Diop de Dakar, FST, DMI, LACGAA, Dakar, Senegal
{ousmane3.ndiaye,massamba2.sow}@ucad.edu.sn

Abstract. In this paper, we propose a design and an implementation of an efficient Public Key Encryption based on quasi-centrosymmetric Goppa codes, a structure that enables both compactness and robust security. As quantum computing advances, traditional cryptographic methods face potential vulnerabilities, necessitating the development of post-quantum cryptography. Code-based cryptosystems, such as the McEliece scheme, have shown remarkable resilience to quantum attacks, but suffer from large public key sizes. Our proposed scheme introduces quasicentrosymmetry to Goppa codes, significantly reducing the public-key size while retaining the security benefits of the original structure. We also employ the Fujisaki-Okamoto construction to ensure CCA2 security, protecting against adaptive chosen-ciphertext attacks. A thorough security analysis confirms that our approach withstands key recovery and algebraic attacks, while our implementation demonstrates competitive performance. This work highlights the potential of quasi-centrosymmetric Goppa codes as a promising foundation for efficient and secure post-quantum cryptographic applications.

Keywords: Post-quantum Cryptography · Coding-based Cryptography · Goppa Code · McEliece · Quasi-Centrosymmetric · Classic McEliece

1 Introduction

Contemporary cryptographic protocols rely on asymmetric schemes grounded in computationally intractable mathematical problems. However, quantum computers will be able to solve these problems quickly, threatening current cryptographic systems. This has created an urgent need for new standards, leading to the development of post-quantum cryptography, which prepares for a future where attackers may have access to quantum technology.

Many encryption schemes, believed to be quantum resistant, have been proposed. These include various approaches such as lattice-based cryptography, isogeny-based methods, hash-based signatures, multivariate cryptography, and code-based systems. After several rounds of evaluations, NIST narrowed down the pool to 7 finalists and 8 alternate candidates for public-key encryption and

D. Bassole et al. (Eds.): InterSol 2025, LNICST 671, pp. 180–191, 2026.
https://doi.org/10.1007/978-3-032-15154-4_14

key establishment. Currently, the lattice-based algorithm Crystals-Kyber has been selected for standardization, while three code-based cryptosystems—BIKE [1], Classic McEliece [9], and HQC—are moving forward to the fourth round.

Known for its conservative design, Classic McEliece offers robust long-term protection even against quantum adversaries. Using binary Goppa codes in the Niederreiter framework, it enables fast encryption and efficient decryption. It has remained resilient to attacks for over 40 years, unlike some other approaches like lattice-based cryptography, which have seen significant security reductions.

Despite its strong resistance to quantum attacks, Classic McEliece has a significant downside: the large size of its public keys, which range from 255 KB to 1326 KB, depending on the security level. This drawback is a key reason why it remains under further review in NIST's fourth round of evaluation.

Related Work: Many researchers have explored the use of redundant matrices, where certain rows are generated through permutations of others. This has led to the development of Goppa codes with non-trivial permutation groups. Notable examples include quasi-cyclic codes [6], quasi-dyadic codes [2,3], and quasi-monoidic codes [5], which achieve key sizes of just a few tens of kilobytes . However, several attacks have emerged targeting schemes like DAGS, which uses quasi-dyadic Srivastava codes with an extension degree of 2. Despite the fact that quasi-dyadic and quasi-cyclic binary alternant codes [3] have remained unbroken, they were eliminated after the first round of the NIST Post-Quantum Cryptography competition.

A major challenge with using these codes is that they make algebraic attacks more unfeasible. This is because the order of the permutation group allows a reduction in the number of unknowns, simplifying the attack by working on the folded code [14]. Thus, the reduced key size offered by these codes often comes at the cost of decreased security.

This work builds upon our previous study in [17] Ousmane Ndiaye, where the quasi-centrosymmetric code structure was initially introduced for key generation purposes.

Our Contribution: We present an iimplementation of a new code-based KEM built on quasi centrosymmetric Goppa codes, which extend classical Goppa structures by leveraging quasi centrosymmetry to enable compact and secure public key representations through symmetric half-block matrix design.

We further propose a CCA2-secure variant using the Fujisaki–Okamoto transformation, reducing ciphertext redundancy while ensuring strong adaptive chosen-ciphertext resistance. Our scheme is formally proven secure against both classical and quantum attacks, with a complexity of $2^{\frac{n}{2}} + WF\left(\frac{n}{2}, \frac{k}{2}, \frac{r}{2}\right)$. Using folding, we reduce the overall complexity to the square root of that of the original McEliece scheme via an optimized key generation process.

Finally, we provide a C implementation of our PKE and benchmark it against comparable schemes, demonstrating superior efficiency in key size and computational cost, making it a promising candidate for post-quantum applications.

Organization of the Paper: We organize this work as follows. Section 2 provides the necessary preliminaries, covering notation and background on code-based cryptography and quasi-centrosymmetric Goppa codes. In Sect. 3, we introduce our proposed Key Encapsulation Mechanism (KEM), explaining the key generation, encryption, decryption processes in detail and the theorical security proof. Section 4 describes the pratical security. Section 5 discusses the implementation and performance of our KEM, with comparative analysis against similar schemes. Finally, Sect. 6 presents our conclusion and suggests directions for future research.

2 McEliece Cryptosystem

2.1 Notation and Definitions

In what follows, we shall use the notation defined below:

- $(\mathbf{a} \parallel \mathbf{b})$: the concatenation of vectors $\mathbf{a}$ and $\mathbf{b}$
- $\xleftarrow{\$}$: choosing a random element from a set or distribution

- $\mathcal{E}^{Mc}_{\mathcal{K}_{\text{pub}}}(x, e)$ encryption scheme of the McEliece PKC, x is the plaintext and e the error vector.
- $\mathcal{D}^{Mc}_{\mathcal{K}_{\text{priv}}}(z)$ decryption scheme of the McEliece PKC, return the corresponding plaintext x of the ciphertext z and y the error vector.
- $H : \mathbb{F}_2^k \mapsto \mathbb{F}_2^l$, where $l \leq k$ and $l = \lceil \log_2 \binom{n}{r} \rceil$: a One-Way Hash function .
- Gen : $\mathbb{F}_2^l \mapsto \mathbb{F}_2^k$: a Cryptographically secure Pseudo random sequences Generator.

2.2 Code-Based Cryptography

Definition 1. *An $[n, k]$-linear code $\mathcal{C}$ of length n and dimension k over $\mathbb{F}_q$ is a k-dimensional vector subspace of $\mathbb{F}_q^n$.*

Definition 2. (Hamming Metric). *The **Hamming weight** $wt(x)$ of a vector $x \in \mathbf{F}_q^n$ is the number of its non-zero entries. The Hamming distance $d(x, y)$ between two vectors $x, y \in \mathbf{F}_q^n$ is defined as the weight of their difference, i.e.,*

$$d(x, y) = wt(x - y).$$

*The **minimum distance** d of a code C is defined as the minimum distance between any two different codewords of C, or equivalently as the minimum weight over all non-zero codewords.*

Definition 3. *Let $\mathcal{C}$ be a $[n, k]$-linear code over $\mathbb{F}_q$, a generator matrix $\mathbf{G}$ is a $(k \times n)$ matrix whose lines are basis of $\mathcal{C}$. If c belongs to $\mathcal{C}$ then c is linear combination of those lines. We can write*

$$\mathcal{C} = \{m \cdot \mathbf{G}, m \in \mathbb{F}_q^k\}.$$

If $\mathbf{G} = (I_k \mid A)$ with I_k the identity matrix of order k and A a $k \times (n-k)$-matrix, we say that $\mathbf{G}$ is under systematic form.

Definition 4. *(Parity-Check Matrix). Let $\mathcal{C}$ be a (n,k)-code over $\mathbb{F}_q$. Then there is a $(n-k) \times n$-matrix $\mathbf{H}$ over $\mathbb{F}_q$ of rank $n-k$ such that*

$$\mathcal{C} = \{c \in \mathbb{F}_q^n | \mathbf{H} \cdot c^\top = 0\}$$

Theses matrix are called Parity-check matrices of the code $\mathcal{C}$.

Definition 5. *(Syndrome) Let $\mathcal{C}$ be a (n,k)-code over $\mathbb{F}_q$ and $\mathbf{H}$ a Parity-check matrix of $\mathcal{C}$.*
For all $x \in \mathbb{F}_q^n$, the syndrome of x is the vector $s_x = \mathbf{H} \cdot x^\top \in \mathbb{F}_q^{n-k}$.

Problem 1. (Syndrome Decoding Problem). Let $\mathbf{H}$ be an $r \times n$ full-rank matrix, and let s be a vector, both with entries in $\mathbf{F}_q$. Let t be a non-negative integer. Find a vector $e \in \mathbf{F}_q^n$ of weight t such that $\mathbf{H}e^T = s^T$.

The Syndrome Decoding Problem (SDP) is indeed a fundamental problem in complexity theory, particularly in the context of coding theory and cryptography. The SDP has been shown to be NP-complete in [7]. This is directly connected to the general decoding problem for the following reason: Consider an $[n,k]$ linear code C with a generator matrix $\mathbf{G}$ and a parity-check matrix $\mathbf{H}$. For a message vector $m \in \mathbb{F}_q^k$ and an error vector $e \in \mathbb{F}_q^n$ with Hamming weight $w_H(e) \leq w$, decoding involves recovering m from the received vector $c = m\mathbf{G} + e$, which includes errors. By using $\mathbf{H}$, one can compute the syndrome $s = \mathbf{H}c^T = \mathbf{H}e^T$, which depends only on the error vector e.

2.3 Goppa Codes

Let $\mathbb{F}_{2^m}$ be the finite field with 2^m elements. Let $n \leq 2^m$, the support $L = (\beta_0, \ldots, \beta_{n-1})$ be an ordered sequence of distinct elements of $\mathbb{F}_{2^m}$, and a square-free degree-r polynomial $g \in \mathbb{F}_{2^m}[x]$ such that $g(\beta_0)g(\beta_1)\cdots g(\beta_{n-1}) \neq 0$. The binary Goppa code with support L and generator polynomial g is defined as:

$$\Gamma(L,g) = \left\{ (a_0, \ldots, a_{n-1}) \in \{0,1\}^n \mid \sum_{j=0}^{n-1} \frac{a_j}{z - \beta_j} \mod g(z) = 0 \right\}.$$

As a subclass of alternant codes, the parity-check matrix of the Goppa code $\Gamma(L,g)$ is well defined as

$$H = \left[\frac{\beta_j^i}{g(\beta_j)} \right]_{0 \leq i < r,\ 0 \leq j < n}$$

When we want to construct efficiently codes with compact (symmetric) generator matrix or run an attack, we deal with a very important concept call permutation group of the code acting on coordinate or in globally isomorphism group acting on codewords which we will define in the following.

Definition 6. *(Permutation group)*
Let $\mathcal{C}$ be a linear code of length n on $\mathbb{F}_q$. Let $\sigma \in S_n$ acting on $\mathcal{C}$ by $\forall c \in \mathcal{C}, \sigma(c) = (c_{\sigma^{-1}(0)}, \ldots, c_{\sigma^{-1}(n-1)})$. The code $\mathcal{C}$ is said σ-invariant if $\sigma(\mathcal{C}) = \mathcal{C}$. The permutation group of $\mathcal{C}$ is: $Perm(\mathcal{C}) = \{\sigma \in S_n | \sigma(\mathcal{C}) = \mathcal{C}\}$

2.4 Quasi-Centrosymmetric Goppa Codes

Quasi-centrosymmetric Goppa codes were introduced by Ndiaye in [17] and made it possible to propose a balance between key size and security using a permutation group of order 2.

Definition 7. *A centrosymmetric matrix is a matrix which is symmetric about its center. More precisely, an $r \times n$ matrix $A = (a_{ij})$ is centrosymmetric when its entries satisfy:*

$$a_{ij} = a_{r-i-1,n-j-1} \quad \textit{for} \quad 0 \leq i \leq r-1, \quad 0 \leq j \leq n-1.$$

Definition 8. *A quasi-centrosymmetric matrix is defined as a block matrix in which each block is a centrosymmetric submatrix.*

The set of $r \times r$ centrosymmetric matrices over a field K is a sub-algebra of the associative algebra of all $r \times r$ matrices which will allow to have a Gauss-Jordan reduction which preserves the centro structure centrosymmetric.

Building Quasi-Centrosymmetric Subfield Subcodes

Goppa quasi-centrosymmetric codes have several constructions but for reasons of simplicity and speed in key generation it is preferable to use parity matrices in the form of Cauchy matrices as in [16] by Misoczki and Barreto.

Cauchy-like Parity Matrices. Parity-check matrices are crucial in the construction of Goppa codes. A Cauchy-like parity matrix, denoted by $\mathbf{H}$, is defined by the following elements:

$$\mathbf{H} = \left[\frac{1}{d_i - S_j}\right]_{0 \leq i < r,\ 0 \leq j < n}$$

where d and L are disjoint sequences of distinct elements from a finite field $\mathbb{F}_q$, with $q = 2^m$. The objective is to design such a matrix $\mathbf{H}$ that is centrosymmetric—exhibiting symmetry around its center—while maintaining the properties required for a Goppa code.

Theorem 1. ([17]). *Let $q = 2^m$, $n = n_0 r$, $s = s_0 r$ with r even number. Let $H \in \mathbb{F}_q^{s \times n}$ is simultaneous a (s_0, n_0) quasi-centrosymmetric of order r and Cauchy matrix $H = C(d, S)$ for two disjoint sequences $z \in \mathbb{F}_q^s$ and $L \in \mathbb{F}_q^n$ of distinct elements. Then z and L satisfy:*

$$d_{(c+1)r-1-i} = d_{cr+i} + \beta_c, \ \textit{and} \ S_{(b+1)r-1-j} = S_{br+j} + \beta_c$$

for some $\beta_c \in \mathbb{F}_q$, $0 \leq i, j \leq r-1$, $0 \leq c \leq s_0 - 1$ and $0 \leq b \leq n_0 - 1$

Corollary 1. ([17]). *Let $H \in \mathbb{F}_q^{r \times n}$ with r an even number, $q = 2^m$, $n = n_0 r$ be simultaneous a $(1, n_0)$ quasi-centrosymmetric of order r and Cauchy matrix $H = C(z, L)$ for two disjoint sequences $z \in \mathbb{F}_q^r$ and $L \in \mathbb{F}_q^n$ of distinct elements. Then z and L satisfy: $d_{r-1-i} = d_i + \beta$, and $S_{(b+1)r-1-j} = S_{br+j} + \beta$ for some $\beta \in \mathbb{F}_q$, $0 \leq i, j \leq r-1$ and $0 \leq b \leq n_0 - 1$.*

Algorithm 1: Constructing a Goppa code in quasi-Centrosymmetric form

Input: n_0, r, $q = 2^{n_0 r}$
Output: L, g,parity-check matrix H

$R \leftarrow \mathbb{F}_q^*$, $\beta \xleftarrow{\$} \mathbb{F}_q^*$;
for $i = 0$ **to** $\frac{r}{2} - 1$ **do**
  $d_i \xleftarrow{\$} R$, $d_{r-1-i} \leftarrow d_i + \beta$;
  $R \leftarrow R \setminus \{d_i, d_{r-1-i}\}$;
for $b = 0$ **to** $\frac{n}{r} - 1$ **do**
  for $j = 0$ **to** $\frac{r}{2} - 1$ **do**
    $S_{br+j} \xleftarrow{\$} R$, $S_{br+r-1-j} \leftarrow S_{br+j} + \beta$;
    $R \leftarrow R \setminus \{S_{br+j}, S_{br+r-1-j}\}$;
$g \leftarrow 1$;
for $i = 0$ **to** $r - 1$ **do**
  $g \leftarrow g \cdot (x - d_i)$;
  for $j = 0$ **to** $n - 1$ **do**
    $H_{ij} \leftarrow \frac{1}{d_i - S_j}$;
return L, g, H;

The algorithm below outlines the steps necessary for constructing a quasi-centrosymmetric Goppa code. For some $\beta \in \mathbb{F}_q$, $0 \leq i, j \leq r - 1$ and $0 \leq b \leq n_0 - 1$. We present the key generation, encryption, and decryption processes of the Niederreiter cryptosystem based on quasi-centrosymmetric Goppa codes capable of correcting r errors.

3 Quasi-Centrosymmetric Goppa for McEliece

3.1 Key Generation

Algorithm 2: Construction of the public and private keys for Goppa codes in quasi-centrosymmetric form

Input: m, r, n
Output: Public key $\mathbf{H}_{\text{pub}}$, Private key (L, g)

Function `KeyGeneration`(m, r, n):
  Step 1: Call `GenParityCheck`(m, r, n) to construct $\mathbf{H} \in \mathbb{F}_{2^m}^{r \times n}$, a parity-check matrix of a Goppa code $\mathcal{G}(L, g)$ in Cauchy and quasi-centrosymmetric form;
  Step 2: Transform this matrix into a binary matrix $\mathbf{H}_{\text{bin}} \in \mathbb{F}_2^{mr \times n}$ using the co-trace function;
  Step 3: Apply the Gaussian elimination algorithm to $\mathbf{H}_{\text{bin}}$ to obtain the systematic form $(\mathbf{M} \mid I_{rm})$;
  Step 4: The public key is half of the quasi-centrosymmetric matrix $\mathcal{K}_{\text{pub}} = S_r(\mathbf{M}^T) \in \mathbb{F}_2^{(n-rm) \times \frac{rm}{2}}$;
  Step 5: The private key consists of (L, g);
  return $\mathcal{K}_{\text{pub}}, \mathcal{K}_{\text{priv}} = (L, g)$;

A Toy Example 2: Quasi-Centrosymmetric Goppa Let $\mathbb{F}_{2^5} = \mathbb{F}_2[u]/(u^5 + u^2 + 1)$, $n = 7 * 4$, $r = 4$.
The offset $\alpha = 1, z = (u^5, u^6, u^{27}, u^2)$,
$L = (u^{25}, u^{20}, u^8, u^{21}, u^{30}, u^{12}, u^{23}, u^{17}, u^{19}, u^7, u^{22}, u^{11}, u^{14}, u^3, u^{29}, u^{13}, u^9, u^{18}, u^1, u^{16}, u^4, u^{28}, u^{26}, u^{10}, u^{24}, u^{31}, u^0, u^{15})$ and $g(x) = (x - u^5)(x - u^6)(x - u^{27})(x - u^2)$. The associated parity-check matrix is:

$$H = \left(\begin{array}{cccc|cccc|cccc|cccc|cccc|cccc|cccc} u^{18} & u^2 & u^{28} & u^{17} & u^5 & u^4 & u^{25} & u^3 & u^{13} & u^{21} & u^{27} & u^{30} & u^{10} & u^{23} & u^{11} & u^6 & u^{16} & u^{12} & u^{20} & u^7 & u^9 & u^{14} & u^1 & u^{24} & u^{15} & u^{26} & u^{29} & u^{22} \\ u^{14} & u^{12} & u^{20} & u^1 & u^{10} & u^{29} & u^{26} & u^6 & u^{11} & u^7 & u^{16} & u^{23} & u^5 & u^{30} & u^{13} & u^3 & u^{27} & u^2 & u^{28} & u^{21} & u^{22} & u^{18} & u^{17} & u^{15} & u^{24} & u^{25} & u^4 & u^9 \\ u^1 & u^{20} & u^{12} & u^{14} & u^6 & u^{26} & u^{29} & u^{10} & u^{23} & u^{16} & u^7 & u^{11} & u^3 & u^{13} & u^{30} & u^5 & u^{21} & u^{28} & u^2 & u^{27} & u^{15} & u^{17} & u^{18} & u^{22} & u^9 & u^4 & u^{25} & u^{24} \\ u^{17} & u^{28} & u^2 & u^{18} & u^3 & u^{25} & u^4 & u^5 & u^{30} & u^{27} & u^{21} & u^{13} & u^6 & u^{11} & u^{23} & u^{10} & u^7 & u^{20} & u^{12} & u^{16} & u^{24} & u^1 & u^{14} & u^9 & u^{22} & u^{29} & u^{26} & u^{15} \end{array}\right) \quad (1)$$

a corresponding co-trace matrix in systematic form is

$$H_{bin} = \left(\begin{array}{cccc|cccc|cccc|cccc|cccc||cccc|cccc}
0&1&1&0&1&1&0&0&1&0&0&0&0&0&0&0&0&0&0&0&0&0&0&0&0&0&0&0\\
1&1&1&1&0&0&0&0&0&1&0&0&0&0&0&0&0&0&0&0&0&0&0&0&0&0&0&0\\
1&1&1&1&0&0&0&0&0&0&1&0&0&0&0&0&0&0&0&0&0&0&0&0&0&0&0&0\\
0&1&1&0&0&0&1&1&0&0&0&1&0&0&0&0&0&0&0&0&0&0&0&0&0&0&0&0\\
\hline
1&1&0&1&1&1&0&1&0&0&0&0&1&0&0&0&0&0&0&0&0&0&0&0&0&0&0&0\\
1&0&0&0&0&1&1&1&0&0&0&0&0&1&0&0&0&0&0&0&0&0&0&0&0&0&0&0\\
0&0&0&1&1&1&1&0&0&0&0&0&0&0&1&0&0&0&0&0&0&0&0&0&0&0&0&0\\
1&0&1&1&1&0&1&1&0&0&0&0&0&0&0&1&0&0&0&0&0&0&0&0&0&0&0&0\\
\hline
1&0&0&1&1&1&1&1&0&0&0&0&0&0&0&0&1&0&0&0&0&0&0&0&0&0&0&0\\
0&0&1&1&0&0&1&0&0&0&0&0&0&0&0&0&0&1&0&0&0&0&0&0&0&0&0&0\\
1&1&0&0&0&1&0&0&0&0&0&0&0&0&0&0&0&0&1&0&0&0&0&0&0&0&0&0\\
1&0&0&1&1&1&1&1&0&0&0&0&0&0&0&0&0&0&0&1&0&0&0&0&0&0&0&0\\
\hline
1&1&1&0&0&0&0&0&0&0&0&0&0&0&0&0&0&0&0&0&1&0&0&0&0&0&0&0\\
0&0&1&0&0&1&1&1&0&0&0&0&0&0&0&0&0&0&0&0&0&1&0&0&0&0&0&0\\
0&1&0&0&1&1&1&0&0&0&0&0&0&0&0&0&0&0&0&0&0&0&1&0&0&0&0&0\\
0&1&1&1&0&0&0&0&0&0&0&0&0&0&0&0&0&0&0&0&0&0&0&1&0&0&0&0\\
\hline
1&0&1&1&1&0&0&0&0&0&0&0&0&0&0&0&0&0&0&0&0&0&0&0&1&0&0&0\\
1&1&0&0&1&0&1&0&0&0&0&0&0&0&0&0&0&0&0&0&0&0&0&0&0&1&0&0\\
0&0&1&1&0&1&0&1&0&0&0&0&0&0&0&0&0&0&0&0&0&0&0&0&0&0&1&0\\
1&1&0&1&0&0&0&1&0&0&0&0&0&0&0&0&0&0&0&0&0&0&0&0&0&0&0&1
\end{array}\right)$$

3.2 Encryption

Algorithm 3: Algorithm for Ciphertext Computation

Input: $\mathbf{m} \in \mathbb{F}_2^k$, $\mathcal{K}_{\text{pub}}$
Output: Ciphertext $\mathbf{c} \in \mathbb{F}_2^n$

Function `GenerateCiphertext`($\mathbf{m}$, $\mathcal{K}_{pub}$):
- **Step 1:** Define $G \leftarrow (I_{n-rm} \mid \mathcal{K}_{\text{pub}})$;
- **Step 2:** Generate $e \xleftarrow{\$} \mathcal{W}_{n,r}$;
- **Step 3:** The ciphertext is the public syndrome:
- $\mathbf{c} \leftarrow \mathcal{E}^{Mc}_{\mathcal{K}_{\text{pub}}}(m, e) = mG \oplus e = m || m\mathcal{K}_{\text{pub}} \oplus e \in \mathbb{F}_2^n$;
- **return** $\mathbf{c}$;

3.3 Decryption

Decoding is the most complex step of the process, due to the many calculations it requires, often costly and sophisticated. We will first provide a general (see Algorithm 4) presentation before introducing some specific algorithms, in order to facilitate understanding.

Algorithm 4: Decryption Algorithm for McEliece-Based Scheme

Input: Ciphertext $\mathbf{c} \in \mathbb{F}_2^n$, $\mathcal{K}_{\text{priv}} = (L, g)$.
Output: Secret message $\mathbf{x}$.
1. Retrieve the parity-check matrix $\mathbf{H}'$ using the private key (L, g).
2. Use a Patterson algorithm to decode $\mathbf{c}$ and recover the error vector:

$$(m, \mathbf{e}) \leftarrow \mathcal{D}^{Mc}_{\mathcal{K}_{\text{priv}}}(\mathbf{c}).$$

Output: The secret message $\mathbf{m}$.

The Patterson algorithm is widely used for decoding binary irreducible Goppa codes. However, it cannot be directly applied to separable Goppa codes due to the reducibility of g. Since Goppa codes are also Alternant codes, we present a decoding algorithm based on the extended Euclidean algorithm, capable of correcting up to $\frac{r}{2}$ errors. To decode up to r errors, we use the square of the Goppa code, which satisfies $\Gamma(L, g) = \Gamma(L, g^2)$.

3.4 CCA2 Security Conversions

Fujisaki-Okamoto's Generic Conversion: This version, based on One-Way Encryption (OWE), was proposed in [15] to achieve security against CCA2. Since these three schemes are OWE, this conversion can be adapted to them. Consider a plaintext m of length k. The conversion proceeds as follows:

Algorithm 5: Fujisaki-Okamoto's Generic Conversion

Input: Plaintext m of length k.
Output: Ciphertext $c = (c_1, c_2)$.

1 **Steps:**

1. Generate $e \xleftarrow{\$} \mathcal{W}_{n,r}$.
2. Compute $r \leftarrow H(e\|m)$.
3. Encrypt r to obtain $c_1 \leftarrow \mathcal{E}^{Mc}_{\mathcal{K}_{\text{pub}}}(r, \sigma) = rG + e$.
4. Compute $c_2 \leftarrow m \oplus Gen(e)$.
5. Return the ciphertext $c := (c_1, c_2)$.

Theorem 2. ([15]). *Provided that the McEliece PKE satisfies both indistinguishability and decoding hardness, the encryption scheme in Algorithm 5 is secure under the IND-CCA2 model.*

According to [[15], Th. 12], our construction, inspired by [11], meets all conditions from both symmetric (One-Time Pad) and asymmetric encryption (McEliece).

4 Security

4.1 Security Against Decoding Attacks

Among the most studied attacks against code-based cryptosystems is the family of Information Set Decoding (ISD) algorithms, originally introduced by Prange in 1962 [18]. These algorithms aim to recover the original message by identifying a set of error-free positions, known as an information set, from which part of the codeword can be reconstructed. Over the years, several improvements have been proposed [10,13], yet the complexity of ISD remains exponential in the code parameters.

In particular, the asymptotic cost of the best known classical variant of ISD, due to Both and May [10], is roughly $\tilde{O}(2^{0.0885n})$. Further analysis by Torres and Sendrier [20] shows that, under typical parameterizations such as $r = O(n/\log n)$ and $k = Rn$, the ISD complexity can be approximated as $2^{-\log_2(1-R)r(1+o(1))}$. The case of folded or symmetric Goppa codes has also been studied, including the impact of structural symmetries and the use of Sendrier's DOOM strategy [19].

For a complete treatment of these attacks, including their application to folded codes and quantum considerations, we refer the reader to [17].

4.2 Key Recovery Attacks

Recovering the private key from the public matrix is generally hard, but algebraic structures—like quasi-cyclic or dyadic forms—can enable efficient attacks via permutation symmetries. Faugère et al. [12] proposed a powerful structural attack based on Gröbner bases and variable reduction to retrieve the support and multiplier.

For quasi-centrosymmetric Goppa codes in Cauchy form, the attack complexity reduces further by targeting the invariant folded structure. While a brute-force search over all Goppa polynomials and supports costs about 2^{mrn}, solving the associated algebraic system offers a more efficient alternative.

4.3 Algebraic Cryptanalysis

Given the public matrix, an attacker can attempt to find a solution by reducing the problem to the security of a folded Alternant code without centrosymmetric structure. This enables the application of the FOPT attack [13], combined with a guess-and-solve method on support and multiplier, achieving an approximate complexity of $2^{\frac{\deg(\Gamma)}{2}m^2} \cdot \mathrm{poly}(n)$.

Further reduction allows the use of Gröbner basis computation, where the F5 algorithm [4] bounds the complexity asymptotically by terms involving the number of equations, independent variables, and the degree of regularity, achieving efficient recovery in practical scenarios.

5 Environment and Implementation

To implement binary field extensions $\mathbb{F}_2$ of degree $m = 13$, the best approach is to use lookup tables for logarithms and exponentials based on a primitive element β of F_{2^m}. This method remains efficient as long as the tables fit within the processor's cache, ensuring fast and optimized finite field arithmetic computations.

According to the Classic McEliece NIST proposal [9], the ciphertext size is $n - k = (1 - R + o(1))n$ bits, and the public key size is $(c_0 - o(1))b^2(\log_2 b)^2$, where $c_0 = \frac{R}{(1-R)(\log_2(1-R))^2}$, with $c_0 = 0.7418860694$ and $R = 0.7968121300$ (Table 1).

Table 1. Quasi-centrosymmetric Goppa codes [17].

m	n	r	public key Size (bytes)	Security level
12	3488	64	130560	113
13	4608	96	262080	151
13	8192	128	678912	240

5.1 Implementation

The implementation was done in C99 with an adapted library, using exponential/antilog tables for finite field operations and centrosymmetric codes to optimize security and memory. Keccak (SHA-3) hash functions were employed to generate error vectors uniformly. Timings were averaged over 10 runs. The code was compiled using CLANG 8.0.0 on an Intel(R) Core(TM) i5-5300U CPU @ 2.30GHz. The code is available at[1].

5.2 Performance and Comparison

We provide here a comparison with other code-based KEMs, particularly those submitted to NIST. In the Table 2, we present data for **Classic McEliece** and **DAGS_5** in terms of memory requirements for the highest security level (256-bit classical security).

It is easily observed that the size of the public key in our scheme is approximately half that of **Classic McEliece**, although it is larger than that of **DAGS_5**. Regarding the latter, it is worth noting that with equal parameters, our scheme offers a security advantage. The timings are expressed in cycles per byte (cpb).

[1] https://github.com/ouzdeville/centro_keygen/tree/CNRIA2025.

Table 2. Comparison of NIST code-based KEMs (in bytes) for security level 3

Parameter set	Public key	Private key	Ciphertext	Key Generation
Classic McEliece [9]	1047319	6762	226	364 756 564
DAGS_bin_5 [3]	19712	6400	1632	847 980 876
Our PKE	678912	6762	226	518 986 730

6 Conclusion

In this paper, we proposed a public key encryption scheme based on quasi-centrosymmetric Goppa codes, offering a promising post-quantum cryptographic solution. The incorporation of quasi-centrosymmetry reduces the public key size while preserving strong security. Our CCA2-secure construction, based on the Fujisaki-Okamoto approach, ensures redundancy in ciphertext and resilience against adaptive chosen-ciphertext attacks.

Security analysis confirmed the scheme's resistance to ISD and algebraic attacks, particularly with the folding technique. The performance of our PKE, demonstrated through implementation and comparison with existing schemes, highlights its competitive advantages in key size and efficiency.

Future work will focus on optimizing this construction for practical applications and exploring its integration into hybrid encryption schemes.

References

1. Aragon, N., et al.: Bike: "It Flipping Key Encapsulation, NIST PQC Round (2017)
2. Banegas, G., et al.: Dags: key encapsulation using dyadic GS codes. J. Math. Cryptol. **12**(4), 221–239 (2018)
3. Banegas, G., et al.: Dags: reloaded revisiting dyadic key encapsulation. In: Code-Based Cryptography Workshop, pp. 69–85. Springer (2019)
4. Bardet, M., Faugère, J.C., Salvy, B.: On the complexity of the F5 gröbner basis algorithm. J. Symbolic Comput. **70**, 49–70 (2015)
5. Barreto, P.S.L.M., Lindner, R., Misoczki, R.: Monoidic codes in cryptography. In: Yang, B.-Y. (ed.) PQCrypto 2011. LNCS, vol. 7071, pp. 179–199. Springer, Heidelberg (2011). https://doi.org/10.1007/978-3-642-25405-5_12
6. Berger, T.P., Cayrel, P.-L., Gaborit, P., Otmani, A.: Reducing key length of the mceliece cryptosystem. In: Preneel, B. (ed.) AFRICACRYPT 2009. LNCS, vol. 5580, pp. 77–97. Springer, Heidelberg (2009). https://doi.org/10.1007/978-3-642-02384-2_6
7. Berlekamp, E., McEliece, R., van Tilborg, H.: On the inherent intractability of certain coding problems. IEEE Trans. Inform. Theory **24**(3), 384–386 (1978)
8. Bernstein, D.J.: Grover vs. McEliece. In: Sendrier, N., (ed.), Post-Quantum Cryptography, pp. 73–80. Springer, Berlin, Heidelberg (2010)
9. Bernstein, D.J., et al.: Classic McEliece: conservative code-based cryptography. NIST submissions (2017)

10. Both, L., May, A.: Decoding linear codes with high error rate and its impact for LPN security. In: Lange, T., Steinwandt, R. (eds.) Post-Quantum Cryptography, pp. 25–46. Springer International Publishing, Cham (2018)
11. Cayrel, P.L., Hoffmann, G., Persichetti, E.: Efficient implementation of a CCA2-secure variant of McEliece using generalized srivastava codes. In: Fischlin, M., Buchmann, J., Manulis, M. (eds.) Public Key Cryptography - PKC 2012, pp. 138–155. Springer, Berlin Heidelberg (2012)
12. Faugère, J.-C., Otmani, A., Perret, L., Tillich, J.-P.: Algebraic cryptanalysis of mceliece variants with compact keys. In: Gilbert, H. (ed.) EUROCRYPT 2010. LNCS, vol. 6110, pp. 279–298. Springer, Heidelberg (2010). https://doi.org/10.1007/978-3-642-13190-5_14
13. Jean-Charles, F., Ayoub, O., Ludovic, P., de Portzamparc, F., Tillich, J.: Folding alternant and goppa codes with non-trivial automorphism groups. IEEE Trans. Inf. Theory **62**(1), 184–198 (2016)
14. Faugère, J., Otmani, A., Perret, L., de Portzamparc, F., Tillich, P.: Structural cryptanalysis of mceliece schemes with compact keys. Designs Codes Cryptography **79**(1), 87–112 (2016)
15. Fujisaki, E., Okamoto, T.: Secure integration of asymmetric and symmetric encryption schemes. Proc. CRYPTO '99, LNCS **1666**, 535–554 (1999)
16. Misoczki, R., Barreto, P.S.L.M.: Compact mceliece keys from goppa codes. In: Jacobson, M.J., Rijmen, V., Safavi-Naini, R. (eds.) Selected Areas in Cryptography, pp. 376–392. Springer, Berlin Heidelberg, Berlin, Heidelberg (2009)
17. Ndiaye, O.: Moderate classical mceliece keys from quasi-centrosymmetric goppa codes. In: El Hajji, S., Mesnager, S., El Mamoun, S. (eds.) Codes, Cryptology and Information Security, pp. 77–90. Springer Nature Switzerland, Cham (2023)
18. Prange, E.. The use of Information sets in decoding cyclic codes. In: Information Theory, IRE Trans., vol. 8, pp. 5–9 (1962)
19. Sendrier, N.: Decoding one out of many. In: Yang, B.Y. (ed.) Post-Quantum Cryptography, pp. 51–67. Springer, Berlin Heidelberg (2011)
20. Canto Torres, R., Sendrier, N.: Analysis of information set decoding for a sub-linear error weight. In: Takagi, T. (ed.) PQCrypto 2016. LNCS, vol. 9606, pp. 144–161. Springer, Cham (2016). https://doi.org/10.1007/978-3-319-29360-8_10

Secure Device Identification and Authentication Architecture for IoT

Mbemba Hydara[1], Raja Muzammil Muneer[2](✉), Yasir Saleem[2], Afeef Obaid[2], and Bamfa Ceesay[1]

[1] Computer Science Department, University of the Gambia, MDI Rd, Kanifing, The Gambia
{hmbemba,bamfa}@utg.edu.gm

[2] Computer Engineering Department, University of Engineering and Technology, Lahore, Pakistan
rajamuzammil93@gmail.com

Abstract. In this era, the use of Internet of Things (IoT) is growing exponentially. This positive development also raises questions about security of IoT. In the I.T industry, many vendors are producing products that are IP-enabled and can easily be configured by just plug and play. This ease is creating heighten security problems as proper identification and authentication are required for each IP-enabled device. In this study, we extend the work of IoT-Sentinel which has been already reported in the literature. In this work, a security mechanism that identifies devices as well as constrains communication of vulnerable devices has been designed and developed. In this paper, we have been able to optimize the earlier work by demonstrating how to identify devices that could not be identified or declared vulnerable with high accuracy using Machine learning. With Machine learning algorithms, we have been able to classify devices of which Random Forest provided the best performance in terms of accuracy than others. The outcome of our approach is more promising and has added a new optimal level of resilience to security.

Keywords: IoT · Machine Learning · Privacy and Security · Fingerprint · Secure devices

1 Introduction

Internet of Things is spreading everywhere in this era, it is predicted that by the year 2020 IoT devices will reach more than 20 billion. In order to keep with the overwhelming pace in modern life and to have benefits of technology, a lot of people are installing smart devices at home, which are nothing but IoT devices that form a home network or an office network. Being able to control remotely one can do everything as desired. These include devices such as Tv, Ac, smart door, smart toaster etc. as shown in Fig. 1. These devices are either IP- enabled or wired connection with a gateway. Several vendors in the market are selling their products for home automation, office automation, digital labs or classrooms, etc. However, all these products from vendors have missing functionality in terms of security or either vendor not mindful of security vulnerabilities. The effect

D. Bassole et al. (Eds.): InterSol 2025, LNICST 671, pp. 192–203, 2026.
https://doi.org/10.1007/978-3-032-15154-4_15

of the lack of security measures can result in dangerous consequences as reported in [2]. Apart from this, it is also reported in [3] that by a single software lacking security, exposes many devices to attacks leading to losses. Given the security concern, we need to consider the basic element which can save us from vulnerabilities and prevent attackers from launching further attacks.

Device identification underscores the basic element which can help in this matter. After identifying devices, we can dictate security over devices or even split devices into secure or insecure categories. Apart from the security concern, it can also be kept in mind that device identification can also help an administrator to troubleshoot or restrict few devices from communicating in a heterogeneous network environment.

Our approach for identifying devices is by using device Fingerprints. Passive fingerprinting has been reported in [4, 5] and different techniques have been reported using Passive Fingerprinting. However, it is not only one type of fingerprinting that can be used at a single time, both passive and active fingerprinting can be used at the same time. This can be further classified into which information is to be used for a selection of features for device identification, and even outlook the previously installed network IoT devices leaving them with their out-of-date software versions.

Fig. 1. Different IoT devices

2 Literature Review

First of all in [6] a comprehensive overview of existing security challenges is presented and privacy issues in IoT integrated with Edge Computing and related architectures. In [7] a comparative study very useful to the readers and those who want to make research in the area of IoT. The work involve Analysis of existing threats, opportunities, strengths, and weaknesses in IoT based devices. This survey further discusses all aspects of IoT and the current situation. The survey in [8] presents the most related limitations of IoT devices, classification of IoT attacks, architectures for authentication and access control, and lastly security issues. These issues have been categorized in a table in [9].

A lot of devices are getting part of IoT but vendors are not considering security flaws in the devices. Already a lot of attacks have been discovered, some of the problems and their optimized solutions are discussed. Similarly, in [10] one time password scheme is another important techniques use for authentication. In this paper, we analyzed the old schemes for one time password as way for authentication in the field of internet of things. This study contributed by providing a new and efficient scheme for one time password authentication and this OTP is based on ECC. These techniques can also be used to authenticate and identify devices. The authors in [11] contend that when point of trust is based on a third party only is likely to pose a problem as third party involvement is not a reliable solution for data exchange.

To overcome this, we proposed a system which is not based on a centralised system but a decentralized one known as "blockchain" using smart contract and Ethereum. This Technology can also be used to identify and authenticate devices. In [12], a scheme that restricts IoT devices connected over the internet from sharing information against the permission of the user is proposed.

Instead, this scheme will permit devices to only share information based on the consent of the user. The main concept is that some gateways are connected to all devices in IoT and this gateway is made secure using Blockchain, serving as the main key for storing user privacy preferences. In [13] OAUTH2 scheme is presented and token expiration discussed. In this scheme, the user gets the token, processes it so that token expiration can be checked and determine whether the token is still valid or expired.

Apart from Machine Learning techniques discussed above, the scheme was found to be one of the best ways to identify devices. One of the main device identification challenge in Machine Learning is to create the signature of devices called Fingerprints. In [14], different types of fingerprints were examined and active fingerprinting for identification of devices in a network was implemented. However, the down side is that it lacks scalability to thousands of devices because of more bandwidth consumption. On the other hand, passive fingerprinting is also implemented. This type is scalable as in [15] with a prediction accuracy of more than 90%. The fingerprinting technique used in [16] predicts accuracy higher than 0.8 but it is implemented on a small scale and used Active type fingerprinting for this approach.

Packet inter-arrival time is also cited in the literature for device fingerprinting in which average communication time and other parameters relating to time are analyzed by specific software. The software include Wireshark or protocol analyzer that gives information about every sort of packet being transmitted from devices to host or host to device. In this way specific piece of information from these software's with respect to time a signature can be generated and stored in a database. This will have a unique similarity index thus as a new device is identified its signatures will be observed and matched with the database. The database having more value of similarity index will be awarded the type of devices discussed in [17] where two-time-type of fingerprints are being used in this matter: for device identification we mean its model, type, and version. In device identification, we will be using both passive and active types of fingerprinting in which we will observe the behavior of devices and a unique fingerprint (Meta data) will be extracted using this analyses.

3 Discussion of Required Models and Methodology

3.1 Proposed Machine Learning Methods

This section covers all the machine learning techniques utilized in our system in detail.

Random Forest

Random Forest is an efficient estimator with the ability to fit multiple decision tree classifiers on numerous sub-samples of a particular dataset. The algorithm limits overfitting and improves predictive F1 scores by using averaging. As compared to single decision trees, Random Forest offers less variance and higher F1 scores. After careful data preprocessing, number of trees are created based on the selected parameters of the dataset. The more the number of created trees, higher will be the value of F1 score.

The RF's training algorithm employs bagging or bootstrap aggregating to tree learners with a training set of

$$X = x_1, \ldots, x_n \tag{1}$$

Having

$$Y = y_1, \ldots, y_n \tag{2}$$

responses, repeated bagging (B times) generates a random sample, which replaces the training set, and the algorithm then works to fit trees to this sample:

For b = 1,..., B:

1. Sample, with replacement, n training examples from X, Y; call these X_b, Y_b.
2. Train a classification tree or regression tree on X_b, Y_b.

Once the training is complete, taking an average of the predictions from all individual regression trees can help make prediction about an unknown sample x':

$$f = \frac{1}{B}\Sigma_{b=1}^{B}\left(f_b(x')\right) \tag{3}$$

In case of a classification tree, one can also consider taking the majority vote.

Bootstrapping protocol improves model's performance by reducing variance without enhancing the overall bias. In any model, individual trees show high sensitivity to noise existing in the training dataset. However, the overall impact of noise can be reduced by averaging multiple trees together while ensuring that the trees are not very similar to each other. Deterministically training multiple trees on same dataset will increase the likelihood of correlation between them, In order to avoid this, bootstrap sampling plays an important role by generating distinct training sets for every tree and reducing the inter-tree correlation.

$$\sigma = \sqrt{\frac{1}{B-1}\Sigma_{b=1}^{B}\left((f_b(x_F) - f)^2\right)} \tag{4}$$

B (Number of trees/samples) acts as a free parameter. Depending on the nature and size of the training set, hundreds to thousands of trees can be traditionally used.

Gradient Boosting

Gradient boosting combines weak "learners" into a single strong learner in an iterative fashion. It is easiest to explain in the least-squares regression setting, where the goal is to "teach" a model F to predict values of the form $\hat{y} = F(x)$ by minimizing the mean squared error

$$\frac{1}{n}\sum_{i}\left((\hat{y}_i - y_i)^2\right) \tag{5}$$

here i i indexes over some training set of size n n of actual values of the output variable.

Now, let us consider a gradient boosting algorithm with M stages. At each stage m ($1 \leq m \leq M$) of gradient boosting, suppose some imperfect model F_m (for low m, this model may simply return $\hat{y}_i = \overline{y}$ where the RHS is the mean of y).

In order to improve F_m, our algorithm should add some new estimator,

$$h_m(y) = y \text{ or, equivalently, } h_m(y) = y - F_m(x) \tag{6}$$

Therefore, gradient boosting will fit h to the residual $y - F_m(x)$. Just like many other boosting approaches, each subsequent model F_{m+1} works to rectify the mistakes made by its previous model F_m.

This idea can be applied to loss functions beyond the squared error, and also to ranking and classification queries, by taking into consideration that the residuals $h_m(x)$ for a given model are proportional to the negative gradients of MSE or mean squared error loss function with respect to $F(x)$:

$$L_{MSE} = \frac{1}{n}(y - F(x))^2 \tag{7}$$

$$-\frac{\partial L_{MSE}}{\partial F} = \frac{2}{n}(y - F(x)) = \frac{2}{n}h_m(x) \tag{8}$$

In other words, gradient boosting can be taken as a specialized form of gradient descent. Generalization of this algorithm will involve the substitution of a different loss function together with its corresponding gradient.

K Nearest-Neighbor

K-Nearest Neighbors or KNN is an uncomplicated yet effective algorithm that works by storing all the accessible cases followed by using a similarity measure to classify a new case. Any new point included in the sample will be compared to its neighbor points based on the distance. Similarity in the distance will put the new point into the particular class of the neighbor points.

Multiple distance functions have been previously utilized in the available literature to estimate the distance existing between points A and B lying in the feature space.

Euclidean distance function is among the extensively used ones. Let A and B be represented by feature vectors A = $(x1,\ldots., xm)$ and B = $y1,\ldots., yn$, where m is the dimensionality of the feature space. To estimate the distance between the two vectors, the normalized Euclidean metric is generally used by

$$Dist(A, B) = \sqrt{\frac{\Sigma_{i-1}^{m}(xi - yi)^2}{m}} \tag{9}$$

The KNN algorithm is frequently utilized in search applications for finding items similar or related to the query under consideration. The "K" in KNN shows the number of closest neighbors to contemplate when the outcome for the new data point is desired to be predicted. Due to possessing a fast-learning ability and shorter learning phase, KNN algorithm is often referred to as a lazy learner. The model memorizes the training dataset, and once a prediction is requested, it starts functioning with its full efficiency.

3.2 Proposed Methodology

Below section presents the detail of the proposed methodologies to have secure identification and authentication for devices in IoT network. Our scope is limited in this matter as we are concerned only with devices at home, office or small-scale industry or any environment where an automated building management system can work. By introducing both Identification and Authentication, we meant that first device in a network should be identified by technique and method discussed in Fig. 2 and depicted in the architecture.

In this Machine Learning Technique, communication via some authenticated protocol should proceed further. IoT-Sentinel proposed an idea of firewall in which if the device is found to be secure then corresponding levels can be assigned to it, other than this then approach to other authentication components can be joined with identification which may be token-based or alert to the user.

Our proposed work explains how secure device identification can be achieved and at the end of this section, a brief overview of the architecture is also given providing a review of the proposed work.

In this study, we mainly follow IoT-Sentinel approach with basic or few differences.

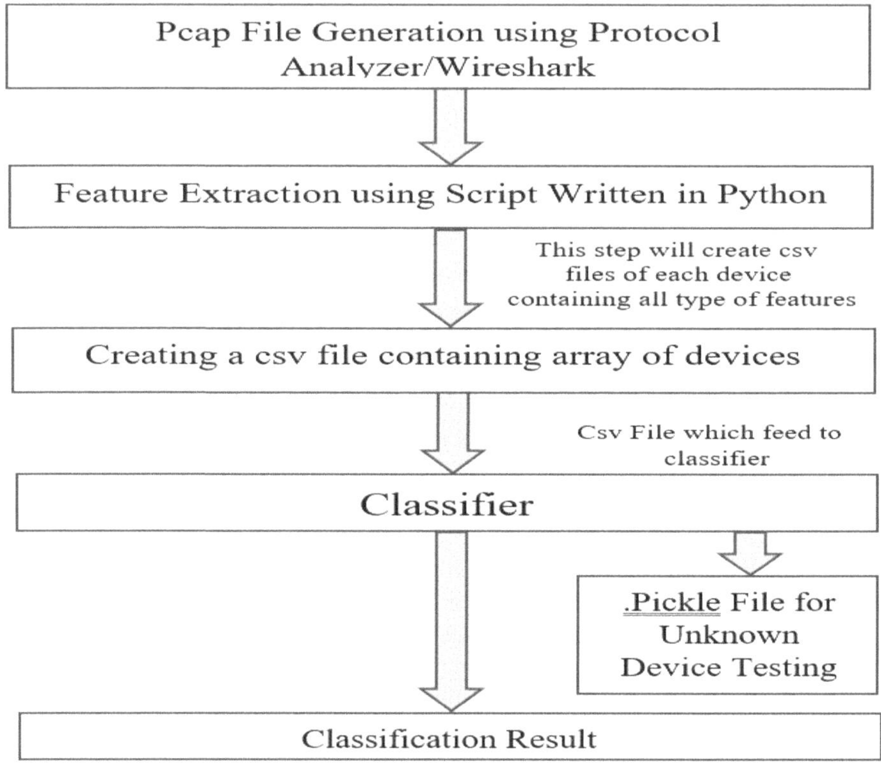

Fig. 2. Overview of Proposed Architecture

Device Fingerprint

The first step to consider in identification of devices is fingerprint generation. In our approach, features will be extracted from the devices by simply creating fingerprint. This will be later used by authorized person to validate any new or previous devices regarding the one installed. Assuming that feature extraction will be done in the initial phase, every device will have unique fingerprint and a total of 33 features out of which 23 features are the same as used in IoT-Sentinel. Ten (10) more features were added which will be based on sequence of packets being transmitted from one device to another as in [18]. On the difference of the subset of parameters, the count of features has increased to 90. This increase in subset features will be further reduce to around 40 to clearly show the addition of more features but has little effect for device identification [19, 20]. Next we will combine both IoT-Sentinel and sequence based types of features in [21].

Device Type Identification

This section explains how an array of 33 features were extracted and a CSV file created and properly labeled with device labeled for further processing. To remain safe from imbalanced data training, we used a threshold of 0.20 as used in IoT-sentinel, or higher as per usage. After balancing the data, we subjected the feature set of all devices (i.e. 33 feature of one device time 31 devices).

In IoT-Sentinel only 27 devices were used, and the dataset given has 31 devices, therefore, we used them in our testing and a single CSV file was extracted from all initial setup of devices and in this single file, all device were balanced giving us an array of 33 times 31. These total devices were then subjected to testing of 5–6 classifiers and the result was found to be the best with more precision using Random forest.

We used binary classifier already used in IoT-Sentinel. This means each device type will be having one classifier. We then subjected fingerprint of unique features to 5 types of classifier. We made the system intelligent such that higher output of classifier will be used and other outputs will be discarded. This will later on be used for device classification. If found to still matched with any of the fingerprints then it will be further subjected to the distance computation, but not to the same algorithm as used in IoT-Sentinel. Two different edit-based algorithms are used which reduces seven times computation of the same fingerprints.

Features Used

Features in Table 1 are combining two different approaches which are packet-based and other behavior-based of devices. The first 23 features are being used in IoT-Sentinel. Other features have been chosen by going through a literature survey on network traffic classification.

Table 1. Features

Features Types
Link Layer Protocol (2)
Network Layer Protocol (4)
Transport Layer Protocol (2)
Application Layer Protocol (8)
IP Options (2)
Packet Content (2)
IP address (1)
Port Class (2)
Packet inter-arrival time (2)
Ethernet Packet size (2)
IP payload size
IP packer header size
Packet count
Packet Direction
Inter- Packet length

Validation

We used 10 fold cross-validation for training the classifier and 5-fold validation for 9 iterations, training classifier a unique model was generated loaded into a pickle file which later on will be compared with any new device or any device whose identification is to be done, within limited time it will predict either device type as "known or unknown", it will let user or administrator know about prediction probability and how many devices are getting matched and how many steps are required to reach known device type.

Metrics
We used different parameters to check prediction for device identification in which we considered recall, precision, and F1-score. These parameters provided the exact prediction. For each individual device, recall, precision, and F1-score were calculated.

In addition, IoT-Sentinel was implemented to compare and evaluate our results, our confusion matrix for the ten devices is also given in Table 2 which has increased rate for true prediction in the same class.

4 Results

By extracting features from the initial phase and then generating fingerprint of each device a model can be made which later on can be used for predicting or testing any unknown device manually or by introducing automation in the testing unknown devices can be identified.

The proposed model was implemented on Scikit-learn, which is a python-based and open-source ML toolbox. Model's performance was evaluated based on the parameters given below:

- **Precision:** This parameter provides the ratio of fingerprints that are accurately identified by the Secure Device Identification and Authentication Architecture to the total number of fingerprints identified. $Precision(Prec) = \frac{TP}{TF+TP}$
- **Recalls:** This parameter provides the ratio of fingerprints that are accurately identified by the Secure Device Identification and Authentication Architecture among all the fingerprints Recalls $= \frac{TP}{TP+FN}$
- **F1-Score:** It is the harmonic mean of precision and recall. $F1 - score = \frac{2*Prec*rcl}{prec+rcl}$

where, TP, FP and FN represent the true positives, false positives and false negatives, respectively.

Table 2. Confusion Matrix A/P

A/P	1	2	3	4	5	6	7	8	9	10
1	179	12	0	0	14	0	0	0	0	0
2	0	99	76	40	0	0	0	0	0	0
3	0	81	70	65	0	0	0	0	0	0
4	8	70	30	90	0	0	0	0	0	0
5	0	0	10	0	150	40	0	0	0	0
6	0	0	0	0	69	152	0	0	0	0
7	0	0	0	0	0	0	165	20	10	0
8	0	0	0	0	0	0	84	116	0	0
9	0	0	0	0	0	0	0	24	60	110
10	0	0	0	0	0	0	021	02	135	21

Confusion matrix depicts that for class actual class 1 it was predicted 179 times as class1 and 12 times as other class during K-Fold cross-validation, these results are shown for 10 times K- fold that in each individual iteration which device mismatch happened.

Classification report of all the techniques is as follows:

Table 3. Classification Report

Sr. No	Precision	Recall	F1-score
Random Forest	0.91	0.91	0.91
Gradient Boosting	0.87	0.89	0.879
K-Neighbor	0.74	0.77	0.756

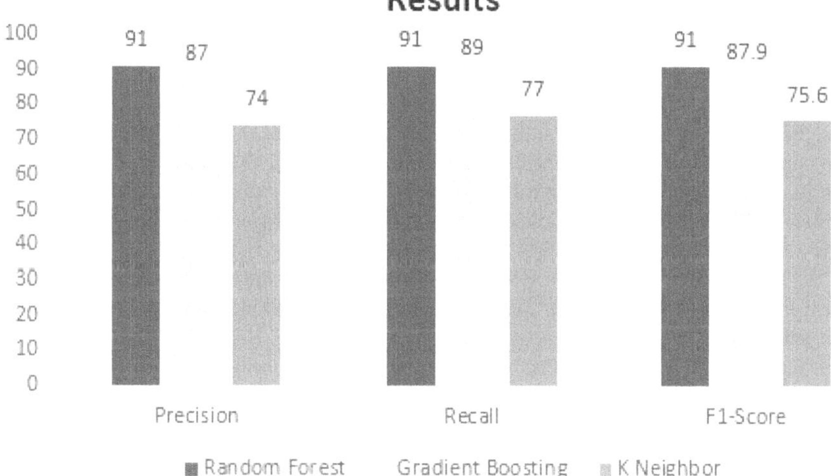

Fig. 3. Results of different classification techniques

All the techniques are effective and efficient to predict the fingerprints but the Random Forest classification model gives the maximum f1 score of 91% as shown in Table 3 and in Fig. 3

Results show Random Forest achieves increased classification performance and yield results that are accurate and precise. Therefore, for the classification problems, if one has to choose a classifier among the tree-based classifiers set, we recommend using the Random Forest with confidence for a variety of classification problems.

5 Conclusion

We have demonstrated that in the study by adding more features and combining them with 23 features of IoT-Sentinel, the device can have a hard and strong fingerprint which can be a great source to optimize security. By generating a pickle modal, it can be used in the future for unknown devices or any security level can be assigned to identified devices. Moreover, this approach can be used to classify heterogeneous devices in any network as above. The type of features used are very important for any type of network classification which may be embedded as important elements in device classifications in a heterogeneous network.

Acknowledgment. Special acknowledgment to Dr. Sheraz Naseer for consistent guidance. Secondly to Authors of IoT-sentinel [1] for sharing dataset so this research could be accomplished.

Data for Research. This research is based on the dataset used by [1], therefore these authors may be contacted to get access to all datasets used.

References

1. Miettinen, M., Marchal, S., Hafeez, I., Asokan, N., Sadeghi, A., Tarkoma, S.: IoT SENTINEL: automated device-type identification for security enforcement in IoT. In: 2017 IEEE 37th International Conference on Distributed Computing Systems (ICDCS), Atlanta, GA, pp. 2177–184 (2017). https://doi.org/10.1109/ICDCS.2017.283
2. Core Security. AVTECH DVR multiple vulnerabilities, Aug. 2013. http://www.coresecurity.com/advisories/avtech-dvr-multiple-vulnerabilities. Accessed 29 Mar 2016
3. Senrio. 400,000 publicly available IoT devices vulnerable to single flaw. http://blog.senr.io/blog/400000-publicly-available-iot-devices-vulnerable-to-single-flaw. Accessed 07 July 2018
4. Letaw, L., Pletcher, J., Butler, K.: Host identification via USB fingerprinting. In: 2011 Sixth IEEE International Workshop on Systematic Approaches to Digital Forensic Engineering, pp. 1–9 (2011)
5. Desmond, L.C.C., Yuan, C.C., Pheng, T.C., Lee, R.S.: Identifying unique devices through wireless fingerprinting. In: Proceedings of the First ACM Conference on Wireless Network Security, WiSec'08, (New York, NY, USA), pp. 46–55, ACM (2008)
6. Lin, J., Yu, W., Zhang, N., Yang, X., Zhang, H., Zhao, W.: A survey on Internet of Things: architecture, enabling technologies, security and privacy, and applications. IEEE Internet of Things Journal, pp. 1–1
7. El-Shweky, B.E., et al.: Internet of things: a comparative study. In: 2018 IEEE 8thAnnual Computing and Communication Workshop and Conference (CCWC), Las Vegas, NV, pp. 622–631 (2018)
8. Zhang, J., Wang, Z., Yang, Z., Zhang, Q.: Proximity based IoT device a uthentication. IEEE INFOCOM 2017 - IEEE Conference Computer, Communications, Atlanta, GA, p. 19 (2017)
9. Maire O'Neill. Insecurity by Design: Today's IoT Device Security Problem. Engineering, Volume 2, PP. 48–49. https://doi.org/10.1016/J.ENG.2016.01.014
10. Shivraj, V.L., Rajan, M.A., Singh, M., Balamuralidhar, P.: One time password authentication scheme based on elliptic curves for Internet of Things (IoT). In: 2015 5th National Symposium on Information Technology: Towards New Smart World (NSITNSW), Riyadh, pp. 1–6 (2015)
11. Huang, Z., Su, X., Zhang, Y., Shi, C., Zhang, H., Xie, L.: A decentralized solution for IoT data trusted exchange based-on blockchain. In: 2017 3rd IEEE International Conference on Computer and Communications (ICCC), Chengdu, pp. 1180–1184 (2017)
12. Cha, S., Tsai, T., Peng, W., Huang, T., Hsu, T.: Privacy-aware and blockchain connected gateways for users to access legacy IoT devices. In: 2017 IEEE 6th Global Conference on Consumer Electronics (GCCE), Nagoya, pp. 1–3 (2017)

13. Gantait, A., Patra, J., Mukherjee, A.: Securing IoT Devices and Gateways 2016, IBM Developer Work. https://www.ibm.com, Part-1, PP. 1–23. Accessed 10 May 2018
14. Bratus, S., Cornelius, C., Kotz, D., Peebles, D.: Active behavioral fingerprinting of wireless devices. In: Proceedings of the First ACM Conference on 61 Wireless Network Security, WiSec '08, (New York, NY, USA), pp. 56–61, ACM (2008)
15. Gao, K., Corbett, C., Beyah, R.: A passive approach to wireless device fingerprinting. In: 2010 IEEE/IFIP International Conference on Dependable Systems Networks (DSN), pp. 383–392 (2010)
16. Sieka, B.: Active fingerprinting of 802.11 devices by timing analysis. In: CCNC 2006. 2006 3rd IEEE Consumer Communications a nd Networking Conference, 2006, vol. 1, p. 15 19, Jan (2006)
17. Noguchi, H., Demizu, T., Hoshikawa, N., Kataoka, M., Yamato, Y.: Autonomous device identification architecture for Internet of Things. In: 2018 IEEE 4th World Forum on Internet of Things (WF-IoT), Singapore, pp. 407–411 (2018). https://doi.org/10.1109/WF-IoT.2018.8355100
18. Althuge and Nishad. IoT-Device Fingerprinting with Sequence Based Features. https://helda.helsinki.fi/handle/10138/234247
19. Granata, D., Rak, M., Salzillo, G., Barbato, U.: "Security in IoT Pairing & Authentication protocols, a Threat Model and a Case Study Analysis" Università della Campania "Luigi Vanvitelli", Dipartimento di Ingegneria, Aversa (CE), 81031 Italy
20. Ali, K., Askar, S.: Security Issues and Vulnerability of IoT Devices. Volume: 5, Issue: 3, pp. 101–115 (2021)
21. Azrour, M., Mabrouki, J, Guezzaz, A., Farhaoui, Y.: New Enhanced Authentication Protocol for Internet of Things. ISSN 2096 – 0654 01/07, pp. 1–9, Volume 4, Number 1, March (2021)

Towards a Fully-Fletched African Register of Implanted Pacemakers

Servule O. F. Kouzonde[1], Ginette Kpadjouda[1], Vinasetan Ratheil Houndji[1], S. Arnaud R. M. Ahouandjinou[1], Jules Degila[1], and Mouhamadou Lamine Ba[2(✉)]

[1] Université d'Abomey-Calavi, Cotonou, Bénin
[2] Université Cheikh Anta Diop, Dakar, Senegal
mouhamadoulamine.ba@uadb.edu.sn

Abstract. Like in any health-critical area, rigor and precision are essential in cardiology. This paper presents an overview of implantable cardiac devices that can be used to devise a pacemaker wearers registry in Africa. The main problem with the setting up of this African register being resolved is the hard access to the history of the control data for patients with pacemakers because that data is stored in servers in foreign countries. This situation heavily impacts the monitoring of the pacemaker wearers and an improvement of the decision-making process by analyzing the historical information. In addition, information sharing between the cardiologists in Africa and the ease of the mobility of the pacemaker wearers are accurate. To propose a solution to these problems, we begin by taking stock of the work carried out in the field, starting with a bibliometric study carried out in three points: the number of annual productions, the countries, and the most productive countries. Following the bibliometric study, we propose a data collection network architecture for the pacemaker environment in Africa and a precise architecture for the solutions provided. There are two solutions: a data collection system and a web platform. We have opted for stable, secure, and scalable technologies to ensure reliable implementation of our solutions. Our data collection device uses a microcontroller integrating an ESP8266 Wi-Fi SoC and a short-range Bluetooth receiver/transmitter. The data delivery platform has been developed using Nest.Js and Angular, two robust and secure JavaScript frameworks. Implementing this registry will undoubtedly help the pacemaker ecosystem in Africa.

Keywords: registry · pacemaker · bibliometric study · state of the art · IoT · data

1 Introduction

A pacemaker is a device that constantly monitors the patient's heart and sends tiny electrical impulses to remedy the situation. It is equipped with numerous

D. Bassole et al. (Eds.): InterSol 2025, LNICST 671, pp. 204–216, 2026.
https://doi.org/10.1007/978-3-032-15154-4_16

sensors to perform its role effectively. While listening to the heart's activity, the pacemaker stores data in its memory. A second device, called the programmer, usually from the same manufacturer, sets the patient's pacemaker parameters. The programmer also enables data stored by the pacemaker to be read and exported to various targets. After pacemaker implantation, and given the connectivity of most devices, rhythmologists have a pressing need to have ubiquitous and long-term access to patient data to guarantee the effectiveness of their care. . Unfortunately, manufacturers are not adequately meeting this need for cardiologists practicing in Africa. The diversity of manufacturers further aggravates this problem by adding an additional layer of complexity. Additionally, to our knowledge, no data center offers an API[1] on implantable cardiac devices to bring together the major players in this field, and most cardiology departments in Africa have no way of easily accessing historical data on pacemaker monitoring. In this paper, we consider centralizing the data of African implantable cardiac device wearers, regardless of the manufacturer. The goal is to enhance data availability about patients with cardiac implants across diverse domains, including clinical, academic, and decision-making spheres.

Before developing the registry prototype, we reviewed the existing literature, including a state-of-the-art and a bibliometric study. The bibliometric research was carried out with R and R.Studio tools. It was based on a database of 1129 documents from PubMed with the search string"pacemaker AND registry". The generalities of pacemakers revolve around the manufacturers, the aggregation system for collecting cardiac implant data, and the elements involved in the design of a registry. To alleviate the lack of infrastructure in the field in Africa, we propose the design of a data collection device and the design of a web application. These solutions combined will allow practitioners and actors in the sector to be up-to-date and improve patient management.

The remainder of this paper is organized as follows. Section 2 begins with a bibliometric analysis, including the methodology, data collection, and main results; then concludes with general information on pacemakers and reviews the registers of implantable cardiac devices with their characteristics, implementation, and limitations. Section 3 presents our contribution to improving the ICT environment in the cardiology field in Africa. Finally, a discussion of this paper is presented in Sect. 4.1.

2 Research Studies on Pacemakers

In this section, we discuss the current state of pacemaker registries in the world and in Africa, as well as the scientific work carried out in the field. We present the components of pacemakers and discuss their internal and external communication architecture, to situate the registries in this system. Among the articles on implantable cardiac devices, we focused on documents dealing with African registries, but not only. We also focused on articles presenting aspects of register design and possible architectures. This focused approach allows us to delve into

[1] Application Programming Interface.

the complexities and unique challenges faced in establishing and maintaining pacemaker registries in varying healthcare infrastructures, particularly in the African context where digital health infrastructure may still be in developmental phases. Through this examination, we aim to highlight significant trends, pinpoint gaps in the current knowledge base, and propose pathways for future research and development in the field of cardiac device registries. This analysis is critical for optimizing registry functionality and enhancing patient outcomes through improved monitoring and data management strategies in cardiology.

2.1 Bibliometric Analysis Methodology

As guiding principles, we adopted elements from the Preferred Reporting Items for Systematic Reviews and Meta-Analyses (PRISMA). Our bibliometric analysis leveraged several open-access databases. These include Google Scholar, Web of Science, and Scopus, encompassing various scientific disciplines. Additionally, PubMed was utilized for its exclusive focus on medicine and biomedical sciences. With the search string"pacemaker AND registry", we had 1129 documents only of article type from 1974 - 2022.

This part provides a comprehensive overview of existing scholarly work, focusing on Africa's involvement in implantable cardiac device registry research. To achieve this, after compiling our database of relevant literature, we employed RStudio for our analysis. We specifically utilized the Bibliometrix library within RStudio, a tool well-suited for conducting detailed bibliometric analyses (Fig. 1).

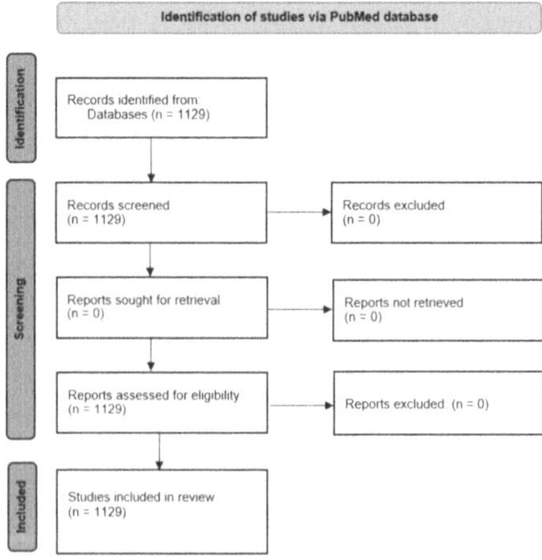

Fig. 1. Flow Prisma diagram of papers selection. Prisma diagram showing the sequences used to select articles from our PubMed database

2.2 Bibliometric Analysis Results

Dataset Overview. Our research yielded a data set over 48 years. The size of the collection in terms of the number of documents, the period of publication, the number of sources, the articles in clinical trials, the comments, and comparative studies are presented in Table 1.

Table 1. Dataset primary information

Category	Description	Result
General	Period	1974 - 2022
	Source	254
	Documents	1129
	Average years from publication	7,49
Clinical trial	Journal article	6
	Journal article on multicentre study	11
	Journal article on a multi-center, observational study	2
Commentary	Editorial	8
	Letter	9
Comparative study	Journal article	40
	Journal article on multi-center study	14
	Journal article on a multi-center, observational study	12
	Journal article on multicentre study and research support, non-us gov't	9

Annual Scientific Production. The first factor in our bibliometric study is the annual production curve on implantable cardiac device registers.

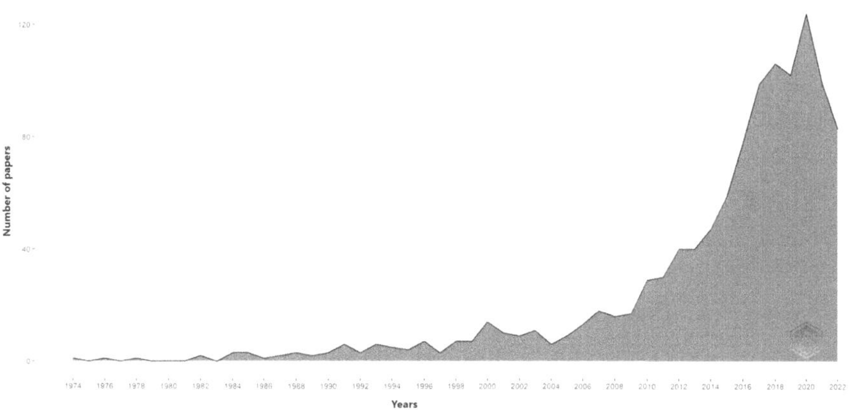

Fig. 2. Annual scientific production. It shows the number of items produced per year

Figure 2 shows the number of papers produced per year and country. One can see an "exponential" growth in the number of documents between 2004 and 2022 and a spike in the number of papers produced in 2020, with more than 120 papers globally, a slight decrease in 2019. Therefore, there is good production in implantable cardiac device registries.

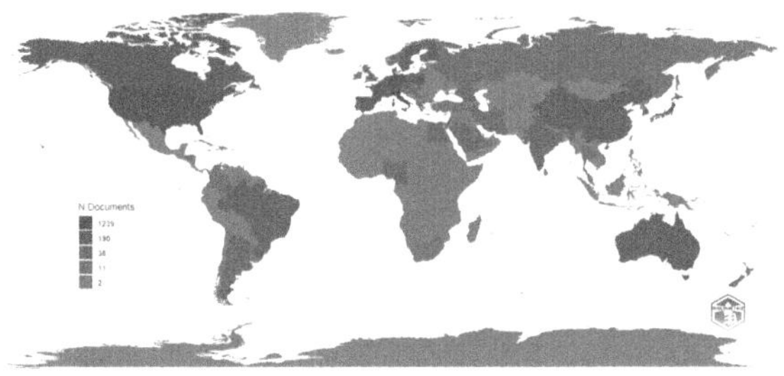

Fig. 3. Country scientific production

Country Scientific Production. Figure 3 shows a map of the world areas with the number of published documents. In the illustration, we observe that those countries with the most published articles are colored in pure royal blue. These countries are on the continents with at least one implantable cardiac device manufacturer: America, Europe, and Asia. Conversely, the continent of Africa exhibits a stark under-representation in the academic literature, with fewer than 12 documents identified in the field. This discrepancy highlights a significant disparity in research output and reflects the limited presence associated technological infrastructure within the continent.

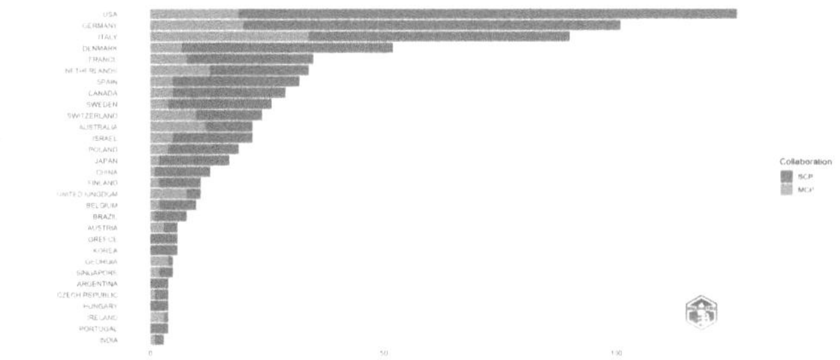

Fig. 4. Relevant countries

Most Relevant Countries. In Fig. 4, publications from a single country (SCP) are shown in green. These are the publications in which all the authors belong to the same country and represent an intra-country collaboration. Multi-country publications (MCP), shown in red, are the publications in which the authors belong to different countries, meaning an international partnership. We have the USA, Germany, and Italy leading the most productive countries with more than 100, 80, and 50 documents written by authors from the same country. Italy dominates with more production between authors from different countries with 34 papers.

2.3 Zoom on Pacemakers

Implanted cardiac devices are commonly used to treat a wide range of life-threatening heart conditions, including arrhythmias and cardiac resynchronization in some heart failure patients. Approximately 400,000 devices are implanted annually, and more than 3 million patients currently wear implanted devices in the United States [3]. All of this is supported by up-to-date registries that allow effective monitoring of implanted patients. In Africa, according to a 2014 demographic study of 31 countries by the World Bank, none had a national pacemaker registry despite the rapid growth in the number of implants. Almost 26% of countries had no pacemaker services [1].

Being electronic devices, pacemakers are composed of an energy source, an electronic system allowing the delivery of electrical pulses calibrated in frequency, amplitude, and width of amplitude; a detection system of the spontaneous electrical activity of the heart, allowing them to operate only in case of failure of this one (sentinel mode); a measurement system to know the resistance of the probes (impedance), the battery charge, the operating statistics; a radio frequency antenna allowing data communication through the skin to an external device. Note that the pacemaker battery has a life span of approximately 5 to 12 years, except for temporary pacemakers, which have a life span of a few days.

2.4 The Manufacturers

There are five manufacturers of implantable cardiac devices and related devices. Medtronic, Abbott, and Boston Scientific are American manufacturers; Biotronik is a European manufacturer, and Microport is an Asian manufacturer.

Each manufacturer offers a wide range of multifunction pacemakers, programmers, and transmitters to facilitate parameter setting and remote cardiology via their monitoring platforms.

2.5 Pacemaker: Data-Sending

The pacemaker ecosystem has three main players: the manufacturer, the patient, and the doctor (hospital/clinic). The doctor, after implanting the pacemaker in the patient, configures the programmer (a device supplied by the manufacturer of the implanted pacemaker and designed to read the information stored on the battery) located in the cardiology department to prepare it to receive data from the patient's pacemaker during possible face-to-face visits. After reading the data, the cardiologist can not only recalibrate or reprogram the device but also export the data to a digital medium. The patient with the implanted pacemaker also has a bedside or mobile monitor (also supplied by the manufacturer) responsible for periodically retrieving pacemaker data for the manufacturers' servers. Low-level Bluetooth technology is used between the pacemaker and the two devices for data transmission.

2.6 Studies on Pacemaker Registries

Four (4) of the twelve (12) papers reviewed summarized the previous works on pacemaker registries. We have the National Tunisian Registry of Cardiac Implantable Electronic Devices [4], The Oregon Health & Science University Cardiac Implantable Electronic Device Extraction Registry [2], Pacemaker Registry Design and Implementation for Global and Local Integration [5], Cardiac Implant Registries 2006–2016: a systematic review and summary of global experiences [7]. They are presented as follows:

National Tunisian Registry of Cardiac Implantable Electronic Devices. The aim of the observational, prospective, multicentre study was to assess the epidemiological, clinical, and therapeutic profile of implantable cardiac devices in Tunisia. It began in January 2021 and ends on 31 May 2023. Sponsored by Dacima Consulting and the Tunisian Society of Cardiology and Cardiovascular Surgery, it involves only Tunisian patients with implantable cardiac electronic devices from all private and public implantation centers.

Among the features promised by this register are the number of implantations per year, per region and per center for each device, the type of device implanted and its compliance with recommendations, the rate and types of short- and medium-term complications for each device, and details of the risk factors associated with each difficulty.

Data collected by cardiologists, electrophysiologists, and implanting surgeons are stored in a Dacima Consulting database per requirements of FDA 21 CFR part 11 (Food and Drug Administration 21 Code of Federal Regulations part 11), HIPAA (Health Insurance Portability and Accountability Act) and ICH (International Conference on Harmonization) [4]

The Oregon Health & Science University Cardiac Implantable Electronic Device Extraction Registry. Begun in September 2013 for 12 years, it is a retrospective review of data on patient characteristics (such as age, gender, and comorbidities), specifications, indications for the procedure, and results of probe extraction performed at Oregon Health & Science University (OHSU).

According to the Heart Rhythm Society (HRS) consensus document, its main objective is the safety of the lead extraction procedure in terms of acute complications [6].

It covers pacemakers and defibrillators only. Patients with a pacemaker or defibrillator lead extraction will have their records reviewed for desired data, which will then be compiled into a database. [2].

Cardiac Implant Registries 2006–2016: A Systematic Review and Summary of Global Experiences. The study aims to standardize the structure and critical elements of the CIR (Cardiac Implant Registry) and provides recommendations on best practice approaches. After the results of the primary research (source from PubMed (Medline), ScienceDirect, and the Scopus database, EMBASE), 82 registers were counted until 2016, of which 18 automatic implantable defibrillators (AID) registries, 7 cardiac resynchronization therapy (CRT) registries, 5 pacemaker registries, 6 cardiovascular implantable electronic device registries that combined ICD, pacemaker, and CRT implantation data, 22 coronary stent registries, 24 transcatheter heart valve registries. Of the 82 registries, 35 were ongoing in 2018 [7].

This study shows that cardiac tolerance device implant registries are approved and recognized as essential but poorly structured and neglected. We, therefore, have a guideline to follow for structuring and designing a Cardiac Implant Registry (CIR) while adding our strengths according to the objectives of the CIR.

3 Contributions

In the face of all this, Africa remains at the back of the pack due to the considerable lack of IT infrastructure for cardiology services and the sidelining of manufacturers. Therefore, a federated African solution is needed to facilitate access to cardiac device data and address most problems related to monitoring implantable cardiac device wearers.

Our solution, whose main components are depicted in Fig. 6, focuses on the transit of cardiac health data across all the different practitioners on the African continent. Initially, we focused on the data collected by pacemakers and not transmitted to rhythmologists by the manufacturers. Then, we focus on the interoperability between the different cardiological services in Africa.

The latter will allow practitioners to reduce the time managing a patient at risk and have up-to-date information about patients with pacemakers. All these elements converge towards our theme of designing and implementing an African registry of pacemaker wearers.

3.1 The Data Covered by the Register

We consider three (03) categories of data in our solution:

1. Patient identification data. This includes the patient's name, first name, date of birth, gender, origin, nationality, weight, family history and occupation. The cardiologist records this data only once when the patient is added to the registry.

2. Clinical data of the patient. At this level, we work with pre-, intra-, and postoperative data and consultation data. The pre-op data revolves around the patient's health, medical history, and lifestyle. The data during and after the operation refers to the operative report, the type of implanted device, the battery and lead brands, the settings made, and the complications during the operation. The rhythmologist who performed the implantation, the location of the implantation, and the patient's primary cardiologist will also be indicated. The control data will include anomalies or problems that occur daily after the implant and the settings of the device parameters.
3. The pacemaker collected data. These data are around all the parameters configured and data collected natively by the device. These include the remaining life of the device, lead status and modes, lead impedance, polarity, pacing frequency, and A & V pacing.

All this data and events are constantly time-stamped and cover all the information related to the life of a patient with an implantable cardiac device.

3.2 General Architecture of the African Pacemaker Registry

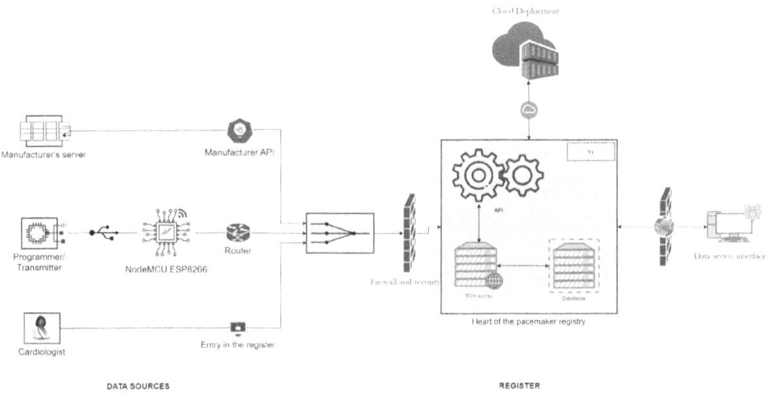

Fig. 5. Architecture of the African Pacemaker Registry

Figure 5 shows the registry architecture emphasizing the different means of data transmission. We have three sources of supply for the registry: manufacturers via an API (application programming interface), programmers installed at the hospital level via a collection module connected to the Internet, and cardiologists via the registry's input interface. The collection module, developed by us, will be connected to an access point to transmit the data read from the transmitter. When routing the data to the registry, the data will go through a security mill (encryption, decryption, request analysis, authentication token verification) and filtering before reaching the implantable pacemaker registry API. The registry provides a man-machine interface to view the registry information through a web client application.

3.3 Data Collection Solution

To ensure the proper functioning of our solution, we rely on three (03) essential data sources: cardiologists, manufacturers and programmers. An IoT data collection device has specifically designed for the registry. This collection system is an integral part of the solutions the register offers.

This device is based on a PCB[2] based on the ESP8266 microcontroller, also known as NodeMCU, a standalone system-on-chip (SOC) with an integrated TCP/IP protocol stack.

The functional prototype of the data collection device is designed to work exclusively with Biotronik's Renamic programmer, complying with a set of technical specifications including data format, type of connection established and security. To transmit data to the register, the device first establishes a Bluetooth connection with Biotronik's Renamic programmer. Next, we ensure that the data collection device has Internet access. Finally, once these operations have been successfully completed, the cardiologist can easily transfer the patient's data to the African registry.

We opted for the design of our data collection device for four (04) reasons:

1. There is difficulty accessing data from pacemakers worn in Africa;
2. Lack of IT infrastructure for patient monitoring;
3. The data collected by the pacemaker is encrypted and, therefore, must be processed by the manufacturer, which hinders and prolongs the patient's treatment time;
4. Have a universal Africa-specific device for data collection.

3.4 Security and Privacy

Data from pacemakers follows a secure path, starting with transmission to the manufacturer's programmer before being routed to our data collection module. This first step benefits from increased security thanks to measures integrated by manufacturers.

To ensure the security of transactions on the ledger network, various security protocols and algorithms have been implemented, including HL7, FHIR, TLS connection, JWT, the use of API keys and the C-CDA standard. These measures secure all interactions, from data collection to transmission to rights holders.

More specifically, our data collection module is reinforced by the use of the AES encryption algorithm in CBC mode with a 256-bit key, supplemented by an upstream key authentication mechanism.

3.5 Application Solution

Continuing in the solutions of the African Pacemaker Registry, the web application is the most important one as it makes the collected data easily available.

[2] Printed circuit board.

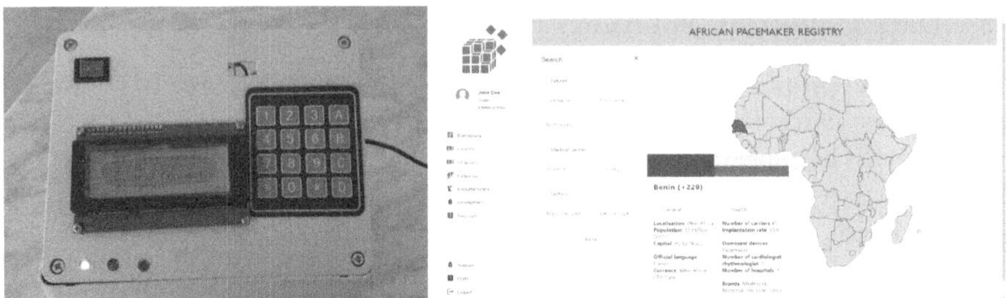

(a) Registry Control Data Collection Device from a programmer.

(b) Registry Web Application.

Fig. 6. Main components of the African Registry of Implanted Pacemakers

The application is divided into several modules with well-defined functionalities. Three actors run the system:

1. The patient is at the heart of the platform's information. He/she can access his/her personal and cardiological data and authorizes a rhythmologist other than the one who performed the implantation to have access to this information;
2. The cardiologist will have to add a patient to the registry by recording personal information and information about the operation, upload the information from the programmer to the registry through the data collection device, and finally access the history of the report of a patient;
3. A general registry administrator will ensure the system works correctly and the right users have the proper permissions.

4 Discussion and Collaboration

4.1 Discussion

The bibliometric study shows that many studies exist in this field. However, Africa still needs to catch up in production and collaboration. Among the studies carried out in Africa, we have a few registries under development. This is mainly the study [7], which outlines the primary elements of designing and setting up a registry. [5] states that the registers follow the standard rules according to the desired functionalities in terms of modeling. Compared to other continents, until 2017, implants in Africa are becoming increasingly larger [1]. Given all this, Africa needs a registry of cardiac device implants, fed on the one hand by pacemaker manufacturers and on the other hand by cardiologists. This will provide the African continent with precise statistics on pacemaker implantations to help monitor patients and promote scientific research in rhythmology. This paper has drawn the first steps to set up a register of African pacemaker wearers that combines efficiency and usefulness. We have designed An IoT device to collect data from programmers and a secure web platform to make the data available to the rightful owner. The web application associated with the registry has been developed using a client-server architecture, using JavaScript frameworks adapted to the hardware specifications. This application allows patients to access their health data. Also, it enables cardiologists to monitor pacemaker patients effectively while providing researchers access to large datasets to facilitate their research in this field. While implementing our solutions, we have identified several significant challenges. The main obstacle remains the restricted access to cardiological data, collected by pacemakers and transferred to manufacturers' servers. This limitation of access is particularly problematic because it is intrinsic to the framework of the study. Most of the manufacturers exercise strict control over the information. To reduce this dependence on manufacturers, we developed a stand-alone data collection module. Budget constraints led us to opt for a prototype based on the NodeMCU, while waiting to develop it with a Raspberry Pi 3. However, two major problems persist with this solution. Firstly, the latency in updating patient data is problematic, as these updates only occur during patients' physical consultations with the rhythmologist. Secondly, the lack of stable and reliable Internet connectivity in many parts of Africa represents a considerable obstacle to efficient data transmission. These challenges highlight the need to adapt digital healthcare technologies to African regional specificities to optimize access and quality of cardiac care across the continent.

4.2 Collaborating Hospital

To successfully design these solutions for the African Pacemaker Registry, we have worked with practitioners from the cardiology service of the CNHUHKM[3] located in Cotonou, Benin, and the Hospital Artistic Le DANTEC located in Dakar, Senegal. This work has been done in the context of the AI4CARDIO research project supported by the ACE-MITIC[4] of Senegal and the ACE-SMIA[5] of Benin.

5 Conclusion

In this paper, we have presented a bibliometric study and state-of-the-art on implementing an African pacemaker system and prototype solutions. The bibliometric study used the PRISMA method with a PubMed database of 1129 documents and a data processing and statistical analysis tool. The United States of America, Germany, and Italy are the most productive countries in terms of the number of papers published in this field. We also noted that the total number of documents produced grew exponentially between 2004 and 2022, from 5 to 120. This demonstrates the growing interest in the subject. In terms of collaboration, there needs to be more collaboration between African countries and those on other continents. Few African countries are studying this subject, unlike Europe and America. The state-of-the-art guides us in two aspects. First,

[3] Centre National Hospitalier Universitaire Hubert Koutoukou MAGA.

[4] African Center of Excellence in Mathematics, Computer Science and ICT.

[5] African Center of Excellence in Mathematics, Computer Science and Applications.

the critical elements of designing a standards-compliant registry, and second, the population of the registry. Following these elements, we have created a prototype of a nodemcu-based IoT data collection solution and a web-based solution to make the collected data available. As part of our future work, we plan to roll out and evaluate the proposed registry in partner cardiology departments. We recommend future research and production collaborations between the African continent and other continents.

References

1. Bonny, A., al: Statistics on the use of cardiac electronic devices and interventional electrophysiological procedures in africa from 2011 to 2016: report of the pan african society of cardiology (pascar) cardiac arrhythmias and pacing task forces. https://academic.oup.com/europace/article/20/9/1513/4772290#120967040 (2017), Accessed 17 Oct 2022
2. Charles Henrikson MD, O.H., University, S.: Pacemaker and defibrillator lead extraction registry. https://clinicaltrials.gov/ct2/show/NCT03847025 (2021), Accessed 29 July 2022
3. Health, O., University, S.: Pacemaker and defibrillator lead extraction registry. https://clinicaltrials.gov/ct2/show/NCT03847025 (2021), Accessed 28 May 2022
4. NATURE-CIED: National Tunisian registry of cardiac implantable electronic devices (nature-cied). https://clinicaltrials.gov/ct2/show/results/NCT05361759 et http://www.stcccv.org.tn/registreEnCours (2021), Accessed 29 July 2022
5. da Silva, K.R., Roberto Costa, E.S.C.e.a.: Glocal clinical registries: pacemaker registry design and implementation for global and local integration – methodology and case study. Plos One (2013)
6. Towbin, J.A.: 2019 hrs expert consensus statement on evaluation, risk stratification, and management of arrhythmogenic cardiomyopathy. https://www.hrsonline.org/guidance/clinical-resources/2019-hrs-expert-consensus-statement-evaluation-risk-stratification-and-management-arrhythmogenic (2019), Accessed 30 July 2022
7. Zhang, S., Gaiser, S, K.R.P.: Cardiac implant registries 2006-2016: a systematic review and summary of global experiences. BMJ Open. National Leading-Edge Cluster Med. Technol. "Medical Valley EMN" **8**(4), e019039 (2018). https://doi.org/10.1136/bmjopen-2017-019039

Information and Communication Technology

Ontology Population and Maintenance Based on Web Scraping: Case of OntoSYSPARCOTCI

Téhia Kouaho N'guessan Narcisse[1](✉), Kaboré Ben Abdoul Nassire[2], Kouakou Malanno[1], Bini Kouadio Kra Norbert[1], and Malo Sadouanouan[2]

[1] Centre National de Recherche Agronomique, Bouake, Côte d'Ivoire
tehiako@gmail.com

[2] Université Nazi Boni, Bobo-Dioulasso, Burkina Faso

Abstract. This paper discusses the populating of an ontology dedicated to the phytosanitary surveillance of cotton plants. This ontology was built with the aim of annotating the data from phytosanitary surveillance of cotton in Côte d'Ivoire and facilitating collaboration between actors with different skills. Its implementation led to the creation of a semantic Wiki. Populating an ontology consists in associating concrete instances with the concepts and relations defined in ontology. In the life cycle of ontologies, it is recommended that they be constantly updated and maintained. This task can be difficult, costly and tedious when it is dedicated solely to humans and carried out manually. In this paper, we present a semi-automatic approach to ontology populating based on web scraping. This approach combines natural language processing (NLP) and Hearst pattern extraction techniques to automatically detect relevant instances in documents collected from the web. Implementation of this approach resulted in a satisfactory accuracy rate of 79%.

Keywords: Ontology · Web scraping · Information extraction · Natural Language Processing (NLP)

1 Introduction

In the context of knowledge management related to pests, diseases, and the phenology of cotton plants in Côte d'Ivoire, a domain ontology for phytosanitary surveillance has been constructed [1]. This ontology has been built to annotate data from the phytosanitary surveillance of cotton plants in Côte d'Ivoire, and to enable surveillance stakeholders with different skills to communicate more easily using the same language [1]. Given the possibilities offered by ontologies for reasoning about data, surveillance stakeholders will be able to derive new knowledge from existing knowledge. An ontology is defined as "a formal and explicit specification of a shared conceptualization" [2]. Essentially, it provides a structured, consensus-based, and reusable representation of domain-specific knowledge.

To evaluate the results obtained from the constructed ontology, we manually populated it [3]. Ontology populating consists in associating concrete instances with the

D. Bassole et al. (Eds.): InterSol 2025, LNICST 671, pp. 219–229, 2026.
https://doi.org/10.1007/978-3-032-15154-4_17

concepts and relations defined in the ontology [4]. As for evaluation, it enabled us to check that ontology met requirements specifications defined on basis of exchanges with domain experts [4].

Sources used to populate ontology manually came from the Centre National de Recherche Agronomique (CNRA). However, there are other sources on the web that could be used to populate the ontology. Moreover, manual populating is a difficult activity to carry out [5]. Additionally, manual population is a challenging task [5]. It can be tedious and difficult to scale for large volumes of data [6].

To overcome these challenges and limitations, we propose an automated populating approach. Manual populating requires human intervention to add new instances, whereas automated populating allows knowledge to be extracted and integrated using automated techniques. The particularity of the automated populating approach we propose in this paper compared with other automated approaches is that it is based on web scraping. Indeed, web scraping in our approach represents the main source of data acquisition, reinforcing the automation and dynamism of the cotton pest surveillance system in Côte d'Ivoire (SySParCot-CI).

Apart from the introduction and conclusion, this paper is divided into four (04) parts. The first part discusses related work, the second presents the ontoSYSPARCOTCI ontology, the third is devoted to our population approach and its implementation, and the fifth part presents the obtained results.

2 State of Art

Ontology population supports the ontology construction process by enriching the associated knowledge base. It involves adding new instances of concepts and relationships to an existing ontology. Due to the limitations of manual methods, automating this process has been widely studied. For example, Lubani et *al.* provides an analysis of various data extraction and integration techniques used for ontology population [7]. According literature [8, 9], these methods can be grouped into three main categories: rule-based approaches, statistical approaches, and machine learning approaches.

Below, we present several research works aimed at automating ontology population.

Hearst [10] defined a set of generic extraction patterns, now widely adopted in the literature, for guiding the extraction of hyponymy relations (i.e., "is-a" relationships) [11–13]. He developed a comprehensive set of rules based on the syntactic and grammatical characteristics of terms, along with specific keywords, to create an adaptable extraction tool for any domain. However, many researchers have highlighted the substantial manual effort required to define these rules.

Chatterjee and Kaushik [14] developed the RENT algorithm, a rule-based system designed to identify domain-specific terms in unstructured text within the agricultural field (e.g., plant species, fruits, pesticides). While this algorithm is replicable in other domains, its effectiveness relies heavily on the extraction patterns used patterns that often include domain-specific vocabulary. Therefore, applying RENT to a new domain requires domain experts to redefine appropriate extraction patterns.

Makki et *al.* [15] approached the problem from a different angle, focusing specifically on the relationships between concepts in an ontology to detect their instances.

Their system, OntoPRiMa, combines rule-based extraction, ontology relationships, and natural language processing techniques to identify concept instances expressed through representative verbs in text.

ArtEquAKT [13] is a system that automatically extracts information about artists from the Web, populates a knowledge base, and uses it to generate personalized biographies. It employs syntactic analysis to determine grammatical categories and semantic analysis to perform named entity recognition and extract binary relations between instances. ArtEquAKT also uses a set of heuristics and reasoning methods to eliminate redundant instances from the ontology.

Miguel Ramos [16] used web scraping and lexical similarity techniques to populate an ontology in the field of engineering. He scraped data from online electronic product retailers and then used lexical similarity between the extracted instances and ECLASS, a lexical database, to determine relevant domain classes. However, this approach has performance limitations, as it relies solely on lexical similarity and does not leverage grammatical features of terms that could enhance the algorithm's accuracy.

Holzinger [17] proposed an ontology population approach using the AllRight Scraper tool to locate and download HTML pages. Instead of using HTML source code, the authors relied on the visual rendering of pages to extract tabular data. They claimed that any element aligned in a tabular format on a web page could be interpreted and extracted as a table. Regular expressions were then used to map extracted data to ontology concepts. However, reliance on visual rendering led to the loss of information often embedded in the HTML source.

Patel et *al.* [18] developed OntoGenie, a semi-automatic tool that leverages lexical databases like WordNet to convert web-extracted data into structured knowledge. Their proposed framework is domain-independent and uses WordNet to bridge between the input domain ontology and web pages.

Finally, Lomov et *al.* [19] trained a neural network to recognize concepts similar to those already present in an ontology by analyzing the context in which associated terms appear in textual data. The most relevant elements identified by the model are then validated by experts and, when appropriate, added to the ontology as new instances.

In view of these different approaches, we focus on a rule-based method, exploiting grammatical properties of terms to extract relevant information from documents retrieved from web pages. In our approach, unlike others, we prefer to collect data directly from the web.

3 OntoSYSPARCOTCI: Ontology Related to Phytosanitary Surveillance of Cotton Crops in Côte D'Ivoire

ontoSYSPARCOT is an ontology dedicated to the phytosanitary surveillance of cotton in Côte d'Ivoire [4]. It describes the data collected from the phytosanitary surveillance of cotton in Côte d'Ivoire [1]. It is used to semantically annotate resources on a semantic web platform called SySParCot-Ci WikiS. This platform facilitates collaboration between CNRA researchers, cotton companies, members of the cotton industry and the public interested in cotton growing. ontoSYSPARCOTCI is composed of 306 identified classes, 307 "Object Property", 113 "Data Property", 146 individuals. These individuals were added manually for testing purposes (Fig. 1).

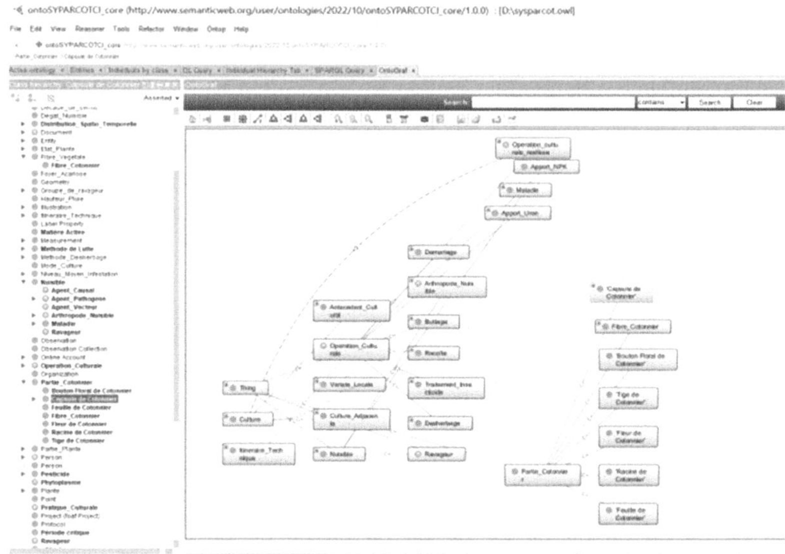

Fig. 1. View of ontoSYSPARCOTCI through 'Protégé' software [4].

4 Ontology Population and Implementation

Process of ontology population can be defined as "the task of updating an ontology with new facts from a knowledge input resource" [7]. Performing this task manually is both time-consuming and costly, which has led to the development of Ontology-Based Information Extraction (OBIE) systems.

In this article, M. Lubani et *al.* [7], has shown aspects to be taken into account when designing ontology populating systems, including:

- Data acquisition – gathering raw textual or structured data from relevant sources;
- Text preprocessing, which involves natural language processing (NLP) techniques such as tokenization, lemmatization, and part-of-speech tagging;
- Candidate instance identification, typically performed using named entity recognition (NER) techniques;
- Concept instantiation, where identified entities are mapped to existing ontology concepts or used to create new instances.

4.1 Web Scraping-Based Ontology Population Approach

The approach we propose is composed of four (04) steps, namely: (i) information extraction from base ontology, (ii) development of web mining engine, (iii) implementation of information extraction engine, (iv) ontology populating, which involves validation and insertion of extracted instances. This approach is based on rules using Hearst patterns [10]. These patterns, originally designed for the English language, are used to detect hyponymy relations in texts. They are based on the assumption that hyponymy relations follow recurrent linguistic structures.

In his article, Hearst describes six (06) patterns based on noun phrases as concepts (NPc) and candidate instances in the extracted hyponymy relation (NPi). Application of these patterns requires prior processing (Tokenization, Lemmatization, Part-of-speech tagging) or annotation, in particular identification of the noun phrases on which rules can be applied. Although modern models exist (BERT, openIE, LLMs), our choice of Hearst's models is explained by the fact that we have limited corpora at our disposal, and Hearst's models are specific to detection of hyponymic relations.

4.2 Implementing

This section builds upon the conceptual framework previously outlined to guide the population of the ontology related to phytosanitary surveillance of cotton crops in Côte d'Ivoire. Tools and technologies employed throughout the implementation process are:

- SpaCy (v 3.0.1): used to perform natural language processing tasks such as tokenization, lemmatization, and part-of-speech tagging.
- Owlready (v 0.20): used to facilitate the reading and writing of ontologies in OWL format.
- Flask (v 3.0.2): provides tools for developing web applications. In this study, it was used to implement the human–machine inter-face of the prototype.
- Scrapy (v 2.11): a versatile framework offering a wide range of tools for web scraping and data extraction from websites.
- Requests (2.32.3): it offers a user-friendly interface for sending HTTP requests and retrieving web content.

Implementation and operation of these tools and technologies are based on architecture below (Fig. 2).

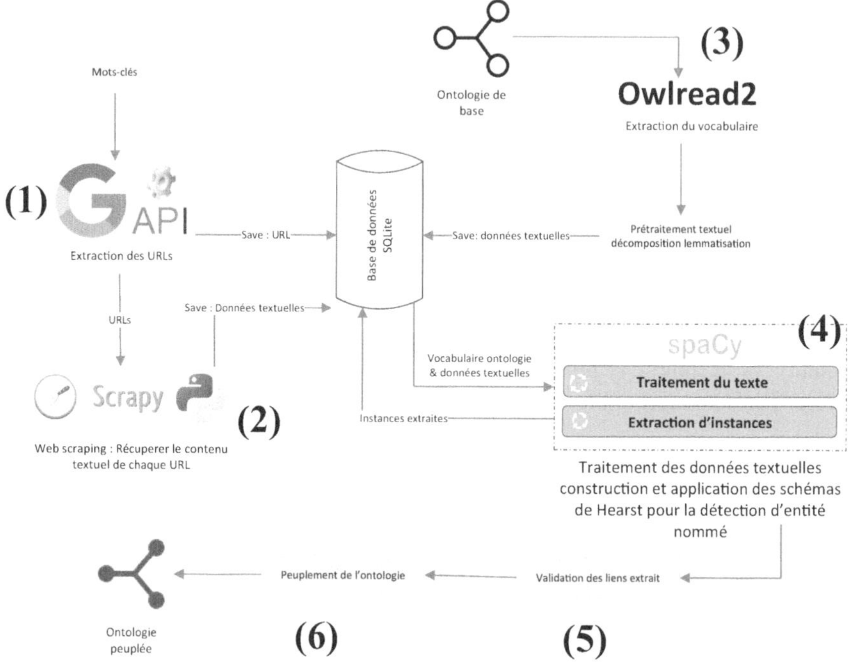

Fig. 2. General architecture of proposed system

(1) Extraction of URLs using Google API from a list of keywords entered as parameters. These URLs are saved in a database and then made available to a web scraping tool (Scrapy).
(2) Extraction of textual data linked to each URL obtained in step 1. During extraction, Scrapy performs technical processing of irregular expressions and then stores this data in a database.
(3) Extraction of the ontology vocabulary to be populated using the Owlread2 library. At this stage, concept names are extracted from the ontology of phytosanitary surveillance of cotton in Côte d'Ivoire (ontoSYSPARCOTCI). Each extracted term is processed (decomposition, lemmatization, …) and stored in a database.
(4) Instance extraction using the results of the previous steps.
(5) Instances extracted in step 4 are submitted to domain experts for validation via a graphical interface and stored in a database.
(6) Add extracted instances to the ontology (ontoSYSPARCOTCI).

Instance extraction algorithm (step 4) is presented below (Algorithm 1). Execution of this algorithm provides us with a list of instances, which after validation are integrated into knowledge base via instantiation process. During validation, the expert has in front of him information linked to each instance, notably presupposed instance, concept referred to in ontology and context in which presupposed instance was selected. This information allows the expert to validate or invalidate definitively.

Algorithm 1: Information extraction algorithm

```
Input:
   Ont: domain ontology
   Ct:Text corpus from web scraping
Output:
   Extracted instances with corresponding concepts
Start
ontology vocabulary ← extract ontology vocabulary (Ont)
matcher ← Initialized Matcher
for each concept in ontology vocabulary do:
   Schemas ← Create extraction schemas
   Enrich (matcher, Schemas)
end for
extracted instances ← Detect Instance (matcher, Ct)
Save in database (extracted instance)
End
```

It is also possible to perform ontology maintenance following or during validation or invalidation of instances detected by experts. When a presupposed concept is discovered, experts hold consensus meetings to validate or invalidate the new concept [5].

5 Results

This section presents the results obtained at each stage of the process. Given the semi-automatic nature of our solution, with human intervention to control and validate, we have developed an ontology populating system (SyPONT) (Fig. 4). This system integrates all the stages of our approach. The system is made up of several interconnected modules for performing tasks related to data extraction, processing, validation and ontology populating. These tasks include:

- URL identification, filtering and validation based on a set of keywords.
- Automated extraction of web page content.
- Cleaning, pre-processing and analysis of extracted texts.
- Identification of concept instances in collected text corpus.
- Validation of extracted instances according to their relevance to associated concepts.
- Insertion of validated instances into ontology knowledge base, guaranteeing consistency and coherence.

Interactions between man and machine and between machines are represented by the use case diagram below (Fig. 3).

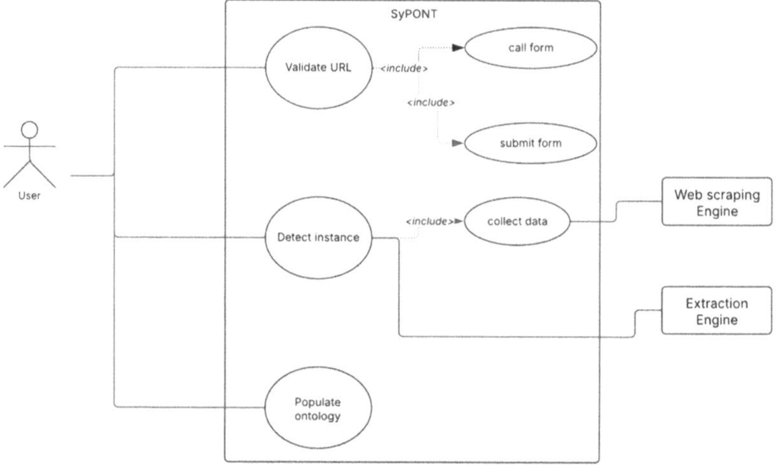

Fig. 3. SyPONT case diagram

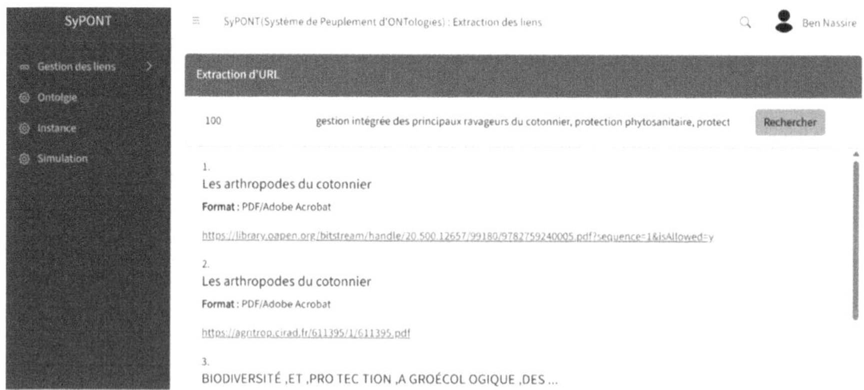

Fig. 4. Screenshot of an interface to our ontology populating system

Searching by keywords related to the domain of phytosanitary surveillance of cotton in general, we obtained a list of files of different typologies (Fig. 4).

Based on keywords identified, we obtained a total of 74 documents after web scraping. As keywords are French, documents obtained are of French language in PDF, HTML, XML format. Mainly PDFs.

Given detection of instances based on ontology concepts, we found that presence of advertising in code had no negative impact.

Fig. 5. Extracted instances validation screen

The selection of an instance necessarily involves human validation or invalidation. Interface for this selection is shown in Fig. 5. Validation of the instance leads to its storage in a database and populating the ontology.

To ensure that our system is working properly, we evaluated it. Evaluation consisted in calculating precision (Table 1). Indeed, given the lack of annotated data due to a large corpus, we did not consider it useful to calculate recall. Most information retrieval systems face a trade-off between improving precision and recall. It is possible to increase recall by performing many retrievals, but this may reduce precision. Similarly, it is possible to increase precision by performing only a few extractions that are clearly correct, but which would reduce recall.

Table 1. Link extraction screen with a list of keywords

Number of elements extracted	Number of correct elements	Accuration
149	117	79%

Each element extracted by system is manually validated after checking its relevance to the associated concept. This method makes it possible to assess the quality of extracted results based on their accuracy.

As the corpus we obtained from scraping was voluminous, we were unable to annotate it. Without this, we cannot detect or identify instances as false negatives. In contrast, we have obtained false positives. To exclude these false positives, we integrated a validation step for the detected instances.

In context of populating our ontology, current paper focuses on taxonomic relations and hyponymy indices. Hyponymy is defined as a hierarchical relationship where a more specific word called hyponym is an instance of a more general word called hyperonym.

6 Conclusion et Perspectives

Faced with data openness and the challenges of data management, the automation of knowledge extraction is an essential lever for improving decision support systems. In this article, we propose a semi-automatic ontology populating approach. One of the distinctive features of this approach is that it is based on web scraping. Based on Hearst patterns, this approach combines both automatic language processing and rule-based information extraction. It efficiently identifies and extracts instances of concepts from data collected on the web. The implementation of this approach to feed the ontology dedicated to the phytosanitary surveillance of cotton in Côte d'Ivoire resulted in an accuracy rate of 79% in the detection of taxonomic relationships. It is also possible to add new concepts and relationships to ontoSYSPARCOTCI using the same approach.

Perspectives for improvement generally include enhancing system performance by, among other things, integrating linguistic expertise to refine extraction schemes, and extending these schemes to non-taxonomic relationships, to further enrich the knowledge base. This approach is an effective alternative to manual approaches, offering time savings, reliability and scalability in specialized contexts. It can also be used to feed other ontologies in various fields.

References

1. N'Guessan Narcisse, T.K., et al.: IEEE multi-conference on natural and engineering sciences for Sahel's sustainable development (MNE3SD). Bobo-Dioulasso, Burkina Faso: IEEE, févr. **2023**, 1–8 (2023). https://doi.org/10.1109/MNE3SD57078.2023.10079897
2. Studer, R., Benjamins, V.R., Fensel, D.: Knowledge engineering: principles and methods. Data Knowl. Eng. **25**(1-2), 161–197 (1998)
3. Amardeilh, F., Damljanovic, D.: Du texte à la connaissance: annotation sémantique et peuplement d'ontologie appliqués à des artefacts logiciels. In: 20èmes journées francophones d'ingénierie des Connaissances, p. 29. Consulté le: 21 avril 2025 (2009). [En ligne]. Disponible sur: https://hal.science/hal-00380551/
4. Téhia, K.N.N.: APPLICATION DES TECHNOLOGIES DU WEB SEMANTIQUE A LA GESTION DES CONNAISSANCES SUR LES NUISIBLES DU COTONNIER EN COTE D'IVOIRE. Université Nazi BONI, Burkina Faso (2024)
5. Tehia, K.N.N., Malo, S., Kouamé, A., Kouakou, M., Bini, K.K.N., Ochou, O.G.: Cotton plant pests and phenology knowledge management in Côte d'Ivoire using semantic web technologies. In: Innovations and Interdisciplinary Solutions for Underserved Areas, Seeam, A., Ramsurrun, V., Juddoo, S., Phokeer, A. Éd., In: Lecture Notes of the Institute for Computer Sciences, Social Informatics and Telecommunications Engineering. Cham: Springer Nature Switzerland, pp. 205–217 (2024). https://doi.org/10.1007/978-3-031-51849-2_14
6. Makki, J., Alquier, A.-M., Prince, V.: Ontology Population via NLP Techniques in Risk Management. HAL Post-Print (2008)
7. Lubani, M., Noah, S.A.M., Mahmud, R.: Ontology population: approaches and design aspects. J. Inf. Sci. **45**(4), 502–515 (2019). https://doi.org/10.1177/0165551518801819
8. Rule-based and Machine Learning Approaches to AI|Canadian Journal of Nursing Informatics. Consulté le: 24 avril 2025. [En ligne]. Disponible sur: https://cjni.net/journal/?p=11562
9. Rule Based Approach in NLP, GeeksforGeeks. Consulté le: 24 avril 2025. [En ligne]. Disponible sur: https://www.geeksforgeeks.org/rule-based-approach-in-nlp/

10. Hearst, M.A.: Automatic acquisition of hyponyms from large text corpora. In: COLING 1992 volume 2: The 14th international conference on computational linguistics, Consulté le: 24 avril 2025 (1992). [En ligne]. Disponible sur: https://aclanthology.org/C92-2082.pdf
11. Roller, S., Kiela, D., Nickel, M.: Hearst Patterns Revisited: Automatic Hypernym Detection from Large Text Corpora. 8 juin 2018. arXiv: arXiv:1806.03191. https://doi.org/10.48550/arXiv.1806.03191
12. Chiticariu, L., Krishnamurthy, R., Li, Y., Reiss, F., Vaithyanathan, S.: Domain adaptation of rule-based annotators for named-entity recognition tasks. In: Proceedings of the 2010 conference on empirical methods in natural language processing, pp. 1002–1012 (2010). Consulté le: 24 avril 2025. [En ligne]. Disponible sur: https://aclanthology.org/D10-1098.pdf
13. Kim, S., et al.: Artequakt: Generating tailored biographies from automatically annotated fragments from the web (2002). Consulté le: 24 avril 2025. [En ligne]. Disponible sur: https://oro.open.ac.uk/20056/
14. Chatterjee, N., Kaushik, N.: RENT: regular expression and NLP-based term extraction scheme for agricultural domain. In: Proceedings of the International Conference on Data Engineering and Communication Technology, vol. 468, S. C. Satapathy, V. Bhateja, et A. Joshi, Éd., in Advances in Intelligent Systems and Computing, vol. 468. , Singapore: Springer Singapore, pp. 511–522 (2017). https://doi.org/10.1007/978-981-10-1675-2_51
15. Makki, J.: ONTOPRIMA: a prototype for automating ontology population. Int. J. Web Semantic Technol. **8**(4), 1–11 (2017). https://doi.org/10.5121/ijwest.2017.8401
16. Ramos De La Peña, M.: Development of a framework for ontology population using web scraping in mechatronics. Master's Thesis, Universitat Politècnica de Catalunya, 2021. Consulté le: 24 avril 2025. [En ligne]. Disponible sur: https://upcommons.upc.edu/handle/2117/365371
17. Holzinger, W., Krüpl, B., Herzog, M.: Using ontologies for extracting product features from web pages. In: The Semantic Web - ISWC 2006, vol. 4273, Cruz, I., et al. (eds.) in Lecture Notes in Computer Science, vol. 4273, Berlin, Heidelberg: Springer Berlin Heidelberg, pp. 286–299 (2006). https://doi.org/10.1007/11926078_21
18. Patel, C., Supekar, K., Lee, Y.: OntoGenie: Extracting ontology instances from WWW. Hum. Lang. Technol. Semantic Web Web Serv. ISWC, vol. 3, 2003, Consulté le: 24 avril (2025). [En ligne]. Disponible sur: http://c.web.umkc.edu/copdk4/Papers/OntoGenie.pdf
19. Lomov, P., Malozemova, M., Shishaev, M.: Training and application of neural-network language model for ontology population. In: Software Engineering Perspectives in Intelligent Systems, vol. 1295, Silhavy, R., Silhavy, P., Prokopova, Z. (ed.) in Advances in Intelligent Systems and Computing, vol. 1295. Cham: Springer International Publishing, pp. 919–926 (2020). https://doi.org/10.1007/978-3-030-63319-6_85

CADAPPAR: An Integrated and Modular System for Crash Data Collection and Analytics

Awa Tiam(✉), Ibrahima Gueye, and Oumar Niang

Thies Polytechnic, BP A10, Thies, Senegal
awa.tiam@univ-thies.sn, {igueye,oniang}@ept.edu.sn

Abstract. The present paper describes an integrated and modular computerized system for road crash data collection. Unlike the commonly used 2-tier architecture, this system leverages a 4-tier architecture including a mobile application for on-site data collection, a synchronization server, a distributed NoSQL database for data storage and a web application for data analysis and visualization. The system makes use of containerization to ensure scalability, ease of deployment and fault-tolerance. The offline-first approach ensures resiliency on connectivity restrained areas. The system incorporates a collaborative approach that allows multiple data collectors to contribute seamlessly. To evaluate its effectiveness, Proof of Concept tests, simulated scenarios, and resiliency assessments were conducted. The results highlight the system's efficient offline-first synchronization and its adaptability to diverse deployment environments. Collaboration tests showed that enabling multiple collectors reduced data collection time by 50%. However, the evaluation also revealed key insights regarding real-world deployment challenges and the need for comprehensive performance benchmarking.

Keywords: n-tier architecture · road crash · on-site data collection · collaborative collection · distributed database · containerization · offline-first

1 Introduction

The data presented in table (Table 1), which illustrate reported and estimated road traffic fatalities, highlight a challenge that is prevalent across many low-and-middle-income countries. Notably, there is a significant discrepancy between the figures reported by national authorities and those estimated by the World Health Organization (WHO). In general, WHO estimates suggest that actual road traffic fatalities are approximately four times higher than the numbers reported by these countries. Figure 1 illustrates the ranking of countries based on the extent of discrepancies between fatality estimates from the two principal international sources on road safety: the Global Status Report on Road Safety

D. Bassole et al. (Eds.): InterSol 2025, LNICST 671, pp. 230–246, 2026.
https://doi.org/10.1007/978-3-032-15154-4_18

(GSRRS) and the Global Burden of Disease (GBD) study. In response to this issue, various stakeholders have initiated efforts to strengthen data systems. One such initiative was the first regional congress on road mortality data, held in Senegal in March, 2023. This congress aimed to address the barriers to the implementation of the *Global Plan for the Second Decade of Action for Road Safety*. As a result, the *Dakar Declaration of June 2023*, endorsed by 21 African countries, outlines a series of commitments aimed at enhancing the collection, analysis, and dissemination of road crash data.

Table 1. Senegalese profile 2007 [1], 2010 [2], 2016 [3], and 2021 [4]

Element	2007	2010	2016	2021
Population	12378532	12433728	15411614	-
Reported deaths	345	277	604	877
Estimated deaths by WHO	4023	2421	3609	3502

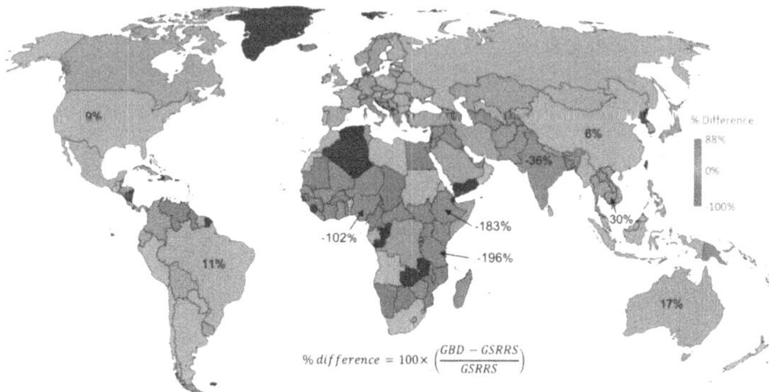

Fig. 1. Senegal, in the *red* (Color figure online) zone in terms of discrepancies between road traffic fatality estimates from GBD 2019 and GSRRS 2018, from [5].

While considerable efforts have been dedicated to analysing crash data for decision-making, comparatively less attention has been given to developing efficient systems for collecting this data in the first place. However, as highlighted by the"Garbage In, Garbage Out" (GIGO) principle, ensuring reliable outcomes requires careful attention to both input quality and processing methods [6].

As the WHO defines it, a road crash data system is comprised of the people, the processes, the hardware and software involved in collecting and managing information about road traffic crashes [7]. Traditional road crash data collection methods often involve paper-based forms or fragmented digital tools, leading to inefficiencies, delays, or incomplete data. A review of fully computerized road crash data collections systems highlights a lack of robust offline capabilities and the reliance on relational data models for storage. Due to the transactional nature of these relational data models, data transfer may be disrupted particularly in areas with limited connectivity. We present CADAPPAR an integrated road crash data system with subsystems for crash data capture, transfer, storage, and analysis. In this paper, we are focusing on the processes, the hardware and software applied in the capture, transfer, storage and analytics subsystems. The mains points of the system presented here are—to allow systematic on-site collaborative data collection in diverse connectivity areas using affordable hardwares and softwares and—ensure data quality and timely availability through the building of a single source of truth. This work builds upon and extends the contributions previously presented in [8] and [9]. In this extended version, we introduce a more comprehensive framework that reinforces the system's integrated design and provides performance insights based on semi-controlled experimental evaluations. The rest of this paper is organized as follows: in Sect. 2 we review the architecture of existing crash data collection systems, Sect. 3 describes the system covered by this paper, Sect. 4 presents the evaluation approach, and Sect. 5 discuss the present system limitations and future directions.

2 A Literature Review on Setting up Road Crash Data Collection Systems

2.1 Literature Review

The Transportation Research Laboratory (TRL) proposed a methodology to collect data following a road crash with the main objectives of collecting the maximum data elements on-site and speeding up on-site data collection [10]. The technique involves taking 2 or 3 laser scans of the accident scene (Fig. 2). Experiments show that a single scan of the scene takes between two and three minutes. These images can contain up to several hundred thousand data points. These measurements can form a three-dimensional model of the scene, including the positions of infrastructure, vehicles (including damage), the position and extent of debris, visual obstructions and so on.

According to the authors, this technique is not cost-effective for most accident scenes due to the costs involved in developing applications for laser scanning systems. The materials (equipment, electricity, data connectivity and laptops) must be usable in any weather conditions. It has also been shown that in many experiments on the classification of accident conditions, the terrestrial laser is capable of effectively classifying conditions during the day and night, but the results can be influenced by atmospheric conditions, particularly in humid meteorological conditions. This system also requires a continued data connectivity and power source. The road crash data collection system in Abu Dhabi initially relied on paper-based forms. The legacy system faced significant limitations, including delayed data recording, frequent omissions, and inconsistencies during manual data transfer. Updates to existing records were also impossible. Therefore, the proposed system in [11] integrates an Geographic Information System (GIS), the

Fig. 2. Sample installation of the TRL 3D scanner, from [10].

Global Positioning System(GPS) with Mobile Data Terminals (MDT) installed in police vehicles. These MDT, equipped with GPS receivers, enabled real-time localization and collection of standardized crash data elements. It was planned to use the GPRS network in the future to automatically send the data collected from mobile terminal. In scenarios where GPRS connectivity was unavailable, data could be stored locally on the MDTs and synchronized later. This system is an example of a process of improving an existing crash data collection system by revisiting his main components. Recognizing that a crash involves a sequence of events rather than a single incident, it is essential to adapt data collection guides to account for events sequentiality. In this context, [12] proposed updating the Spanish road crash data collection guide. METRAS, a software developed for this purpose, enables detailed descriptions of each traffic unit (e.g., vehicles, fixed or mobile objects) and assigns them to specific portions of traffic. Traffic units are entered chronologically using non-complex events. The second phase of data entry involves documenting the sequence of events leading to the collision in their chronological order, including the involvement of each vehicle. Additionally, the system allows users to mark the most lethal event in the sequence. The description highlights METRAS as a tool for systematically capturing crash events sequence. However, the document does not specify the computer hardware and software used to implement METRAS, nor does it detail its integration into broader data collection systems. [13] introduced a centralized, cloud-based system with an integrated client-server architecture designed to streamline crash data collection and analysis. The system utilizes a relational database (MySQL) to manage data storage and provides a web-based interface for on-site data collection and analysis. Accessible via a URL, the web application can be used on both mobile and desktop devices. Data is collected through six structured tabs corresponding to crash general characteristics, the road and its immediate surroundings, vehicles, drivers, passengers, and pedestrians. The database structure follows the Model Minimum Uniform Crash Criteria (MMUCC) guidelines. GPS and GLONASS are used for geolocation with manual correction options available when necessary. The system supports collaborative data collection though the specific mechanisms for collaboration are not fully detailed. The system uses Bootstrap and JQuery on the client side, while Linux, Apache Tomcat, MySQL, and PHP are employed on the server side to manage collection, storage, and analysis. The MySQL database comprises 19 tables and 580 variables. Additionally, the system is connected to other road safety information systems, such as vehicle registration databases and emergency or medical service systems. In [14], an upgraded crash data system is developed. The system aims to address several key objectives: improving accident localization data, reducing time spent on-site, ensuring flexibility in data collection, automating the generation of diagrams from collected data, enabling the attachment of multimedia files (images, videos), automating license plate and driver's license reading, and providing database querying through Application Programming Interfaces(APIs). The system architecture relies on a relational database, with data collected via a mobile application and a web portal. The mobile application primarily facilitates the collection of mandatory data elements using GPS, bar code scanners, and cameras, prioritizing the safety of data collectors. The web application complements this by enabling the collection of additional information and providing access to statistics computed from the data. To enhance data accessibility, REST APIs are available, allowing collected data to be downloaded at various levels of aggregation. Results demonstrated the localization data retrieved in five seconds and crash scene data collected within ten seconds. A crash data collection system was developed by [15] in partnership with the National Police in Ouagadougou, Burkina Faso, over six months. The system's primary goal was to improve the accuracy of accident localization. Operational police teams collected data using GPS trackers installed on patrol vehicles, which transmitted location data via SMS to the Ushahidi platform through a 3G network. data—such as gender, age, vehicle make and model, casualties, and fatalities—were manually collected on forms and subsequently entered into a database. From a hardware perspective, the system's central server ran on Ubuntu 12.04 LTS with 4 GB of RAM, 2 CPUs, and 20 GB of disk space. The server hosted Ushahidi, a database management system, SMS interpretation and de-duplication logic, and a web application for road accident cartography. Ushahidi, an open-source platform based on Swift River, uses crowdsourcing mechanisms to collect and restore data from various sources, including Twitter, SMS, email and RSS feeds. The authors highlighted the benefits of using open-source technologies and cost-effective hardware. Police officers expressed positive feedback about the system. Data validation involved comparing platform entries with intervention team reports. However, several limitations were noted. GPS tracker setup and synchronization required approximately a month, and some trackers malfunctioned due to high vehicle temperatures. The authors emphasized that while the system significantly improved localization, localization alone represents only a narrow scope of a comprehensive data system. They recommended expanding the system to include a smartphone application for broader and more efficient data collection. The Traffic Police in Kenya are responsible for collecting road accident data at crash sites using a form called *P41*. However, the summarized data, often presented in Excel workbooks, introduce significant biases. For instance, victims who are transported directly to hospitals are excluded from the statistics. The study by [16] addresses these issues by proposing a system to improve data completeness and accelerate collection. This system includes a mobile application for on-site data collection. The system uses a centralized client-server architecture to manage data collection and processing. The mobile application is developed using the Java API of Android 4.3 platform (API 8), with backward compatibility extending to API 2.2. On the server side, the system utilizes PHP, HTML, and JavaScript to process and interpret the data received from the mobile application. Data entered via the mobile interface is transmitted to the server through web services, where it is stored and managed on a database server. The DRIVER [17] system is a web-based platform developed by the Global Road Safety Facility (GRSF) and the World Bank to support road accident data management, particularly for low-and middle-income countries. To address the limitations of proprietary accident data collection (cost, isolation, lack of critical features), the DRIVER system was designed as an open-source solution with the objectives of ow deployment costs (open-source license), comprehensive data tools, anonymized data access, localization coding and multi-language support. Despite its strengths, DRIVER is primarily designed for the analysis and visualization of road accident data. It relies on existing processes to manage the collection of raw data. Deploying DRIVER in a country requires retrieving and customizing its source code, which is openly accessible via the World Bank's repository [18]. Integrating DRIVER involves familiarity with tools such as Ansible, Docker, and Vagrant, as well as experience with relational databases to model the system according to local collection guidelines. Additionally, web development expertise in Python, Django, JavaScript/Angular, HTML, and CSS is necessary. For security, DRIVER employs OAuth2 protocols.

2.2 Identified Gaps

Lack of Offline Capabilities. On-site data collection ensures the most exhaustive possible collection of alterable data such as skid marks, vehicle debris, final positions of vehicles and people [19]. Electronic or computerized collection ([20,21]) are to ensure quality of data by avoiding subsequent data entry from paper forms to data store. Some of the systems studied here lack offline capabilities in particular given the on-site collection. Often web-based application are used to collect data on-site. This may limit usability in low-connectivity or offline environments. In case of mobile applications, web services are used to transfer collected data. This design introduces challenges for on-site data collection as data must be continuously transferred to a central data store for consistency.

When connectivity is lost, data must be temporarily stored locally, often in terminal memory. This reliance can lead to potential data loss or inconsistencies, especially if the temporary storage is not robust or fails to synchronize correctly when the connection is restored.

Centralized Relational Database. Most systems use relational databases relying on centralized data storage. The use of a centralized relational database with predefined tables may make the system less flexible when new data elements need to be added or schema changes are required. While the system uses single transaction web services, this could be a bottleneck. The transaction-like data transfer ensures data consistency through transactional storage, following ACID properties. However they can pose challenges for systems like on-site data collection in the following ways :

- Connectivity dependency : transactions typically require a stable connection to the central data store to ensure atomic operations causing delays or failures in disconnected areas.
- Conflict resolution : when using local storage for temporary data merging with central database upon connection can lead to conflict.

These points emphasize the need for more resilient, distributed or hybrid data models that can adapt to intermittent connectivity, improve real time data processing and adapt seamlessly to schema changes.

Real Time Collaboration To accelerate data collection, use of bar code scanners, images capture or video captures are proposed. We have seen that images or scans may miss certain details of the crash scenes [22]. Collaboration is recognized to help reduce overall collection time and thus ensure rapid closure of traffic lanes, avoiding subsequent accidents, traffic jams and the risk of impact on accident responders ([14,23]). However, documented studies aiming to enable real time collaboration are not available.

3 System Design and Implementation

3.1 Key Architectural Propositions of CADAPPAR

Integrated and Modular System. CADAPPAR integrates data collection, transfer, storage, and analysis as cohesive subsystems connected through standardized interfaces and protocols (Fig. 3). It adopts a modular, containerized 4-tier architecture—comprising a mobile application (presentation tier), data transfer, data storage, and analytics (processing tier). Each tier handles specific responsibilities, promoting fault tolerance and flexibility. REST APIs and other protocols enable communication between components, while containerization supports scalable and independent module updates.

Lazy Offline-First. To ensure the usability of the collection system in diverse connectivity environments, we propose to apply the lazy offline-first paradigm [24]. The collected data will be saved at local mobile level regardless of the connectivity state. Depending on the availability of the connectivity, this data is replicated to the final data store. In this lazy loading, data is synchronized depending on device or network conditions.

Exploration of NoSQL Data Model. Often, countries have a minimum guide including data elements that need to be collected for most of their analytical or statistical needs. Data elements describing a crash may evolve. Furthermore, the transaction-like data transfer appears to be a concern in an on-site data collection schema. To grasp these challenges, we propose to explore the usage of a NoSQL data model.

Real-Time Collaboration. The system proposes a documented approach to allow collaboration for on-site road crash data collection. The NoSQL based data model is at the center of the proposition. If data elements can be saved with the least amount of relations between them, different users may be involved in the process. As synchronization requirements could be kept as simple as possible. The real-time collaboration implies that crash data elements are identified and categorized; a team of collectors are located in the same site and tasks are allocated to the different collectors.

3.2 The System Components

The system includes the following components :

- Presentation tier: a mobile application for on-site data collection, using GPS and offline storage to ensure data capture even in resources-restrained areas. The application help avoid data entry from paper forms to data store. It offers functionalities to collect data related to crash, involved vehicle details, involved person details, road description and surroundings. To ensure data integrity fields validation are implemented. Localization and timestamp are also automatically associated.
- Synchronization tier via a synchronization module: serves as an interface for real-time or batch data transfer to allow the system to operate efficiently in both offline and online modes.
- Data tier: a distributed database with a NoSQL data model to provide storage for evolving crash data and unstructured data such as crash scenes pictures.
- Processing tier : a web application with background of business rules and analytics to perform update on collected data, data visualization on dashboards, geographic crash mapping, querying capabilities and interactive dashboard creation and management.

3.3 Technical Implementation

Tools and Technologies. The functional programming languages Scala and Kotlin are used in this system setup. Kotlin is used in the mobile application setup while Scala is used for web application via Play Framework. The Couchbase Sync Gateway [25] is used to ensure data synchronization between the database Couchbase Server [26,27] and mobile clients. Couchbase Lite is used as a local database within mobile clients [28]. Open Street Map is used in geographic crash mapping.

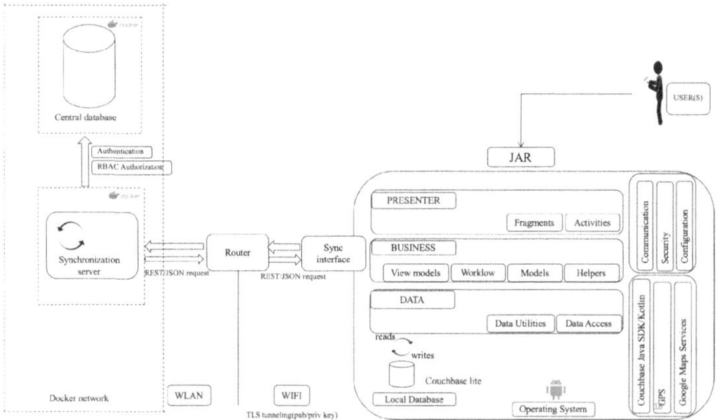

Fig. 3. The three components of the system : collection, transfer and storage.

Containerization. Three of the modules (synchronization, database and web application) are containerized. We use Docker to fully encapsulate each of these module with their respective environment and dependencies. To enable communication between those containers, a network is created and shared between the three modules.

Integration. Below we detail the protocols used between tiers in the system:

1. The replication protocol is based on RESTful APIs/WebSockets. Websockets are used to secure data synchronization between the mobile database and the synchronization server. To further secure communications, we have added a process of certificate pinning between the mobile application and the synchronization server. This helps ensure that only trusted synchronization servers communicate with the mobile application.
2. A Software Development Kit(SDK) protocol built over TCP/IP by Couchbase is used to ensure communications between the data tier and the synchronization tier.

3. SQL++ protocol [29] is used to perform queries and data retrieval upon the database tier and the processing tier. Role-based access control (RBAC) is used to enable further secure communication between the synchronization module and the database.

Collaboration.

Crash Modeling and Unique Identifier By collaboration, we aim to allow multiple officers to work on the collection process. The database model consists of documents of four type respectively *Crash*, *Vehicle*, *Person*, *Road*, and *Multimedia* representing data related to pictures or videos of crash scenes. A road crash unique identifier is created partly from the crash localization, the crash date and the crash time. All documents are linked to this identifier in order to get a full view of the crash details. Our approach of collaboration imply that this unique identifier be shared between a group of collectors. Figure 4 shows the algorithm behind the sharing of a crash identifier.

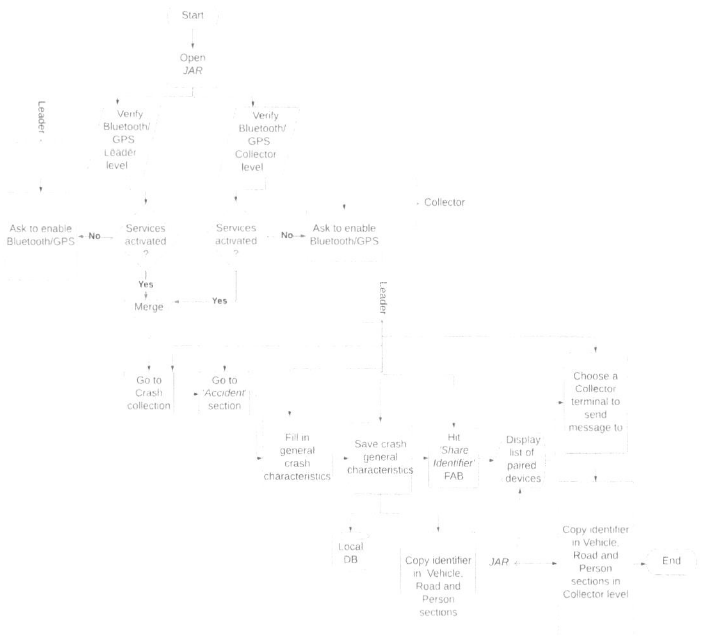

Fig. 4. Schematized algorithm for sharing crash identifier.

The leading collector has to share the unique identifier to fellow collectors. The mobile terminal of the leader and collectors are paired via Bluetooth. Once the crash identifier is deduced, the list of paired devices of other collectors are displayed in the leader's mobile application instance. To share the identifier via Bluetooth, the leader must select the collector terminal.

Conflict-Resolution. We expect no conflicts to occur at the final database. Thanks to the Couchbase "conflict-free" resolution mechanism, no conflicts occur at the database level, as documents that could potentially create conflicts during concurrent writes are rejected during synchronization. Deletes operations are not allowed at the mobile application level. As of now, there is no pull replication implemented at mobile level. That is to prevent the mobile database size to grow. On local level, the Last-Writes-Wins algorithm is applied to handle updates by a specific collector. Thanks to this process, whenever a document is modified through JAR, his content is updated with the latest data. The replication process is schematized on Fig. 5.

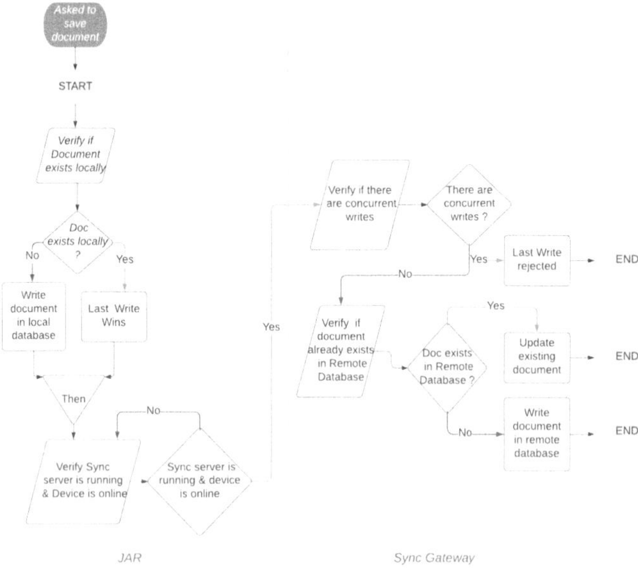

Fig. 5. Schematized algorithm of the replication process.

4 System Evaluation

4.1 Proof of Concept

The different tiers of the system architecture were deployed on testing environment (Table 2). We set up a 3-nodes database cluster using Docker and the latest image of Couchbase Server as the remote distributed database. Each of these nodes runs as container on the same physical machine. The synchronization server and the analytics application run also on the same physical machine. The mobile application is deployed on two mobile phones. A WLAN network connects the smartphones and synchronization server.

Table 2. Test environment

Tier	Hardware/Software	Properties
Application	Huawei Nova 3i	Android 8.1 (Oreo)
Application	X-TIGI-JOY7 Mate	Android 8.1 (Oreo)
Synchronization	macOS Mojave 10.14.6	Intel Core i7-16 Go
Data	macOS Mojave 10.14.6	Intel Core i7-16 Go
Processing	macOS Mojave 10.14.6	Intel Core i7-16 Go
Containerization	Docker Desktop	Community 19.03.13

Figure 6 shows a sample cartographic visualization of a crash.

Fig. 6. Crash cartography from web application interface with details from a sample crash.

4.2 Impacts of Collaboration on Collection Duration

In this evaluation, two crash scenarios are simulated: the first is about a motorist thrown off the roadway onto the pavement and the last is about a motorist striking a pedestrian. The data elements were identified and made available prior to collection. Two testers, with varying expertise levels, using the two smartphones available in the testing environment were involved. An average of 60 data elements were set to be collected for each of these scenarios [30]. Four set of tests were conducted, collection durations were retrieved in minutes. The results are presented on Fig. 7a and Fig. 7b.

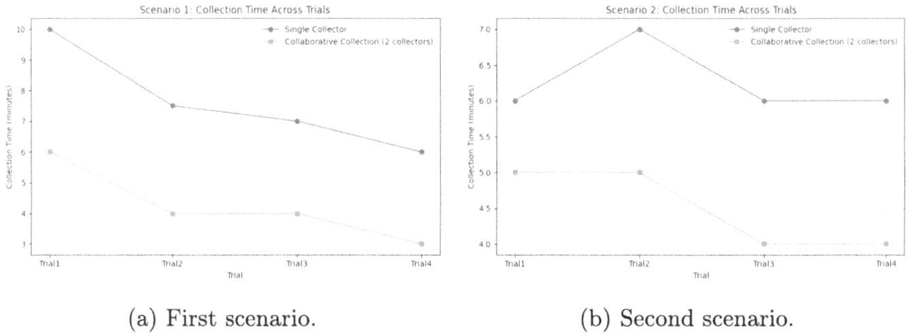

(a) First scenario. (b) Second scenario.

Fig. 7. Collections durations across the semi-controlled four-trials tests, in minutes.

Quantitative analysis. On average, data collection took 8 min when performed by a single collector, whereas collaborative collection with two collectors reduced the time to 4 min across all four trials. This represent a 50% decrease in duration across all four trials. This suggests that distributing tasks among multiple users improves efficiency, likely due to parallel execution of data entry tasks such as localization, vehicle and person details.

4.3 Resiliency Tests

In this experiment, we evaluate the database system resiliency.

1. Database high availability
   - Methods: To simulate a node failure, one of the cluster nodes was intentionally disconnected by removing it from the shared Docker network. The node was later rejoined to the cluster using the same procedure. During disconnection, the server appeared unreachable to the cluster manager; The system successfully triggered the automatic failover process, removing the unresponsive node from the cluster and redistributing its data to the remaining nodes.
   - Results : after the server came back online, the rebalance process was initiated, and the data was redistributed across all three nodes of the cluster.

2. Data resiliency
   - Methods: To simulate a loss of data residing in the remote database due to server failure, we have simply deleted the running Docker containers. The database was recreated and reconnected with the synchronization server via the shared virtual Docker network and the role-based access control authentication/authorization processes;
   - Results: when the database came online, the synchronization server recreated deleted data in the database by using the contents of local databases on mobile clients. In this case, there was a full re-upload of data from mobile to server. The documents residing in the local database are associated with a Time To Live (TTL) property which indicates the amount of time before they are deleted from the database. In our testing environment, the documents are set to never expire which allowed the system to rebuild data on the remote database. In case of intentional data deletion however, resulting in a tombstone, the documents will not be recreated.

4.4 Synchronization Time and Throughput

In this experiment, we evaluate the impact of data size on synchronization time and throughput. To conduct the analysis, we developed a debug version of the application with two data-saving modes: a bulk-saving method and a sequential saving method, which introduces a delay of 5,000 milliseconds (5 s) between each batch. The following steps are performed.

- Crash data points are generated using the Python Faker library, resulting in four files: crashes, vehicles, persons, and roads.
- The mobile application is launched in debug mode on a physical device;
- The synchronization tests are initiated.

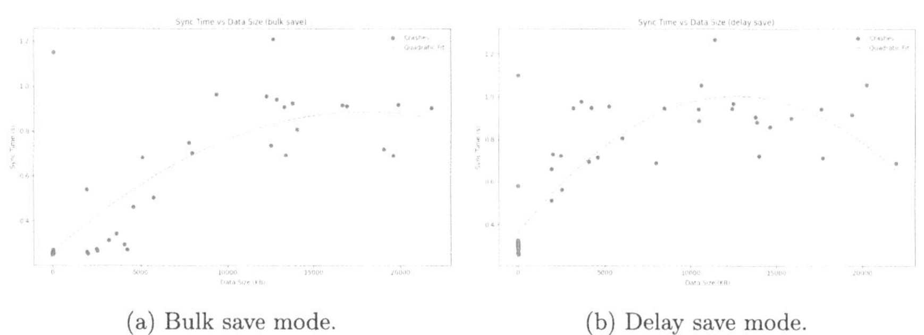

(a) Bulk save mode. (b) Delay save mode.

Fig. 8. Synchronization time for different batch size, in seconds.

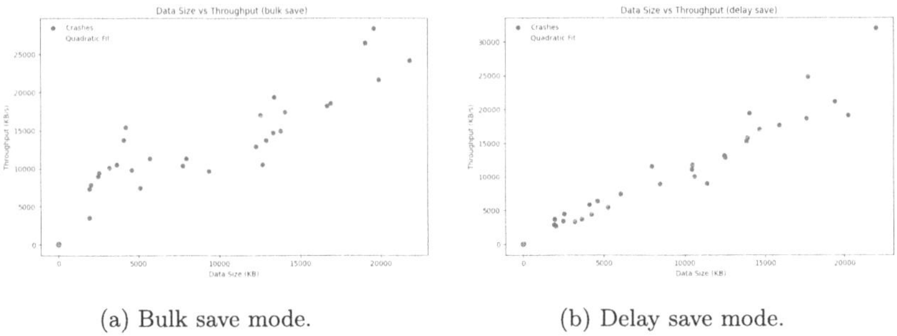

(a) Bulk save mode.

(b) Delay save mode.

Fig. 9. Throughput for different batch size, in KB/s.

Results. From this experiment, we can see that synchronization time does not strictly linearly increase with data size. There is no exponential growth in synchronization time. The figures (Fig. 8band Fig. 8a) show that the system handles increasing data sizes efficiently, maintaining scalable performance. Either case of data saving seem to follow the same pattern. The throughput does not seem to be negatively impacted by the data size in general. With low data sizes, the throughput is relatively low. The experiment suggests that as data size increases, the throughput generally improves. The system demonstrates scalability under increasing data loads, with throughput increasing across batch sizes—even under bulk transmission conditions (Fig. 9band Fig. 9a).

5 Discussion

This paper presents the design, implementation, deployment and evaluation of CADAPPAR, a road crash data collection system. The system's architecture was driven, among other reasons, by the need to enhance modularity, scalability, data accuracy, support offline functionality, and ensure collaboration among collectors. While the system's modular architecture enhances scalability and flexibility, the absence of benchmarking data from the literature or the industry, particularly regarding data collection durations limits direct comparisons with similar systems. Future work will focus on piloting the system in collaboration with local road safety agencies to validate its usability in real-world scenarios. Collaborative collection tests suggest a significant reduction in collection time. However as only four trials were conducted, larger-scale experiments would provide more generalizable conclusions. Furthermore, tests are needed to determine the optimal number of simultaneous users before coordination eventually degrades performance. Road accident fatalities reporting are also affected by the follow-up of victims taken to hospitals. The mobile application presented here integrates the option to enter hospital identification. The analytics application allows to update the information collected for a specific victim. However a more integrated approach is required to ensure effective updating of data from hospital records to the crash data system.

Disclosure of Interests. The authors have no competing interests to declare that are relevant to the content of this article.

References

1. WHO: Global status report on road safety: time for action. In: Global Status Report on Road Safety: Time for Action, pp. 244–245. World Health Organization, Geneva, Switzerland (2009)
2. WHO: Global status report on road safety 2013: supporting a decade of action. In: Global Status Report on Road Safety 2013: Supporting a Decade of Action, p. 248. World Health Organization, Geneva, Switzerland (2013)
3. WHO: Global status report on road safety 2018. In: Global Status Report on Road Safety 2018, p. 227. World Health Organization, Geneva, Switzerland (2018)
4. GRSF: Global status report on road safety 2023 : Senegal (2023). https://cdn.who.int/media/docs/default-source/country-profiles/road-safety/road-safety-2023-sen.pdf?sfvrsn=bab35d3f_3&download=true
5. Mitra, S., Bhalla, K.: Improving Road Traffic Injury Statistics In Low and MiddleIncome Countries: Addressing Discrepancies Between Official Statistics and Global Statistical Models. Washington, DC. (2023). https://www.globalroadsafetyfacility. org/sites/default/files/2023-11/Improving
6. Oliveira, P., Rodrigues, F., Henriques, P.R.: A formal definition of data quality problems. In: ICIQ (2005)
7. WHO, et al.: Data systems: a road safety manual for decision-makers and practitioners (2010)
8. Tiam, A., Gueye, I., Niang, O.: An on-site collaborative approach of road crash data collection. In: Ngatched Nkouatchah, T.M., Woungang, I., Tapamo, J.-R., Viriri, S. (eds.) Pan-African Artificial Intelligence and Smart Systems, pp. 423–437. Springer, Cham (2023)
9. Tiam, A., Gueye, I., Wade, A.-M., Sidibe, S., Niang, O.: Design and implementation of an offline-first road crash data collection system. World J. Adv. Res. Rev. **13**(2), 095–107 (2022)
10. Forman, P., Parry, I.: Rapid data collection at major incident scenes using three dimensional laser scanning techniques. In: Proceedings IEEE 35th Annual 2001 International Carnahan Conference on Security Technology (Cat. No.01CH37186), pp. 60–67 (2001). IEEE
11. [11] Khan, M.A., Al Kathairi, A.S., Grib, A.: A GIS based traffic accident data collection, referencing and analysis framework for Abu Dhabi. Proceeding Codatu XI in (2004)
12. Tormo, M.T., Sanmartin, J., Pace, J.F.: Update and improvement of the traffic accident data collection procedures in Spain: The Metras method of sequencing accident events. 4th IRTAD Conference (2009)
13. Montella, A., Chiaradonna, S., Criscuolo, G., De Martino, S.: Development and evaluation of a web-based software for crash data collection, processing and analysis. Accident Anal. Prevention **130**, 108–116 (2019)
14. Paz, A., Arteaga, C., Gaviria, C.: Integrated system for collecting and reporting crash and citation data. In: Proceedings of the 4th International Conference on Vehicle Technology and Intelligent Transport Systems-Volume 1: VEHITS, pp.225–230 (2018). Scitepress

15. Bonnet, E., Niki'ema, A., Traor'e, Z., Sidbega, S., Ridde, V.: Technological solutions for an effective health surveillance system for road traffic crashes in burkina faso. Global Health Action **10** (2017). https://doi.org/10.1080/16549716.2017.1295698
16. [16] Derdus, K.M., Ozianyi, V.G.: A mobile solution for road accident data collection. In: Proceedings of the 2nd Pan African International Conference on Science, Computing and Telecommunications (PACT 2014), pp. 115–120 (2014). IEEE
17. GRSF: DRIVER. Last accessed May 5, (2025). https://www. globalroadsafetyfacility.org/driver
18. WorldBank: DRIVER Github. Last accessed May 5, (2025). https://github.com/WorldBank-Transport/DRIVER
19. Singh, K., Chawla, A., Mukherjee, S., Agrawal, P.: A pilot study at national highway-8 for on-site crash data collection and in-depth investigation in India, vol. 2017-January (2017). https://doi.org/10.4271/2017-26-0001
20. Verhulst, M., Rutkowski, A.-F.: Catch me if you can: Technological constraints/affordances and mindfulness during collaborative police emergency response (2017)
21. Lichtbraun, P.M.: The nypd mobility initiative and its impact on police officers (2023)
22. Pagounis, V., Tsakiri, M., Palaskas, S., Biza, B., Zaloumi, E.: 3D Laser scanning for road safety and accident reconstruction. In: Proceedings of the XXIIIth International FIG Congress, vol. 8, pp. 13–27 (2006)
23. Walton, J.R., Barrett, M.L., Agent, K.R.: Evaluation of methods to limit the time taken to investigate crash sites. Accident Invest. Quart. **46**, 30–40 (2007)
24. Developers: Build an offline-first app. Last accessed May 5, 2025. (2023). https://developer.android.com/topic/architecture/data-layer/offline-first#lazy_writes
25. Couchbase: Sync Gateway: Data Modeling. May 5, 2025. https://docs.couchbase.com/sync-gateway/current/data-modeling.html
26. Ostrovsky, D., Haji, M., Rodenski, Y., Ostrovsky, D., Haji, M., Rodenski, Y.: Getting started with couchbase server. Pro Couchbase Server, 3–18 (2015)
27. Messina, A.: Architectural Overview of Couchbase Server (2018)
28. Documentation: Couchbase Lite. Last accessed May 5, (2025). https://docs.couchbase.com/couchbase-lite/current/index.html
29. Hubail, M.A., et al.: Couchbase analytics: NOETL for scalable NOSQL data analysis. Proc. VLDB Endowment **12**(12), 2275–2286 (2019)
30. Awa, T.: Experiments Repository. Last accessed May 5, 2025. (2025).https://github.com/Tiamawa/Experiments/blob/master/Scenario_simulation_data_elements.tex

Review of Gambia's Healthcare System and Adaptation of Health Information System

Mbemba Hydara(✉), Bamfa Ceesay, and Adamu Aminu

Department of Computer Science, University of The Gambia, MDI Rd, Kanifing, PO Box 3530, Serrekunda, Gambia
{hmbemba,bamfa,aadamu}@utg.edu.gm

Abstract. The Gambia government has set an ambitious goal to establish an E-government aimed at promoting service efficiency, productivity, and accountability. The Public Healthcare System is one of the primary sectors to benefit from this initiative where healthcare service and service delivery sector faces difficult challenges. These challenges in the public health sector include lack of Healthcare Information Systems, electronic medical record systems and quality service delivery. In this study, we provide situation analysis of the healthcare system, policies, and practices. The objectives are to identify structural and policy gaps; based on the outcome of the analysis, we present a design and development framework of an interoperable Healthcare Information System (HIS) for a nationwide adoption. The focus is about interoperability between Public Health Information Platform (PHIP) and Health Information System (HIS). The goal is about Integration of regional Population Health Information Platforms (PHIP) with HIS at healthcare service delivery levels. The framework will allow analysis of data collected from multiple sources and the recommendations provided will also serve as implementation guide for policy for informed decision making.

Keywords: Healthcare Information Systems · Policy · Interoperability · Services

1 Introduction

There is an increasing demand for healthcare services and service deliveries in The Gambia. However, the major challenges responsible are issues of demography, fragmented healthcare systems to uneven distribution of healthcare service and resources. Manual paperwork and record keeping of data and information still remain the primary patient information processing method in public healthcare service and ser-vice delivery. This approach continues to pose significant problems especially information achieving, sharing, and maintenance of patients' medical information into addition the following challenges:

1. Inefficient tracking of patient medical history or information for diagnosis,
2. Needs for physical storage facilities for keeping records.
3. Cases of missing patient's record led to:

D. Bassole et al. (Eds.): InterSol 2025, LNICST 671, pp. 247–257, 2026.
https://doi.org/10.1007/978-3-032-15154-4_19

a. Delay in diagnosis and treatment.
b. Repetition of medical test or diagnosing.
c. Death of patient due to service delay.

Information technology (IT) is no longer perceived as mare supporting tool but has become a strategic necessity for developing an integrated healthcare IT infrastructure that can improve services and reduce medical problems [1]. This situation has made HIS an important requirement for an effective and efficient healthcare system. The objective of this study is to review and analyse the existing Healthcare system, evaluate the policies and complexity of the problems, build on the identified gaps, and finally provide a design and implementation framework for an integrated interoperable HIS for nation-wide adoption. The goal is to propose an effective solution and make recommendations on best practice to guide policy implementation. The rest of the paper is organized as follows: Sect. 2 explores a desk review of related work. Section 3 provide methodology use in the study and Sect. 4, explains details of the Healthcare System and structure in Gambia.

2 Related Works

HIS is a system designed to manage health care data in an effective and efficient manner. Many countries face challenges and failures in their implementation of nationwide HIS [2]. The advent of healthcare information technology provides an important impetus for countries to adopt and deploy efficient and effective healthcare system [3]. Many researchers contend that integrated medical information systems now forms an essential part of modern healthcare systems to the extent of evolving into an integrated enterprise-wide system.

Regional and national bodies including develop societies around the world have supported the shift towards an integrated, patient-centered healthcare information system. Prominent among these are WHO [4], African Union [5] and Ecowas [6]. These entities have all prioritized the need to develop integrated HIS as well as relevant policies in member countries. According to WHO 3rd Programme of Work HISs report, the lack of robust and effective HIS often results in a significant gap between what policymakers, health professionals and researchers know and what they need to know to improve the health of the population.

In The Gambia for example, the key objective and priorities outlined in Sect. 3.2 of the National Health Policy 2021–2030 are the establishment and implementation of an Integrated HIS and Health Research. The objective of this policy is to 'establish a robust integrated HIS that will pro-vide secured, timely, reliable, accurate, relevant, and complete information for in-formed decision making [4]. The policy also provides the basis for institutional and legal framework for the implementation of the sectors priorities.

A careful review of the national Healthcare Systems shows that several countries have launched integrated healthcare initiatives with the objective of implementing a nationwide interoperable HIS [7–9] system. A good healthcare information system does not only provide quality and optimized healthcare service but also provides low medical cost [10]. This is particularly important for a population with low middle class income families. Denmark for example, has earned recognition to have some success in the implementation of eHealth for their public hospitals. The most challenging condition for the adaptation of a useful HIS is sharing of health data and information among healthcare service providers. This is apparent in the case of Denmark where interoperability problem has not been addressed because the leadership has failed in providing sufficient solutions when deployed [9]. Despite been one of the smallest countries in Africa, there is a huge disparity among different regions in the Gambia in terms of healthcare services and service deliveries. This is further compounded by uneven distribution of healthcare services and re-sources. To overcome this challenge, The Gambia government set an ambitious goal to provide an eHealth service to her population as part of sustainable development goal [4].

Medical service providers require comprehensive and accurate data on patients at the point-of-care if they are to provide high quality health services to their patients. To be able to achieve meaningful interoperable Healthcare Information System in the country, policy study and structural situation analysis is required. A good national healthcare system will provide solution to several information sharing and interoperable environment in healthcare service [11]. In addition, it will provide an unprecedented level of efficiency and improvement in data sharing, quality data, security, and availability, minimizing errors in data and information; empowering patients and efficient time management for healthcare staff and personnel. To implement this in practice can sometimes be challenging because factors underlining interoperable HIS adoption are multi-faceted ranging from organizational complexity, social, to technical factors.

Nonetheless, the commitment to implement national electronic health systems has also led to an increasing research interest in identifying meaningful implementation strategies. In this study, some common strategies adopted by countries drawn from the topology of national programs of England, USA, and Australia are considered. In these countries, three different implementation strategies were adopted: top-down, bottom-up and middle-out respectively [12]. The top-down approach aimed at creating one Single Shared Electronic Record (SSEHR) that will store data centrally. All local or regional healthcare service providers can add or read data for the centralize record. The National Health System of England delivers majority of healthcare in UK.

It served as model example for many other countries that adopt the top-down approach [13]. This approach proposes several primary challenges due to the scales and complexity involved. In a much fragmented and decentralized healthcare system, national scale management of healthcare is impossible due to differences in Governance structures, standards of compliance and procurement process.

In the bottom-up approach, integration of healthcare information systems being implemented at local or regional level is the focus. Compared with the top-down, the bottom–up approach addresses challenges in a fragmented or decentralized healthcare system. The United States Health Information Exchanges (HIE) use bottom-up approach toward implementing national HIS. In contrast, this approach does not create a single record, but instead allow virtual views of local or regional records, that are abstracted or aggregated from regional systems. Based on the analysis of the two approaches, the following flaws have been observed. In the top-down approach, all existing systems that do not meet defined standards for national HIS will not be integrated and the local standards or requirements that do not comply may be abandoned and replaced by compliant ones [3].

3 Findings on Gambia's Adoption of HIS and Methodology

The study conducted a comprehensive desk review of the literature, personal interviews, and use of survey data on the Gambia healthcare sector. The study adopted mix methods (Qualitative and Quantitative) data collection research approach. The goal is to review and evaluate the existing system, identify policy, technology infrastructure and organizational gaps and finally propose an integrated, interoperable HIS solution framework for policy implementation. We also investigated the factors underpinning implementation challenges of HISs in the country.

3.1 Healthcare System and Structure in Gambia

The provision of healthcare service in the Gambia are two categories: public healthcare system provided by the government and private healthcare system pro-vided by private businesses. The healthcare system is built around three tier levels; Primary, Secondary and Tertiary. Until now, there are four referral hospitals operated by the government. In addition, there are eight main health centers, sixteen smaller centers, and more than 200 mobile clinics. There are also several privately run clinics as well as a few health focused NGOs operating in country.

The primary health care (PHC) system focuses on the provision of basic healthcare services and education for small communities. Primary healthcare services are usually provided by trained individuals in the communities. The services provided at this level are out-patient care. The secondary healthcare system focusses on the sub-urban communities through the provision of health centers in selected communities.

These centers provide both outpatient and inpatient care and treatment. The third level in the healthcare system is the tertiary healthcare where Healthcare services and treatment are provided within the framework of hospitals.

3.2 Factors to Enhance Implementation Strategies in the Gambia

Countries all around the world are faced with various challenges in delivering standard healthcare services to citizens. These challenges vary from one country to another and are determined by various factors such as demographic and government policies. The human development index (HDI) performance indicator for example is a key determining factor to healthcare challenges individual countries face. Countries with high HDI usually have healthcare challenges towards healthcare delivery services and less challenges towards healthcare resources including human resources [14].

Globally, countries facing health system problems vary from one country to the other. While health service delivery challenges are more often seen in countries with a very high Human Development Index (HDI). Human resources challenges tend to attract more attention compared to those with a low HDI. In describing healthcare systems in countries with low HDI, the World Health Organization (WHO) provide the following six components.

- Service delivery;
- Healthcare workforce;
- Healthcare information systems;
- Medicines and technologies;
- Financing; and
- Leadership/governance.

Institutional Factors

The existing institutional structure of the Gambia healthcare system is defined by three tier levels of healthcare service and service delivery. Primary Health Care (PHC) communities are usually served by trained community health workers that package of prevention, promotion, and Social and Behavior Change Communication (SBCC) services. This includes training of families in optimal maternal and child health behaviors, nutrition, hygiene, and other key family practices [4]. The objective of PHC is to provide basic PHC services to small and remote settlements through community based trained workers, and community clinics. They work with hardly any supervision and only make referrals to healthcare centers or hospitals for cases that require more than basic primary healthcare service. A community nurse may sometimes be working with multiple small communities. Patients' data and record keeping are usually done to keep track of patients in various parts of the communities for follow up or service delivery. In certain cases, information is recorded for patients that need more than basic primary care and requiring referrals to a health center or hospital. The standards and information collected can also vary from one community nurse to another. The secondary healthcare level is composed of health centers and hospitals. This tertiary level of care is envisaged to comprise of general, teaching, and specialized hospitals to handle advanced and specialized healthcare needs of the population. Figure 1 below illustrate the three-tier architecture of healthcare system in the Gambia including facilities at each level. The Ministry of Health holds responsibility for central functions such as policy and priority setting, financial management, budget execution, and audits. In Fig. 1, the service providers include:

- Healthcare staff
- Community Health Nurses
- Village Health Workers
- Voluntary Health Care Services

Human Resources and Financial Challenges

Gambia's public healthcare service is currently undergoing a transition to a new hope characterized by more efficient care delivery, affordable public service, accountability, steady and sustainable healthcare system that supports equity and social service for all. Every healthcare system relies on services from different sets of professionals to provide care to patients. As in many other African countries, the workforce within the healthcare system in the Gambia is not given the priority it de-serves. More priorities have been given to provision of commodities, healthcare equipment and facilities. Many

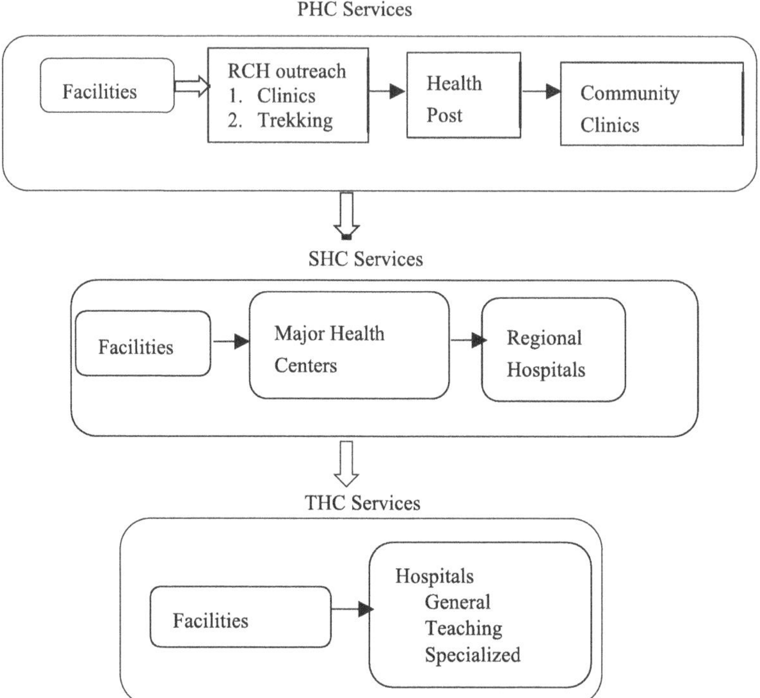

Fig. 1. Gambia Health System Tiers and other facilities.

factors, such as the educational system, payment schemes and working environments are essential and determining factors in the availability of healthcare professionals and quality of services within a given healthcare system. The University of The Gambia and the Gambia College are currently the only public institutions that provides professional education and training in the fields of medicine and nursing. This development is affected by high attrition rate of personnel. Many young medical practitioners do not stay in the country after their educational careers. The Human flight and brain drain indicators also ushered an economic impact of human displacement (for economic or political reasons) and the consequences it has on a country's development. The higher the index, the greater the human displacement [15]. Statistical data of the Gambia from 2007 to 2022 shows an average index for the Gambia during the period as 7.19 index points with a minimum of 6 index points in 2007 and a maximum of 8.4 index points in 2016. The latest value for 2022 is 7.2 index points. Compared to the world average in 2022 based on 177 countries is index 5.21 points. This problem has also been cited in the national health policy plan 2022 to 2030 [4]. According to the world health organization's report [16], total expenditure on health as percentage of national GDP was 7.3 by 2014 and total expenditure on health per capita by the same by 118 as shown in Table 1 below. Gambia's healthcare sector highly relies on funding from partner organizations such as World Health Organization, United Nation Development Fund, and other organizations.

Political Developments

The Ministry of Health (MoH) governs the healthcare system of the Gambia in partnership with United Nations (UN) agencies such as WHO and UNDP. MoH also establishes policies, legislation, systems, and structures with the primary objectives of ensuring transparency and accountability in the management of health services and resources. The UN agencies provide both technical, financial and provision of re-sources and capacity building. These agencies also play an important role in the formulation of policies and strategies for the government. The increase in healthcare need and the fragmented structure of the system has given rise to poor service delivery in several programs because of unstable leadership. Lack of good governance also contributes to poor quality of care and inefficiency in the allocation of resources.

Table 1. Health Financing Indicators in The Gambia

Indicator	Number
Total health expenditures as a % of GDP	4.68%
Percent of government budget allocated to health	7%
General government expenditure on health as a percentage of total health expenditure	32.78%
Total health expenditures per capita (international $)	$118
Out-of-pocket expenditures as a % of total health expenditures	24.4%
External resources for health as a percentage of total health spending	36.45%

Adoption of new technology in the medical and healthcare system in general spans a range of activities-from basic and applied research to development efforts that yield product creation. Gambia like many other developing countries have been experiencing rapid technological revolution ranging from growth in internet to cellular technologies [17]. According to the Gambia Health Policy 2021–2030, there is no existing dedicated HIS in all the public healthcare institutions in the Gambia, Patient information recording and processing is still done manually. Challenges in the adoption of integrated healthcare systems is attributed to technical and workforce challenges.

3.3 Infrastructure

Lessons learned from developed countries that have successfully implemented robust healthcare with healthcare information system have substantial funding and support from government [18]. Developing countries implementing HIS solutions for healthcare sector lack funding, resources, and weak IT infrastructure. There is no IT infrastructure in many components of the healthcare system. Any incentives to develop HIS die out or fade away before they are executed. Even whereas there exists an IT infrastructure, initiatives die out due to unreliable and sustainable resources.

3.4 Political Will

In many cases, there is lack of acceptance of new technologies due to associated risk with cost and sustainability. There is also lack of political foresight in the benefit and significance of its introduction. In some cases, there is a lack of understanding of what is modern HIS and its benefits for policy and decision-making.

3.5 Workforce Challenges

There is a major need for building the capacity of the workforce in the healthcare system towards understanding the used and adaptation of HIS. Training of healthcare professionals in the use of new system do not only come with additional cost but also require huge efforts due to unfamiliarized content or concept to these professionals. The national education system and policies does have direct influence on the training of professionals. This is particularly true for those professionals that are produced locally or have no access to academic training and resources outside the country. Any implementation of HIS will require a careful balance between user-friendliness and the advanced features. This often result to a compromise of system's functionalities in favor of user-friendliness. This challenge becomes tougher at the PHC level where clinicians are less IT savvy. Adoption of any approach will have to fine tune between the levels of technology acceptable to healthcare professionals in general and the acceptable ease of use.

4 Interoperability and Data Exchange Standards of the HIS

Interoperability is essential for information to flow freely, accurately, efficiently, and securely between health information technology (HIT) systems and across healthcare networks—systems and networks that support hospitals and clinicians in the delivery of patient care [19]. However, in the context of The Gambia, the challenges in the implementation of interoperability between any meaningful HIS in the healthcare system varies from one approach to another. The institutional structure of the healthcare systems source and the level of healthcare service provided at the three-tiers also varies from basic to most advanced healthcare.

Similarly, resource availability and skill professionals required for the adoption of HIS varies in each stage of the healthcare system. At the PHC level, there is services provided by less qualified or student medical practitioners. This individual sometime lack formal clinical education in their practice. Their skills are acquired from government sponsors trainings and workshops. At this level, there is no feasibility of implementing any HIS without infrastructure reforms and capacity building. Resources and skill availability are much improved at secondary and tertiary level of healthcare (SHC, THC). Although, there is need for improvement in resource availability and capacity building to achieve any meaningful HIS. A top-down approach of interoperability ensures that there is a centralized system that serves multiple healthcare units. However, as pointed out in other studies, this can be very challenging for situation where the number of systems is very high. A general defined policies will override the policies of those systems that do not comply [13]. Considering the small number of healthcare institutions in the

SHC and THC levels of the Gambia, top-down approach is very feasible. The existing institutions are not using meaningful HIS and central system with rules and policies will not be over-riding any existing ones. In contrast, bottom-up approach is equally feasible but with tougher challenges such as prioritization and funding. Healthcare authorities and policy makers must prioritize allocation of resources and funds in top-down fashion.

4.1 Data Exchange Standards

Electronic Data Interchange (EDI) is the generic term for "intervention-free" ex-change of messages for controlling processes. The organizations that create or use data exchange standards fall into one of two categories. They are either creators of new standards or users of existing standards who modify an interoperability specification for a specific purpose. They are called Standards Developing organizations (SDO) and Profile Development organizations (PDO) respectively. There are several data exchange standards some of which includes the following:

- The Health Insurance Portability and Accountability Act (HIPAA) establishes national standards for protecting the privacy and security of individuals' health information.
- Joint Commission Standards is an independent, non-profit organization that accredits and certifies healthcare organizations in the United States. The Joint Commission sets standards for patient safety and quality of care.
- ISO 9001 is an international standard that outlines the requirements for a quality management system. Healthcare
- Health Level Seven (HL7) is a set of international standards for the exchange, integration, sharing, and retrieval of electronic health information. It covers areas such as clinical and administrative data, as well as messaging and document standards.
- International Classification of Diseases (ICD) is a standard classification system for diseases and health conditions used worldwide. It is maintained by the WHO and provides a common language for reporting and analyzing health information [20].

However, the most well-known and widely used data exchange standard in healthcare worldwide is HL7 Version 2.x. This standard is employed mainly for the transmission of messages to support data exchange within hospitals, between providers and hospitals, and between providers and registries [19]. To pull data from multiple and disparate sources would also require system integration. The adoption of a data warehousing strategy based on DHIS2 for example is an effective strategy for integrating different information flows. The data warehouse approach will allow different data collection forms to be imported into a common repository and enables the use of common Intelligence tools including that of GIS and a dashboard which enables users to gain outputs locally relevant to them.

4.2 Conclusion

In the Gambia, healthcare is very fragmented and unevenly distributed. For healthcare authorities and policy makers, the challenge for the adoption ranges from understanding the use and benefit of HIS, to financial cost and implications. The proliferation of information technology has not had an observable impact on the healthcare service and service delivery. Any meaningful implementation of HIS is now being pursued in several countries to improve the quality, safety, and efficiency of affordable healthcare.

The work of Coiera et al. [13] presented a conceptual model to implementation of HIS. The authors contend that an initial bottom-up or top-down strategy may evolve into a middle-out approach over time. However, it can also be argued that such adoption will still faces the challenge of weak infrastructure to support such systems. In addition, the effort to provide user-friendly system for low IT skill professionals also compromise functionality and quality. Such a system could equally face sustainability problems. The system will have short life cycle when the cost of maintenance is too high in comparison to benefit realized. For the Gambia to make significant progress to the adoption of HIS and achieved meaningful success, healthcare authorities and policy play a significant role in the promotion and financing of such initiative. Government policies should direct as well as prioritize the use of IT and support financing of both infrastructure and capacity building in this regard. In summary, to achieve the overall objectives set out in line with international best practice, it is recommended that Gambia government:

- Legislate a policy specifically targeting HIS.
- Embark on implementation of the proposed HIS and train skill professionals
- Build an electronic Healthcare record system.
- Develop a policy to serve to regulate, facilitate and coordinate the information system processing points.
- Develop an interoperable mechanism for effective integration of dataflow be-tween multiple entities.
- Use International Standard best practice as reference tool.
- Implement the HIS gradually on a pilot basis.

References

1. Mantzana, V., Themistocleous, M., Irani, Z., Morabito, V.: Identifying healthcare actors involved in the adoption of information systems. Eur. J. Inf. Syst. **16**, 91–102 (2007)
2. Liu, G.G., Chen, Y., Qin, X.: Transforming rural health care through information technology: an interventional study in China. Health Policy Plan. **29**, 975–985 (2014)
3. Guo, Y., Shibuya, K., Cheng, G., Rao, K., Lee, L., Tang, S.: Tracking China's health reform. The Lancet **375**, 1056–1058 (2010)
4. Africa, W.R.O.f.: National Health Policy of The Gambia, 2021–2030. WHO (2021). https://www.afro.who.int/countries/gambia/publication/national-health-policy-gambia-2021-2030
5. Reynhardt. Mark and others. Global Space Governance: Africa's contribution to the United Nations Committee on the Peaceful Uses of Outer Space (UNCOPUOS) (2019)
6. Aidam, J., Sombi{\'e}, I.: The West African Health Organization's experience in improving the health research environment in the ECOWAS region. Health Res. Policy Syst. **1**, 1–11 (2016)
7. Abraham, C., Nishihara, E., Akiyama, M.: Transforming healthcare with information technology in Japan: a review of policy, people, and progress. Int. J. Med. Inform. **80**, 157–170 (2011)
8. Dixon, B.E., Vreeman, D.J., Grannis, S.J.: The long road to semantic interoperability in support of public health: experiences from two states. J. Biomed. Inform. **49**, 3–8 (2014)

9. Kierkegaard, P.: Interoperability after deployment. Int. J. Qual. Health Care **27**, 147–153 (2014)
10. Health, M.o.: Gambia National Health strategic Plan 2014–2020. In: Gambia National Health strategic Plan, pp. 1–142
11. Car, J., et al.: The impact of eHealth on the quality & safety of healthcare: a systematic overview and synthesis of the literature, NHS Connecting for Health Evaluation Programme (2008)
12. Morrison, Z., Robertson, A., Cresswell, K., Crowe, S., Sheikh, A.: Understanding contrasting approaches to nationwide implementations of electronic health record systems: England, the USA and Australia. J. Healthc. Eng. **2**, 25–41 (2011)
13. Coiera, E.: Building a national health IT system from the middle out. J. Am. Med. Inform. Assoc. **16**, 271–273 (2009)
14. Roncarolo, F., Boivin, A., Denis, J.-L., H{\'e}bert, R., Lehoux, P.: What do we know about the needs and challenges of health systems? A scoping review of the international literature. BMC Health Serv. Res. **17**, 1–18
15. TheGlobalEconomy.com. Gambia: Human flight and brain drain. TheGlobalEconomy.com (2022). https://www.theglobaleconomy.com/Gambia/human_flight_brain_drain_index. Accessed 12 2022
16. Organiztion, W.H.: Country information. World Health Organiztion. https://www.afro.who.int/countries/gambia. Accessed 12 2022
17. Sood, S.P., et al.: Electronic medical records: a review comparing the challenges in developed and developing countries. In: Proceedings of the 41st Annual Hawaii International Conference on System Sciences (HICSS 2008), pp. 248–248. IEEE (2008)
18. Hillestad, R., et al.: An electronic medical record systems transform health care? Potential health benefits, savings, and costs. Health Aff. **24**, 1103–1117 (2005)
19. Oemig, F., Snelick, R.: Healthcare standards landscape. In: Healthcare Interoperability Standards Compliance Handbook, Springer, pp. 75–103 (2016)
20. Chronicle, T.: Physical Violence on Women – Survey Indicates 46% Raise in the Gambia (2021). https://www.chronicle.gm/physical-violence-on-women-survey-indicates-46-raise-in-the-gambia/
21. Tao, W., et al.: Towards universal health coverage: lessons from 10 years of healthcare reform in China. BMJ Global Health **5**, 2086 (2020)

Short Papers

Vehicle Routing Optimization for Medical Product Distribution in Regional Capitals of Burkina Faso: A Linear Programming Approach with Gurobi

Saan-Nonnan Olivier Dabire[1](✉), Boureima Zerbo[2], and Désiré Guel[1]

[1] University of Joseph KI-ZERBO, Ouagadougou, Burkina Faso
oliviersdabire@gmail.com, desire.guel@ujkz.bf
[2] University of Thomas SANKARA, Saaba, Burkina Faso
boureima.zerbo@uts.bf

Abstract. This study presents a MILP based approach to the Vehicle Routing Problem (VRP) for optimizing medical product distribution in Burkina Faso. The model accounts for critical real-world constraints including restricted areas and road inaccessibility while ensuring equitable service to priority healthcare centers. Implemented using the Gurobi solver, it achieved exact solutions rapidly (662 variables post-preprocessing, 62 constraints) with a near-zero optimality gap. While results demonstrate efficient route allocation, the reliance on synthetically generated data and the model's static nature limit operational realism. Future improvements will include integration of dynamic variables, field-collected data, and scalable heuristics such as Ant Colony Optimization to enhance adaptability and practical deployment.

Keywords: MILP · VRP · Healthcare logistics · Gurobi · Security Constraint

1 Introduction

Optimizing healthcare logistics is crucial for equitable access to care, particularly in low-resource settings like Burkina Faso, where road infrastructure, geographic dispersion, and security concerns hinder medical distribution.

To address this, we formulate a Vehicle Routing Problem (VRP) using a Mixed-Integer Linear Programming (MILP) model that integrates practical constraints such as vehicle capacity, restricted zones, and road conditions. MILP provides exact solutions and serves as a reliable baseline despite known limitations in scalability and responsiveness.

Our model, implemented with the Gurobi solver, aims to minimize travel distance while ensuring coverage of priority healthcare centers. Due to incomplete field data, demand and capacity values were synthetically generated, limiting real-world validation. Nonetheless, the approach offers a solid foundation for future integration of heuristics, real-time variables, and sustainable logistics considerations.

D. Bassole et al. (Eds.): InterSol 2025, LNICST 671, pp. 261–267, 2026.
https://doi.org/10.1007/978-3-032-15154-4_20

2 Literature Review

MILP models have proven effective in logistics optimization across sectors such as transportation [1], energy [7], and telecommunications [3], offering exact solutions under multiple constraints.

In healthcare logistics, MILP is widely applied to routing problems with capacity and time windows [9]. Variants address multi-depot routing [8] and improve relaxations for faster convergence [6]. However, scalability and real-time adaptability remain major challenges.

Many models assume static demand and lack field validation [5], which undermines operational realism. As problem size grows, exact methods become computationally intensive, reinforcing the need for hybrid approaches combining MILP with heuristics or AI techniques.

Given these insights, our work builds on MILP's strengths while acknowledging its limitations, proposing it as a baseline for healthcare routing in Burkina Faso under real-world constraints.

3 Methodology

We model the distribution of medical products in Burkina Faso using a Mixed-Integer Linear Programming (MILP) approach to solve the Vehicle Routing Problem (VRP) under practical constraints.

Healthcare center locations and distances were sourced from the national health authority [2]. Due to missing data, healthcare demand and vehicle capacities were synthetically generated within realistic bounds. Data cleaning involved deduplication and standardization to ensure usability for optimization.

The MILP model aims to minimize total travel distance while balancing vehicle workloads and respecting operational constraints. It integrates vehicle capacities, road access limitations, and priority service zones.

Data and Parameters:

- N : Set of healthcare centers ($i \in N$).
- 0 : Initial depot (starting point of the vehicles).
- K : Set of available vehicles ($k \in K$).
- Q_k : Maximum capacity of vehicle k (in units).
- d_i : Demand of center i (in units).
- c_{ij} : Distance traveled between centers i and j.
- R_f : Set of restricted roads.
- Z_r : Set of high-risk zones.

Decision Variables:

- $x_{kij} \in \{0, 1\}$: 1 if vehicle k travels on arc (i, j), 0 otherwise.
- u_{ki} : Load of vehicle k after visiting node i.
- $d_{\max}, d_{\min}$: Auxiliary variables to balance route distances.

Objective Function:

$$\min Z = \sum_{k \in K} \sum_{(i,j) \in C} c_{ij} \cdot x_{kij} + (d_{\max} - d_{\min}) \tag{1}$$

Constraints:

$$\sum_{(i,j) \in C} c_{ij} \cdot x_{kij} \leq d_{\max}, \qquad \forall k \in K \tag{2}$$

$$\sum_{(i,j) \in C} c_{ij} \cdot x_{kij} \geq d_{\min}, \qquad \forall k \in K \tag{3}$$

$$d_{\max} - d_{\min} \leq 500 \tag{4}$$

$$\sum_{k \in K} \sum_{j \in C, j \neq i} x_{kij} \geq 1, \qquad \forall i \in \text{Strategic Cities} \tag{5}$$

$$\sum_{k \in K} \sum_{j \in C, j \neq i} x_{kij} \leq 1, \qquad \forall i \in C \setminus \{0\} \tag{6}$$

$$x_{kij} = 0, \qquad \forall (i, j) \in R_f \cup Z_r, \forall k \in K \tag{7}$$

Solver and Parameters: The model was implemented using Gurobi, leveraging presolve, cutting planes, and parameter tuning (MIPGap: 0.01-0.05, Heuristics: 0.3-0.8, MIPFocus: 2). Solver efficiency was evaluated through sensitivity analyses.

Performance Summary: The final model included 912 variables and 62 constraints, reduced post-presolve to 662 and 23, respectively. The optimal solution (960 km total travel) was found in under 1.5 s with a 0% MIP Gap.

Scalability and Limitations: MILP ensures solution quality but remains limited for large-scale dynamic networks. This issue is further discussed in Sect. 4, including hybrid extensions to improve scalability.

Table 1. Summary of Infeasible Solutions

Execution	Parameters Used	Reason for Infeasibility
Run 1	MIPGap = 0.05, Heuristics = 0.8	Too many route constraints, preventing feasible vehicle assignments.
Run 2	MIPGap = 0.02, Heuristics = 0.5	Vehicle capacity exceeded in multiple routes, violating constraints.
Run 3	MIPGap = 0.01, Heuristics = 0.3	Presolve removed necessary constraints, causing an inconsistent model.
Run 4	MIPGap = 0.05, Heuristics = 0.8	Infeasible due to an excessive maximum distance constraint per vehicle.

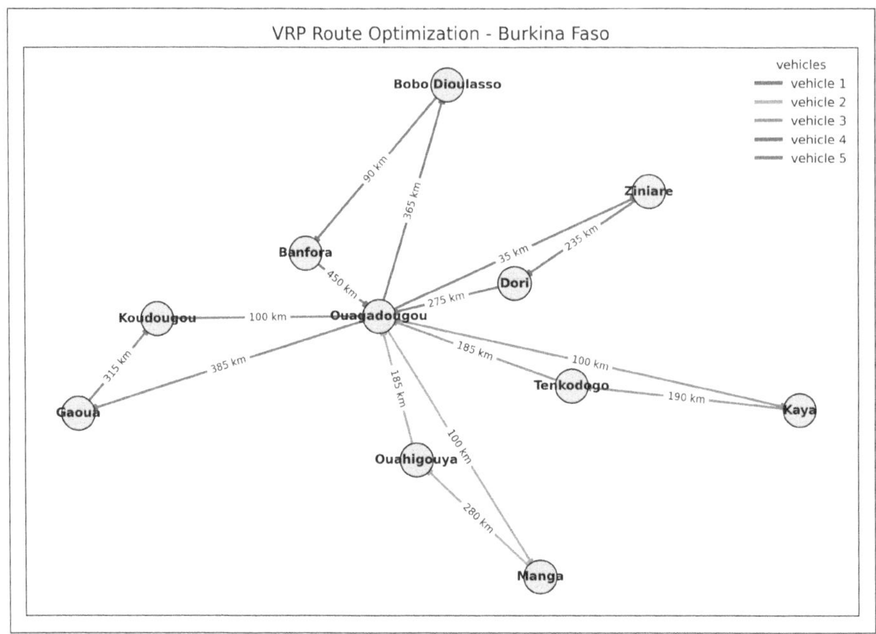

Fig. 1. Optimization of vehicle routes.

4 Results and Discussion

The MILP model solved with Gurobi yielded optimal routes for distributing medical supplies in Burkina Faso, achieving a MIP gap of 0.000% within two seconds for medium-sized instances. As shown in Fig. 1, vehicle routes were optimized to minimize total distance while avoiding high-risk zones. This led to reduced fuel consumption and maintenance costs, enhancing overall logistics efficiency.

The model respected constraints such as vehicle capacities, road restrictions, and priority areas [4], resulting in balanced trip assignments (Fig. 2). However, some distance disparities remained (Fig. 3), partly due to uneven health center distribution. Assigning vehicles to specific zones helped reduce route overlap.

Sensitivity analysis over 10 runs showed low variability (mean: 962.4 km, SD: 3.5 km), confirming robustness. Solver parameters (MIPGap, Heuristics) influenced convergence: lower MIPGap improved precision, and reducing Heuristics (0.3) enhanced convergence quality. Solver iterations and cutting-plane techniques contributed to performance gains.

Despite strong performance on small datasets, the model's scalability is limited. As the number of health centers and vehicles increases, so does the complexity, leading to infeasibility or prolonged runtimes (Table 1). To address this, clustering techniques (e.g., K-means, DBSCAN) and local search heuristics (e.g., 2-opt, Tabu Search) could decompose and accelerate the solution process.

A hybrid approach combining MILP for initial assignment and metaheuristics (e.g., ACO, GA) for refinement appears promising. Future developments will incorporate dynamic parameters, such as time-dependent demand and traffic conditions, to enhance realism. Additionally, integrating delivery time windows and IoT/GPS technologies would enable real-time route adjustments.

While the current model assumes fixed demand and omits real-time disruptions, synthetic data were calibrated using national health reports. Future validation with Burkina Faso's medical supply agency (CAMEG) is planned to ensure operational realism.

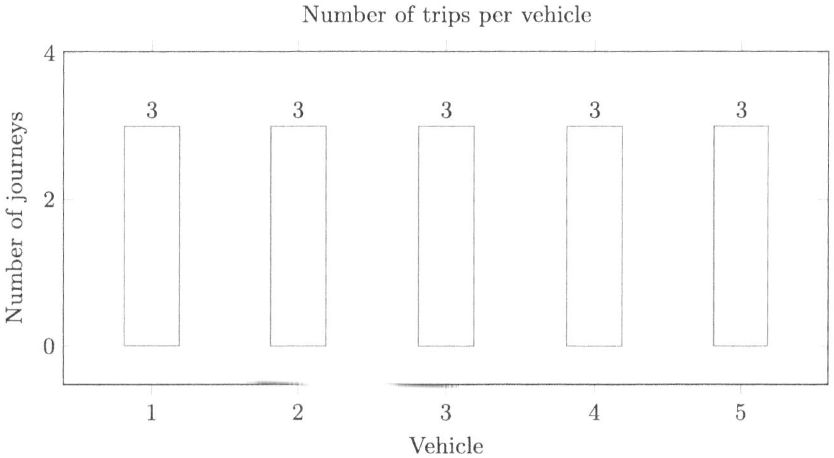

Fig. 2. Number of trips per vehicle.

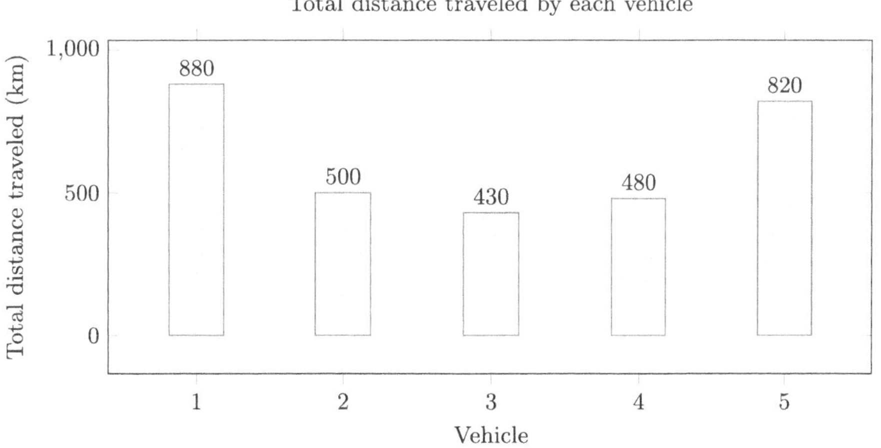

Fig. 3. Total distance traveled by each vehicle.

Total distance currently serves as a proxy for cost. Future iterations will include explicit logistics costs (fuel, labor) and environmental metrics (e.g., CO_2 emissions). To support reproducibility and adoption, all code, parameters, and scenarios will be made publicly available via a GitHub repository.

5 Conclusion and Perspectives

This study validated the effectiveness of a MILP model solved with Gurobi for optimizing medical supply distribution in Burkina Faso. The model minimized travel distances and ensured balanced resource allocation under realistic constraints.

Despite strong performance, scalability remains limited for larger networks. To address this, future work will combine MILP with heuristics (e.g., Clarke-Wright, ACO) for faster, scalable routing. Incorporating GPS, IoT, and dynamic data (e.g., traffic, variable demand) will enhance adaptability and operational realism.

The approach offers a transferable framework for healthcare logistics in similar contexts, with future research focusing on hybrid modeling and field validation to support broader deployment.

References

1. Chang, D.: GUROBI-based modeling optimization of railway containerized transportation for passengers. In: Easa, S., Wei, W., eds, Eighth International Conference on lectromechanical Control Technology and Transportation (ICECTT 2023), p. 225, Hangzhou, China, September 2023. SPIE.
2. Directorate General of studies and sectoral statistics/ministry of health of Burkina Faso (DGESS/MSB). Data on Healthcare Centers in Burkina Faso, (2024). Accessed: 2024-09-25
3. Yun-Fan Huang and Wei-Kuo Chiang. Gurobi optimization for 5gc refactoring. In: 2023 International Conference on Consumer Electronics - Taiwan (ICCE-Taiwan), pp. 115–116 (2023)
4. Laporte, G., Toth, P., Vigo, D.: Vehicle routing: Problems, methods, and applications. Transp. Sci. **54**(3), 1–25 (2020)
5. Lukitosari, V., Subriadi, A.P.: Supply-demand optimization in the product distribution process through the branching method. IOP Conf. Series: Mater. Sci. Eng. **1072**(1), 012026 (2021)
6. Mandal, U., Regan, A., Rousseau, L.M., Yarkony, J.: A new class of compact formulations for vehicle routing problems (2024)
7. Qi, X., Liu, L., Zhang, Z., Pan, Z., Wu, W.: Study on the cooperative optimized operation of power system source-grid-load-storage based on gurobi mathematical programming. In: 2023 IEEE 7th Information Technology and Mechatronics Engineering Conference (ITOEC), volume 7, pp. 1085–1092 (2023)
8. Sierra, M., Casanova, M., García-Sánchez, Á., Larzabal, H., López, D.: Milp model for a generalized capacitated vehicle routing problem with multiple depots and multiple pickup and delivery requests. In: Bautista-Valhondo, J., Mateo-Doll, M., Lusa, A., Pastor-Moreno, R., eds, Proceedings of the 17th International Conference

on Industrial Engineering and Industrial Management (ICIEIM) – XXVII Congreso de Ingeniería de Organización (CIO2023), pp. 306–311, Cham, (2024). Springer Nature Switzerland

9. Tóth, M., Hajba, T., Horváth, A.: MILP models of a patient transportation problem. Central Eur. J. Oper. Res. (2024)

5G-NR PRACH Detection Using an AutoEncoder Under Interference

Ahmed Sawadogo[1(✉)], Désiré Guel[1], and Boureima Zerbo[2]

[1] Université Joseph KI-ZERBO (U-JKZ), Ouagadougou, Burkina Faso
amedsavadogo45@gmail.com, desire.guel@ujkz.bf

[2] Université Thomas SANKARA (UTS), Ouagadougou, Burkina Faso
boureima.zerbo@uts.bf

Abstract. Efficient detection of the Physical Random Access Channel (PRACH) is vital for reliable initial access in 5G New Radio (5G-NR), yet it remains challenged by intra- and inter-cell interference. This paper proposes a deep learning-based solution leveraging an Autoencoder (AE) trained on synthetic PRACH data under noisy conditions. The model detects valid preambles by minimizing reconstruction error, effectively distinguishing them from interference. Simulation results demonstrate improved detection accuracy and reduced RMSE, especially with optimized latent dimensions (3264), offering a practical balance between performance and complexity. These findings support the integration of AI-based detection in future adaptive 5G-NR systems.

Keywords: 5G-NR · PRACH · Autoencoder · Interference · Machine Learning · Deep Learning

1 Introduction

The advent of fifth-generation (5G) mobile networks marks a major leap in wireless communications, enabling ultra-reliable low latency communication (URLLC), massive machine-type communication (mMTC), and enhanced mobile broadband (eMBB) [1]. These capabilities support billions of devices, including IoT sensors, autonomous vehicles, and high-speed mobile applications.

A core challenge in 5G-NR is the initial access via the Physical Random Access Channel (PRACH), which enables synchronization between User Equipment (UE) and base station (gNB) [2]. Accurate PRACH detection is essential for low-latency and reliable network access.

In dense deployments, PRACH detection suffers from intra/inter-cell interference, multipath effects, and signal collisions, leading to increased miss rates and degraded quality of service (QoS) [3]. Traditional correlation-based methods using Zadoff-Chu sequences struggle in such conditions [4].

To address this, AI and deep learning—particularly Autoencoders (AEs)—have shown promise in denoising and feature extraction [5]. An AE learns to reconstruct clean signal patterns, enabling it to differentiate valid preambles from noise [6].

D. Bassole et al. (Eds.): InterSol 2025, LNICST 671, pp. 268–273, 2026.
https://doi.org/10.1007/978-3-032-15154-4_21

This study proposes an AE-based PRACH detection framework trained on synthetic data with varying interference, aiming to enhance detection in complex 5G environments.
The paper is organized as follows: Sect. 2 reviews related work; Sect. 3 outlines the proposed method; Sect. 4 presents simulation results; and Sect. 5 concludes the study.

2 Background and Related Work

This section presents the theoretical foundation of autoencoders in PRACH detection and reviews key classical and AI-based approaches from the literature.

An autoencoder consists of an **encoder** and a **decoder** [7]. It maps input $\mathbf{x} \in \mathbb{R}^d$ to a latent space $\mathbf{z} \in \mathbb{R}^m$ as:

$$\mathbf{z} = \sigma(\mathbf{W}_e \mathbf{x} + \mathbf{b}_e), \tag{1}$$

and reconstructs $\hat{\mathbf{x}}$ via:

$$\hat{\mathbf{x}} = \sigma'(\mathbf{W}_d \mathbf{z} + \mathbf{b}_d). \tag{2}$$

The model minimizes:

$$\mathcal{L} = \frac{1}{n} \sum_{i=1}^{n} \|\mathbf{x}_i - \hat{\mathbf{x}}_i\|^2. \tag{3}$$

This structure enables effective feature extraction under noise and interference.

Traditional PRACH detection, based on Zadoff-Chu correlation, performs poorly in noisy settings. AI-driven approaches now offer enhanced robustness and adaptability. Table 1 summarizes key contributions.

Table 1. Summary of Related Work

Authors	Method	Strengths	Weaknesses	Details/Results
Pastukh et al. [8]	Correlation using Zadoff-Chu	Good in low noise	Poor robustness	~80% detection at SNR > 10 dB
Guel et al. [9]	CNN detection	Robust in noise	High complexity	89% accuracy on synthetic data
Dahal et al. [3]	Multi-agent RL	Adaptive in interference	Complex model	+15% SINR gain in simulations
Chinchali et al. [5]	Autoencoder filtering	+18 dB SNR gain	Needs interference model	Trained on noisy simulated data
Fang et al. [2]	FNN for PRACH	High accuracy	Not scalable	>90% accuracy in simple scenario
Zehra et al. [10]	RL + cognitive radio	Spectrum efficiency	Slow convergence	Converges after 1000 iterations

3 Proposed Methodology

This section presents an autoencoder-based PRACH detection pipeline for noisy and interference-prone 5G environments. The methodology includes signal generation, channel modeling, and detection based on reconstruction error.

The system (Fig. 1) processes PRACH signals corrupted by Rayleigh fading and noise. A deep autoencoder learns signal features by minimizing the reconstruction error:

- Encoder: compresses input to latent representation.
- Decoder: reconstructs the original signal.
- Detection: if reconstruction error (MSE) is below a threshold, PRACH is detected; otherwise, it is interference.

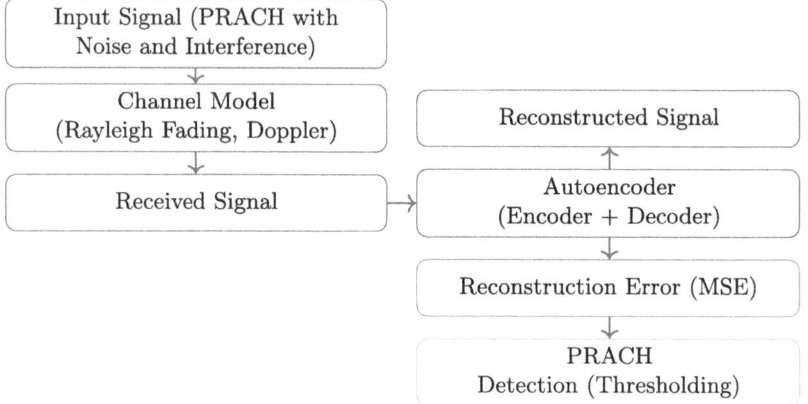

Fig. 1. System Model for PRACH Detection Using Autoencoder.

Key parameters are listed in Table 2, including SNR values, delay profile, Doppler frequency, and model training setup (e.g., optimizer: Adam, loss: MSE). The autoencoder uses varying latent dimensions (e.g., 16, 32, 64) for performance benchmarking.

Table 2. Key Configuration Parameters

Category	Description	Value(s)
PRACH	Detection threshold	0.0001
Channel	Doppler frequency	70 Hz
Training	Optimizer/Loss	Adam/MSE
Autoencoder	Latent Dimensions	[16, 32, 64]

The model classifies signals as PRACH if reconstruction error is below threshold; otherwise, they are labeled as interference.

4 Results and Analysis

This section presents simulation results and complexity analysis of the autoencoder-based PRACH detection model. Evaluations focus on reconstruction accuracy and computational cost across varying latent dimensions (`LatentDim`).

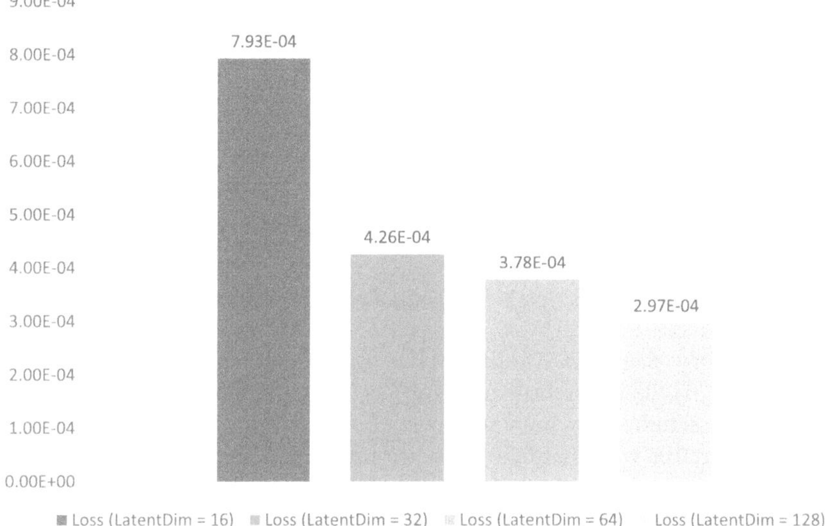

(a) Loss across different latent dimensions.

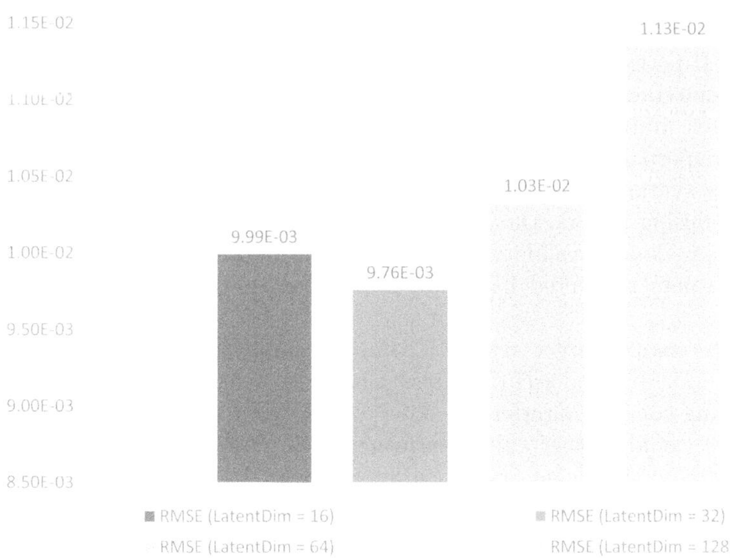

(b) RMSE across different latent dimensions.

Fig. 2. Evaluation of PRACH Autoencoder Performance.

Figure 2 show the evolution of loss and RMSE across latent dimensions from 16 to 128. Increasing `LatentDim` improves performance up to 64, beyond which benefits diminish or degrade due to possible overfitting and increased complexity.

A latent dimension of 64 yields the best balance between detection accuracy and training cost, showing minimal reconstruction error without excessive resource demands. The model's complexity is primarily due to the encoder/decoder layers, with cost proportional to:

$$\mathcal{O}(2NL), \tag{4}$$

where N is the input size and L the latent dimension. Increasing L linearly scales compute and memory needs. The Adam optimizer adds overhead:

$$\mathcal{O}(2 \cdot \#\text{parameters}), \tag{5}$$

doubling memory use over vanilla SGD. Empirical analysis shows that a `LatentDim` of 3264 offers the best trade-off, as higher values yield minimal accuracy gains with significantly increased cost.

Thus, `LatentDim` values of 64 or less are preferred for practical implementations balancing accuracy and efficiency.

5 Conclusion

This study validates the potential of autoencoder (AE)-based detection to enhance PRACH performance in 5G-NR networks, particularly under noisy and interference-prone conditions. Simulations show that the AE effectively extracts PRACH features, improving detection accuracy and reducing reconstruction error. Proper hyperparameter tuning and preprocessing contributed to model efficiency across synthetic channel conditions.

Despite promising results, the study is limited by its reliance on simulated data and lack of real-world validation. Interference scenarios were simplified, and practical constraints prevented hardware implementation. These factors limit generalizability.

Future work should target real 5G datasets, hardware deployment (e.g., FPGA/GPU), and advanced architectures such as GANs or hybrid AE-CNN-RL models. Including complex interference sources and benchmarking against classical techniques would further assess performance in realistic settings, moving toward adaptive and intelligent 5G detection systems.

References

1. Hassan, A.N., Al-Chlaihawi, S., Khekan, A.R.: Artificial intelligence techniques over the fifth generation (5G) mobile networks: a review. In: Indonesian Journal of Electrical Engineering and Computer Science (2021)
2. Fang, R., Chen, H., Liu, W.: Deep learning-based PRACH detection algorithm design and simulation. In: 2022 2nd International Conference on Frontiers of Electronics, Information and Computation Technologies (ICFEICT), pp. 505–511. IEEE (2022). https://doi.org/10.1109/icfeict57213.2022.00094

3. Dahal, M., Vaezi, M.: Multi-agent deep reinforcement learning for multi-cell interference mitigation. In: 2023 57th Annual Conference on Information Sciences and Systems (CISS). IEEE (2023). https://doi.org/10.1109/ciss56502.2023.10089622
4. Robinson, C.P., Uvaydov, D., D'Oro, S., Melodia, T.: Narrowband interference detection via deep learning. In: ICC 2023 - IEEE International Conference on Communications, pp. 6379–6384 (2023). https://doi.org/10.1109/ICC45041.2023.10278618
5. Chinchali, S., Tandon, S.: Deep learning for wireless interference segmentation and prediction. In: Proceedings of Citeseer (2012)
6. Oyedare, T.R.: A Comprehensive Analysis of Deep Learning for Interference Suppression, Sample and Model Complexity in Wireless Systems. PhD thesis. Virginia Tech (2024)
7. Joshi, A.V.: Introduction to AI and ML. In: Machine Learning and Artificial Intelligence. Springer International Publishing, pp. 3–7 (2019). isbn: 9783030266226. https://doi.org/10.1007/978-3-030-26622-6_1
8. Pastukh, A., Tikhvinskiy, V., Devyatkin, E., Kostin, A.: Interference analysis of 5G NR base stations to fixed satellite service bent-pipe transponders in the 6425-7125 MHz frequency band. In: Sensors, vol. 23(1), pp. 172 (2023). https://doi.org/10.3390/S23010172
9. Guel, D., Kabore, A., Bassolé, D.: 5G NR PRACH Detection with Convolutional Neural Networks (CNN): Overcoming Cell Interference Challenges (2024). eprint: 2408.11659
10. Zehra, S.S., Qureshi, R., Aamir, M., Magarini, M.: Utilizing cognitive radio and reinforcement learning for multiple preamble detection in 5GPRACH. In: 2022 25th International Symposium on Wireless Personal Multimedia Communications (WPMC) (2022). https://doi.org/10.1109/WPMC55625. 2022.10014807

Maize Productivity Optimization: An Analysis of Hybrid, Cobb-Douglas, and CES Models

Ezra Daniel Dzarma[1] (✉), Theophile Komlan Dagba[2], and Guy Degla[1]

[1] Department of Computer Science and Operations Research, University of Abomey-Calavi/IMSP Dangbo, Porto-Novo, Benin
{daniel.dzarma,gdegla}@imsp-uac.org

[2] Department of Computer Science and Operations Research, University of Abomey-Calavi, Cotonou, Benin
tdagba@hotmail.com

Abstract. This study investigates the optimization of maize farming productivity using three different models: Cobb-Douglas, Constant Elasticity of Substitution (CES), and a hybrid optimization model. Data on farm inputs and output were collected from Northeast Nigeria between October and December 2023. The study compares the performance of these models in predicting optimal maize yields based on labour, fertilizer, herbicides, pesticides, seeds, and land inputs. While the Cobb-Douglas model demonstrated moderate yield predictions, it resulted in unrealistic input allocations, especially for seed quantities. The CES model provided greater flexibility in input substitution but underperformed in yield optimization due to calibration challenges. In contrast, the hybrid optimization model integrated strengths from both approaches, achieving the highest yield of 6.5t/ha with practical and balanced input distributions. This model outperformed both the Cobb-Douglas and CES models, highlighting its potential for improving agricultural productivity through better optimization and real-world applicability in resource-limited regions like Northeast Nigeria.

Keywords: Hybrid Model · Cobb-Douglas · CES · Maize Farming · Input Optimization

1 Introduction

Maize (Zea mays) is a vital staple crop in North-East Nigeria as well as many Western African Countries, essential for food security, income, and economic stability. It serves both food and industrial purposes, supporting smallholder farmers and local industries. Despite its importance, production remains below potential, requiring yield-improving interventions. Recent studies emphasize maize's socioeconomic value, particularly its role in reducing poverty and malnutrition in rural communities [1].

Several studies have examined maize production in North-east Nigeria, focusing on yield improvement and limiting factors. Abdoulaye *et al.* [2] highlighted the role

D. Bassole et al. (Eds.): InterSol 2025, LNICST 671, pp. 274–280, 2026.
https://doi.org/10.1007/978-3-032-15154-4_22

of improved seed varieties and modern farming practices, while Musa and Abdullahi [3] emphasized soil fertility management and irrigation systems. These underscore the promise of innovative methods in bridging yield gaps. However, comprehensive strategies addressing broader cultivation constraints are still lacking. Though CES and Cobb-Douglas models aid productivity analysis, each has limitations: Cobb-Douglas assumes constant elasticity, Fixed Elasticity of Substitution while CES, though flexible, is computationally intensive and may misrepresent real-world input interactions [4].

Low maize yields in North-East Nigeria result from poor soil fertility, erratic rainfall, pests, and weak agronomic practices. Limited input access and inadequate extension services hinder modern farming adoption. Climate change worsens rainfall unpredictability, affecting planting and harvesting. Adebayo et al. [5] highlight sustainable land use and better-input access. Recent study also recommends adaptive policies and climate-smart agriculture to boost maize productivity [6].

The aim of this research is to develop a robust mathematical model that can optimize maize yields per hectare in North-east Nigeria by addressing the identified constraints. By a new integrating factor as the input efficiency, the model seeks to provide practical recommendations for farmers to maximize their output [7].

2 Methodology

Crop yield optimization relies on models like Cobb-Douglas, CES, and hybrid functions to analyze the relationship between farm inputs and output for improved productivity [8]. In this research, 752 valid data samples was collected from farmers in Northeast Nigeria using structured questionnaire plus 747 simulated data total 1499. The data were processed and analyzed using Python and excel solver to identify the most efficient input combinations for enhancing maize yield and resource use efficiency.

2.1 Cobb-Douglas Production Function

The original Cobb-Douglas production function is a mathematical model that represents the relationship between two or more inputs (typically capital and labour) and the output of a firm or economy is expressed as:

$$Y = AK^{\alpha}L^{\beta} \quad (1)$$

Where:

Y = Output (e.g., total production, such as maize yield in the context of agriculture) K = Capital input (e.g., machinery, buildings, equipment); L = Labour input (e.g., human workers); A = Total Factor Productivity (TFP) or technology level, representing the efficiency with which inputs are used; α = Output elasticity of capital, representing the percentage change in output resulting from a 1% change in capital; β = Output elasticity of labor, representing the percentage change in output resulting from a 1% change in labour.

3 Constant Elasticity of Substitution (CES)

The CES production function is a widely used production function in economics. It represents the relationship between multiple inputs and output, allowing for varying degrees of substitutability between inputs.

General CES Production Function

$$y=\theta\left(\sum_{i=1}^{n}\alpha_i x_i^{\rho}\right)^{\frac{1}{\rho}} \tag{2}$$

Where

y = the output (maize yield per hectare in kg/ha); $\theta =$ Total productivity factor

$\alpha_i =$ share parameter for inputs x_i (how much each input contribute to the output with $\sum_{i=1}^{n}\alpha_i = 1$); x_i= farm inputs (labour, fertilizer (bags of 50 kg), herbicides (litres), pesticides (litres), seeds (kg) and land in thousands of naira; ρ = substitution parameter, which governs the elasticity of substitution between the inputs; n = number of the farm inputs.

4 Hybrid Model Formulated Optimization Model

The hybrid model was created by integrating the Cobb-Douglas production function with the CES model, aiming to address the limitations of each individual model. This hybrid approach combines the strengths of both models with minimal adjustments as shown in Fig. 1 and Eq. 3.

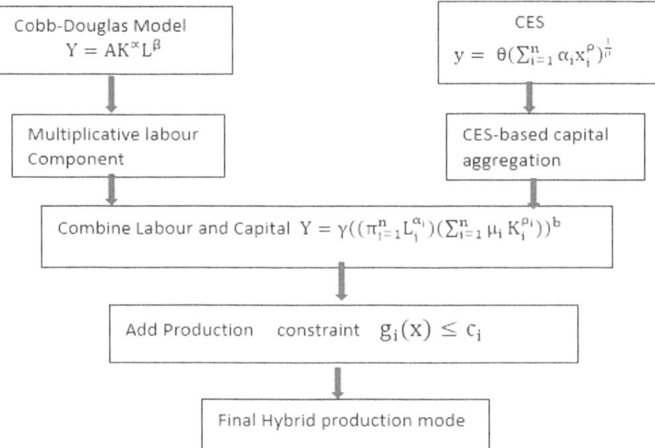

Fig. 1. Hybrid formulation process

$$Y = \gamma[\left(\pi_{j=1}^{n}L_j^{\alpha_i}\right)\left(\sum_{i=1}^{n}\mu_i K_i^{\rho_i}\right)]^b \tag{3}$$

$$g_i(x) \leq c_i \tag{4}$$

Where

Y = farm output; $\gamma = \frac{\beta}{\theta}$; K_i = the quantities of the six factors of production (capital which refers to six farm inputs in our in this research; L_j = the quantities of the six factors of production (labour which is also refers to six farm inputs); α_j = the output elasticities of the farm inputs in the Cobb-Douglas part of the function; μ_i = the output elasticities of capital in the CES part of the function; b = the overall elasticities of CES and CDPF which is the average of the two elasticities; $g_i(x)$= production constraints.

5 Mathematical Formulation of the Model

A mathematical optimization model equation was developed using CES and Cobb-Douglas production functions applied via Python to field data from North-East Nigeria. Equation (5) were obtained from the relationships between key inputs included labour (b), fertilizer (f), herbicides (h), pesticides (p), and seeds (s) land rental (l) and corresponding yield (y) while Eq. (6)-(9) reflected variable interactions, unit input costs, and resource availability based on the data obtained from the field.

$$Y = 8.34[(b^{\frac{1}{5}} f^{\frac{1}{9}} h^{\frac{1}{16}} p^{\frac{1}{9}} s^{\frac{1}{84}} l^{\frac{4}{91}})(\frac{3}{7}b^{-\frac{5}{6}} + \frac{5}{9}f^{-\frac{5}{6}} + \frac{4}{7}h^{-\frac{5}{6}} + \frac{4}{7}p^{-\frac{5}{6}} + \frac{1}{3}s^{-\frac{5}{6}} + \frac{3}{7}l^{-\frac{5}{6}})]^{0.5} \tag{5}$$

$$24f^2 + 2.5s^3 \leq 144.185 \text{ (fertilizer and seeds constraints)} \tag{6}$$

$$7h^2 + 5.5p^3 \leq 70.2 \text{ (Chemical constraints)} \tag{7}$$

$$4b + 30l \leq 228 \text{ (labour and land constraints)} \tag{8}$$

$$b, f, h, p, s, l > 0 \tag{9}$$

Excel Solver was employed as a data analysis tool to determine the optimal allocation of farm inputs and the corresponding outputs.

6 Results and Discussion

6.1 Farm Inputs-Outputs Optimization

Table 1 presents the results of the optimal farm inputs and outputs as determined through the application of Cobb-Douglas production function, CES and hybrid optimization model.

The comparison of Cobb-Douglas, CES, and Hybrid models reveals varying efficiencies in optimizing maize yield. The Cobb-Douglas model increased yield to 4.1t/ha from the field average of 3.9t/ha by intensifying labour (80 man-days) and fertilizer (10 bags), though it showed limitations in realistic seed allocation (30 kg) and overreliance on inputs, raising sustainability concerns. In contrast, the CES model yielded 3931 kg/ha and allowed flexible substitution among inputs, especially benefiting labour (60 man-days) and seed (30 kg), yet underperformed in yield and practicality The hybrid model outperformed both, achieving 6.5 t/ha with balanced inputs, 60 man-days of labour, 10 bags of fertilizer, and 22 kg of seed, offering both high efficiency and real-world applicability [9, 10].

Table 1. Cobb-Douglas, CES and Hybrid Optimal Inputs

Inputs/Outputs/ha	CDPF	CES	Hybrid
Labour (Man-day)	80	60	60
Fertilizer (50kg)	10	11	10
Herbicides (L)	15	10	8
Pesticides (L)	4	5	3
Seeds (Kg)	30	30	22
Land (₦000)	50	25	30
Optimal yield (t)	4.1	3.9	6.5

7 Hybrids Result Consideration vs IITA

Table 2 reveals that the New Hybrid yields 6.5 t/ha, aligning with IITA's benchmark of ≥6 t/ha and clearly outperforming Aduba Hybrid (2.4 t/ha) and Girma & Tadesse Hybrid (2.52 t/ha). Despite using more fertilizer (12 bags), herbicides (10 L), and pesticides (3 L), the New Hybrid delivers superior output efficiency. Compared to IITA, which achieves similar yields with less fertilizer (8 bags) and labour (68.96 person-days), the new Hybrid still surpasses older hybrids in productivity. This supports findings by Patel & Lee [11] and Zhu *et al.* [12] that modern hybrids efficiently convert inputs into higher yields.

Table 2. New Hybrid Vs Aduba and Girma & Tadesse Hybrid

Inputs/output/ha	Hybrid	Aduba Hybrid [14]	Girma&Tadesse Hybrid [15]	IITA [13]
Labour (man/day)	60	145	150	68.96
Fertilizer (50kg)	12	2.3	2.4	8
Herbicides (litres)	10	3.1	3.3	15.6
Pesticides (litres)	3	1.7	1.6	0.2–3
Seeds (kg)	22	20	24	15–20
Land (₦)	30,000	16,500	15,500	-
Yield (t)	6.5	2.4	2.52	y >= 6t

7.1 7.1Performance of Maize Yield Prediction Models Using Absolute Gross Profit

The analysis of absolute gross profit for the maize varieties shows clear differences in economic performance. The absolute gross profit was calculated as the product of the estimated yield of each model and the estimated maize price per kg by NEARLS [16]

₦559/kg). The Hybrid variety is the best-performing model, generating an absolute gross profit of ₦3,633,500. The CDPF variety produced ₦2,291,900, which is ₦1,341,600 less than Hybrid. CES yielded ₦2,180,100, a margin of ₦1,453,400 lower than Hybrid. Among the lower-performing models, Aduba Hybrid generated ₦1,341,600, which is ₦2,291,900 less than Hybrid, while Girma & Tadesse Hybrid achieved ₦1,408,680, a difference of ₦2,224,820 less than the best-performing Hybrid. These figures highlight that Hybrid has a substantially higher absolute gross profit than all other models, demonstrating its superior economic potential and making it the most profitable choice among the tested maize varieties.

8 Conclusion

The comparison of actual field data with optimization models shows that the Cobb-Douglas model produced high yields (5168.61 kg/ha) but with impractical input levels, especially for seed. The CES model improved flexibility and substitution but faced calibration challenges and yielded moderately (4152.85 kg/ha). The hybrid optimization model outperformed both, achieving 6481.91 kg/ha with realistic, balanced inputs. It combined the strengths of Cobb-Douglas and CES, adapting well to real farm conditions. This highlights hybrid models as promising tools for improving yield prediction and resource use efficiency in agriculture, overcoming limitations of traditional models.

Acknowledgement. The authors gratefully acknowledge RSIF-PASET for their generous sponsorship, which supported the publication of this article and contributed significantly to the advancement of research on optimizing maize yields in Nigeria.

References

1. Olayide, T., Adebisi, A., Umar, S.: Socioeconomic contributions of maize to rural livelihoods in Nigeria. Agri. Policy Rev. **14**(2), 78–92 (2023). https://doi.org/10.1016/j.apr.2021.02.003
2. Abdoulaye, T., Abass, A., Maziya-Dixon, B., Tarawali, G., Alene, A.: Impacts of improved maize varieties in Nigeria: ex-post assessment of productivity and welfare outcomes. Int. Inst. Tropical Agri. (2018). https://doi.org/10.1007/s12571-018-0772-9
3. Musa, Z., Abdullahi, B.: Soil fertility management and its effect on maize yield in North-east Nigeria. Int. J. Soil Sci. **15**(4), 341–356 (2023)
4. Arrow, K.J., Chenery, H.B., Minhas, B.S., Solow, R.M.: Capital-labor substitution and economic efficiency. Rev. Econ. Stat. **43**(3), 225–250 (1961). https://doi.org/10.2307/1927286
5. Adebayo, R.A., Ige, T.A., Yusuf, A.: Sustainable land management practices for improved crop yields in sub-Saharan Africa. J. Agri. Sci. Pract. **8**(2), 123–135 (2021)
6. Okonkwo, C.E., Bello, A.M.: Climate variability and its effect on smallholder maize yields in North-East Nigeria. J. Climate Agri. Sustain. **12**(3), 78–89 (2023)
7. Peter, E., Hassan, R., Abdulkadir, A., Bala, A.: A multi-objective mathematical programming model for optimizing smallholder-cropping systems in North-East Nigeria. Ann. Oper. Res. (2025). https://doi.org/10.1007/s10479-023-05718-1
8. Ahmed, M.A., Salisu, I., Ojo, A.T.: Advances in modeling agricultural production systems: a case of maize optimization. Afr. J. Agric. Res. **19**(3), 199–210 (2023)

9. Aliyu, J., Bello, M., Ibrahim, T.: Optimization of fertilizer use in sub-Saharan agri culture. J. Agric. Res. **13**(4), 145–162 (2021)
10. Mbah, L., Ugwu, A.: Sustainability in fertilizer application. Niger. Agric. J. **54**(1), 32–44 (2023)
11. Patel, R., Lee, K.Y.: Hybrid maize and land-use efficiency: a global synthesis. Agric. Syst. **202**, 103482 (2023). https://doi.org/10.1016/j.agsy.2023.103482
12. Zhu, H., He, X., Wang, X., Long, P.: Increasing hybrid rice yield, water productivity, and nitrogen use efficiency: optimization strategies for irrigation and fertilizer management. Plants **13**(12), 1717 (2024). https://doi.org/10.3390/plants13121717
13. Kamara, A.Y., Kamai, N., Omoigui, L.O., Togola, A., Ekeleme, F., Onyibe, J.E.: Guide to maize production in Northern Nigeria. International Institute of Tropical Agriculture: Ibadan, Nigeria (2020)
14. Aduba, J.: Technical efficiency of smallholder maize farmers in Nigeria: The stochastic frontier approach (2017). https://www.academia.edu/32373695/
15. Girma, A., Tadesse, T.: Analysis of technical efficiency in maize production in Guji Zone: stochastic frontier model. Agric. Food Secur. **9**(1), 11 (2020). https://doi.org/10.1186/s40066-020-00270-w
16. National Agricultural Extension and Research Liaison Services (NAERLS) (2025). Wet season agricultural performance survey report: Maize prices by zone (July 2023). NAERLS. Retrieved from https://naerls.gov.ng/wp-content/uploads/2025/04/Agricultural-Performance-Survey-of-2024-Wet-Season-in-Nigeria.pdf

Author Index

D. Bassole et al. (Eds.): InterSol 2025, LNICST 671, pp. 281–282, 2026.
https://doi.org/10.1007/978-3-032-15154-4

The manufacturer's authorised representative in the EU is Springer Nature Customer Service Centre GmbH, Europaplatz 3, 69115 Heidelberg, Germany. If you have any concerns regarding our products, please contact ProductSafety@springernature.com

Printed and bound by CPI Group (UK) Ltd, Croydon, CR0 4YY
07/07/2026
02160913-0007